A practical foundation in accounting

A practical foundation
in accounting

HARRY JOHNSON and AUSTIN WHITTAM

Fourth edition revised by Harry Johnson
assisted by Roy Lee-Faulkner

London and New York

First published 1982 by the Academic Division of
Unwin Hyman Ltd

Second edition 1982
Third edition 1987
Third impression 1990

Fourth edition published 1992
by Routledge
11 New Fetter Lane, London EC4P 4EE

Simultaneously published in the USA and Canada
by Routledge
a division of Routledge, Chapman and Hall, Inc.
29 West 35th Street, New York, NY 10001

© Harry Johnson and Austin Whittam 1982, 1984, 1987, 1992

Typeset by Leaper & Gard Ltd, Bristol
Printed and bound in Great Britain by Biddles Ltd, Guildford and King's Lynn

British Library Cataloguing in Publication Data
A catalogue record for this book is available from the British Library
    0–415–07864–4

Library of Congress Cataloging in Publication Data
Has been applied for
    0–415–07864–4

Contents

Preface to the Fourth Edition

As with previous editions, this edition is intended mainly for students studying for foundation and preliminary examinations set by the various examining bodies. It is devoted primarily to accounting practice, with emphasis on modern presentation. The intention is to give a sound training in basic accounting so that examinations can be attempted with confidence and questions answered with style. There are several excellent texts on the market dealing with accounting theory and the student's attention will doubtless be drawn to one or more of these books by his tutor, according to the depth of study required. However, the appendix to this book should not be overlooked.

Many first year accounting degree students will also find use for the text. A common assumption that is made regarding these students is that they will find double entry accounting easy. This is not so for many. Yet a thorough knowledge of the interrelationship between T accounts, profit and loss accounts, balance sheets and other accounting statements is necessary before the strengths and weaknesses of accounting practices can be understood.

The questions at the end of each chapter should be regarded as an integral part of the chapter. Most accountancy examinations still place a great deal of emphasis on the ability to work quickly and accurately, and practice is therefore essential. The questions have been arranged in approximate order of increasing difficulty, first through the 'S' suffixed questions and then through the non S suffixed. A great improvement in this edition is that the full answers to the S suffixed questions can be found at the end of the book. The answers are given in full because presentation is such an important part of any accounting solution. A solutions manual for the remaining 'non-S' questions is available to teachers and lecturers.

Regular users of the book will recognise it easily. However, there are some changes. Value added tax is here to stay, and an introduction to this subject has been brought to an early part of the book; the chapter on goodwill has been substantially re-written and simplified; cash flow replaces funds flow and has been given a separate chapter; suspense accounts are dealt with earlier, but not too early. There are many other minor modifications and updatings.

The generous co-operation of the Institute of Chartered Accountants in England and Wales, the Chartered Association of Certified Accountants, and the Chartered Institute of Management Accountants is acknowledged in allowing the use of their past examination questions.

Finally, teachers and students are thanked for the comments they have made on previous editions; these are always most welcome.

Harry Johnson

Introduction

History informs us that all but the most primitive of societies have required some form of accounting. As soon as economic conditions develop beyond the simplest exchange of goods, methods of recording transactions and possessions become necessary. It is only by maintaining records that a business man knows how much he owns, and/or how much another man owes him. The steward or agent of a landowner, by keeping records of how he has collected and used his master's goods and money, can *account* for his dealings to his master.

This *stewardship* role has had a great influence on the development of accounting. Much of accounting has been concerned with the reporting or accounting of a steward to a landowner, or a manager to a business owner, or a businessman to a tax collector. More recently the stewardship role has taken legal form in that limited companies are required by law to disclose information to their shareholders and others.

The stewardship role of accounting in its modern context is usually described as *financial accounting*. Most of this book is devoted to an introduction to *financial accounting*. It is concerned with the recording of business transactions, facts and events in monetary terms and the subsequent provision of relevant information to interested parties. The information provided is largely historical in that the transactions and events recorded have already taken place, although some may have occurred only recently. Financial accounting also encompasses the summarising of information and the presentation of periodic reports such as profit and loss statements and balance sheets. The interpretation of financial reports in order to evaluate past performance is a further important area which is introduced in the book.

A relatively modern development of accounting is *management accounting*. Management accounting is much more concerned with the control of costs and looking forward, rather than reporting on a past period. The analysis of past events does, of course, play an important part when making forecasts for the future. Management accounting is not covered in this book. Many text books specialise in introductory management accounting, just as this text is mainly concerned with financial accounting.

The historical forms of accounting referred to earlier in this introduction were of differing degrees of sophistication according to the needs and techniques of the time. Modern accounting is based on the double entry system and the recognition of the dual nature of each transaction and this provides a co-ordinated framework for the control of all the transactions of a business. Decisions can thus be made on the basis of accurate information. The double entry system is introduced in Chapter 1 following.

1 Introduction to the double entry system of book-keeping

Aims of the chapter:

> To introduce the concept of double entry
> To consider the business entity convention
> To look at the accounting equation

The double entry system of book-keeping is basically a simple concept. But, as with many simple ideas, it is touched with genius.

It is believed to have originated in the Italian city-states during the thirteenth and fourteenth centuries. In its early form, as described by the Franciscan monk, Luca Pacioli, it was a rather primitive form of accounting. However, the original idea was capable of development into the present comprehensive system, dealing with most business situations, which will be progressively introduced in this book. The system also has a certain beauty and symmetry of its own.

Typical information which the owner of any business would wish to have available is:

> What is owned by the business?
> What is owed to and by the business?
> Is the business operating at a profit?

Ideally the above information would always be available, and in a sophisticated computer system of accounting it is either immediately accessible or can be obtained very quickly. But not every business is large enough to afford a computer system for its accounting records. In any event, computers can only deal with data in accordance with set procedures. It follows, therefore, that there will always be a need for people to understand how to process data in such a way that the output of a computer is meaningful. The same data can, of course, be processed manually to give exactly the same end product – but not nearly so quickly.

The aim of this book is to show the reader HOW business transactions are recorded to give at least the minimum amount of information required by the owner of a business and WHY those transactions are recorded in that particular way.

One of the fundamental conventions of accounting is the *business entity* convention.[1] This means that the firm or the business is dealt with completely separately from any other personal dealings of the owner(s). All, and only, the transactions of the firm pass through the accounting

---

[1] The major accounting conventions are listed and briefly explained in the Appendix.

system. Sometimes this is a legal necessity, as with a limited company. But in any case it is always much more convenient and good business practice to keep the transactions of the firm separate from those of its owner(s).

The simplest model of the firm or business is the sole trader (i.e. the proprietor/manager) buying and selling goods with the intention of making a profit. An example of this type of trader might be the local newsagent or grocer, or possibly a wholesaler of goods.

Imagine then a sole trader commencing business with £70,000 in a separate business bank account. He is using a separate business bank account because he very sensibly consulted an accountant before commencing business and was put wise to the business entity concept!

His overall position could be shown initially thus:

	£		£
Cash at bank	70,000	= Capital (or 'owner's interest')	70,000

If our sole trader then purchased some premises for £55,000, paying by cheque, his overall position would become:

	£		£
Cash at bank	15,000	Capital	70,000
Buildings	55,000		
	70,000		70,000

Next he buys a van for £4,000, and some shopfittings for £5,000, so he now has:

	£		£
Buildings	55,000	Capital	70,000
Van	4,000		
Shopfittings	5,000		
Cash at bank	6,000		
	70,000		70,000

The trader's capital is still £70,000, but instead of it being only in the form of cash at the bank, it is made up of buildings, a van, shopfittings, and of course a reduced amount of cash at the bank.

The trader would now like to spend some money on a typewriter costing £500 and a cash register also costing £500. However, he thinks his £6,000 at the bank is the minimum he will need when he later commences buying goods for resale. Fortunately he has a good friend, L. Grayson, who will lend him £1,000. So after taking advantage of the loan and purchasing the typewriter and cash register his position is:

	£		£
Buildings	55,000	Capital	70,000
Van	4,000	Loan –	
Shopfittings	5,000	L. Grayson	1,000
Equipment	1,000		
Cash at bank	6,000		
	71,000		71,000

The above represents the *accounting equation,* i.e.

Assets = Capital (or owner's interest) + Liabilities (amounts owed)

or alternatively

Capital = Assets − Liabilities

which is very probably the way in which any intelligent layman would describe the *capital* of a firm. Capital is what is owned by a business, less what is owed to outsiders.

Another way of showing the current position would be:

		£
Assets		
	Buildings	55,000
	Van	4,000
	Shopfittings	5,000
	Equipment	1,000
	Cash at bank	6,000
		71,000
Financed by		
	Capital	70,000
	Loan − L. Grayson	1,000
		71,000

and this quite accurately could be described as the opening *balance sheet* of 'A. Trader' before he actually commences trading in goods.

You will note that all the above transactions have been recorded at cost according to the *cost convention* as this is the most objective measure at the time the transactions take place.

Questions

1.1S   Define briefly (a) assets, (b) liabilities, (c) capital.

1.2S   What is the *accounting equation*? What does it mean?

1.3S   Categorise the following as assets or liabilities or capital.
(a) Buildings
(b) Loan to the firm
(c) Equipment
(d) Cash
(e) Cash paid into the firm's bank account by the proprietor.

1.4S   A. Sparrow commenced business on the 1 January 19X1 by paying £50,000 into a separate business bank account. He then transacted the following business:

Jan.   3 Paid J. Wren £21,000 for the purchase of shop premises
Jan. 10 Paid Shopfitters Ltd £3,000 by cheque for fixtures and fittings
Jan. 17 C. Gull gives a cheque for £5,000 to A. Sparrow as a loan
Jan. 24 Bought a motor van for £3,500 paying by cheque
Jan. 31 Bought a typewriter for £250 paying by cheque

Using the method shown in the chapter, build up a balance sheet for
A. Sparrow as at the end of January.

1.5   Using the balance sheet equation calculate the missing figures from the
following:

		£		£		£
(i)	Assets	25,000	Capital	12,000	Liabilities	?
(ii)	Assets	376,000	Capital	?	Liabilities	145,000
(iii)	Assets	?	Capital	589,000	Liabilities	36,000
(iv)	Assets	267,000	Capital	?	Liabilities	99,000
(v)	Assets	?	Capital	421,000	Liabilities	210,000
(vi)	Assets	964,000	Capital	618,000	Liabilities	?

1.6   G. Peake used £3,000 of his own savings and £2,000 borrowed from his
father to open a business bank account on 1 March.

March 2 Bought some shelving and a till for £1,500 paying by cheque
March 5 Transferred £100 from the bank as a cash float
March 9 Issued a cheque for £2,700 for more shop fittings
March 12 Paid a cheque for £5,000 from a Premium Bond win into the
business and paid off the loan in full
March 17 Purchased a second-hand delivery van which cost £2,200,
payment being made by cheque
March 21 Returned as unsuitable some of the shelving which had cost
£400. A full refund was made by cheque
March 25 A typewriter costing £90 was bought for cash
March 31 Bought a display cabinet by cheque – £350

Construct a balance sheet for G. Peake at the end of the period showing all
your workings.

2 Ledger accounts or 'T' accounts

Aims of the chapter:

> To explain how assets and liabilities are recorded in the books of account
> To show how accounts are balanced

The transactions, so far, of A. Trader have been so few and so simple that the recording of them has been achieved by simple mental arithmetic and by re-drawing the balance sheet after each transaction. This is not possible when the transactions become more frequent and more complex.

The accountant therefore uses a *ledger*. In its simplest form it could consist of a single book with suitable rulings. It will probably, for convenience, be separated into several books, but together they form the one ledger.

The ledger contains *accounts*. These are often described as 'T' accounts because in their simplest ruling they form a T, thus:

| *Dr.* | Bank account | *Cr.* |

This simple form of ruling is very useful for rough work, for examination work and for illustration purposes. It will be used in this form in this book where appropriate.

In its more conventional or traditional ruling an account might appear as below:

Dr.				Name of account					*Cr.*
Date	Details	Folio	£	p	Date	Details	Folio	£	p

Each transaction of a particular kind or with a particular person requires a separate account. In the case of A. Trader, he would require a bank account to record all the bank transactions. Accounts would also be required for buildings, vans, shopfittings and equipment. Others would be opened subsequently as required.

Every account has a debit (i.e. *Dr.*) side which is the left-hand side, and a credit (i.e. *Cr.*) side which is the right-hand side. The reason for the *Dr.* side being on the left and the *Cr.* side on the right appears to be lost in history, but the convention is strictly followed.

An inflow of money or value is entered on the *Dr.* side of an account. Debit originates from the Latin and means 'to receive' or 'value received'. An outflow of money or value is entered on the *Cr.* side of an account. Credit also originates from Latin and means 'to give' or 'value given'.

The first and most important rule in book-keeping is that each transaction affects two accounts. For every inflow of value to an account there is a corresponding outflow from a different account. Each and every *Dr.* entry requires a corresponding *Cr.* entry, and vice versa.

The first transaction of A. Trader was to pay £70,000 into a separate business bank account. This would be entered as follows:

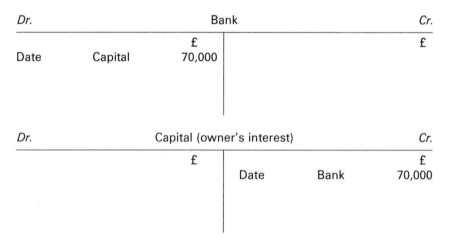

Dr.			Bank				*Cr.*
			£				£
Date	Capital		70,000				

Dr.			Capital (owner's interest)				*Cr.*
			£				£
				Date	Bank		70,000

There has been an inflow to the bank account (the word 'account' can be omitted in the ledger as it is understood) and an outflow from the owner as represented by the capital account.

Also note that in both entries the other account involved in the transaction has been shown; i.e. the word 'capital' appears in the bank account, and the word 'bank' appears in the capital account. This is done for cross-reference purposes. With a traditional ruling, as illustrated previously, the 'folio' column would also indicate the page on which the other affected account appears.

Subsequent transactions of A. Trader are listed below, showing the accounts debited and the accounts credited and the reasoning involved.

		Dr. £	Cr. £
(1)	Buildings account	55,000	
	Bank account		55,000
	An outflow from the bank account with a corresponding inflow into the buildings account on purchase of premises.		
(2)	Van account	4,000	
	Bank account		4,000
	An outflow from the bank account with a corresponding inflow into the van account on purchase of a van.		
(3)	Shopfittings account	5,000	
	Bank account		5,000
	An outflow from the bank account with a corresponding inflow into the shopfittings account on purchase of shopfittings.		
(4)	Bank account	1,000	
	Loan – L. Grayson		1,000
	An outflow from L. Grayson with a corresponding inflow into the bank account on receiving a loan from L. Grayson.		
(5)	Equipment account	500	
	Bank account		500
	Purchase of a typewriter.		
(6)	Equipment account	500	
	Bank account		500
	Purchase of a cash register.		

After making the above entries the T accounts would now appear as follows:

Dr.	Bank			*Cr.*
	£			£
Capital	70,000	(1) Buildings		55,000
(4) Loan – L. Grayson	1,000	(2) Van		4,000
		(3) Shopfittings		5,000
		(5) Equipment		500
		(6) Equipment		500

Dr.	Capital		*Cr.*
	£		£
		Bank	70,000

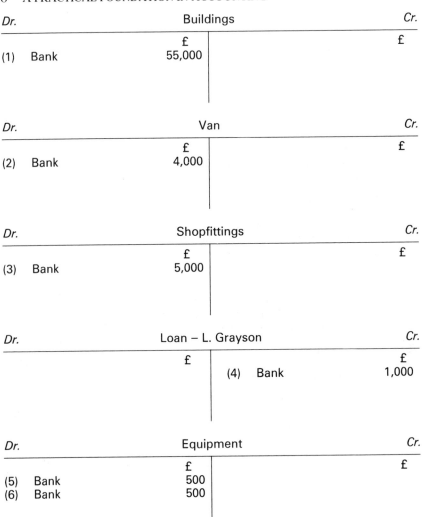

Dr.	Buildings		Cr.
	£		£
(1) Bank	55,000		

Dr.	Van		Cr.
	£		£
(2) Bank	4,000		

Dr.	Shopfittings		Cr.
	£		£
(3) Bank	5,000		

Dr.	Loan – L. Grayson		Cr.
	£		£
		(4) Bank	1,000

Dr.	Equipment		Cr.
	£		£
(5) Bank	500		
(6) Bank	500		

It will have been noted that both the typewriter and the cash register have been included in the equipment account, rather than a separate typewriter account and separate cash register account. The degree of analysis required is a matter for the user to decide. There will also probably be a subsidiary record available if A. Trader chooses to use the generic description 'equipment' for these fairly similar items. If A. Trader wishes to know how the equipment account has been built up, he will refer to this subsidiary record, possibly an asset register, an example of which is shown in a later chapter.

Balancing accounts

The next stage is *balancing off* the accounts. For this purpose the bank account is repeated below.

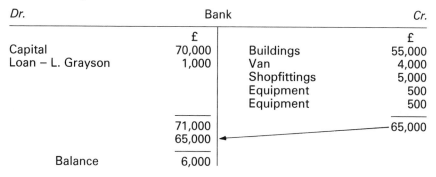

Dr.		Bank	Cr.
	£		£
Capital	70,000	Buildings	55,000
Loan – L. Grayson	1,000	Van	4,000
		Shopfittings	5,000
		Equipment	500
		Equipment	500
	71,000		65,000
	65,000		
Balance	6,000		

It is quite clear that the total of the *Dr.* side is £71,000 (i.e. £71,000 has been received or paid into the bank). The total of the *Cr.* or payment side is found to be £65,000. If the lesser side were transferred to the greater side and deducted as shown above, the balance would be shown quite clearly and correctly as a *Dr.* balance of £6,000. It would be transparently obvious that £6,000 still remained with the bank.

Somewhat unfortunately accounts are not balanced off by this method. To maintain the symmetry of book-keeping and the necessity for a double entry, the following method is adopted, though the end result is the same.

Dr.		Bank	Cr.
	£		£
Capital	70,000	Buildings	55,000
Loan – L. Grayson	1,000	Van	4,000
		Shopfittings	5,000
		Equipment	500
		Equipment	500
		Balance c/d	6,000
	71,000		71,000
Balance b/d	6,000		

The balance c/d (or *carried down* or *carried forward*) is inserted to bring the total of the lesser side to agree with the greater. This is then repeated on the other side of the account, below the total, as the balance b/d (or *brought down* or *brought forward*). The account totals are always shown opposite each other on the same level.

The 'brought down' balance which is below the total *always* indicates whether the balance is *Dr.* or *Cr.*, e.g. in the bank account illustrated above the balance is a *Dr.* balance of £6,000 just as it was previously.

It is worth remembering that if the *Dr.* side totals more than the *Cr.* side, there must be a *Dr.* balance. If the *Cr.* side has the higher total, there must be a *Cr.* balance.

The other accounts of A. Trader would be balanced off similarly:

Dr.		Capital			Cr.
		£			£
Balance c/d		70,000	Bank		70,000
			Balance b/d		70,000

Dr.		Buildings			Cr.
		£			£
Bank		55,000	c/d		55,000
	b/d	55,000			

Dr.		Van			Cr.
		£			£
Bank		4,000	c/d		4,000
	b/d	4,000			

Dr.		Shopfittings			Cr.
		£			£
Bank		5,000	c/d		5,000
	b/d	5,000			

Dr.		Loan – L. Grayson			Cr.
		£			£
c/d		1,000	Bank		1,000
			b/d		1,000

Dr.		Equipment			Cr.
		£			£
Bank		500	c/d		1,000
Bank		500			
		1,000			1,000
	b/d	1,000			

Note particularly that a line is *not* put under the brought down balance, i.e. it is not ruled off. This is now the opening balance for the next period and is the first entry for that new period.

Note also that if there is only one entry, as in, say, the buildings account, it may be used as its own total.

Trial balance

The balances are now listed in what is called a *trial balance*:

Trial Balance – A. Trader

	Dr. £	Cr. £
Bank	6,000	
Capital		70,000
Buildings	55,000	
Van	4,000	
Shopfittings	5,000	
Loan – L. Grayson		1,000
Equipment	1,000	
	71,000	71,000

If all the entries have been made correctly, the two sides must agree because a *Dr.* entry has not been made without a similar *Cr.* entry having been made.

This may appear a long winded way of arriving at the same position as at the end of Chapter 1, but the need for this will become very clear when A. Trader actually commences trading in the next chapter.

Balance sheet

To conclude this stage the trial balance can be re-arranged in the form of a balance sheet, as previously shown in Chapter 1.

Balance Sheet of A. Trader

	£
Assets	
Buildings	55,000
Van	4,000
Shopfittings	5,000
Equipment	1,000
Cash at bank	6,000
	71,000
Financed by	
Capital	70,000
Loan – L. Grayson	1,000
	71,000

The assets have been deliberately arranged in the above order with the more permanent first and more liquid last. More will be said of this later.

Questions

2.1S   Name the accounts to be debited and to be credited to record the following transactions of A. Sparrow.

(a) Introduced capital by paying a cheque into the bank
(b) Gave a cheque to J. Wren for the purchase of shop premises
(c) Paid Shopfitters Ltd by cheque for fixtures and fittings
(d) Received a cheque from C. Gull as a loan
(e) Bought a motor van paying by cheque
(f) Bought a typewriter paying by cheque

2.2S   Record the following transactions in the ledger of A. Sparrow and then prepare a trial balance and balance sheet as at 31 January 19X1.

19X1
Jan.   1   Sparrow introduced capital by paying a cheque for £50,000 into the bank
Jan.   3   Gave a cheque for £21,000 to J. Wren for the purchase of shop premises
Jan. 10   Paid Shopfitters Ltd £3,000 by cheque for fixtures and fittings
Jan. 17   C. Gull gives a cheque for £5,000 to A. Sparrow as a loan
Jan. 24   Bought a motor van for £3,500 paying by cheque
Jan. 31   Bought a typewriter for £250 paying by cheque

2.3S   Open up the appropriate ledger accounts to record the following transactions for G. Peake. Balance the accounts at the end of the month, construct a trial balance and prepare a balance sheet on 31 March.

19X9
March   1   G. Peake opened a business bank account using £3,000 from his own savings and £2,000 borrowed from his father
March   2   Bought some shelving and a till for £1,500 paying by cheque
March   5   Transferred £100 from the bank as a cash float
March   9   Issued a cheque for £2,700 for more shop fittings
March 12   Paid a cheque for £5,000 from a Premium Bond win into the business and paid off the loan in full
March 17   Purchased a second-hand delivery van which cost £2,200, payment being made by cheque
March 21   Returned as unsuitable some of the shelving which had cost £400. A full refund was made by cheque
March 25   A typewriter costing £90 was bought for cash
March 31   Bought a display cabinet by cheque – £350

2.4   Show which accounts are to be debited and which are to be credited to record the following transactions of J. Bennett.

(a) Introduced capital by paying a cheque into the bank
(b) Purchased a shop and shopfittings from D. Rhodes – paid by cheque
(c) Paid M. Dover by cheque for equipment
(d) Bought a second-hand display cabinet – paid by cheque

2.5 Record the following transactions in the ledger of J. Bennett and then prepare a trial balance and balance sheet as at 31 January 19X2.

19X2

Jan. 2 Bennett introduced capital by paying a cheque for £30,000 into the bank

Jan. 5 Gave a cheque for £20,000 to D. Rhodes for shop premises valued at £18,000 and shop fixtures and fittings valued at £2,000

Jan. 20 Paid M. Dover £1,200 by cheque for equipment

Jan. 28 Bought a second-hand display cabinet for £400 – paid by cheque

2.6 Prepare full ledger accounts from the following information relating to the first month's transactions for Andrew Barry, who has just opened a take-away restaurant. Balance the accounts at the end of the month and prepare a trial balance and a balance sheet at that date.

19X3

April 1 Opened a business bank account with £5,000 borrowed from Natpro Bank Plc

April 9 Purchased various items of kitchen equipment for £2,700 by cheque

April 15 Bought £1,600 of shop fittings paying by cheque

April 19 Paid out a cheque for £500 for more equipment

April 21 Returned some of the shop fittings as they were damaged. A full refund was made in cash for £120

April 28 Took £100 cash from the bank for business use

April 30 Bought replacements for the damaged fittings by cash – £210 – and issued a cheque for a deep-freeze which cost £250

Comment on the situation regarding the bank account at the end of the month.

3 Trading

Aims of the chapter:

> To show how revenue transactions are recorded in the
> books of account
> To explain how unsold stock is dealt with in calculating
> the profit for a particular period of time
> To describe how assets and liabilities are listed in the
> balance sheet

The original objective of A. Trader was to buy and sell goods at a profit. So far he has only acquired assets, and a liability in the form of a loan from a friend. He now must buy goods, sell goods, meet any miscellaneous and additional expenses and meet his main objective of making a profit.

It is not only assets and liabilities that are recorded in the ledger accounts, as shown so far. All the subsequent transactions, facts and events related to the trader which can be shown in monetary terms will be recorded and then collated in such a way that it will be possible to see whether or not he has achieved his aim of making a profit. The period of time chosen for determining a profit is usually and conventionally a year. Just one of the many reasons for this is that the income tax period is of one year's duration, though the accounting year need not end on the same date as the tax year or the calendar year.

There are no reasons why a profit or loss should not be calculated more often, and indeed many firms will prepare interim statements at frequent intervals, though they may consider a year to be their normal period of account (see periodicity convention).

The recording of transactions is, as before, carried out through T accounts. In the case of A. Trader, he might be involved in many hundreds of transactions in a year. For convenience, therefore, it is intended to regard his first period of account as one month. In this way all the transactions can be recorded and illustrated through T accounts without inordinate length.

The first month's transactions of A. Trader were as follows (subsequent, of course, to his acquisition of assets):

Jan. 2   Withdrew £200 from bank for cash transactions
　　 3   Bought goods for £4,000, paying by cheque
　　 4   Purchased stationery by cash £15
　　 5   Sold goods for £2,500 receiving cheque

6	Sold goods for £50 received in cash	
9	Paid for cleaning of shop £20 in cash	
10	Paid for electricity £35 by cheque	
11	Sold goods for £1,000 receiving cheque	
12	Paid petrol bill for van £12 by cheque	
13	Purchased additional shop fittings £200 by cheque	
16	Bought goods for £1,000 on credit from D. Flint	
17	Withdrew £500 cash from bank for potential purchases	
18	Bought goods for £500 cash	
19	Paid £40 for servicing of van by cheque	
21	Sold goods for £600, receiving cheque in payment	
22	Sold goods on credit to B. Smith for £500	
23	Sold goods for £200 receiving cheque	
24	Received part payment from B. Smith of £250 by cheque	
25	Goods returned by B. Smith valued at £100 selling price	
27	Paid D. Flint £800 on account by cheque	
28	Sold goods for £400 receiving cheque	
31	Paid for shop cleaning £20 by cash	

At the end of the month A. Trader held a stock of goods valued at cost at £1,380.

Before illustrating the T accounts, one or two important points are worth noting.

A. Trader is not selling goods at the same price that he bought them. After all, he intends to make a profit. Therefore a separate account is maintained for *purchases* and a separate account for *sales*. These words have a special meaning in accounting.

Purchases are goods bought with the intention of selling, and *sales* refers to the sale of goods which have been bought with the intention of selling.

Eventually a comparison will be made, but in the T accounts it is essential that purchases and sales are not confused.

Most of the goods bought are paid for by cheque or cash. The entry is *Dr.* Purchases and *Cr.* either Bank or Cash. However, note carefully the treatment of goods purchased from D. Flint for £1,000. These are not paid for at all initially, and by the end of the month are only partly paid for. A somewhat similar situation exists with the sale of goods to B. Smith.

Following the practice in the previous chapter the transactions are listed below showing the accounts debited and the accounts credited. An explanation is also given where the type of transaction has not previously been met.

Don't forget, an inflow of value is debited, and an outflow is credited.

			Dr. £	Cr. £
Jan.	2	Cash (account)	200	
		Bank (account)		200
		An outflow from the bank into the cash account (probably kept in the till).		

			Dr. £	Cr. £

Jan.	3	Purchases
		    Bank
		    An outflow from the bank into the
		    purchases account.
			4,000	4,000

	4	Stationery
		    Cash
		    An outflow of cash into stationery.
			15	15

	5	Bank
		    Sales
		    An inflow to the bank, sales account being
		    regarded as notionally providing the outflow.
			2,500	2,500

	6	Cash
		    Sales
		    An inflow of cash, sales account being
		    regarded as providing the outflow.
			50	50

	9	Cleaning
		    Cash
		    Payment for cleaning.
			20	20

	10	Lighting and heating
		    Bank
		    Payment for electricity.
			35	35

	11	Bank Sales	1,000	1,000
	12	Motor expenses Bank	12	12
	13	Shopfittings Bank	200	200

	16	Purchases
		    D. Flint (creditor)
		    Note especially in this case that D. Flint
		    provides the outflow, *not* the bank. He is
		    called a *creditor* because his account
		    appears as a credit balance in the
		    accounts until it is paid.
			1,000	1,000

	17	Cash Bank	500	500
	18	Purchases Cash	500	500
	19	Motor expenses Bank	40	40
	21	Bank Sales	600	600

		Dr. £	Cr. £
Jan. 22	B. Smith	500	
	Sales		500
	Note in this case that the inflow is to B. Smith. He is called a *debtor* because his account appears as a debit balance until he pays what he owes.		
23	Bank	200	
	Sales		200
24	Bank	250	
	B. Smith		250
	Note that this is B. Smith paying part of the £500 he owes. Therefore the account in his name is credited. It is not another sale. The sale was recorded in full on 22 January. His debit balance as a 'debtor' is reduced by this entry.		
25	Sales	100	
	B. Smith		100
	This is a further reduction in the amount owed by B. Smith. The sales are also reduced because goods have been returned. It has nothing to do with purchases. Often a separate *sales returns* or *returns inwards* account is opened for convenience, but eventually debited to sales.		
27	D. Flint	800	
	Bank		800
	Here D. Flint is part paid and the account in his name is debited, so reducing the credit balance and the amount owed to him. It is not a purchase; this took place on 16 January.		
28	Bank	400	
	Sales		400
31	Cleaning	20	
	Cash		20

Accounts have already been opened and balanced off for assets and capital and the loan. This example now commences with those brought forward balances. The best practical approach is to make both the debit and credit entries for a particular transaction before moving on to the next transaction. New accounts are opened as the need arises. A reasonable amount of space should be left for each account, especially bank, cash, purchases and sales, as these accounts usually have most entries.

At this stage ignore the remarks in brackets at the foot of some accounts (i.e. Transferred to Trading a/c, Transferred to P and L a/c).

Dr.		Bank			Cr.
		£			£
Jan. 1 b/d		6,000	Jan. 2 Cash		200
5 Sales		2,500	3 Purchases		4,000
11 Sales		1,000	10 Lighting and heating		35
21 Sales		600	12 Motor expenses		12
23 Sales		200	13 Shopfittings		200
24 B. Smith		250	17 Cash		500
28 Sales		400	19 Motor expenses		40
			27 D. Flint		800
			c/d		5,163
		10,950			10,950
b/d		5,163			

Buildings

		£			£
Jan. 1 b/d		55,000	c/d		55,000
b/d		55,000			

Van

		£			£
Jan. 1 b/d		4,000	c/d		4,000
b/d		4,000			

Shopfittings

		£			£
Jan. 1 b/d		5,000	c/d		5,200
13 Bank		200			
		5,200			5,200
b/d		5,200			

Equipment

		£			£
Jan. 1 b/d		1,000	c/d		1,000
b/d		1,000			

Capital

		£			£
c/d		70,000	Jan. 1 b/d		70,000
			b/d		70,000

Dr.		Loan – L. Grayson		Cr.

		£				£
	c/d	1,000	Jan.	1	b/d	1,000
					b/d	1,000

Cash

			£				£
Jan.	2	Bank	200	Jan.	4	Stationery	15
	6	Sales	50		9	Cleaning	20
	17	Bank	500		18	Purchases	500
					31	Cleaning	20
						c/d	195
			750				750
		b/d	195				

Purchases

			£			£
Jan.	3	Bank	4,000		c/d	5,500
	16	D. Flint	1,000			
	18	Cash	500			
			5,500			5,500
		b/d	5,500	(Transferred to Trading a/c 5,500)		

Sales

			£				£
Jan.	25	B. Smith	100	Jan.	5	Bank	2,500
		c/d	5,150		6	Cash	50
					11	Bank	1,000
					21	Bank	600
					22	B. Smith	500
					23	Bank	200
					28	Bank	400
			5,250				5,250
	(Transferred to Trading a/c 5,150)					b/d	5,150

Stationery

			£			£
Jan.	4	Cash	15		c/d	15
		b/d	15	(Transferred to P and L a/c 15)		

Dr.		Cleaning		Cr.
	£			£
Jan. 9 Cash	20	c/d		40
31 Cash	20			
	——			——
	40			40
	══			══
b/d	40	(Transferred to P and L a/c 40)		

Lighting and heating

	£		£
Jan. 10 Bank	35	c/d	35
	══		
b/d	35	(Transferred to P and L a/c 35)	

Motor expenses

	£		£
Jan. 12 Bank	12	c/d	52
19 Bank	40		
	——		——
	52		52
	══		══
b/d	52	(Transferred to P and L a/c 52)	

D. Flint (creditor)

	£		£
Jan. 27 Bank	800	Jan. 16 Purchases	1,000
c/d	200		
	——		——
	1,000		1,000
	══		══
		b/d	200

B. Smith (debtor)

	£		£
Jan. 22 Sales	500	Jan. 24 Bank	250
		25 Sales	100
		c/d	150
	——		——
	500		500
	══		══
b/d	150		

The accounts have been balanced off and a trial balance prepared below. In theory the balances should be calculated without actually writing them in the accounts, for sound reasons which will be explained later.

In practice, for illustration purposes, it is more convenient to show the balance on the account so that you can see how the trial balance is built up.

Trial Balance at 31 January

	Dr. £	Cr. £
Bank	5,163	
Buildings	55,000	
Van	4,000	
Shopfittings	5,200	
Equipment	1,000	
Capital		70,000
Loan – L. Grayson		1,000
Cash	195	
Purchases	5,500	
Sales		5,150
Stationery	15	
Cleaning	40	
Lighting and heating	35	
Motor expenses	52	
D. Flint (creditor)		200
B. Smith (debtor)	150	
	76,350	76,350

If the two sides do not balance, an error has been made. This could be in *posting*, which is the term used for entering the transactions in an account, or it could be in calculating or extracting balances.

The two sides could agree and there still be an error. For example, an entry could have been posted correctly as to the amount, but entered in the wrong account. Care is therefore needed.

Extended trial balance

At this stage of study the calculation of profit is best illustrated by the method known as the extended trial balance. In this way a clear picture is built up showing how and why the accounts dovetail together. A shorter method will be demonstrated in the next chapter when the student is familiar with the principles involved. It is not necessary to use an extended trial balance in a short exercise.

The one item of original information on which no action has yet been taken is the stock held by A. Trader at the month end, valued at cost at £1,380.

A glance at the trial balance shows that Purchases cost £5,500, whilst Sales only amount to £5,150 – an apparent loss. But £1,380 of these purchases are still held in stock. To find the cost of the goods actually sold, therefore, it is necessary to deduct £1,380 from £5,500. The £1,380 is carried forward as an asset into the next period when the goods may be sold.

It should also be noted that, in the simple model dealt with here, stock is only valued at the end of the period. There is no continuous control of stock, nor is there likely to be at the local newsagent or corner shop.

The first column of the extended trial balance shown below is therefore a repeat of the original trial balance plus a *Dr.* entry of £1,380 and a *Cr.*

Extended Trial Balance

	Trial balance Dr. £	Trial balance Cr. £	Trading account Dr. £	Trading account Cr. £	Profit and loss account Dr. £	Profit and loss account Cr. £	Balance sheet Dr. £	Balance sheet Cr. £
Bank	5,163						5,163	
Buildings	55,000						55,000	
Van	4,000						4,000	
Shopfittings	5,200						5,200	
Equipment	1,000						1,000	
Capital		70,000						70,000
Loan – L. Grayson		1,000						1,000
Cash	195						195	
Purchases	5,500		5,500					
Sales		5,150		5,150				
Stationery	15				15			
Cleaning	40				40			
Lighting and heating	35				35			
Motor expenses	52				52			
D. Flint (creditor)		200						200
B. Smith (debtor)	150						150	
Closing stock		1,380		1,380				
Closing stock c/f	1,380						1,380	
Gross profit			1,030			1,030		
Net profit					888			888
	77,730	77,730	6,530	6,530	1,030	1,030	72,088	72,088

entry of £1,380 for stock at the end of the period. This maintains the rule that each *Dr.* entry requires a corresponding *Cr.* entry, and the reason for this stock entry will become clear very shortly.

The second column of the extended trial balance is headed 'Trading account'. Most traders would wish to know how much they have made simply by buying and selling goods without confusing the issue with other expenses. All the items of the original trial balance concerned with buying and selling goods are transferred to this column. The *Cr.* entry for stock is one of these, and as purchases are a *Dr.*, it is equivalent to making a deduction from purchases. A balance is taken on the column amounting to £1,030, and this is described as the *gross profit*. It is interesting to note that this is 20% of sales, thus providing the sort of information useful to a business man.

This figure of £1,030 is transferred to the next column headed 'Profit and loss account'. The other expenses figures in the original trial balance are now transferred to this column and a balance taken to give the *net profit*. Essentially the whole operation is one of *netting off* many balances and replacing them with one balance, i.e. the net profit.

The remaining balances are transferred to the end column headed 'Balance sheet' along with the figure of net profit. The figure of net profit in fact becomes part of the capital. The reason for this is quite simple. If the owner of a business buys goods for £20 cash and sells them for £30 cash, he has made a profit of £10 and he has also increased his assets (i.e. cash) by £10. Therefore he has increased his capital by £10. (Capital = assets − liabilities). The same applies to A. Trader, except that there are many transactions involved in calculating his profit.

It will be noted also that the *Dr.* entry for stock has been transferred to the 'Balance sheet' column. This will be carried forward and used in the next period's trading account as the opening balance of stock.

In fact it is only the balances listed in the balance sheet that are carried forward, and they provide the opening account balances for the next period. Just, indeed, as was done with the balance sheet calculated in Chapter 2 after acquiring the assets.

The other account balances are transferred to either the trading account or the profit and loss account. They are there 'netted off', and only the net profit is carried forward by adding it to the capital. So, in theory, the T accounts should not be balanced off for the trial balance as many balances are transferred and not carried forward. Those that are transferred have been indicated in the T accounts in brackets (Transferred to Trading a/c, Transferred to P and L a/c).

Final accounts

The extended trial balance is not the form in which the *final accounts* (the common name given to the trading and profit and loss account and balance sheet, although the balance sheet is a list of balances − not an account) will be presented to a client by an accountant. The extended trial balance will be regarded as a working paper and re-arranged and re-written as follows without mention of *Dr.* or *Cr.*

A. Trader
Trading and Profit and Loss Account (Income Statement)
for the month ended 31 January 19XX

	£	£
Sales		5,150
Cost of sales		
Purchases	5,500	
less Closing stock (Inventory)	1,380	4,120
Gross profit (Gross margin)		1,030
Stationery	15	
Cleaning	40	
Lighting and heating	35	
Motor expenses	52	142
Net profit (Net income)		888

(The words in brackets are 'Americanisms' now found in some English textbooks, but not in general use here.)

A. Trader
Balance Sheet as at 31 January 19XX

	£	£
Assets		
Fixed assets		
Buildings		55,000
Van		4,000
Shopfittings		5,200
Equipment		1,000
		65,200
Current assets		
Stock	1,380	
Debtors	150	
Bank	5,163	
Cash	195	
	6,888	
less Current liabilities		
Creditors	200	
Working capital		6,688
		71,888
Financed by		
Capital	70,000	
add Profit for period	888	70,888
Loan – L. Grayson		1,000
		71,888

Note particularly the headings. The trading and profit and loss account is concerned with profits and losses *over a period of time*. The balance sheet lists assets and liabilities at *a point in time*.

The assets described as *fixed assets* are those which will provide service to the business for a longer period than one year. Obviously the van will not last for ever, and the student may feel that a charge for this and other fixed assets should be made against profits. This is a valid observation and the subject of charging for fixed assets will be discussed in detail in the chapter dealing with *Depreciation* (see Ch. 5).

Current assets are those which are continuously changing and will not normally have a life of one year. They should be arranged with the most liquid at the bottom and the least liquid at the top. The order shown is the one usually adopted. The most liquid asset is cash.

Current liabilities are liabilities of a temporary and continuously changing nature – unlike the loan which is of a more long term nature.

Current liabilities are deducted from current assets to give *working capital*, another concept requiring further discussion later.

A more traditional presentation of a trading and profit and loss account and balance sheet is shown below. It is most unlikely that any accountant would now present final accounts in this format. The balance sheet below is illogically presented with the *Cr.* balances on the left-hand side and the *Dr.* balances on the right. This form of balance sheet was a long-standing English custom causing endless confusion for new students. The practice was not followed by the Americans, or the Irish and other European countries, who sensibly still kept to the left for *Dr.* and the right for *Cr.* in their balance sheets.

You will still meet the trading and profit and loss account and balance sheet presented as below, and should become familiar with the format.

A. Trader
Trading and Profit and Loss Account
for the month ended 31 January 19XX

	£		£
Purchases	5,500	Sales	5,150
less Closing stock	1,380		
Cost of goods sold	4,120		
Gross profit c/d	1,030		
	5,150		5,150
Stationery	15	Gross profit b/d	1,030
Cleaning	40		
Lighting and heating	35		
Motor expenses	52		
Net profit	888		
	1,030		1,030

Balance Sheet as at 31 January 19XX

	£		£
Capital	70,000	Fixed assets	
add Profit for period	888	Buildings	55,000
		Van	4,000
	70,888	Shopfittings	5,200
Loan – L. Grayson	1,000	Equipment	1,000
			65,200

Current liabilities		Current assets		
Creditors	200	Stock	1,380	
		Debtors	150	
		Bank	5,163	
		Cash	195	6,888
	72,088			72,088

Questions

3.1S   Record the following transactions in the appropriate ledger accounts of D. Johnstone, antique dealer, and then, using the extended trial balance method, prepare a trading and profit and loss account for the month of January 19X1, and a balance sheet as at 31 January 19X1.

19X1
Jan.   2 Paid £50,000 into a business bank account
     3 Bought shop premises £20,000, paid by cheque
     5 Bought shop fittings, paid by cheque £2,500
     9 Bought goods for resale £14,000, paid by cheque
    10 Withdrew £100 cash from the bank
    12 Bought stationery, paid in cash £20
    16 Bought a van, paid by cheque £2,500
    19 Sold goods for £8,500, received payment by cheque
    23 Paid petrol bill for van, £15 by cheque
    26 Sold goods on credit to J. Parker £3,500
    28 Paid for shop cleaning £20 cash
    31 Received cheque from J. Parker for £2,000 in part payment of his account

Stock in hand, at cost price, was valued at £4,000 on 31 January.

3.2S   Record the following transactions in the appropriate ledger accounts of P. Brown, hardware merchant, and then, using the extended trial balance method, prepare a trading and profit and loss account for the month of July 19X2, and a balance sheet as at 31 July 19X2.

19X2
Jul.   1 Paid £20,000 into a business bank account
       Bought shop fittings £2,000 and a van £3,200, both paid by cheque
     2 Paid rent by cheque £200
     3 Bought goods for resale on credit from J. Smith, £2,500
     5 Cash sales £260
     8 Paid wages of assistant in cash £35
    10 Paid insurance by cheque £12
    12 Cash sales £400
    15 Paid wages of assistant in cash £35
       Goods returned to J. Smith, £480
    17 Paid J. Smith £1,500 by cheque
    19 Bought goods for resale on credit from I. Thomas, £1,400
       Cash sales £480
    22 Paid wages of assistant in cash £35
    24 Bought stationery, paid in cash, £25
    26 Cash sales £600
    27 Paid I. Thomas £700 by cheque

29 Paid wages of assistant in cash £35
31 Paid £1,375 cash into the bank

Stock in hand, at cost price, was valued at £2,715 on 31 July.

3.3S   Steve O'Hare set up in business on 1 June 19X8 selling car spares. His initial bank deposit was £10,000 of his own cash.

You are asked to record the following transactions for his first month of trading, extract a trial balance at the end of the month and prepare a set of final accounts.

19X8
June   1 Paid the first month's rent by cheque – £550
          Purchased shop fittings £4,200 and goods for resale £3,000 by cheque
       3 Bought more stock on credit from B. Whiteley – £4,000
       4 Withdrew £600 cash from the bank for business use
          Sold £700 of goods on credit to D. Karsa
       7 Banked £1,500 takings for the week
          Paid wages in cash £120
          Paid £10 cash for window cleaning
       9 Bought goods on credit for £1,500 from R. Knowles
      10 Paid B. Whiteley £2,500 on account by cheque
      14 Returned £150 of damaged stock to R. Knowles
          Paid £2,400 for sales into the bank
          Wages paid in cash £130
      16 Bought a motor van on credit from AB Cars for £8,400, paying a deposit of £2,100 by cheque
      18 Issued a cheque for £150 for installation of a telephone
      21 Settled the wages in cash £105
          Banked the week's takings £1,900
      23 Bought £2,300 stock on credit from R. Knowles
      25 Sold £620 goods on credit to J. Markham
      27 Markham returned £60 of the goods as unsuitable
      28 Banked takings totalling £2,800
          Wages paid in cash £135
      30 Received a cheque from Karsa in full settlement

Notes: Closing stock valued at £5,320
          Daily cash takings have not been recorded

3.4   Enter the following transactions in the books of M. Booker and then, using the extended trial balance method, prepare a trading and profit and loss account for the month of May 19X3 and a balance sheet as at 31 May 19X3.

19X3
May   1 Started business with £13,000 in the bank and £500 cash
      2 Paid rent by cheque £350
         Bought office equipment £2,500, paid by cheque
      3 Bought goods on credit from: W. Piper £2,500 L. Price £1,900
         Bought goods for cash £120
      5 Sold goods for cash £380
      7 Sold goods on credit to A. Flowers £820
      8 Returned goods to W. Piper £200
         Paid the following amounts in cash: Wages £50 Stationery £25 Insurance £15
     10 Sold goods for cash £520

11 Paid £600 cash into the bank
13 Paid by cheque: W. Piper £1,500 L. Price £1,500
15 Paid wages in cash £50
17 Sold goods for cash £600
18 A. Flowers returned goods valued at £120 and paid the balance of his account by cheque
20 Bought goods on credit from W. Piper £2,000
21 Sold goods for cash £650 and on credit to E. Kenworthy £1,650
22 Paid wages in cash £50
24 E. Kenworthy returned goods valued at £165
26 Sold goods for cash £700
27 Paid £2,190 cash into the bank
29 Paid wages in cash £50
31 Paid the following amounts by cheque: W. Piper £800 L. Price £400
Received cheque from E. Kenworthy for £1,200

Stock in hand, at cost price, was valued at £2,300 on 31 May.

3.5   Write up the following transactions in the books of J. Buck for the month of February 19X6. At the end of the month, prepare a trading and profit and loss account and balance sheet using the extended trial balance method.

19X6
Feb. 1 Started business with £8,000 in the bank and £200 cash
2 Paid rent by cheque £300
Bought goods on credit from:
P. Rice   £1,200   S. Baxter £1,850   K. Deal £1,600
3 Sold goods for cash £200 and on credit to P. Lewis for £550
4 Paid insurance by cheque £25 and bought stationery for cash £15
5 Paid wages in cash £50
Sold goods for cash £350
8 Paid £500 cash into the bank and returned goods to P. Rice £240 and S. Baxter £170
9 Paid by cheque:
P. Rice £960   S. Baxter £1,680   K. Deal £1,600
11 Sold goods on credit to J. Dover £800
12 Paid wages in cash £50 and sold goods for cash £570
14 Paid £520 cash into the bank
Goods returned by P. Lewis £25
Bought shopfittings, paid by cheque £1,700
15 Cheque received from P. Lewis for £525
Sold goods for cash £600
16 Sold goods on credit to R. Poole £820
17 Cheque received from J. Dover £400
19 Paid wages in cash £50 and sold goods for cash £620
21 Paid £1,070 cash into the bank
22 Goods returned by R. Poole £160
Sold goods for cash £520
23 Bought goods on credit from:
P. Rice £1,520   K. Deal £930
24 Sold goods for cash £800 and on credit to P. Lewis for £630
26 Paid wages in cash £50
28 Paid £1,250 into the bank and bought postage stamps and stationery for cash £20
Bought van, paid cheque for £2,500

Stock in hand, at cost price, was valued at £1,925 on 28 February.

3.6   At the end of her first year of trading Anne Burton has extracted the following trial balance from her ledger. Using this information and the closing stock figure you are asked to prepare Anne's trading and profit and loss accounts and balance sheet.

Anne Burton's Trial Balance on 31 December 19X2

	Dr. £	Cr. £
Capital		20,000
Motor vehicles	8,000	
Fixtures and fittings	5,000	
Purchases	33,000	
Sales		55,000
Purchase returns		1,000
Sales returns	3,000	
Wages	11,500	
Rent and insurance	6,200	
Heat and light	4,100	
Motor expenses	2,400	
Creditors		6,300
Debtors	7,800	
Bank	1,200	
Cash	100	
	82,300	82,300

Closing stock valued at £9,700

4 Final accounts

Aims of the chapter:

To examine in greater detail the trading and profit and loss accounts
To introduce the matching (or accruals) convention

The previous chapter (Ch. 3) dealt with the general approach to T accounts, and the preparation of a fairly simple trading and profit and loss account and balance sheet from those T accounts.

This subject of final accounts now requires additional explanation in some areas and further development to cover common situations not previously considered.

It will have been noted that it is the normal practice to present the trading and profit and loss account under a single heading. You should follow this practice, whilst being fully aware that the section down to gross profit is the trading account, and the section between gross profit and net profit is the profit and loss account.

Trading account

There are one or two items in the trading account requiring further attention.

Many goods are bought with carriage paid. Transport costs are thus included in the purchase price. But sometimes the cost of carriage is shown as a separate item on the invoice (i.e. bill) sent by the supplier. These costs are called *carriage inwards* and a separate account is opened. For consistency carriage inwards is added to purchases in the trading account. Carriage inwards should not be confused with *carriage outwards*, which is the cost of sending goods to customers. Carriage outwards is a selling expense and is always included in the profit and loss account.

In the simple model for A. Trader shown in Chapter 3, the return of goods from a customer was debited to the sales account. However, most firms wish to keep a separate record of the goods returned for statistical and analytical purposes. It is useful to know, for example, just what percentage of goods are being returned by customers, and conversely the percentage of goods that are being returned to suppliers. Further investigation might be required should either of these figures be regarded as too high. It is therefore usual practice to maintain a *sales returns* (or *returns inwards*) account, and a *purchases returns* (or *returns outwards*) account. The actual adjustments to sales and purchases can be shown in the trading account.

One other item which might possibly appear in a trading account is labour, or wages. Under normal circumstances, with a firm which buys and sells goods but does not manufacture them, wages will appear in the profit and loss account as explained below. But occasionally a trader will in some way alter the goods he is selling. A transistor radio imported from Hong Kong could be modified to meet British specifications. The cost of doing this might reasonably be shown in the trading account as part of the *cost of goods sold*. In examinations a specific instruction will be given if an element of labour or wages is to be shown in the trading account. Otherwise wages should be shown in the profit and loss account.

Note also that the situation described above only covers a minor modification of goods. The complete manufacture of goods requires a somewhat different model which is explained in the chapter on *manufacturing accounts* (see Ch. 16).

An example of a trading account is shown below, which incorporates all the points discussed above, and also includes stock brought forward.

Trading Account

	£	£	£
Sales			15,000
less Sales returns (returns inwards)			300
			14,700
Cost of goods sold			
Stock brought forward			
(opening stock)		1,380	
Purchases	12,000		
less Purchases returns			
(returns outwards)	150	11,850	
Carriage inwards		170	
		13,400	
less Stock carried forward			
(closing stock)		1,350	
		12,050	
Labour		200	
			12,250
Gross profit			2,450

Note particularly that the labour figure is shown quite separately from, and not confused with, stock and purchases. Also note once again that labour appears very infrequently in the trading account.

The order in which the figures dealing with stock and purchases appear is not critical, provided that the calculations are carried out accurately (resulting in £12,050 here), but the above layout is recommended.

Goods are sometimes purchased (or sold) subject to a *trade discount*. This is a method of charging different types of customer different prices.

For example, a member of the public buying some goods or parts from an electrical dealer/wholesaler might pay a certain 'retail' price. But a professional electrician or a good customer purchasing the same goods could be allowed a substantial discount. The invoice to the electrician would probably show the retail price, the trade discount and the net price to be paid. It would be normal practice for the electrician to record the net price paid in his purchases account.

In the same way it is usual to record sales in the sales account at the price actually charged (i.e. the net price after deducting any trade discount). When answering examination questions an account for trade discount is most unlikely to be required, although it might be necessary to calculate the net price. In practice some firms may vary the method.

Trade discounts should not be confused with *discounts for prompt payment* which are mentioned in the next section.

Profit and loss account

All expenses other than purchases and the associated items referred to in the previous section are shown in the profit and loss account.

Wages, or labour costs, are normally shown in the profit and loss account. With a sole trader any payment made to himself or to anyone else for the trader's personal benefit is called a *Drawing*. A sole trader can pay wages to any employee, including his wife or any other member of his family, and these wages will appear in the profit and loss account. But he should not describe payments to himself as wages. Any payment of this nature should be debited to a *drawings account*. If drawings have been confused with wages, a correction is required. Drawings are regarded as a payment on account of profit and the total of the drawings account is normally deducted from capital in the balance sheet, as shown below.

	£	£
Financed by		
Capital	30,000	
add Net profit	888	
	30,888	
less Drawings	500	30,388

A sole trader may also take goods from the business for his own use. The Inland Revenue ruling is that these goods should be charged at selling price, so the correct entry is

Dr. Drawings account
Cr. Sales account.

On the other hand if, in an examination question, the transfer has been made at cost price the entry is

Dr. Drawings account
Cr. Purchases account,

despite the fact that this is strictly speaking incorrect for tax purposes.

A trader may receive income from a source other than his normal trading function. The upper floor of a shop might be rented out as offices. Commission could be received for collecting hire purchase instalments or insurance premiums. This miscellaneous income would normally appear in the profit and loss account before the expenses as follows:

	£	£
Gross profit		2,450
add Rents receivable	150	
Commission receivable	45	195
		2,645
less Expenses		
Wages	300	
Cleaning	50	
Lighting and heat	35	
Other expenses	20	405
Net profit		2,240

It is quite possible that a firm could make payments for rent and/or commission (e.g. for the introduction of new customers), whilst at the same time be receiving rent income and income from commission. Rent paid is a different type of transaction to rent received. Separate accounts should be maintained and rent should appear in the profit and loss account separately as both income and expenditure. The figures should not be netted off. Commission received and commission paid should be dealt with similarly.

Discounts for prompt payment are another example where there could be both a benefit and an expense. Discounts allowed and discounts received should appear as separate items in the profit and loss account. Discounts will be considered further in the chapter dealing with the cash book (see Ch. 6).

Accruals and prepayments

An important convention in accounting is that of *matching*. It is associated with the *accruals* convention. This means that the expenses for a period should be matched against related income. It is not an easy exercise in complex situations. There is always the possibility that an item should have appeared in a previous period, or be deferred until a future period. If expenses are not properly offset against income, the resulting profit or loss will be incorrect.

This theme will be pursued further in the chapter on depreciation (see Ch. 5), when the treatment of fixed assets will be considered.

However, the convention does have implications on what should appear in the profit and loss account as an expense.

It is normal practice, particularly with a small firm, to *Dr.* expenses to an account as a transaction occurs. But it is unlikely that the billing of, say, electricity will take place on precisely the year end date of the firm (assuming the period of account to be the conventional one year). The recognition of the expense normally only takes place when the electricity invoice is received.

It may therefore be necessary for an adjustment to be made to ensure the proper matching of expenses with revenue.

In the example mentioned, an estimate should be made of the value of electricity consumed and not accounted for at the year end, and it should be brought into the accounts for the period. The original electricity account might appear:

Dr.		Electricity	*Cr.*
19X1		£	
Feb. 1 Bank		203	
May 3 Bank		146	
Aug. 2 Bank		76	
Nov. 4 Bank		120	

Assume that the firm's year ends on 31 December and it is estimated that electricity to the value of £153 has been consumed but not invoiced at that date. It would be recorded as follows:

Dr.		Electricity		*Cr.*
19X1	£	19X1		£
Feb. 1 Bank	203	Dec. 31 Profit and loss a/c		698
May 3 Bank	146			
Aug. 2 Bank	76			
Nov. 4 Bank	120			
Dec. 31 Accrual c/d	153			
	698			698
		19X2		
		Jan. 1 Accrual b/d		153

It will be seen that the correct figure of £698 will now appear as an expense in the profit and loss account for 19X1. But there is also a *Cr.* balance of £153 carried down on the account. This is called an *accrual* and appears as a current liability in the balance sheet. *Creditors and accruals* are sometimes shown as a composite item in the balance sheet.

In 19X2 an automatic adjustment will take place in the electricity account. Assume for example that £225 is paid on 2 February, £156 on 1 May, £80 on 4 August, £130 on 3 November, and it is estimated that £160 worth of electricity has been consumed but not billed on 31 December 19X2.

The account will appear thus:

Dr.		Electricity	Cr.
19X2	£	19X2	£
Feb. 2 Bank	225	Jan. 1 Accrual b/d	153
May 1 Bank	156	Dec. 31 Profit and loss a/c	598
Aug. 4 Bank	80		
Nov. 3 Bank	130		
Dec. 31 Accrual c/d	160		
	751		751
		19X3	
		Jan. 1 Accrual b/d	160

It will be noted that in effect the payment of £225 made on 2 February will be automatically reduced by the accrual of £153, so effectively charging the correct figure of £72 for January consumption in 19X2.

There should probably have been an accrual b/d in 19X1, unless 19X1 was the first year of trading, but for illustration purposes one has to start somewhere!

This matching convention, then, requires that expense accounts should be examined carefully to ensure that the proper charge has been made for the period.

Occasionally too much will have been paid.

A rent will often be payable in advance. Assume a quarterly rent of £240 payable on 1 December 19X1 which is increased to £300 quarterly payable on 1 March, 1 June, 1 September and 1 December 19X2, with an accounting year ending on 31 December. It is obvious that the rent payable on 1 December also covers the months of January and February.

The account for 19X2 would appear:

Dr.		Rent payable	Cr.
19X2	£	19X2	£
Jan. 1 Prepayment b/d	160	Dec. 31 Prepayment c/d	200
Mar. 1 Bank	300	Dec. 31 Profit and loss a/c	1,160
Jun. 1 Bank	300		
Sep. 1 Bank	300		
Dec. 1 Bank	300		
	1,360		1,360
19X3			
Jan. 1 Prepayment b/d	200		

In this way the account is adjusted so that once again the correct amount has been charged to the profit and loss account for the year. The amount paid in advance, shown as a debit balance brought down on the rent account, is called a *prepayment*. This is shown as a current asset in the balance sheet, or sometimes as a composite item, *debtors and prepayments*.

It may also be necessary to adjust an income account in a similar manner. If, for example, an amount of commission was outstanding at the year end, the commission account would be credited and the amount carried down as a debit. This amount carried down would appear as a debtor in the balance sheet.

Dr.		Commission receivable	Cr.
19X2	£	19X2	£
Dec. 31 Profit and loss a/c	149	Mar. 31 Bank	30
		Jul. 1 Bank	27
		Oct. 3 Bank	52
		Dec. 31 Amount due c/d	40
	149		149
19X3			
Jan. 1 Amount due b/d	40		

When dealing with accruals and prepayments it is necessary to bear in mind the materiality convention. Suppose a firm had a van with a substantial amount of petrol in its tank at the year end, and this petrol had been already charged to motor expenses. An adjustment could be made to carry forward the unused petrol to the next period. However, a measure of common sense has to be applied, and adjustments should only be made when the amount is material. What is, or is not, material is a matter of judgement and depends on the size of the firm and the circumstances. Trivial amounts can safely be ignored.

Example of preparation of final accounts

The final part of this chapter sets out a worked example of final accounts, bringing together many of the situations previously described.

An examination question will often commence with a trial balance. Sometimes it might give a single column of balances which need to be re-organised into a trial balance. Occasionally a list of balances is provided without a figure for capital. In the last-mentioned circumstance the balancing figure is capital, but the accuracy of this figure depends upon your recognising correctly those balances which are debits and those which are credits.

After the trial balance (or list of balances) there will usually appear a number of *adjustments*, which have also to be taken into the final accounts.

The practice of using an extended trial balance to build up the trading and profit and loss account and balance sheet is extremely useful for illustration purposes. It does however require a good deal of additional work in re-writing the trial balance and extending the columns.

The method is therefore not really suitable for examination purposes where some speed is essential. Most students should by now recognise without too much difficulty those items which appear in the trading account, those which appear in the profit and loss account, and those in the balance sheet. A shorter method than the extended trial balance (and one which has been long tried and tested) is to examine the trial balance and place a 'T' or 'P' or 'B' in front of each item to indicate where it appears in the final accounts. You can then proceed directly to the trading account, ticking off the Ts as they are entered in the account, and similarly on to the profit and loss account and the balance sheet.

The adjustments are dealt with in a somewhat similar way, as will be demonstrated shortly.

By the end of the exercise all the Ts, Ps and Bs should have been ticked, and the balance sheet should balance. However, it is very easy to make an error so that the balance sheet does not, in fact, balance. You should not become obsessed with balancing in examinations. It is much more important to ensure so far as possible that what is done is correct, and that the time available is allocated properly over all the questions.

EXAMPLE 4.1

The following trial balance was extracted from the books of J. Foster, a trader, as at 31 December 19X2.

		£	£
B	Capital		25,460
B	Loan – B. Jones		8,000
T	Purchases	58,992	
T	Sales		75,330
P	Repairs to buildings	1,128	
B	Buildings	25,300	
B	Van	4,200	
B	Equipment	3,700	
T	Stock – 1 Jan 19X2	3,723	
P	*Lighting and heating	672	
P	Cleaning	430	
P	Motor expenses	1,256	
B	Balance at bank		1,200
P	Wages	2,436	
B	Cash in hand	272	
P	Discounts allowed and received	345	652
B	Drawings	6,480	
P	*Rates	1,275	
P	*Insurance	93	
B	Debtors	743	
B	Creditors		625
P	Miscellaneous expenses	107	
T	Carriage inwards	274	
P	Carriage outwards	632	
P	Commission received		754
T	Returns inwards	270	
T	Returns outwards		307
		112,328	112,328

The following matters are also to be taken into account:

1. Stock in trade at 31 December 19X2 valued at cost £4,135
2. Rates paid in advance amount to £270; insurance paid in advance amounts to £16
3. The loan from B. Jones is at 8% per annum interest which has not yet been paid
4. Electricity consumed but not paid for is estimated at £137 (electricity is included in lighting and heating)
5. Ignore depreciation.

A trading and profit and loss account for 19X2 is required, and a balance sheet as at 31 December 19X2.

The trial balance has already been examined and a T, P or B placed in front of each item as appropriate. The adjustments referred to in the question as 'The following matters ...' still remain to be dealt with.

Each one of these adjustments requires both a *Dr.* and a *Cr.* adjustment. Otherwise the essential duality and the balance will be disturbed. An easy way of incorporating these adjustments into the final accounts is to complete a working paper as follows:

Note			Dr. £	Cr. £
1.	Stock carried forward	B	4,135	
		T		4,135
2.	Rates prepaid	B	270	
		P		270
	Insurance prepaid	B	16	
		P		16
3.	Interest owing	P	640	
		B		640
4.	Electricity accrual	P	137	
		B		137

An asterisk, or some other marking, can be placed against an amount in the trial balance if it requires adjustment. Thus when the figure for rates of £1,275 in the trial balance is to be entered in the profit and loss account, your attention will be drawn to the need to deduct the £270 prepaid. Even if an error is made initially, the fact should become obvious if the items are carefully ticked off when entered; i.e. all the Ts should have been ticked on both the trial balance and the adjustment working paper, otherwise the trading account is not complete, and so on.

The answer to the question is given below. This solution should be carefully worked through. Note that the balance at the bank is a *Cr.* balance and indicates that the bank account is overdrawn. It is impossible, of course, for cash to be overdrawn.

J. Foster
Trading and Profit and Loss Account
for the year ended 31 December 19X2

	£	£	£
Sales			75,330
less Sales returns			270
			75,060
Cost of goods sold			
Opening stock		3,723	
Purchases	58,992		
less Purchases returns	307	58,685	
Carriage inwards		274	
		62,682	
less Closing stock		4,135	58,547
Gross profit			16,513
add Discounts received		652	
Commission		754	1,406
			17,919
less Expenses			
Wages		2,436	
Repairs to buildings		1,128	
Lighting and heating		809	
Cleaning		430	
Motor expenses		1,256	
Discounts allowed		345	
Rates		1,005	
Insurance		77	
Carriage outwards		632	
Miscellaneous expenses		107	
Interest on loan		640	8,865
Net profit			9,054

Balance Sheet as at 31 December 19X2

	£	£	£
Assets			
Fixed assets			
Buildings			25,300
Van			4,200
Equipment			3,700
			33,200
Current assets			
Stock		4,135	
Debtors		743	
Prepayments		286	
Cash		272	
		5,436	

	£	£	£
less Current liabilities			
Creditors[1]	1,265		
Accruals	137		
Bank overdrawn	1,200	2,602	
Working capital			2,834
			36,034
Financed by			
Capital		25,460	
add Profit for period		9,054	
		34,514	
less Drawings		6,480	28,034
Loan from B. Jones			8,000
			36,034

Notes:
1. Creditors £625 + interest owing £640.

The traditional (but not recommended) presentation of the trading and profit and loss account is also shown below:

	£	£		£
Opening stock		3,723	Sales	75,330
Purchases	58,992		*less* Sales returns	270
less Purchases returns	307			75,060
		58,685		
Carriage inwards		274		
		62,682		
less Closing stock		4,135		
Cost of goods sold		58,547		
Gross profit c/d		16,513		
		75,060		75,060
Wages		2,436	Gross profit b/d	16,513
Repairs to buildings		1,128	Discounts received	652
Lighting and heating		809	Commission	754
Cleaning		430		
Motor expenses		1,256		
Discounts allowed		345		
Rates		1,005		
Insurance		77		
Carriage outwards		632		
Miscellaneous expenses		107		
Interest on loan		640		
Net profit		9,054		
		17,919		17,919

Personal and impersonal accounts

Accounts which record assets are known as *real* accounts. Accounts which record expenses and income are known as *nominal* accounts, and nominal accounts together with real accounts are collectively described as *impersonal* accounts. Accounts which record transactions of debtors and creditors are called *personal* accounts. These traditional classifications are still used occasionally.

Questions

4.1S   John Pink rents shop premises at an annual cost of £400 payable quarterly in arrears. In the year to 31 December 19X5, his first year of business, Pink made the following payments to his landlord by cheque in each case:

Mar. 30	£100
Jun. 28	£100
Sep. 27	£100

The rent due on 31 December 19X5, was not paid until January 8 19X6.
Write up Pink's rent account for the year ending 31 December 19X5, showing the correct transfer to the profit and loss account and bringing down any remaining balance.

4.2S   Charles Indigo rents premises at an annual rental of £1,000. The rates payable for the accounting year 1 July 19X6–30 June 19X7, his first year of business, were £360. Cheques for rent and rates were paid as follows:

19X6		£
Jul. 28	Rates for 9 months to 31 March 19X7	220
Sep. 28	Rent for 3 months to 30 September 19X6	250
19X7		
Jan. 3	Rent for 3 months to 31 December 19X6	250
Mar. 28	Rent for 3 months to 31 March 19X7	250
Apr. 30	Rates for 6 months to 30 September 19X7	280

Write up Indigo's rent and rates accounts for the year ending 30 June 19X7, showing the charge to profit and loss account in each case and bringing down any remaining balances.

4.3S   The following trial balance was extracted from the books of J. Black at 31 December 19X8.

	£	£
Capital 1 January 19X8		30,000
Sales		63,000
Purchases returns		2,000
Lighting and heating	440	
Purchases	53,500	
Rent and rates	2,520	
General expenses	1,000	
Fixtures and fittings	12,800	
Motor vehicles	7,500	
Drawings	9,560	
Bank overdraft		4,780
Debtors and creditors	4,450	2,870
Cash in hand	80	
Stock at 1 January 19X8	10,800	
	102,650	102,650

At 31 December 19X8:

> Stock was valued at £11,900
> Electricity accrued £30

Prepare a trading and profit and loss account for the year ended 31 December 19X8, and a balance sheet as at that date.

4.4S   The following trial balance was extracted from the books of S. White at 30 June 19X6.

	£	£
Capital at 1 July 19X5		30,000
Freehold premises	15,000	
Fixtures and fittings	6,750	
Stock at 1 July 19X5	7,296	
Purchases	17,434	
Sales		24,708
Purchases returns		199
Sales returns	180	
Debtors	3,180	
Creditors		2,244
Drawings	2,250	
Salaries	1,245	
Lighting and heating	172	
Rates	400	
Sundry expenses	162	
Discounts allowed	330	
Discounts received		186
Balance at bank	2,908	
Cash in hand	30	
	57,337	57,337

At 30 June 19X6:

Stock was valued at	£7,144
Rates paid in advance	£100
Electricity accrued	£28

Prepare a trading and profit and loss account for the year ended 30 June 19X6, and a balance sheet as at that date.

4.5S   The rent and rates account in the ledger of B. Riley showed that on 31 December 19X2 the rent for the quarter to 31 December was outstanding and that the rates for the half-year ended 31 March 19X3, amounting to £176, had been paid. During the year to 31 December 19X3, the following payments relating to rent and rates were made, all by cheque:

		£
Jan. 4	Rent for the quarter to 31 December 19X2	190
Mar. 29	Rent for the quarter to 31 March 19X3	190
Jun. 26	Rates for the half year to 30 September 19X3	184
Jul. 7	Rent for the quarter to 30 June 19X3	190
Sep. 30	Rent for the quarter to 30 September 19X3	190
Dec. 28	Rent for the quarter to 31 December 19X3	190

The rates for the half year ending 31 March 19X4, which amount to £184, were paid on 6 January 19X4.

You are required to show the rent and rates account as it would appear after the books for the year ended 31 December 19X3 had been closed.

4.6   During the year to 31 December 19X0, A. Ball made the following payments for rent and rates.

19X0		£
Jan. 10	Rent, three months to 31 December 19X9	275
Mar. 31	Rent, three months to 31 March 19X0	275
Apr. 30	Rates, six months to 30 September 19X0	350
Jul. 8	Rent, three months to 30 June 19X0	275
Oct. 15	Rent, three months to 30 September 19X0	300
Oct. 15	Rates, six months to 31 March 19X1	350

The balances on the account (i.e. the rent and rates account) at 1 January 19X0 were:

Rates prepaid   £150
Rent accrued   £275.

From 1 July 19X0 the annual rent was increased to £1,200.
You are required:

(a) To write up the rent and rates account in the ledger of A. Ball for the year to 31 December 19X0, showing clearly any prepayment or accrual at that date and the transfer to profit and loss account for the year.
(b) To state the accounting convention involved in the question and to show the split between the amount charged for rent and the amount charged for rates for the year.

4.7   From the information given below you are required to show the rent, rates and insurance account in the ledger of S. Forshaw for the year ended 30 June 19X6, showing clearly the prepayments and accruals at that date and the transfer to profit and loss account for the year.
The balances on the account at 1 July 19X5 were:

	£
Rent accrued	200
Rates prepaid	150
Insurance prepaid	180

Payments made during the year ended 30 June 19X6 were as follows:

19X5		£
Aug. 10	Rent, three months to 31 July 19X5	300
Oct. 26	Insurance, one year to 31 October 19X6	600
Nov. 2	Rates, six months to 31 March 19X6	350
Dec. 12	Rent, four months to 30 November 19X5	400
19X6		
Apr. 17	Rent, four months to 31 March 19X6	400
May 9	Rates, six months to 30 September 19X6	350

(Chartered Institute of Management Accountants)

4.8   The trial balance prepared from the books of P. Green at 30 June 19X4 was as follows:

	£	£
Capital at 1 July 19X3		50,850
Drawings	7,400	
Freehold premises	20,000	
Debtors and creditors	8,500	5,350
Stock 1 July 19X3	10,000	
Wages	3,650	
Carriage inwards	3,600	
Rates and insurance	2,900	
Purchases and sales	101,100	121,550
Returns inwards and outwards	435	210
Carriage outwards	1,100	
Advertising	515	
Rent received		800
Office equipment	3,050	
Fixtures and fittings	6,400	
Lighting and heating	1,240	
Balance at bank	8,795	
Cash in hand	75	
	178,760	178,760

At 30 June 19X4:

1. Stock was valued at £15,500
2. Rates prepaid £400
3. Insurance owing £320; electricity accrued £135
4. An invoice amounting to £80 had been posted to the carriage inwards account instead of carriage outwards account
5. Rent receivable outstanding £200.

Prepare a trading and profit and loss account for the year ended 30 June 19X4, and a balance sheet as at that date.

4.9   The trial balance extracted from the books of D. Brown at 30 September 19X5, was as follows:

	£	£
Capital at 1 October 19X4		27,000
Fixtures and fittings	9,500	
Van	2,500	
Purchases and sales	26,100	38,700
Lighting and heating	320	
Discounts allowed and received	1,380	1,150
Wages	2,450	
Rent and rates	1,760	
Telephone	220	
Insurance	270	
Stock at 1 October 19X4	8,200	
Debtors and creditors	2,530	2,570
Drawings	6,800	
Cash in hand	50	
Balance at bank	7,340	
	69,420	69,420

At 30 September 19X5:

1. Stock was valued at £8,500
2. Rent owing £500
3. Rates paid in advance £120
4. Insurance paid in advance £60
5. Telephone charges accrued £40
6. Electricity accrued £60.

Prepare a trading and profit and loss account for the year ended 30 September 19X5, and a balance sheet as at that date.

4.10   The balances extracted from the books of G. Lewis at 31 December 19X6 are given below:

	£
Drawings	7,180
Heating and lighting	1,234
Postages and stationery	268
Carriage outwards	1,446
Insurances	1,818
Wages and salaries	18,910
Stock at 1 January 19X6	42,120
Purchases	74,700
Sales	131,040
Rent and rates	2,990
General expenses	1,460
Discount received	426
Plant and machinery	9,060
Cash at bank	3,222
Cash in hand	65
Debtors	1,920
Creditors	630
Sales returns	1,310
Purchases returns	747

At 31 December 19X6:

1. Stock was valued at £33,990
2. Rent owing £310
3. Insurance paid in advance £220
4. The balance on the capital account is the balance brought forward at 31 December 19X5.

Prepare a trading and profit and loss account for the year ended 31 December 19X6 and a balance sheet at that date.

5 Depreciation

Aims of the chapter:

> To consider how the matching convention applies to fixed assets
> To introduce the going concern and the money measurement
> conventions

Depreciation means a reduction of value through physical wear and tear or other form of deterioration. Fixed assets have previously been defined as assets which will provide service for a period longer than one year. They will have been acquired for use in the business and not for resale. The majority of fixed assets are subject to depreciation and have a limited productive life. Land is a possible exception, and even land in some forms of use will reduce in value (e.g. a mine or quarry).

Provision for this depreciation of fixed assets should therefore be made in an accounting system. The matching convention and common sense indicate that the most appropriate way of achieving this would be to allocate the cost of the asset, over its useful life, against the income generated by the asset.

The subject of depreciation is, however, fraught with difficulties, some of which are outside the scope of this book but nevertheless deserve at least a brief mention.

The *going concern* convention assumes that a business entity will remain operational indefinitely, unless there is clear evidence to the contrary. If this assumption were not made, it would be most difficult to apportion the cost of a fixed asset over its life, as the possibility of cessation of business would always have to be borne in mind. The full cost of an asset might have to be charged against income immediately, so causing a wide variation of net profits from year to year.

Another problem is created by the *monetary measurement* convention which requires that only transactions, facts and events recordable in monetary terms should be brought into the accounts. This has advantages in that money is a common measure or common denominator in terms of which transactions, facts and events can be recorded. It also has disadvantages in that money does not tell the whole story regarding the quality of the business, or the product, or the management. A major disadvantage is that money is not a stable unit of measurement as a result of inflation.

Depreciation is usually based on the cost price of assets under the convention that cost is the most objective measurement as it is supported by an actual transaction. But at the end of the useful life of an asset inflation is frequently the cause of a substantial increase in its replacement cost, so requiring an increase in the monetary capital required for the firm to maintain its trading base.

Price changes also cause *appreciation* of some asset values in monetary terms, though not necessarily in real terms. A prime commercial site with buildings may increase in monetary value due to a combination of good fortune in terms of situation, and pure inflationary tendencies. The actual buildings, nevertheless, must be physically deteriorating, whilst appreciation simultaneously takes place for other reasons. At the present time accountants are wrestling with these problems in terms of recognising them in accounting statements.

The remainder of this chapter will be devoted to dealing with depreciation on the basis of the historical cost of acquisition of fixed assets. It will be primarily concerned with the conventional approach to depreciation, i.e. the allocation of the historical cost of an asset over its useful life against income.

The arithmetic of depreciation is reasonably simple once the life of the asset has been determined. It may be relatively easy to forecast the life of an asset if there has been substantial past experience of the type of asset, or if it has a fixed legal life, as with a copyright or patent. Problems can occur with new technology and here most accountants will probably adopt their usual conservative approach and err on the side of a short life.

In a worked example of a profit and loss account, in Chapter 4, repairs to buildings were correctly charged to the profit and loss account. On the other hand, any expenditure which might improve or prolong the life of an asset should be capitalised and debited to the asset account. (Expenditure on fixed assets is referred to as *capital expenditure.*) Additionally, any costs of acquiring assets, including legal charges, and installation costs should also be debited to the asset account and written off over the anticipated useful life of the asset.

Methods of calculating depreciation

1   Straight line method

This is probably the most commonly used method for calculating depreciation. The cost of the asset less any anticipated residual value is divided equally over the estimated life.

Vehicle cost	£20,000
Life	6 years
Residual value	£2,000.

$$\text{Annual depreciation} = \frac{£20,000 - £2,000}{6} = £3,000.$$

A particular point to note is that in examination questions annual depreciation by the straight line method is often expressed as a percentage of the original cost price, i.e. in this case 15%. This should not be confused with the next method described, where a percentage is also used.

In the straight line method the residual value can be, and often is, ignored if the amount is trivial, e.g. scrap value only.

2   Reducing balance method

(This method is also known as the *diminishing* or *declining balance method* or as the *reducing instalment method.*)

From a student's point of view this method is equally as important as the straight line method. A percentage is applied to the original cost after deducting any depreciation already provided. Taking the facts as before, i.e.

Vehicle cost	£20,000
Life	6 years
Residual value	£2,000

the following formula is applied.

$$\text{Rate of depreciation} = 1 - \sqrt[n]{\frac{\text{Residual value}}{\text{Cost}}},$$

where n represents the life of the asset (in years).

Applying the formula to the original data:

$$\text{Rate of depreciation} = 1 - \sqrt[6]{\frac{2,000}{20,000}}$$
$$= 0.319 \text{ or } 32\%.$$

The depreciation for each year is therefore:

	£
Cost	20,000
Depreciation	
Year 1 at 32% (of £20,000)	6,400
	13,600
Year 2 at 32% (of £13,600)	4,352
	9,248
Year 3 at 32% (of £9,248)	2,959
	6,289
Year 4 at 32% (of £6,289)	2,012
	4,277
Year 5 at 32% (of £4,277)	1,369
	2,908
Year 6 at 32% (of £2,908)	930
	1,978

By this method the percentage is applied to the reducing balance, not the original cost as in the straight line method. A percentage cannot be calculated without an estimated residual value, as is obvious from an examination of the above formula.

The rounding off of the percentage and the pounds has produced a residual value of £1,978 rather than £2,000. This is quite near enough for all practical and examination purposes. Calculations should normally be made to the nearest per cent and nearest pound.

An advantage sometimes claimed for this method of depreciation is that the charge to profit and loss account for depreciation decreases as the cost of repairs tends to increase. In theory the charge for depreciation plus the cost of repairs should remain approximately constant. In practice repair costs do not often conform to this pattern.

3 Revaluation method

Occasionally an asset is revalued at the end of each year. Small tools are often dealt with in this way. In this case the depreciation for any one year is given by

Valuation at start of year + additions − valuation at end
Year 1   £20,000 + £5,000 − £17,000 = £8,000
Year 2   £17,000 + £6,000 − £16,000 = £7,000

and so on.

4 Production method

In a manufacturing concern a machine might be depreciated according to the number of units produced in a year compared with the total anticipated unit production of that machine over its life.

Machine cost	£50,000
Expected production	96,000 units
Residual value	£2,000.

The depreciation charge per unit would be

$$\frac{£50,000 - £2,000}{96,000} = £0.50 \text{ per unit.}$$

A similar alternative is to use annual machine hours in use compared with total anticipated machine hours over the life of the machine:

Machine cost	£50,000
Expected production	8,000 hours
Residual value	£2,000.

The depreciation charge per machine hour would be

$$\frac{£50,000 - £2,000}{8,000} = £6 \text{ per machine hour.}$$

5 Sum of years digits

This is an American method not frequently met in this country. If an asset is to be depreciated over six years, the years are arranged thus:

							Total
Year	1	2	3	4	5	6	21
Years reversed	6	5	4	3	2	1	21

In year 1 the depreciation provided is 6/21 of the original cost. In year 2 it is 5/21 of the original cost, and so on. It produces a depreciation pattern somewhat similar to the reducing balance method, except plotted graphically the annual depreciation calculated by this method would produce a downward sloping straight line, whereas the reducing balance method would produce a curve.

Vehicle cost	£20,000
Life	6 years
Residual value	£2,000.

Depreciation
Year 1 6/21 × £18,000 = £5,143
Year 2 5/21 × £18,000 = £4,286
Year 3 4/21 × £18,000 = £3,429
Year 4 3/21 × £18,000 = £2,571
Year 5 2/21 × £18,000 = £1,714
Year 6 1/21 × £18,000 = £857

Accounting for depreciation

Fixed assets of a similar type will normally be grouped into one account. All motor cars would appear in one account, whilst buildings would appear in another account. The degree of analysis for account headings (e.g. between motor cars and motor vans) is to a large extent a matter of choice. It will always be necessary in practice to maintain an asset register showing the underlying details of each asset account, and the depreciation provided for each individual asset.

A minor problem is sometimes met regarding the treatment of depreciation in the year of acquisition of an asset. An examination question will usually indicate whether a full year's depreciation should be provided, or whether depreciation should be ignored in the year of acquisition. If there is no indication, the depreciation should be apportioned on a monthly basis if sufficient information is available.

In practice the normal procedure is to provide for a full year's depreciation in the year of acquisition, with no depreciation charge in the year of sale.

The accounting entries are shown in Example 5.1 for the depreciation of the vehicle considered in methods 1 and 2. These methods (i.e. straight line and reducing balance) are the most frequently required and are shown side by side for the first three years for comparison purposes.

It will be seen that an account is opened called *provision for depreciation* account and the entries are

Dr. Profit and loss account
Cr. Provision for depreciation account,

with the amount of the depreciation charge for the year.

EXAMPLE 5.1

STRAIGHT LINE
Vehicle

	£
19X1 Jan. 1 Bank	20,000

Provision for depreciation of vehicle

	£		£
19X1 Dec. 31 Balance c/d	3,000	19X1 Dec. 31 Profit and loss	3,000
19X2 Dec. 31 Balance c/d	6,000	19X2 Jan. 1 Balance b/d	3,000
		Dec. 31 Profit and loss	3,000
	6,000		6,000
19X3 Dec. 31 Balance c/d	9,000	19X3 Jan. 1 Balance b/d	6,000
		Dec. 31 Profit and loss	3,000
	9,000		9,000
		19X4 Jan. 1 Balance b/d	9,000

Balance sheets (extract)

	Cost	Depreciation	Net value
	£	£	£
31 Dec. 19X1 Vehicle	20,000	3,000	17,000
31 Dec. 19X2 Vehicle	20,000	6,000	14,000
31 Dec. 19X3 Vehicle	20,000	9,000	11,000

REDUCING BALANCE
Vehicle

	£
19X1 Jan. 1 Bank	20,000

Provision for depreciation of vehicle

	£		£
19X1 Dec. 31 Balance c/d	6,400	19X1 Dec. 31 Profit and loss	6,400
19X2 Dec. 31 Balance c/d	10,752	19X2 Jan. 1 Balance b/d	6,400
		Dec. 31 Profit and loss	4,352
	10,752		10,752
19X3 Dec. 31 Balance c/d	13,711	19X3 Jan. 1 Balance b/d	10,752
		Dec. 31 Profit and loss	2,959
	13,711		13,711
		19X4 Jan. 1 Balance b/d	13,711

Balance sheets (extract)

	Cost	Depreciation	Net value
	£	£	£
31 Dec. 19X1 Vehicle	20,000	6,400	13,600
31 Dec. 19X2 Vehicle	20,000	10,752	9,248
31 Dec. 19X3 Vehicle	20,000	13,711	6,289

In this way depreciation for the year is matched against the income for the year.

Whenever there is a separate asset account, there should also be a separate 'provision for depreciation' account.

The cost price of the asset is only brought together with the depreciation provision at the balance sheet stage. This method of presentation continues until the asset is disposed of, when the two amounts are brought together as shown later in this chapter.

It should also be noted that the accounting is precisely the same for both the straight line and reducing balance methods, and indeed any other method. It is only the amounts that vary according to the method used.

A slightly more complex situation is now illustrated in Example 5.2.

EXAMPLE 5.2

At 31 December 19X1 a firm owned the following assets and had at that date already made provision for depreciation as indicated.

	Cost price £	Depreciation £
Motor vans	65,400	17,560
Equipment	12,300	6,200

During the year ending 31 December 19X2 further motor vans costing £7,800 and additional equipment costing £2,800 were acquired. The motor vans are depreciated at 20% per annum by the straight line method, and the equipment at 25% per annum by the reducing balance method. A full year's depreciation is provided in the year of acquisition. Prepare the appropriate accounts for the year ending 31 December 19X2, and show how the balances would be presented in the balance sheet.

Solution:

Motor vans

19X2	£	19X2	£
Jan. 1 Balance b/d	65,400	Dec. 31 Balance c/d	73,200
X X Bank	7,800		
	73,200		73,200
19X3			
Jan. 1 Balance b/d	73,200		

Equipment

19X2	£	19X2	£
Jan. 1 Balance b/d	12,300	Dec. 31 Balance c/d	15,100
X X Bank	2,800		
	15,100		15,100
19X3			
Jan. 1 Balance b/d	15,100		

Provision for depreciation of motor vans

19X2	£	19X2	£
Dec. 31 Balance c/d	32,200	Jan. 1 Balance b/d	17,560
		Dec. 31 Profit and loss	14,640
	32,200		32,200
		19X3	
		Jan. 1 Balance b/d	32,200

Note: The depreciation for the year is 20% of £73,200 = £14,640.

Provision for depreciation of equipment

19X2	£	19X2	£
Dec. 31 Balance c/d	8,425	Jan. 1 Balance b/d	6,200
		Dec. 31 Profit and loss	2,225
	8,425		8,425
		19X3	
		Jan. 1 Balance b/d	8,425

Note: The depreciation for the year is 25% of (£15,100 − £6,200) = £2,225.

Balance Sheet (extract) as at 31 December 19X2

	Cost £	Depreciation £	Net £
Motor vans	73,200	32,200	41,000
Equipment	15,100	8,425	6,675

Disposal of assets

The annual charge made for depreciation of an asset is, at best, no more than an estimate. Its accuracy depends on the accuracy of the original forecast of the life of the asset and its residual value. It is only on disposal of, or scrapping of, an asset that the true picture can be determined.

On disposal the cost price of the asset is transferred to a *disposal of assets* account, as is the accumulated depreciation and any cash or consideration received for the asset. The result is often described as a 'profit' or 'loss' on the sale of the asset. Strictly speaking this is incorrect. The difference represents under- or over-depreciation of the asset. This difference is debited or credited as appropriate to the current year's profit and loss account.

EXAMPLE 5.3

Once again, consider the example of the vehicle depreciated by both methods 1 and 2 (i.e. straight line and reducing balance) shown in Example 5.1. Assume that it was decided to dispose of this vehicle during the fourth year, i.e. 19X4, and £8,000 was received for the vehicle on 1 May. The accounting entries would be as shown on page 54, again shown side by side.

The accounting is once again the same for both methods. However, due to the differing methods of calculation, a further charge to the profit and loss account is required under the straight line method, whilst under the

EXAMPLE 5.3

STRAIGHT LINE
Vehicle

		£			£
19X4			19X4	Dec. 31 Disposal of	
Jan. 1	Balance b/d	20,000		vehicle	20,000

Provision for depreciation of vehicle

		£			£
19X4	Dec. 31 Disposal of		19X4		
	vehicle	9,000	Jan. 1	Balance b/d	9,000

Disposal of vehicle

		£			£
19X4			19X4		
Dec. 31	Vehicle	20,000	May 1	Bank	8,000
			Dec. 31	Depreciation	9,000
			Dec. 31	Profit and loss	3,000
		20,000			20,000

REDUCING BALANCE
Vehicle

		£			£
19X4			19X4	Dec. 31 Disposal of	
Jan. 1	Balance b/d	20,000		vehicle	20,000

Provision for depreciation of vehicle

		£			£
19X4	Dec. 31 Disposal of		19X4		
	vehicle	13,711	Jan. 1	Balance b/d	13,711

Disposal of vehicle

		£			£
19X4			19X4		
Dec. 31	Vehicle	20,000	May 1	Bank	8,000
Dec. 31	Profit and loss	1,711	Dec. 31	Depreciation	13,711
		21,711			21,711

reducing balance method the asset has been over-depreciated, resulting in a credit to profit and loss account.

Note that it is not necessary to provide the 'normal' depreciation in the year of disposal. The disposal of asset account takes care of all depreciation required in that year.

The entries to be made on the disposal of a fixed asset can therefore be summarised as under:

Disposal of asset account	Debit	
Fixed asset account		Credit
With the original cost of the asset sold.		
Provision for depreciation of fixed asset account	Debit	
Disposal of asset account		Credit
With the depreciation provided to date on the asset sold.		
Bank account (or other asset account)	Debit	
Disposal of asset account		Credit
With the cash or other asset received on the sale of the fixed asset.		
Profit and loss account	Debit	
Disposal of asset account		Credit
With the balance on the disposal of asset account if it is a loss.		
or		
Disposal of asset account	Debit	
Profit and loss account		Credit
With the balance on the disposal of asset account if it is a profit.		

Note: The balance on the disposal of asset account represents either an under-provision (loss) or an over-provision (profit) of depreciation.

A more realistic example is now considered. This is a development and continuation of Example 5.2.

EXAMPLE 5.4

The firm considered in Example 5.2 acquired and sold the following assets in the year ending 31 December 19X3:

In 19X3 a further motor van was acquired costing £4,050, and additional equipment costing £1,200.

In the same year a vehicle originally purchased for £3,500 in 19X0 was disposed of for £1,100, and equipment costing £1,000 in 19X0 was sold for £550. Prepare the appropriate accounts for the year ending 31 December 19X3 and show how the balances would be presented in the balance sheet.

Solution:

It is first necessary to calculate the accumulated depreciation on the assets disposed of. In the case of the motor van depreciated by the straight line method this is quite simple:

$$3 \text{ years (i.e. 19X0, 19X1, 19X2)} \times 20\% = 60\%,$$
$$60\% \times £3,500 = £2,100.$$

The equipment, having been depreciated by the reducing balance method, is slightly more difficult and has to be scheduled:

	£	Total depreciation £
Cost	1,000	
Depreciation		
19X0 at 25%	250	250
	750	
19X1 at 25%	188	188
	562	
19X2 at 25%	141	141
	421	579

The appropriate entries in the books of account are therefore:

Motor van

19X3	£	19X3	£
Jan. 1 Balance b/d	73,200	Dec. 31 Disposal of motor vans	3,500
X X Bank	4,050	31 Balance c/d	73,750
	77,250		77,250
19X4			
Jan. 1 Balance b/d	73,750		

Equipment

19X3	£	19X3	£
Jan. 1 Balance b/d	15,100	Dec. 31 Disposal of equipment	1,000
X X Bank	1,200	31 Balance c/d	15,300
	16,300		16,300
19X4			
Jan. 1 Balance b/d	15,300		

Provision for depreciation of motor vans

19X3		£	19X3		£
Dec. 31 Disposal of motor vans		2,100	Jan. 1 Balance b/d		32,200
Dec. 31 Balance c/d		44,850	Dec. 31 Profit and loss		14,750
		46,950			46,950
			19X4		
			Jan. 1 Balance b/d		44,850

Note: The depreciation for the year is 20% of £73,750 = £14,750.

Provision for depreciation of equipment

19X3		£	19X3		£
Dec. 31 Disposal of equipment		579	Jan. 1 Balance b/d		8,425
Dec. 31 Balance c/d		9,710	Dec. 31 Profit and loss		1,864
		10,289			10,289
			19X4		
			Jan. 1 Balance b/d		9,710

Note: The depreciation for the year is 25% of £15,300 – (£8,425 – £579) = 25% of £7,454 = £1,864.

Disposal of motor vans

19X3	£	19X3	£
Dec. 31 Motor vans	3,500	X X Bank	1,100
		Dec. 31 Provision for depreciation of motor vans	2,100
		Dec. 31 Profit and loss	300
	3,500		3,500

Disposal of equipment

19X3	£	19X3	£
Dec. 31 Equipment	1,000	X X Bank	550
Profit and loss	129	Dec. 31 Provision for depreciation of equipment	579
	1,129		1,129

The suggested presentation in the profit and loss account is as follows:

Depreciation	£	£
Motor vans		
Charge for year	14,750	
Under-provision (add)	300	15,050
Equipment		
Charge for year	1,864	
Over-provision (less)	129	1,735

Balance Sheet (extract) as at 31 December 19X3

	Cost £	Depreciation £	Net £
Motor vans	73,750	44,850	28,900
Equipment	15,300	9,710	5,590

Fixed asset register

The advantage of an asset register, as referred to earlier in the chapter, to assist in the accurate computation of the provision for depreciation will now be apparent. A separate record or memorandum account for each item of plant and machinery, and for each motor vehicle, etc., is maintained giving the relevant information for that individual asset. A typical lay-out is as follows:

Classification, i.e.
 	
    Plant and
    machinery
 	
  Motor
  vehicle
	Description:
	
	Maker:
	
	Invoice
	reference:
			Location	Serial no.
				
				Date
				purchased

Original cost *less* Residual value Net capital cost		£	Disposal: Date Written-down value Net proceeds	£
Estimated Life .... years			Gain/loss on disposal	
Method of depreciation:				

Year	Cost £	Depreciation £	Written-down value £	Notes

As demonstrated in the accounting illustrations, in the ledger there is normally one asset account and one provision for depreciation of that asset account for each main class of asset, e.g. plant and machinery, motor vehicles. At the end of each accounting period, the totals in the asset register are reconciled with the appropriate asset account and the provision for depreciation of the asset account in the ledger. The major advantage of using a fixed asset register arises on the disposal of an asset as all the detailed information required for correctly accounting for the sale is contained in the asset register.

Depreciation of assets and availability of funds

A common misconception is to believe that the balance on the provision for depreciation account somehow represents a fund of available ready cash.

It is true that a charge will have been made to the profit and loss account, so reducing the profits and discouraging the owner from withdrawing from the business more than the stated net profit. If a firm were only trading for cash and only profits were withdrawn, the cash/bank position would improve in line with the depreciation provision if all other things remained static.

However, the owner, noticing that his cash/bank position had improved, might be inclined to make use of these extra funds. He could increase his stock, or buy further fixed assets, or commence giving credit to customers (i.e. introduce debtors) in order to expand his business.

The provision for depreciation might therefore have an influence on the cash/bank position, but it is the cash account and the bank account balances which have also taken into account other transactions which indicate the actual position. There is no other fund of cash available. The method of providing depreciation may affect the profit but it will not affect the cash flow.

Depreciation should be regarded as purely an exercise in the allocation of costs over a period of time.

The subject of *funds* will be dealt with in more detail in the chapter on *cash flow*.

Questions

5.1S   Truck & Co. showed the following balances on the plant and machinery account and the provision for depreciation of plant and machinery account at 30 September 19X7.

	£
Plant and machinery, at cost	10,000
Provision for depreciation of plant and machinery	2,000

Depreciation is provided at 20% per annum on cost.
    You are required to show:
 (a) the plant and machinery account and the provision for depreciation of plant and machinery account at 30 September 19X8
 (b) the balance sheet extract at 30 September 19X8.

5.2S   D. Bird purchased machinery for £3,000 in June 19X2. Its life is estimated
to be six years, and its residual value at the end of this period £534.
    You are required to show the machinery and provision for depreciation
of machinery accounts for the six years, calculating depreciation at a fixed
rate per cent on the reducing value of the asset. Accounts are prepared to 31
December in each year and a full year's depreciation is provided in the year
of purchase.

5.3S   On 1 January 19X3, a manufacturer acquired two identical machine tools at
a cost of £5,000 each, and a reprographic machine for the office at a cost of
£2,000. The machine tools are depreciated at 20% per annum on a
declining balance basis, and the reprographic machine, which has an estimated residual value of £200 and a life of six years, is depreciated on a
straight line basis. On 1 January 19X4 one of the machine tools was sold for
£2,750 and a new one acquired for £8,000.

Required:
(a) Prepare the relevant asset accounts, the provision for depreciation
    accounts, and the sale of assets account, for the year ended 31
    December 19X4.
(b) The manufacturer, observing the sale of asset account and the cost of
    the new machine, notes that 'in future we must increase the depreciation
    rate because we underestimated the amount of cash needed to replace
    the asset'. Discuss this statement.

(Chartered Association of Certified Accountants)

5.4S   A firm acquired two lorries details of which are as follows:

Registration no.	NOL 862 V	NOM 760 W
Date of purchase	31 May 19X6	31 October 19X6
Cost price	£18,000	£24,000

On 1 September 19X7, vehicle NOL 862 V became a total loss. In full
settlement on 20 September 19X7 an insurance company paid £12,500
under a comprehensive policy. The firm prepared accounts annually to 31
December and provided depreciation on a straight line basis at a rate of
20% per annum for motor vehicles, apportioned as from the date of
purchase and up to the date of disposal.
    You are required to record these transactions in the following accounts,
carrying down the balances as on 31 December 19X6 and 31 December
19X7:

(a) Motor vehicles
(b) Provision for depreciation of motor vehicles
(c) Motor vehicles disposals.

5.5S   The following trial balance was extracted from the books of F. Robinson at
30 June 19X9.

Trial Balance at 30 June 19X9

	£	£
Freehold premises at cost	16,000	
Fixtures and fittings at cost	4,000	
Provision for depreciation on fixtures and fittings		1,600
Cash in hand	50	

	£	£
Balance at bank	2,164	
Stock at 1 July 19X8	14,864	
Purchases and sales	116,230	164,720
Returns inwards and outwards	1,330	1,910
Debtors and creditors	12,210	11,694
Drawings	11,200	
Salaries and commission	18,360	
Lighting and heating	1,510	
Rent, rates and insurance	2,600	
Sundry expenses	802	
Discounts	1,220	816
Capital at 1 July 19X8		21,800
	202,540	202,540

The following matters are to be taken into account:

1. Stock at 30 June 19X9, £10,280
2. Rent owing £250
3. Rates prepaid £700; insurance prepaid £100
4. Commission due but unpaid £240
5. Fixtures and fittings are to be depreciated at 10% per annum on cost.

You are required to prepare a trading and profit and loss account for the year ended 30 June 19X9, and a balance sheet as at that date.

5.6S   The following trial balance was extracted from the books of S. Barnard at 31 December 19X8.

Trial Balance at 31 December 19X8

	£	£
Cash in hand	30	
Balance at bank	8,750	
Debtors and creditors	2,530	2,750
Stock at 1 January 19X8	8,200	
Purchases and purchase returns	26,100	1,300
Sales returns and sales	1,650	38,700
Wages	2,450	
Rent and rates	2,110	
Insurance	1,030	
Discount received		1,150
Van at cost	2,500	
Provision for depreciation of van		1,100
Fixtures and fittings at cost	2,590	
Provision for depreciation of fixtures and fittings		1,250
Drawings	6,310	
Capital at 1 January 19X8		18,000
	64,250	64,250

The following matters are to be taken into account:

1. Stock at 31 December 19X8, £11,500
2. Rent owing £250
3. Rates prepaid £360

4. Insurance prepaid £190

5. The van cost £2,500 and has an estimated residual value of £300. The cost less the residual value is to be written off as depreciation over 4 years. The fixtures and fittings cost less residual value of £90 is to be written off over 10 years.

You are required to prepare a trading and profit and loss account for the year ended 31 December 19X8, and a balance sheet as at that date.

5.7   Carriers Ltd purchase four lorries at a cost of £4,000 each. The directors expect to use the lorries for a period of five years, after which time they will be traded in for new vehicles. They are now considering whether to charge depreciation annually at 40% by the reducing balance method or at 18½% by the straight line method; both methods produce an approximately similar residual value for the vehicles.

You are required:

(a) to show the provision for depreciation of lorries account under both methods over the five year period;

(b) to show the balance sheet extract under both methods at the end of the five year period;

(c) to tabulate the advantages and disadvantages of the two methods of depreciation shown.

Note: Carriers Ltd provides for a full year's depreciation in the year of purchase.

5.8   (a) At March 1 19X6, the following balances appeared on the ledger accounts of Hill & Co. Ltd:

	£
Van A account	1,550
Van B account	1,500
Office equipment account	2,100

Each asset account had a corresponding 'provision for depreciation account', the respective balances on each being £1,388, £960 and £780.

Van A was originally acquired in December 19X2, and it was considered that it would last six years with a residual value of £50. It is company policy to provide a full year's depreciation in the year of acquisition, and depreciation of 40% per year is calculated on a declining balance.

Van B was acquired in June 19X4 (depreciation at 40% per year on a declining balance) and was sold in December 19X6 for £230. A new van C was obtained for £1,800 (less trade discount 10%), and was expected to have a five year life, and is to be depreciated on a declining balance at 40% per year. The office equipment is depreciated on a straight line basis at 10% on cost.

Required:
Prepare all the necessary ledger accounts relevant to the above information for the year ended 28 February 19X7.

(b) An employee, observing the depreciation balances on the above accounts, notes with relief that 'the company has plenty of funds for replacement'.

Required:
Comment briefly on the validity of this observation.

(Chartered Association of Certified Accountants)

5.9   Greenacres and Co., a well established company specialising in the distribu-
       tion of agricultural buildings, equipment and fertilisers, commenced a
       machinery repair service on 1 January 19X7.
           From the beginning of the new venture, the repair service used a prefab-
       ricated building which the company bought originally with the intention of
       selling it. In fact, the building was included in trading stock at cost at 31
       December 19X6, at £10,000 and was then displayed for retail sale at
       £13,000. In preparing the building for use as a workshop on 1 January
       19X7, the following expenditure was incurred:

	£
Foundations and erection costs	1,000
Interior and exterior painting	600
Heating and lighting systems	3,000

       On 1 January 19X8, further work was undertaken on the repair service
       building's heating system at a total cost of £1,400, half of which related to
       repairs and the rest concerned the installation of additional thermostatic
       controls.
           On 30 June 19X8, the following work was completed on the workshop
       building:

	£
Installation of partition walls	1,600
Renewal of wooden window frames	1,000

       Early in 19X9, following the closure of the machinery repair service, the
       workshop building, including the heating and lighting systems, was sold for
       £8,000. It is company policy to provide depreciation annually on prefabri-
       cated buildings at the rate of 10% of cost at the end of each financial year
       (31 December).
       Required:
       (a) The following ledger accounts as they would appear in the books of
           Greenacres & Co. for each of the financial years ended 31 December
           19X7, 19X8 and 19X9:
           (i) Repair service workshop building
           (ii) Repair service workshop building provision for depreciation.
           Note: The balances on accounts should be brought down at the end of
           each financial year.
       (b) The repair service workshop building disposal account.
                    (Chartered Association of Certified Accountants)

5.10   J. Foster Ltd, a company with a turnover of £30,000 per year, acquired a
       machine on 1 January 19X5 for £8,000. It was company policy to depreciate
       machinery on a straight line basis at 20% per year. During 19X7 a modifica-
       tion was made to the machine to improve its technical reliability at a cost of
       £800 which it was considered would extend the useful life of the machine by
       2 years. At the same time, an important component of the machine was
       replaced at a cost of £500, because of excessive wear and tear. Routine
       maintenance during the year cost £250.
       Required:
       (i) Show the asset account, the provision for depreciation account, and the
            charge to profit and loss account in respect of the machine for the year
            ended 31 December 19X7.
       (ii) Once an asset such as a machine is installed, what factors should be

considered when deciding whether to capitalise or treat as expense subsequent expenditure relating to that asset?

(Chartered Association of Certified Accountants)

5.11   The following trial balance was extracted from the books of W. Hill at 31 December 19X8.

Trial Balance at 31 December 19X8

	£	£
Stock at 1 January 19X8	14,600	
Purchases	125,020	
Returns outwards		1,060
Cash in hand	340	
Bank	2,266	
Freehold premises at cost	33,860	
Trade expenses	4,840	
Printing, stationery, advertising	1,164	
Debtors	33,600	
Creditors		22,967
Wages	22,900	
Salaries	11,100	
Capital at 31 December 19X8		10,395
Discounts	6,300	4,600
Sales		220,895
Office furniture at cost	13,050	
Rates and insurance	4,200	
Returns inwards	1,055	
Provision for depreciation on freehold premises		10,158
Provision for depreciation on office furniture		4,220
	274,295	274,295

The following matters are to be taken into account:

(a) Stock at 31 December 19X8, £15,200
(b) Rates paid in advance, £650; insurance accrued due, £160
(c) Provide for depreciation as follows: 5% on cost on freehold premises; 10% on reducing balance on office furniture
(d) Drawings of £24,200 have been debited to capital account.

You are required to prepare a trading and profit and loss account for the year ended 31 December 19X8 and a balance sheet as at that date.

5.12   The following trial balance was extracted from the books of K. Inman at 31 March 19X9.

Trial Balance at 31 March 19X9

	£	£
Capital account		16,270
Stock at 1 April 19X8	4,930	
Fixtures and fittings at cost	2,350	
Provision for depreciation of furniture and fittings		2,000
Motor vans at cost	12,640	

	£	£
Provision for depreciation on motor vans		5,400
Disposal of motor van		182
Purchases	58,200	
Sales		91,350
Debtors and creditors	7,818	5,212
General expenses	1,230	
Wages and salaries	7,980	
Discounts	1,413	891
Balance at bank	12,205	
Drawings	11,424	
Motor expenses	475	
Rent and rates	640	
	121,305	121,305

The following matters are to be taken into account:

1. Stock at 31 March 19X9, £5,780
2. Wages and salaries owing £217
3. The credit balance on the disposal of motor van account represents the cash received for an old van sold during the year. The cost price of this van, £4,000, is included in the motor vans at cost account and the depreciation provided to date, £3,200, is included in the provision for depreciation on motor vans account.
4. Depreciation for the year is to be provided as follows: fixtures and fittings, 10% per annum on reducing balance; motor vans, 25% per annum on cost.

You are required to prepare a trading and profit and loss account for the year ended 31 March 19X9, and a balance sheet as at that date.

6 Division of the ledger; books of original entry

Aims of the chapter:

To develop the system of recording transactions

In Chapter 2 reference was made to the fact that, for convenience, the ledger would probably be divided into several books; but together the several books form the one ledger.

In most systems there will almost certainly be a separate *cash book*, a separate *debtors ledger* (or *sales ledger*) and a separate *creditors ledger* (or *purchases ledger*). The remaining accounts might possibly (though not necessarily) be divided into real accounts dealing with assets, liabilities and capital, and nominal accounts dealing with income and expense accounts.

It is important to remember that this division is purely for convenience and is made so that the work can be shared; each person or group of persons specialising in a particular area of work.

Cash book

In the examples considered previously there has been an implicit presumption that separate cash and bank accounts are maintained. The simple concept of a cash book does nothing to disturb this; it is just that cash and bank transactions are shown in columnar fashion in one book. It is as essential as ever that transactions are recorded accurately as being either cash or bank transactions.

In Chapter 3 the cash/bank transactions of A. Trader were recorded in separate accounts. The following example brings these transactions together into one book, but the one book still represents the two separate accounts.

A reference back to Chapter 3 will show that nothing, in fact, has changed. The balances carried down are just as they were, and the two accounts have been maintained separately, but now in columnar form.

On 2 January £200 cash was withdrawn from the bank, and it therefore appears as before as a credit in the bank account and a debit in the cash account. A transaction affecting only the cash and bank accounts is usually described as a *contra* item because it is recorded in the one book, i.e. the cash book. The contra items are marked with a $\mathcal{C}$.

Cash Book of A. Trader for the month of January 19XX

		Cash £	Bank £				Cash £	Bank £
Jan.	1 b/d		6,000	Jan.	2 Cash C			200
	2 Bank C	200			3 Purchases			4,000
	5 Sales		2,500		4 Stationery		15	
	6 Sales	50			9 Cleaning		20	
	11 Sales		1,000		10 Lighting and			
					heating			35
	17 Bank C	500			12 Motor			
					expenses			12
	21 Sales		600		13 Shopfittings			200
	23 Sales		200		17 Cash C			500
	24 B. Smith		250		18 Purchases		500	
	28 Sales		400		19 Motor			
					expenses			40
					27 D. Flint			800
					31 Cleaning		20	
					31 c/d		195	5,163
		750	10,950				750	10,950
Feb.	1 b/d	195	5,163					

Payments are easily identified as either cash payments or bank payments. If the payment is made directly from the bank account (e.g. by cheque or standing order) it appears in the bank account column. Payments of cash are recorded in the cash column.

When an amount is received by cheque it should be recorded directly in the bank column. The cheque may be placed initially in the till, but it only has value when paid into the bank. Only actual receipts of cash are recorded in the cash column. The banking of any of this cash is a separate transaction, i.e. *Cr.* cash and *Dr.* bank.

At any time a balance may be taken on the cash account column, and this should agree with a physical check of the cash in the cash till.

Similarly, a balance can be taken on the bank account at any time, and this should reconcile with the bank statement supplied by the firm's banker.

Cash book with discount column

The traditional cash book also has a 'discount' column on both the *Dr.* and *Cr.* side, so becoming a three-column ruling. This once again is a device used only for convenience.

Suppose A. Trader owes D. Flint £200 for goods purchased on 5 February 19XX.

In A. Trader's books, D. Flint's account would show D. Flint as a creditor thus:

D. Flint

		£
	19XX	
	Feb. 5 Purchases	200

D. Flint is offering 2½% discount to those of his customers who pay within one month, and therefore A. Trader decides to take advantage of this by paying Flint £195 cash in full settlement on 28 February.

After payment, D. Flint's account in A. Trader's books would appear:

D. Flint

19XX		£	19XX		£
Feb. 28 Cash		195	Feb. 5 Purchases		200
	Discount	5			
		200			200

A. Trader's cash book would now appear as follows:

Cash Book

	Discount £	Cash £	Bank £	19XX	Discount £	Cash £	Bank £
				Feb. 28 D. Flint	5	195	

Now suppose J. Thomas purchases £400 of goods from A. Trader on 7 February 19XX. J. Thomas would appear as a debtor:

J. Thomas

19XX	£	
Feb. 7 Sales	400	

A. Trader, to encourage early payment, is offering 3% discount to customers who pay him within seven days. J. Thomas pays £388 by cheque in settlement on 13 February 19XX.

The entries would appear as follows in A. Trader's cash book:

Cash Book

19XX	Discount £	Cash £	Bank £		Discount £	Cash £	Bank £
Feb. 13 J. Thomas	12		388				

J. Thomas's account would now be as follows:

J. Thomas

19XX		£	19XX		£
Feb. 7 Sales		400	Feb. 13 Bank		388
				Discount	12
		400			400

These discounts for early payment are often described as *cash discounts*, even though payment may have been made by cheque.

An example of a three-column cash book showing a week's transactions is given below:

19XX

Mar.   2 Balances brought down: bank £1,700, cash £394

2 Received £98 cash from J. Abbott after he has deducted £2 discount

Paid wages £122 in cash

3 Paid F. Ascot £195 by cheque

4 Paid J. Bloggs cheque £95 having deducted £5 discount

Paid petrol account £27 by cheque

5 Received cheque for £196 from B. Davies, he having deducted 2% discount

Received cheque from A. Jones for £147 after he has deducted £3 discount

6 Cash sales £87

Paid J. Harrison £40 by cash

Received cash from T. Smith for £49, discount of 2% having been deducted

Cash Book

	Discount	Cash	Bank		Discount	Cash	Bank
19XX	£	£	£	19XX	£	£	£
Mar. 2 b/d		394	1,700	Mar. 2 Wages		122	
J. Abbott	2	98		3 F. Ascot			195
5 B. Davies	4		196	4 J. Bloggs	5		95
A. Jones	3		147	Motor			
				expenses			27
6 Sales		87		J. Harrison		40	
T. Smith	1	49		c/d		466	1,726
	10	628	2,043		5	628	2,043
Mar. 7 b/d		466	1,726				

It should be noted particularly that, whilst balances have been carried down on the cash and bank columns, the discount columns have only been totalled.

The reason for this is that the total of the *Dr.* discount column represents discounts allowed and is shown as an expense in the profit and loss account. The total of the *Cr.* discount column represents discounts received and is treated as income in the profit and loss account. It would be bad accounting to net them off against each other.

The total of the *Dr.* discounts column (in this case £10) is transferred to a *discounts allowed* account in the ledger and the total of the *Cr.* discounts column (in this case £5) is transferred to a *discounts received* account in the ledger. Each time a total is taken on the cash book (a week, a month or whenever) the totals of the discount columns are so transferred. But note that the *discounts allowed* are already correctly shown as *Dr.* and are therefore transferred as a *Dr.*, thus:

Discounts allowed

19XX	£	
Mar. 6 Total for the week		
from cash book	10	

The same reasoning applies to the *discounts received*, which are transferred as a *Cr.* thus:

Discounts received

	19XX	£
	Mar. 6 Total for the week	
	from cash book	5

In this way the total discounts for the year can be accumulated more conveniently than in the cash book. The discount columns in the cash book are not the actual accounts, but are there simply for memorandum purposes.

Debtors ledger (or sales ledger)

The *debtors ledger* is a separate book or file containing all the debtors' accounts. It is often described as the *sales ledger* because it contains the personal accounts of customers to whom sales have been made. It is an integral part of the double entry system. As a separate book it can be the special responsibility of one person or a group of persons whose function it is to keep the debtors' accounts. Not all sales appear in this ledger, despite its title. For example, cash sales will not appear as they are a straightforward *Dr.* cash, *Cr.* sales entry.

Linked with the debtors ledger (or sales ledger) is the *sales day book*. The sales day book is not part of the double entry system and it may take any one of several forms. It is a subsidiary record.

In the original form of sales day book, credit sales would be entered in full detail in the sales day book as the sales were made. From this record an invoice or bill was prepared for despatch to the customer. Note should be made here of the use of the term *credit sales* in its normal sense, i.e. a period of credit is given to the customer before he is called upon to pay his debt; the customer will of course appear as a debtor.

A modern sales day book will not contain so much detail and may take any one of several forms. But the importance of the sales day book lies in the fact that the debtors' accounts are debited and the sales account credited from this original source. An abridged example of a sales day book is given below. The debits to the debtors' accounts (in the debtors ledger) will be posted individually, whilst the credit to the sales account can be posted in total at suitable intervals, so reducing considerably the number of entries in the sales account.

Sales Day Book

19X1	Invoice	Folio	Amount £
Jan. 2 R. Fairclough	X1/1	564	71
4 W. Thompson	X1/2	743	27
5 A. Howell	X1/3	217	39
R. North	X1/4	591	123
6 J. Kean	X1/5	198	112
7 L. Hunt	X1/6	327	83
Sales account – sales for week NLS 1			455

Associated with the sales day book is a *sales returns book* (or *returns inwards book*). When goods have been returned by a customer, a *credit note* is usually forwarded to the customer, indicating that the goods have been received and his account has been credited.

The credit notes are recorded in the sales returns or returns inwards book. Each individual debtor is credited with the value of the goods he has returned, whilst the total is debited to a sales returns account (or returns inwards account), as mentioned in Chapter 4.

Sales Returns Book

19X1	Credit note	Folio	£
Jan. 9 W. Thompson	X1/CN1	743	9
11 R. North	X1/CN2	591	15
Sales returns account – returns for week NLS 2			24

The double entries for the sales and sales returns transactions given above would be shown in the accounts as below:

Debtors Ledger

R. Fairclough   Folio 564

19X1		£	
Jan. 2 Sales	SDB	71	

W. Thompson   Folio 743

19X1		£	19X1		£
Jan. 4 Sales	SDB	27	Jan. 9 Sales returns	SRB	9

A. Howell   Folio 217

19X1		£	
Jan. 5 Sales	SDB	39	

R. North   Folio 591

19X1		£	19X1		£
Jan. 5 Sales	SDB	123	Jan. 11 Sales returns	SRB	15

J. Kean   Folio 198

19X1		£	
Jan. 6 Sales	SDB	112	

L. Hunt   Folio 327

19X1		£	
Jan. 7 Sales	SDB	83	

Nominal Ledger

Sales account   NLS 1

	19X1	£
	Jan. 7 Debtors – sales for	
	week ending 7	
	January 19X1	455

Sales returns accounts   NLS 2

19X1	£	
Jan. 14 Debtors – returns		
for week ending		
14 January 19X1	24	

It should be remembered that the sales account will also be credited separately with cash sales direct from the cash book. And indeed, the sales returns account will be debited direct from the cash book where any cash sales are returned and money is refunded to the customer.

Folios

You will note that *folios* have now been introduced. This is a reference system which assists in tracing transactions through the system. It is unlikely to appear in examination questions.

Creditors ledger (or purchases ledger)

The *creditors ledger* (or *purchases ledger*) is a book containing the personal accounts of the persons from whom goods have been bought. It is an integral part of the double entry system.

When an invoice is received from a supplier it is given a reference number and first entered into a *purchases day book*, which is not part of the double entry system. This has a similar format to the sales day book:

Purchases Day Book

19X1	Ref. no.	Folio	£
Jan. 2 T. Grundy	X1/1	4234	98
3 F. Jackson	X1/2	1123	127
4 E. Jones	X1/3	3729	65
5 R. Jacobs	X1/4	2036	192
Purchases account – purchases for week			482

The posting to the creditors' accounts (in the creditors ledger) and the purchases account are from this book of original entry.

Coupled with the purchases day book is a *purchases returns book* (or *returns outwards book*) in which are recorded goods returned to suppliers. The periodic total is credited to a purchases returns account (or returns outwards account) whilst the individual creditors are debited with the value of goods returned.

Purchases Returns Book

19X1	Ref. no.	Folio	£
Jan. 3 T. Grundy	X1/DN1	4234	14
5 E. Jones	X1/DN2	3729	65
Purchases returns account – returns for week			79

The double entry for the purchases and purchase return transactions given above would be shown in the accounts, as on page 74; in this instance the transactions have been displayed diagrammatically to enable you to follow the double entry more easily.

Some firms have discontinued the use of a creditors ledger as such. It is often much simpler to accumulate invoices for, say, a month, and then to batch and pay them. In this way they need only be recorded as a cash transaction, so eliminating the creditor stage. Invoices offering worthwhile discounts can be paid at more frequent intervals. At the end of the year an adjustment of the accounts is required to include as creditors any invoices received but not paid.

However, many other firms still continue with conventional creditors' accounts in a creditors ledger.

Journal

The word *journal* means a diary or day book. The journal in its original form was a written daily record of all business transactions in the order in which they occurred. The postings to the accounts took place from the journal; and the journal provided a reference point for all entries in the accounts. Items were set out to show which account was to be debited and which was to be credited, and the reason for so doing. All the transactions of A. Trader in Chapters 2 and 3 were, in fact, 'journalised' so that you could follow each transaction into the accounts, though at that time the use of the word 'journalise' was deliberately avoided.

Subsequent development of the journal moved sales into the sales day book and purchases into the purchases day book. This is why these books are sometimes called the *sales journal* and the *purchases journal*. The use of the journal for recording cash and bank transactions was also discontinued, as these are adequately dealt with in the cash book.

The journal, the sales day book, the sales returns book, the purchases day book, the purchases returns book and the cash book are all now described as *books of original entry* or *books of prime entry* as they provide the original source for the T accounts. The cash book is also an integral part of the double entry system, whereas the other books are solely subsidiary records.

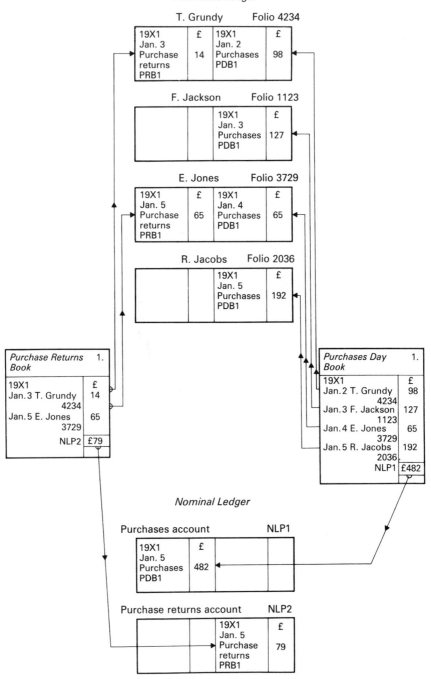

The use of the journal is now usually restricted to

1. Opening entries for a new business
2. Correction of errors
3. Transfers between accounts
4. The purchase and sale of fixed assets on credit.

A simple practical rule to follow is that a transaction must be journalised if it does not appear in one of the other books of prime entry.

Students are often required in examinations to journalise transactions that would now not normally be journalised, e.g. cash transactions. This is to assist the examiner in determining whether the student would make the correct debit and credit entries without the necessity for actual T accounts being shown.

The format of the journal is as shown in Chapters 2 and 3. The accounts to be debited are, by convention, shown first. The accounts to be credited are slightly inset:

Journal

Date	Account to be debited	Dr.	Cr.
	Account to be debited	X	
	Account to be credited		X
	Narrative (or description).		

EXAMPLE OF OPENING ENTRY

John Brown had been running a part time business for some years. On 1 January 19XX he decided to rent a shop and go into full time business. The assets he intended to put into the business were: stock £1,560; van valued at £2,500; equipment valued at £650; cash £503. He owed his mother £1,000 which she had loaned him to help buy the van.

The opening journal entry would be:

Journal

		Dr. £	Cr. £
Jan. 1	Stock	1,560	
	Van	2,500	
	Equipment	650	
	Cash	503	
	Loan – Mrs. Brown		1,000
	Capital		4,213
		5,213	5,213
	Assets and liabilities on commencement of business.		

Note: Capital is a balancing figure calculated from the accounting equation:

$$\text{Capital} = \text{Assets} - \text{Liabilities}$$

EXAMPLE OF TRANSFER BETWEEN T ACCOUNTS

On 1 February 19XX £500 had been charged to the repairs to buildings account. Subsequently it is decided that work to the value of £150 is for improvements and should be charged to the asset account. An adjustment is made at the year end, i.e. 31 December 19XX.

		Dr. £	Cr. £
Dec. 31	Buildings	150	
	Repairs to buildings		150
	Improvement work included in invoice of 1 February 19XX for £500.		

Questions

6.1S   On 1 January 19X2, J. Mowbray, a trader, had cash in hand amounting to £33 and cash at the bank of £625. Write up the following transactions in his cash book and show the balances of cash at the bank and in hand on 31 January 19X2.

19X2
Jan.   3 Received cash of £107 from V. Banyard
       4 Received cash from I. Watson, £20
         Paid J. Greaney's account of £80 by cheque
       5 Paid £40 cash into the bank
       6 Paid wages, £100, by cash
      11 Paid K. Walton's account of £42 by cheque
      12 Received £75 cheque from W. Larkin against his account
      13 Cashed a cheque for £90 and paid wages, £100, by cash
      15 Received cheque of £150 from A. Benthram
      18 Received cheque of £86 from J. Noble
      19 Paid the account of Office Equipment Co., £8, by cash
      20 Received cash, £106, from J. Jones
         Paid wages, £100, in cash
      24 Paid A. Williamson's account of £55 by cheque
      25 Received cheque of £152 from P. Willey in payment of his account
      27 Cashed a cheque for £110 and paid wages £100, by cash

6.2S   (a) From the following transactions of A.M. Smith, write up his cash book in three-column form, bringing down the balances at 31 January 19X3 in the cash and bank columns.

			£
19X3			
Jan.	1	Cash at bank	520
		Drew cheque for office cash	180
	2	Received cheque from N. Walton	494
		Discount allowed to N. Walton	26
	3	Purchased stamps from office cash	15
	8	Paid R. Hayton's account by cheque	342
		Discount deducted from R. Hayton's account	18
	10	Received cheque in payment of W. Bolton's account	653
	11	Paid H. Vanstone on account	300
		Paid wages from office cash	120
	14	Drew cheque for office cash	135
	16	Paid C. Yates by cheque	114
		Discount received on payment of C. Yates account	6

21	Received cheque from D. Webster	399
	Discount allowed to D. Webster	21
25	Paid wages from office cash	120
	Purchased stationery from office cash	28
	Purchased stamps from office cash	26
28	Drew cheque for office cash	174
	Drew cheque for self	280
30	Paid F. Wilson by cheque	153

(b) How would the totals of the discount column be dealt with in the ledger?

6.3S   Details of sales and sales returns of G. Snow, engineer, for the month of April 19X2 are given below:

19X2		Folio	£
Apr.	3 Sold to Robinson & Co.	1201	900
	8 Sold to Brown & Son	1202	1,120
	14 Sold to White & Co.	1203	924
	Returns from Robinson & Co.	1201	240
	18 Sold to M. Vickers	1204	420
	21 Sold to G. Platt	1205	429
	Returns from White & Co.	1203	142
	25 Sold to M. Holt	1206	2,460

Show the entries for the above transactions in the sales day book and sales returns book and the postings to the ledger accounts.

6.4S   Compile the sales day book and purchases day book of E. Booth, wholesale draper, from the following particulars and make the postings to the ledger accounts.

19X8		£
Oct.	1 Sold to M. Greenwood	1,240
	3 Bought from A. Hargreaves	800
	4 Bought from R. Scruton	420
	Sold to A. Gaston	746
	6 Bought from H. Smith	708
	Sold to E. Aldcroft	640
	10 Sold to M. Daniels	480
	14 Sold to M. Greenwood	420
	16 Sold to A. Gaston	264
	18 Bought from A. Hargreaves	680
	Sold to W. Pickles	336
	21 Bought from B. Hubbard	2,240
	24 Sold to E. Aldcroft	348
	Sold to M. Daniels	260
	27 Bought from P. Davies	520
	Sold to M. Heslop	760
	30 Bought from E. Hull	1,460
	Sold to A. Crompton	920
	31 Sold to A. Gaston	647

If you wish, the following references may be inserted. For cross-reference purposes, the sales day book folio is SDB10 and the purchase day book folio is PDB10.

The ledger accounts are to be shown in alphanumeric order prefixed by the letter 'D' for debtors ledger accounts, 'C' for creditors ledger accounts and 'N' for nominal ledger accounts: e.g. M. Greenwood's folio is DG2, A. Gaston's folio is DG1.

6.5S   On 1 January 19X8, the assets and liabilities of J. Shaw, a wholesale toy distributor, were as follows:

	£	£
Assets		
Freehold premises at cost		25,000
Fittings at cost	12,000	
less Depreciation to date	3,000	9,000
Stock at cost		8,000
Debtors		
E. Booth		480
M. Greenough		360
Cash in hand		200
Liabilities		
Loan from J. Buckle		10,000
Bank overdraft		6,800
Creditors		
A. Hargreaves		260

Calculate Shaw's capital and show the journal entry recording the above particulars.

6.6S   Open the ledger accounts in J. Shaw's books from the particulars given in Question 6.5S and record the following transactions in those accounts after first making the entries in the appropriate book of prime entry.

19X8		£
Jan.	2 Sold on credit to E. Booth	290
	5 Sold on credit to M. Greenough	360
	8 Bought on credit from A. Hargreaves	460
	11 Cash sales	320
	12 Banked cash	200
	Paid wages in cash	120
	14 Sold on credit to C. Leydell	420
	18 Purchased fittings on credit from N. Barrow	1,200
	22 Sold on credit to C. Ingin	260
	26 Paid wages in cash	120
	Goods returned by C. Ingin	28
	29 Cheque received from E. Booth	468
	Discount allowed to E. Booth	12
	Cheque received from M. Greenough	351
	Discount allowed to M. Greenough	9
	Cheque paid to A. Hargreaves	260
	30 Bought on credit from J. Gilpin	220

Bring down the balances on the accounts at 1 February 19X8 and take out a trial balance at that date.

6.7   From the following particulars compile the cash book of A.C. Worsick showing the cash and bank columns and bring down the balances at the end of the month.

19X3		£
Mar.	1 Balance at bank	2,010
	Purchased goods, paid by cheque	1,020
	Drew cheque for office cash	150
	Purchased stamps from office cash	25

19X3		£
6	Received cheque from J. Done	132
8	Received cheque from F. Thomas	143
10	Bought stationery from office cash	16
13	Paid wages from office cash	80
	Paid W. Garlick's account by cheque	209
15	Received cheque from J. Done	96
	Purchased stamps from office cash	25
16	Drew cheque for office cash	146
17	Received cheque from P. Hart	134
20	Paid V. Cavey by cheque	175
22	Received cheque from F. Thomas	75
24	Office cleaning account paid from office cash	60
27	Paid wages from office cash	80
	Paid A. Young's account by cheque	189
30	Drew cheque for office cash	140
31	Drew cheque for self	240

6.8   (a) Enter the following transactions in G.J. Wallwork's cash book, showing discount, cash and bank columns, and bring down the balances at 31 January 19X4, in the cash and bank columns.

19X4

Jan.   1 Balance at bank £1,143
        Cash in hand £250
        Purchased for resale, goods at £411, paid by cheque
     2 Received cheque from P. Crawford, £250 on account
     6 Cash sales £182
        Paid in cash: wages £63, postages £21
     7 Cash banked £98
    13 Cash sales £384
        Paid in cash: wages £63, printing and stationery £45
    14 Cash banked £276
        Paid by cheque C. Connelly's account £260 less 5% discount
    18 Received cheque from P. Crawford for £130
        Discount allowed to P. Crawford £20
    19 Cash sales £186
        Paid in cash: wages and commission £163, postages £35
    20 Drew cheque for office cash £12
        Received cheque from N. Horner in payment of his account for £280 less 2½% discount
    26 Cash sales £620
        Paid in cash: wages £63, postages £10
    27 Cash banked £547
    30 Paid D. Steele's account £400 less 2½% discount

      (b) Open a discount allowed account and a discount received account and post the total of the discount columns to the respective account.

6.9   Record the following transactions in the sales day book, purchases day book, sales returns book, purchases returns book and the ledger accounts of J. Whitehead & Co., Furniture Manufacturers.

19X6		Folio	£
Jun.	1 Bought from S. Hayes	C9111	4,333
	4 Bought from P. Highman	C9112	513

19X6		Folio	£
Jun. 6	Sold to J.S. Holt	D4111	1,016
9	Sold to A. Weatherall	D4112	2,106
	Returned goods to P. Highman	C9112	513
12	Goods returned by J.S. Holt	D4111	213
15	Sold to G. McLaren	D4113	521
18	Sold to T. Ives	D4114	710
24	Bought from E. Griffiths	C9113	715
	Goods returned by G. McLaren	D4113	111
28	Bought from A. Ravenscroft	C9114	545
29	Sold to N. Blakeway	D4115	455
30	Goods returned to A. Ravenscroft	C9114	54
	Bought from J. Dixon	C9115	517

6.10   Enter the following transactions in the appropriate day books of M. Higgins & Co., Manufacturers, and make the postings to the ledger accounts. Cross-reference the postings by use of suitable folios.

19X8		£
May 1	Sold to A. Jones	1,090
	Bought from T. Hall	1,398
3	Bought from E. Drake	1,260
5	Sold to R. Hardy	2,120
	Sold to C. Jones	860
8	Bought from D. Steele	1,480
11	Sold to M. Booth	1,260
	Sold to A. Jones	980
13	Bought from E. Drake	540
	Goods returned by C. Jones	240
17	Sold to R. Hardy	1,240
	Goods returned to E. Drake	70
21	Bought from D. Steele	840
24	Sold to C. Jones	980
	Sold to M. Booth	780
26	Goods returned to D. Steele	84
27	Goods returned by M. Booth	117
29	Sold to L. Shepherd	640
	Sold to V. Ward	860
	Bought from J. Bolton	1,290
31	Sold to M. Scriven	1,830
	Sold to C. Jones	1,140

6.11   On 1 July 19X3, the assets and liabilities of G. Mitchell, a wholesale and retail butcher, were as follows:

	£
Freehold premises at cost	30,000
Fittings at cost	3,000
Provision for depreciation on fittings to date	600
Stock at cost	1,200
Debtors	
P. Dillon	450
R. Higham	260
Cash at bank	2,280
Cash in hand	320

	£
Loan from J. Shockledge	15,000
Creditors	
M. Pearson	650
D. Dyson	350

Calculate Mitchell's capital and show the journal entry recording the above particulars.

6.12   Open the ledger accounts in G. Mitchell's books from the journal entry in the solution to Question 6.11 and record the following transactions in those accounts after first making the entries in the appropriate book of prime entry.

19X3		£
Jul. 1	Bought on credit from G. Swann	670
3	Sold on credit to M. Goddard	840
5	Bought on credit from A. Stones	560
6	Cash sales	1,200
7	Wages paid in cash	200
	Cash banked	1,120
10	Bought motor van on credit from J. Slow	3,600
12	Received cheque from P. Dillon in full settlement	440
	Bought on credit from M. Pearson	1,810
14	Received cheque from R. Higham in full settlement	254
	Cash sales	1,360
	Paid M. Pearson in full settlement by cheque	638
	Paid D. Dyson in full settlement by cheque	342
	Bought on credit from D. Dyson	1,480
	Wages paid in cash	200
16	Cash banked	1,160
21	Cash sales	1,580
	Wages paid in cash	220
24	Bought meat for cash	980
28	Cash sales	1,660
	Wages paid in cash	220
	Cash banked	1,500
31	Sold on credit to R. France	860
	Sundry expenses paid by cheque	160

Stock at 31 July 19X3 was £1,500.

Depreciation to be charged on fittings – £25, on motor van – £75.

Prepare a trial balance at 31 July 19X3 and a trading and profit and loss account and balance sheet as at that date.

Use any coding system you feel appropriate for cross-reference purposes.

7 Value added tax (VAT)

Aims of the chapter:

> To introduce 'value added tax'
> To show how it can be recorded in the accounts

Introduction

Value added tax (VAT) is a tax on the supply of goods and services which is eventually borne by the final customer, but it is collected at each stage of the distribution chain. HM Customs and Excise are responsible for the administration of VAT.

Suppose company A produces certain goods, providing all the necessary raw materials and labour. A batch of these goods is sold to company B for £400 (exclusive of VAT). A is required to add VAT (currently $17\frac{1}{2}\%$) to the selling price of these goods and account for this VAT to Customs and Excise. The total selling price to B is therefore £470 inclusive of VAT.

Company B now further refines the goods and then passes them on to wholesaler C for £600 excluding VAT, or £705 including VAT. B is required to account for the VAT of £105 (called *output tax*) but is entitled to deduct the £70 VAT paid to A (called *input tax*).

C next supplies the goods at £720 excluding VAT to retailer D; and retailer D finally sells these to the public, E, at £880 excluding VAT.

The following tabulation shows how the sale price is increased each time by VAT. It also shows how, at each stage, the seller is required to add and collect output VAT. But the seller is also entitled to deduct any input VAT that he has previously borne.

The column headed 'net payment' shows the net amount of VAT that each supplier pays over to Customs and Excise. When this column is totalled it agrees with the total amount of VAT added to the goods. In this example the end customer(s) E is/are not registered (see later) for VAT and cannot reclaim the tax.

Seller	Sale price (ex. VAT) £	VAT £	Total sale price £	Input tax £	Output tax £	Net payment to Customs and Excise £
A	400	70	470		70	70
B	600	105	705	70	105	35
C	720	126	846	105	126	21
D	880	154	1,034	126	154	28
						154

Business expenses

The above example does not tell the full story. It has dealt only with the production and supply of goods for resale. A trader also bears input tax on expenses (e.g. stationery, telephone) and on assets which are for use in the business rather than for resale. This input tax also can be recovered by deduction from output tax. There are a few exclusions to this rule. For example VAT charged on motor cars bought for use rather than for resale and VAT charged on certain business entertaining expenses is irrecoverable.

Standard rate and zero rate

So far it has been assumed that the *standard rate* of VAT (i.e. currently 17$\frac{1}{2}$%) applies to all goods. However, certain goods and services are *zero rated* (e.g. most food stuffs, children's clothing, gas, electricity). A supplier of zero rated items does not add any VAT to the selling price of goods. He is still entitled to recover from Customs and Excise any input tax that he has paid (on supplies or expenses or assets).

Exempt supplies

Some supplies are *exempt* (e.g. insurance, postal services, financial services). This means that the supplier does not add VAT, but he cannot recover his input tax. Of course the price of the product to the final consumer must reflect this irrecoverable VAT if the supplier is not to suffer.

Registration and tax period

All businesses with a taxable turnover over a specified amount (which is usually increased each year in the Budget in line with inflation) are required to register for VAT with Customs and Excise. Businesses with a turnover under the specified amount do not have to register. If they do not register they are effectively in the same position as a person making exempt supplies, i.e. they cannot recover input tax.

The usual period for tax return forms and payments to be sent to Customs and Excise is three months. Should there be an excess of input tax, a repayment is made by the revenue. Monthly tax periods can be requested if regular repayments are expected.

Effect of VAT on businesses

The main effect of VAT on businesses is that they have the task of collecting it. They also have to finance the tax until it can be recovered, though certain small businesses can adopt a cash accounting system. The full burden of VAT normally falls on the final customer.

The problems associated with VAT are therefore of administration and understanding the rules. Basically it is important that all purchases and expenses are analysed and the input tax allocated (i.e. debited) to the VAT account so that the tax can be recovered. Similarly all output VAT must also be allocated (i.e. credited) to the VAT account so that it can be accounted for to Customs and Excise.

A business cannot deduct or reclaim VAT on goods or services acquired for a non-business activity.

Special schemes for retailers

The normal VAT procedure requires records to be kept of each individual transaction. Most retailers would find it impossible to keep such detailed records of sales. There are therefore several alternative special schemes for retailers to enable them to calculate output tax. Once a scheme is chosen it is of course the only scheme to affect that particular retailer. A retailer who has chosen a special scheme must analyse his purchases and expenses and allocate input tax to the VAT account in the same way as any business. But the special scheme will allow him to calculate a proportion of his total sales income as output tax in a way that suits his circumstances, rather than recording each sale individually. Many of the complications of apportioning output VAT are caused when a retailer supplies a mixture of standard rated and/or zero rated and/or exempt items.

Certain items are outside the scope of VAT and are not regarded as a supply. They include wages and salaries, motor vehicle duty, subscriptions and donations to political parties, trade union subscriptions.

The example shown below illustrates a system for an imaginary supplier of office furniture who is registered for VAT. Goods are usually bought and sold on credit.

The accounting entries for outputs are

	Dr.	Cr.
Debtor (or cash) account	With the selling price including VAT	
Sales account		With the selling price excluding VAT
VAT account		With the amount of VAT charged

The accounting entries for inputs are

	Dr.	Cr.
Purchases account or expense account	With the cost price excluding VAT	
VAT account	With the amount of VAT charged	
Creditor (or cash account)		With the cost price including VAT

EXAMPLE 7.1

The transactions for the month of July 19X7 of W. Brooks & Co., office furniture suppliers, included the following:

Purchases on credit, inclusive of VAT at 17½%

19X7	Supplier	£
Jul. 1	Abbess Ltd	470
	Olivetti Ltd	329
	Twinlock Ltd	705
	United Stationers Ltd	141
10	Olivetti Ltd	611
12	Roneo-Vickers Ltd	423
18	United Stationers Ltd	235
22	Twinlock Ltd	376
31	Abbess Ltd	282

Purchase returns, inclusive of VAT at 17½%

19X7	Supplier	£
Jul. 3	United Stationers Ltd	47
24	Twinlock Ltd	94

Credit sales, inclusive of VAT at 17½%

19X7	Customer	£
Jul. 1	T. Hibbit & Co.	517
8	F. Spencer	188
10	R. Moss & Co.	1,034
15	Spinks & Co.	564
16	F. Spencer	376
19	T. Hibbit & Co.	329
23	S. Gratrix Ltd	987
29	R. Moss & Co.	329

Sales returns, inclusive of VAT at 17½%

19X7	Customer	£
Jul. 4	T. Hibbit & Co.	47
12	R. Moss & Co.	47

The following expense invoices were received during the month; VAT is included at 17½% where stated.

19X7		£
Jul. 3	British Telecom (incl. VAT)	282
10	Norweb – electricity (zero rated)	520
12	North West Gas (zero rated)	260
14	Halfway Service Station – petrol (incl. VAT)	47
21	D. Thomson (Insurance Brokers) Ltd (exempt)	396
28	Slow Ltd – purchase of Ford Escort car – this includes VAT but is irrecoverable	5,200
29	Halfway Service Station – petrol (incl. VAT)	47

In the accounting system of W. Brooks & Co. VAT is identified at the time an invoice is entered in a book of prime entry. Five day books are used:

Sales day book	Sales + VAT on sales
Sales returns day book	Sales returns + VAT on sales returns
Purchase day book	Purchases + VAT on purchases
Purchase returns day book	Purchase returns + VAT on purchase returns
Expenses day book	Expense invoices + VAT on expense invoices

Purchase Day Book

		Net price	VAT	Total cost price
19X7		£	£	£
Jul. 1	Abbess Ltd	400	70	470
	Olivetti Ltd	280	49	329
	Twinlock Ltd	600	105	705
	United Stationers Ltd	120	21	141
10	Olivetti Ltd	520	91	611
12	Roneo-Vickers Ltd	360	63	423
18	United Stationers Ltd	200	35	235
22	Twinlock Ltd	320	56	376
31	Abbess Ltd	240	42	282
		3,040	532	3,572

Purchase Returns Day Book

		Net price	VAT	Total cost price
19X7		£	£	£
Jul. 3	United Stationers Ltd	40	7	47
24	Twinlock Ltd	80	14	94
		120	21	141

Sales Day Book

		Net price	VAT	Total sale price
19X7		£	£	£
Jul. 2	T. Hibbit & Co.	440	77	517
8	F. Spencer	160	28	188
10	R. Moss & Co.	880	154	1,034
15	Spinks & Co.	480	84	564
16	F. Spencer	320	56	376
19	T. Hibbit & Co.	280	49	329
23	S. Gratrix Ltd	840	147	987
29	R. Moss & Co.	280	49	329
		3,680	644	4,324

Sales Returns Day Book

		Net price	VAT	Total sale price
19X7		£	£	£
Jul. 4	T. Hibbit & Co.	40	7	47
12	R. Moss & Co.	40	7	47
		80	14	94

Expense Day Book and Analysis

	Total incl. VAT £	Telephone £	Electricity £	Gas £	Petrol £	Insce £	Motor vehicles £	VAT £
19X7								
Jul. 3 British Telecom	282	240						42
10 Norweb	520		520					
12 North West Gas	260			260				
14 Halfway Service	47				40			7
21 D. Thomson	396					396		
28 Slow Ltd	5,200						5,200	
29 Halfway Service	47				40			7
	6,752	240	520	260	80	396	5,200	56

Note: Where a VAT-inclusive figure is given, the amount of VAT can be calculated by multiplying by $17\frac{1}{2}/117\frac{1}{2}$.

Creditors Ledger

Abbess Ltd

19X7		£	19X7			£
Jul. 31	Balance c/d	752	Jul.	1	Purchases	470
				31	Purchases	282
		752				752
			Aug.	1	Balance b/d	752

Olivetti Ltd

19X7		£	19X7			£
Jul. 31	Balance c/d	940	Jul.	1	Purchases	329
				10	Purchases	611
		940				940
			Aug.	1	Balance b/d	940

Twinlock Ltd

19X7		£	19X7			£
Jul. 24	Purchase returns	94	Jul.	1	Purchases	705
31	Balance c/d	987		22	Purchases	376
		1,081				1,081
			Aug.	1	Balance b/d	987

United Stationers Ltd

19X7		£	19X7			£
Jul. 3	Purchase returns	47	Jul.	1	Purchases	141
31	Balance c/d	329		18	Purchases	235
		376				376
			Aug.	1	Balance b/d	329

Roneo-Vickers Ltd

		19X7			£
		Jul. 12	Purchases		423

British Telecom

		19X7			£
		Jul. 3	Expense		282

Norweb

		19X7			£
		Jul. 10	Expense		520

North West Gas

		£
	19X7	
	Jul. 12 Expense	260

Halfway Service Station

19X7		£	19X7		£
Jul. 31 Balance c/d		94	Jul. 14 Expense		47
			29 Expense		47
		94			94
			Aug. 1 Balance b/d		94

D. Thomson (Insurance Brokers) Ltd

		£
	19X7	
	Jul. 21 Expense	396

Slow Ltd

		£
	19X7	
	Jul. 28 Expense	5,200

Value added tax

19X7		£	19X7		£
Jul. 31 Purchases		532	Jul. 31 Purchases returns		21
Sales returns		14	Sales		644
Expenses		56			
Balance c/d		63			
		665			665
			Aug. 1 Balance b/d		63

Debtors Ledger

T. Hibbit & Co.

19X7		£	19X7		£
Jul. 2 Sales		517	Jul. 4 Sales returns		47
19 Sales		329	31 Balance c/d		799
		846			846
Aug. 1 Balance b/d		799			

F. Spencer

19X7		£	19X7		£
Jul. 8 Sales		188	Jul. 31 Balance c/d		564
16 Sales		376			
		564			564
Aug. 1 Balance b/d		564			

R. Moss & Co.

19X7		£	19X7		£
Jul. 10	Sales	1,034	Jul. 12	Sales returns	47
29	Sales	329	31	Balance c/d	1,316
		1,363			1,363
Aug. 1	Balance b/d	1,316			

Spinks & Co.

19X7		£
Jul. 15	Sales	564

S. Gratrix Ltd

19X7		£
Jul. 23	Sales	987

Nominal Ledger

Purchases

19X7		£
Jul. 31	Creditors – per purchase day book	3,040

Purchase returns

			19X7		£
			Jul. 31	Creditors – per purchase rtns book	120

Sales

			19X7		£
			Jul. 31	Debtors – per sales day book	3,680

Sales returns

19X7		£
Jul. 31	Debtors – per sales rtns book	80

Expenses – per day book

19X7		£
Jul. 31	Telephone	240
	Electricity	520
	Gas	260
	Petrol	80
	Insurance	396

Motor vehicle – per day book

19X7	£	19X7	£
Jul. 31 UDB 954	5,200		

The balances extracted from the three ledgers are:

Creditors ledger – all credit balances

	Cr. £
Abbess Ltd	752
Olivetti Ltd	940
Twinlock Ltd	987
United Stationers Ltd	329
Roneo-Vickers Ltd	423
British Telecom	282
Norweb	520
North West Gas	260
Halfway Service Station	94
D. Thomson	396
Slow Ltd	5,200
Value added tax	63
	10,246

Debtors ledger – all debit balances

	Dr. £
T. Hibbett & Co.	799
F. Spencer	564
R. Moss & Co.	1,316
Spinks & Co.	564
S. Gratrix Ltd	987
	4,230

Nominal ledger

	Dr. £	Cr. £
Purchases	3,040	
Purchases returns		120
Sales		3,680
Sales returns	80	
Telephone	240	
Electricity	520	
Gas	260	
Petrol	80	
Insurance	396	
Motor vehicles	5,200	
	9,816	3,800

To prove the arithmetical accuracy of the postings a trial balance can be extracted.

	Dr. £	Cr. £
Creditors		10,246
Debtors	4,230	
Nominal	9,816	3,800
	14,046	14,046

In the above example only one account has been kept for VAT, in which is recorded both the tax on outputs (sales) and the tax on inputs (purchases and expenses). It may be simpler in some instances to keep a separate account for input tax and a separate account for output tax.

Questions in examinations sometimes show a trial balance with a balance on 'VAT account'. You are then expected to know that this shows Customs and Excise as a creditor (most probably) or a debtor (less probably) of the trader. The net amount due to or from Customs and Excise in respect of VAT is normally included as part of creditors or debtors and is not shown separately.

The example displayed in this introduction to VAT dealt with a trader registered for VAT. As such the trader was only a collector of VAT; therefore VAT should not be included in income or expenditure except in the few instances where it is irrecoverable, e.g. the motor car bought for use in the business.

In the case of a business which sells exempt supplies only, or a business which is not registered, input VAT will increase the cost of the goods and services the business purchases. The input VAT should therefore be included as part of those costs.

A more advanced study of VAT would show how complications are created when a business supplies a mixture of taxable supplies and exempt supplies.

Questions

7.1S   The following credit sales were made by J. Madden Ltd during May 19X6. All the items are shown inclusive of VAT at $17\frac{1}{2}\%$.

19X6		£
May 6	H. Smith Ltd	235
9	R. Scruton & Co.	376
13	R. Hollis & Co.	282
16	E. Aldcroft Ltd	470
20	M. Daniels & Co.	188
23	E. Seddon & Co.	329
27	H. Smith Ltd	423

You are required to enter up the sales day book, and post the items to the appropriate ledger accounts.

7.2S   Stanley Jones is the proprietor of Jones DIY. He pays all his bills as he receives them. He allocates his takings under a special scheme for retailers,

$17^1/_2/117^1/_2$ of all takings being regarded as VAT. The transactions for July 19X1 are listed below, including VAT at $17^1/_2\%$ where appropriate. The bank balance brought forward is £25,012 and the cash in hand is £232. Devise a columnar cash book to record the transactions and show VAT. Post the appropriate ledger accounts.

19X1			£
Jul.	1	Bought shop fittings, paid by cheque	4,700
		Bought goods for resale, paid by cheque	18,800
		Bought a second-hand Ford Escort, paid by cheque	2,350
		Takings	1,880
	3	Banked previous takings	1,880
	7	Motor car expenses, paid in cash	47
		Paid wages in cash	360
	8	Takings	2,115
	10	Banked	1,500
	12	Paid Norweb – quarterly electricity bill – cheque	480
	15	Takings	2,303
	17	Banked	2,000
	21	Motor car expenses, paid in cash	47
		Paid wages in cash	360
	26	Paid British Gas – quarterly gas bill – cheque	220
	29	Takings	1,974
	30	Banked	2,000

7.3 The credit sales and purchases of P. Davies Ltd for June 19X6 were as follows:

			Inclusive of VAT at $17^1/_2\%$
19X6			£
Jun.	2	Sold to J. Gilpin & Co.	705
	6	Bought from M. Heslop Ltd	987
	6	Sold to F. Pickles Ltd	1,410
	9	Bought from A. Wilson & Co.	940
	13	Sold to J. Gilpin & Co.	282
	16	Sold to F. Pickles Ltd	470
	18	Goods returned by F. Pickles Ltd	47
	23	Bought from M. Heslop Ltd	517
	26	Sold to E. Hull & Co.	188
	28	Sold to E. Kenworthy Ltd	329
	29	Sold to S. Hayes Ltd	564
	30	Goods returned by E. Kenworthy Ltd	94

You are required to enter up the appropriate day books, post the items to the ledger accounts and bring down the balance on the VAT account.

8 Bad debts; discounts on debtors

Aims of the chapter:

To consider the effect of outstanding debt on profit

In Chapters 6 and 7 it was shown how the periodic totals of the sales day book are posted to the sales account, whilst the individual customers' accounts are separately debited with the amount of each sale.

The effect of this is that the sales account is credited with all sales at the time the sales are made, whether or not the debtors will eventually pay. So far, in fact, it has been assumed that all debtors will pay their debts.

This hardly appears a prudent approach to adopt. Customers may go bankrupt, or disappear, or for other reasons fail to honour their debts. In fact it could be claimed that the most prudent approach would be to adopt a cash approach to accounting. Income would then be taken only when cash was actually received.

However, the majority of customers do meet their debts because credit (note the everyday use of the word credit again) is not usually given to just any casual purchaser. Customers are vetted and references possibly taken (e.g. from a bank). The amount of credit granted will also be restricted initially and only allowed to grow with developing trust. So to adopt a purely cash approach to trading could prove even more unrealistic than the one generally adopted and described so far.

But the accountant's normally conservative attitude dictates that some action should be taken regarding debts that are not likely to be met. Otherwise it is very probable that profits for a period could be overstated, or losses understated.

Action is usually taken on known bad debts immediately they are recognised, e.g. as soon as a customer becomes bankrupt, or becomes untraceable. The amount outstanding in the debtors account is credited and transferred to a *bad debts* account, thus:

E. Kilroy

19XX		£	19XX		£
Feb. 2 Sales		85	Sep. 2 Bad debts		85

W. Orme

19XX		£	19XX		£
Mar. 4 Sales		104	Mar. 31 Cash		20
			Oct. 30 Bad debts		84
		104			104

Bad debts

19XX		£	19XX		£
Sep. 2 E. Kilroy		85	Dec. 31 Profit and loss		169
Oct. 30 W. Orme		84			
		169			169

At the end of the firm's accounting year the balance on the bad debts account is transferred as an expense to the profit and loss account as shown above.

It might be thought more appropriate to charge the bad debts in the trading account as they represent a reduction in sales. However, they are regarded as a selling expense and included in the profit and loss account.

Provision for doubtful debts

The charging to profit and loss account, or *writing off*, of known bad debts is not the whole picture. At the end of each year the unpaid balance on debtors' accounts is carried forward, and there is clearly a possibility for further bad debts.

It is common practice therefore to include a *provision* for potential bad debts in the accounts at the year end.

This provision for potential bad debts can be calculated in one of several ways.

(1) Debtors' accounts are examined individually and any debt likely to become bad is listed.
(2) A percentage of debtors is calculated, based on past experience.
(3) A combination of (1) and (2), i.e. any debt thought likely to become bad plus a percentage of the remaining debtors.

Note: The calculation described in (1) is usually described as a *specific* provision, and (2) as a *general* provision. (3) is, of course, a combination of a specific and a general provision.

Some accountants prefer to call this provision a *provision for doubtful debts* as it is not for known and recognised bad debts. This description also avoids confusion with the known bad debts. However, since in examination questions the provision may be entitled either *provision for bad debts* or *provision for doubtful debts*, the two expressions should be regarded as synonymous.

The accounting for both the provision and known bad debts can be carried out by either of two methods. You should be familiar with both methods so that either can be used, as appropriate to the question asked.

Assume the following information:

Year end	Debtors at year end £	Amounts already written off as bad debts £	Debts thought likely to become bad £
31 Dec. 19X1	5,040	69	40
31 Dec. 19X2	9,032	141	32
31 Dec. 19X3	10,073	197	73

The firm commenced trading on 1 January 19X1 and decided at the first year end to create a provision for doubtful debts. The provision would be calculated by taking any debts thought likely to become bad and adding 1% of other debtors at the year end. The provision was calculated similarly in subsequent years:

$$19X1 \quad £40 + (1\% \times £5,000) \quad = £90$$
$$19X2 \quad £32 + (1\% \times £9,000) \quad = £122$$
$$19X3 \quad £73 + (1\% \times £10,000) = £173.$$

Method 1

This method is generally regarded as the easier to understand, though the final results are the same as in method 2.

The amount in the bad debts account at the end of the year is transferred to profit and loss account. The creation and maintaining of the provision is treated as a completely separate transaction for which the book-keeping entries are:

Profit and loss account   *Dr.*
  Provision for doubtful debts   *Cr.*
with the amount necessary to either (a) create the provision (i.e. in the first year) or (b) increase the provision to the figure required (in subsequent years).

Bad debts

19X1		£	19X1		£
	Various debtors a/cs	69	Dec. 31	Profit and loss	69
19X2			19X2		
	Various debtors	141	Dec. 31	Profit and loss	141
19X3			19X3		
	Various debtors	197	Dec. 31	Profit and loss	197

Provision for doubtful debts (or bad debts)

19X1	£	19X1	£
Dec. 31 Balance c/d	90	Dec. 31 Profit and loss	90
19X2		19X2	
Dec. 31 Balance c/d	122	Jan. 1 Balance b/d	90
		Dec. 31 Profit and loss	32
	122		122
19X3		19X3	
Dec. 31 Balance c/d	173	Jan. 1 Balance b/d	122
		Dec. 31 Profit and loss	51
	173		173
		19X4	
		Jan. 1 Balance b/d	173

The above charges will appear in the profit and loss account as an expense thus:

Profit and Loss Account for the year ending

	£
31 December 19X1	
Bad debts	69
Provision for doubtful debts	90
31 December 19X2	
Bad debts	141
Provision for doubtful debts	32
31 December 19X3	
Bad debts	197
Provision for doubtful debts	51

It should be noted that whereas the whole of the known bad debts are charged as an expense in the profit and loss account, only the increase in the provision needs to be so charged. A decrease in the provision would be credited to the profit and loss account.

In the balance sheet the balance on provision for doubtful debts account is deducted from the debtors as shown below. It should be remembered that in this example the known bad debts have already been credited to debtors prior to the year end, and no further adjustment is required for these.

Balance Sheet as at

	£	£
31 Dec. 19X1 Debtors	5,040	
less Provision for doubtful debts	90	4,950
31 Dec. 19X2 Debtors	9,032	
less Provision for doubtful debts	122	8,910
31 Dec. 19X3 Debtors	10,073	
less Provision for doubtful debts	173	9,900

The provision is deducted from the asset against which it has been made (i.e. debtors) just as a provision for depreciation on plant and machinery would be deducted from the balance on the plant and machinery account in the balance sheet.

Method 2

A firm grasp of method 1 is recommended before proceeding to this method.

In this method only one account is maintained, the bad debts account, and both the bad debts written off and the provision for doubtful debts are shown therein. If it is ensured that the correct provision for doubtful debts is carried forward each year, the total debited to profit and loss account will be the same as in method 1.

Bad debts

19X1	£	19X1	£
Dec. 31 Bad debts	69	Dec. 31 Profit and loss	159
31 Provision for doubtful			
debts c/d	90		
	159		159
19X2		19X2	
Dec. 31 Bad debts	141	Jan. 1 Provision for doubtful	
31 Provision for doubtful		debts b/d	90
debts c/d	122	Dec. 31 Profit and loss	173
	263		263
19X3		19X3	
Dec. 31 Bad debts	197	Jan. 1 Provision for doubtful	
31 Provision for doubtful		debts b/d	122
debts c/d	173	Dec. 31 Profit and loss	248
	370		370
		19X4	
		Jan. 1 Provision for doubtful	
		debts b/d	173

The profit and loss account will show an expense as under:

Profit and Loss Account for the year ending

	£
31 December 19X1	
Bad debts	159
31 December 19X2	
Bad debts	173
31 December 19X3	
Bad debts	248

It will be seen, therefore, that exactly the same amount, but as one item rather than two, is charged to profit and loss account.

The balance sheets remain as before, as in method 1.

Provision for discount allowable

Some firms allow cash discounts to debtors for prompt payment. Not all of the debtors will take advantage of these discount terms. The profit shown for the period in the profit and loss account, and also the debtors figure shown in the balance sheet, will be overstated if no deduction is made for the discount to be allowed when the debts are subsequently paid. This deduction is called a *provision for discount allowable* and is created in the same way as all provisions:

Profit and loss account   *Dr.*
     Provision for discount allowable   *Cr.*
with the amount necessary either (a) to create the
provision (i.e. in the first year) or (b) to increase
the provision to the figure deemed necessary in
subsequent years.

The above entries assume that when the year end debtors pay their debts the discount to which they are entitled will be debited to the discount allowed account and not charged against the provision created.

EXAMPLE 8.1

Year end	Debtors at year end	Provision for discount allowable
	£	£
31 Dec. 19X1	16,000	
31 Dec. 19X2	20,000	} 2½% of debtors at year end
31 Dec. 19X3	24,000	

The above provisions would be recorded in the accounts as follows:

Profit and Loss Account for the year ending
                                       £

31 December 19X1
Provision for discount allowable   400

31 December 19X2
Provision for discount allowable   100

31 December 19X3
Provision for discount allowable   100

Provision for discount allowable

19X1	£	19X1	£
Dec. 31 Balance c/d	400	Dec. 31 Profit and loss	400
19X2		19X2	
Dec. 31 Balance c/d	500	Jan. 1 Balance b/d	400
		Dec. 31 Profit and loss	100
	500		500
19X3		19X3	
Dec. 31 Balance c/d	600	Jan. 1 Balance b/d	500
		Dec. 31 Profit and loss	100
	600		600
		19X4	
		Jan. 1 Balance b/d	600

In the balance sheets, the balance on the *provision for discount allowable account* at the balance sheet date is deducted from the debtors as shown below.

Balance Sheet as at

		£	£
31 Dec. 19X1	Debtors	16,000	
	less Provision for discount allowed	400	15,600
31 Dec. 19X2	Debtors	20,000	
	less Provision for discount allowed	500	19,500
31 Dec. 19X3	Debtors	24,000	
	less Provision for discount allowed	600	23,400

Where there are bad debts to be written off, and a provision for the doubtful debts and a provision for discount allowable have to be made, all referring to the same year end debtors figure, they are dealt with in the following order:

	£
Debtors per debtors ledger, say	10,260
less Bad debts, say	260
	10,000
less Provision for doubtful debts, say 2%	200
	9,800
less Provision for discount allowable, say 2½%	245
Cash expected to be collected from year end debtors	9,555

It will be noted that the deductions are made logically. The bad debts are written off before a provision is made against those debtors not known to be bad, and then the provision for discount allowable is made on the balance. It would be illogical to provide for discount allowable to debtors who were not going to pay their debts.

EXAMPLE 8.2

	Debtors at year end £	Bad debts included in year end debtors figures £
31 March 19X1	12,160	160
31 March 19X2	14,190	190
31 March 19X3	13,720	120

Provisions of $2^{1}/_{2}\%$ for doubtful debts and 5% for discount allowable are to be made.

The amounts of the provisions would be calculated as follows:

	31 Mar. 19X1 £	31 Mar. 19X2 £	31 Mar. 19X3 £
Debtors as per trial balance	12,160	14,190	13,720
less Bad debts	160	190	120
Debtors as shown in balance sheet	12,000	14,000	13,600
less Provision for doubtful debts	300	350	340
	11,700	13,650	13,260
less Provision for discount allowable	585	682	663
	11,115	12,968	12,597

The accounts would be as under:

Bad debts

19X1	£	19X1	£
Mar. 31 Debtors	160	Mar. 31 Profit and loss	160
19X2		19X2	
Mar. 31 Debtors	190	Mar. 31 Profit and loss	190
19X3		19X3	
Mar. 31 Debtors	120	Mar. 31 Profit and loss	120

Provision for doubtful debts

19X1	£	19X1	£
Mar. 31 Balance c/d	300	Mar. 31 Profit and loss	300
19X2		19X1	
Mar. 31 Balance c/d	350	Apr. 1 Balance b/d	300
		19X2	
		Mar. 31 Profit and loss	50
	350		350
19X3		19X2	
Mar. 31 Profit and loss	10	Apr. 1 Balance b/d	350
31 Balance c/d	340		
	350		350
		19X3	
		Apr. 1 Balance b/d	340

Provision for discount allowable

19X1	£	19X1	£
Mar. 31 Balance c/d	585	Mar. 31 Profit and loss	585
19X2		19X1	
Mar. 31 Balance c/d	682	Apr. 1 Balance b/d	585
		19X2	
		Mar. 31 Profit and loss	97
	682		682
19X3		19X2	
Mar. 31 Profit and loss	19	Apr. 1 Balance b/d	682
31 Balance c/d	663		
	682		682
		19X3	
		Apr. 1 Balance b/d	663

The profit and loss accounts would show expenses as below.

Profit and Loss Account for the year ending

	£
31 March 19X1	
Bad debts	160
Provision for doubtful debts	300
Provision for discount allowable	585
31 March 19X2	
Bad debts	190
Provision for doubtful debts	50
Provision for discount allowable	97

31 March 19X3

Bad debts   120

The following items in 19X3 could be added to gross profit in the profit and loss account or alternatively deducted from bad debts and discounts allowed respectively in the profit and loss account:

	£
Provision for doubtful debts no longer required	10
Provision for discount allowable no longer required	19

Balance Sheet as at

		£	£	£
31 March 19X1	Debtors		12,000	
	less Provision for doubtful debts	300		
	Provision for discount allowable	585	885	11,115
31 March 19X2	Debtors		14,000	
	less Provision for doubtful debts	350		
	Provision for discount allowable	682	1,032	12,968
31 March 19X3	Debtors		13,600	
	less Provision for doubtful debts	340		
	Provision for discount allowable	663	1,003	12,597

Provision for discount receivable

It is sometimes argued that where a provision for discount allowable is made, and the firm concerned regularly receives cash discount from its suppliers, a provision for discount receivable should also be made at the year end so that the amount owing to creditors is not overstated. There are sound accounting arguments against this practice, e.g. it is against the prudence (or conservatism) convention and suppliers may decide to alter their terms of trading by stopping cash discounts, but it is accepted that so long as a provision for discount allowable is made, a provision for discount receivable can also be made. Such a provision is created as follows:

Provision for discount receivable	*Dr.*
Profit and loss account	*Cr.*

with the amount necessary either (a) to create the provision (i.e. in the first year) or (b) to increase the provision to the figure required.

The assumption is again made that any discount received will be credited to a discount received account and not credited to the provision account.

In the balance sheet, the balance on the provision for discount receivable account would be deducted from creditors.

Questions

8.1S   Show the journal and ledger entries to record the following:

19X5		£
Jan. 1	Provision for doubtful debts	725
Dec. 31	Total of bad debts account	630
Dec. 31	Adjust the provision for doubtful debts account to show a provision of 5% on the book debts which are £12,870 before the above bad debts have been written off.	

8.2S   At 31 December 19X6, the provision for doubtful debts account in the books of W. Charnock stands at £1,400. During 19X7 debts amounting to £1,840 are written off as bad and at 31 December 19X7, the necessary provision for doubtful debts is calculated at £1,050. In 19X8, debts amounting to £1,410 are written off and at 31 December 19X8, the provision for doubtful debts is calculated to be £1,205.

You are required to show the provision for doubtful debts account and the bad debts account for both 19X7 and 19X8.

8.3S   The following details were extracted from the books of R. Young and Co. on 31 December 19X8.

	£
Debtors – before adjustment for any bad debts	45,000
Provision for doubtful debts	4,200
Amount of bad debts	1,200

The company's policy is to make a provision for doubtful debts of 10% on debtors at the year end and a provision for discounts allowable of 5% on debtors at the year end.

You are required to show:

(a) the provision for doubtful debts account;
(b) the provision for discount allowable account;
(c) the amounts to be charged in the profit and loss account for bad debts, doubtful debts and discounts allowable.

8.4S   On 1 January 19X1, the provision for discount receivable in the books of T. O'Keefe was £600. The discounts received during 19X1 amounted to £3,800. The creditors on 31 December 19X1 were £24,800 and a new provision of 2½% is to be made. No separate provision account is maintained in the books.

You are required to show the discount receivable account and the credit to profit and loss account for the year to 31 December 19X1.

8.5S   The trial balance of S. Urban at 31 March 19X3 was as follows:

	£	£
Stock at 1 April 19X2	18,400	
Purchases	60,080	
Purchase returns		240
Cash in hand	340	
Cash at bank	10,084	
Freehold premises at cost	15,440	
Lighting and heating	836	
Printing, stationery and advertising	112	
Accountancy charges	656	
Provision for doubtful debts		1,400
Sundry debtors	14,400	

	£	£
Sundry creditors		11,868
Wages	10,700	
Salaries	3,500	
Bad debts	900	
Capital account at 1 April 19X2		45,860
Drawings	3,000	
Discount allowed	2,520	
Discount received		1,840
Sales		83,580
Office furniture at cost	2,500	
Provision for depreciation on office furniture		500
Rent, rates and insurance	1,600	
Sales returns	220	
	145,288	145,288

The following matters are to be taken into account:

1. Stock at 31 March 19X3, £20,800
2. Provision for doubtful debts is to be increased to £1,600
3. Rent accrued due £200
4. Insurance paid in advance £80
5. Provide for depreciation on office furniture at 5% on cost.

You are required to prepare a trading and profit and loss account for the year ended 31 March 19X3, and a balance sheet as at that date.

8.6   R. Sharp commenced business on 1 January 19X7. At his year end, on 31 December 19X7, he found that he had written off irrecoverable debts amounting to £280. In addition, he found it necessary to create a provision for doubtful debts of £480. During the year to 31 December 19X8, debts totalling £420 proved to be bad and were written off, and £50 was recovered in respect of bad debts previously written off. The total of debtors' outstanding accounts at 31 December 19X8 was £13,800 (after the bad debts had been written off) and it was decided to increase the provision for doubtful debts up to 5% of this figure.
    You are required to show the bad debts account and the provision for doubtful debts account for both years.

8.7   The provision for doubtful debts on 1 July 19X8 was £860. The bad debts during the year ended 30 June 19X9 amounted to £603. The sundry debtors on 30 June 19X9, after the bad debts have been written off, are £18,860 and a new provision of 5% is required.
    You are required to show the ledger, profit and loss account and balance sheet entries from the above details.

8.8   T. Drury and Co. makes a provision for doubtful debts of 5% on debtors and a provision for discount allowable of 2½% on debtors.
    The balances standing in the relevant accounts on 1 July 19X6 were: provision for doubtful debts £1,672, provision for discount allowable £795.
    During the year ended 30 June 19X7, the company incurred bad debts of £2,840 and allowed discounts of £4,892.
    On 30 June 19X7, debtors amounted to £36,716 after the bad debts of £2,840 had been written off.

You are required to show:

(a) the provision for doubtful debts account;
(b) the provision for discount allowable account;
(c) the appropriate entries as they would appear in the profit and loss account.

8.9   On 1 July 19X5 the balances brought down on the discount accounts of T. Ryan were as follows:

	£
Discount allowed account	800
Discount received account	900

During the year ended 30 June 19X6 discount of £3,200 was allowed to debtors and discount of £2,100 was received when paying creditors.

Provisions of $2\frac{1}{2}$% on both debtors and creditors were made at 30 June 19X6, when debtors totalled £24,000 and creditors totalled £12,000.

Separate provision accounts for discounts are not maintained in the books.

You are required to show the discount allowed account and the discount received account for the year to 30 June 19X6 and to bring down the balance on each account at that date.

8.10   The following trial balance was extracted from the books of B.N. Jackson & Co. on 30 June 19X9.

	£	£
Capital account at 1 July 19X8		30,360
Freehold premises at cost	20,000	
Fixtures and fittings at cost	4,500	
Provision for depreciation on fixtures and fittings		450
Stock on 1 July 19X8	5,684	
Purchases and sales	11,263	22,741
Returns inwards and outwards	191	123
Debtors and creditors	3,380	1,694
Salaries	2,390	
Lighting and heating	512	
Rent, rates and insurance	1,620	
Bad debts	210	
Sundry expenses	204	
Discounts allowed and received	360	280
Cash at bank	2,614	
Cash in hand	120	
Drawings	2,600	
	55,648	55,648

The following items are to be taken into account:

1. Stock at 30 June 19X9 £4,672
2. Rates paid in advance £300
3. Rent accrued due £400
4. Create a provision for doubtful debts of £180
5. Create a provision for discount allowable of $2\frac{1}{2}$% on debtors
6. Provide for depreciation on fixtures and fittings at 5% on cost.

You are required to prepare a trading and profit and loss account for the year ended 30 June 19X9 and a balance sheet as at that date.

9 Control accounts

Aims of the chapter:

> To explain the function of control accounts
> To show how these accounts work in practice

The division of the ledger as previously described is adopted by most firms. This means that they will keep a separate debtors ledger (or sales ledger) and a separate creditors ledger (or purchases ledger).

It is appropriate at this stage to reiterate that the debtors' and creditors' T accounts maintained in these ledgers form part of the double entry system. Whenever a trial balance is taken, therefore, it is essential that the balances on all the debtors' and creditors' accounts are included.

If a firm has a large number of debtors and/or creditors the process of taking a trial balance can become protracted. With a large number of accounts there is also a greater possibility of an error occurring within one of the individual debtor's or creditor's accounts.

It would be of great assistance, therefore, if the debtors ledger could be agreed or balanced separately; and similarly the creditors ledger. In this way an error, on say a debtor's account, will be isolated, rather than appear as an unidentifiable error on the full trial balance.

This separate balancing is the function of *control accounts.*

How then are control accounts prepared?

Taking debtors first, it is helpful to consider the entries that would normally be found on an individual debtor's account, i.e.

Debits	*Credits*
Credit sales	Sales returns
Dishonoured cheques	Cash received
Correction of errors	Discount allowed
	Bad debts written off
	Contra entries
	Correction of errors

If it could be ensured that the debtor's control account contained all these items, in either totals or individual amounts as appropriate, the balance on the control account should agree with a schedule or list of the individual debtor's accounts taken from the ledger.

The way in which information has been previously processed means that some of this information is readily available. For example, in Chapter 6 it was shown how the sales day book would be posted in total at suitable intervals to the sales account. The same totals would be put into the debtors ledger control account on the debit side.

The information required for the debtors' control account can be found as follows:

Debits	Source (book of prime entry)
Credit sales	Sales day book
Dishonoured cheques	Journal
Correction of errors	Cash book

Credits	
Sales returns	Sales returns book
Cash received	Cash book
Discounts allowed	Cash book – discount column
Bad debts written off	Journal
Contra entries	Journal
Correction of errors	Journal

It is necessary therefore that a system is set up to record any of the above transactions in the control account. For example, the cash book might be organised so that all cash received is analysed, and one analysis column would be reserved to record cash received from debtors. The total of this column would then appear in the control account.

The same principles apply to the creditors' control accounts.

The entries that would normally appear on an individual creditor's account are:

Debits	Credits
Purchases returns	Purchases
Cash paid	Correction of errors
Discounts received	
Contra entries	
Correction of errors	

The creditors' control account would be built up from the following sources:

Debits	Source (book of prime entry)
Purchases returns	Purchases returns book
Cash paid	Cash book
Discounts received	Cash book – discount column
Contra entries	Journal
Correction of errors	Journal

Credits	
Purchases	Purchases day book
Correction of errors	Journal

EXAMPLE 9.1

From the following information prepare the purchases ledger and sales ledger control accounts for the month of January 19XX.

	£
Sales ledger balance 1 January 19XX	20,363
Purchases ledger balance 1 January 19XX	15,382
Credit sales for month	12,620
Returns inwards	123
Purchases on credit for month	9,175
Cash paid	14,895
Discounts received	107
Discounts allowed	201
Cash received	13,150
Returns outwards	67
Bad debt written off	23

In addition an amount owing to Mr T. Jones of £100 was offset against an amount of £150 owed by him.

Solution

Sales ledger (or debtors ledger) control account

	£		£
Balance b/d	20,363	Returns inwards	123
Credit sales	12,620	Cash received	13,150
		Discounts allowed	201
		Bad debt written off	23
		Purchases ledger – contra	
		T. Jones	100
		Balance c/d	19,386
	32,983		32,983
Balance b/d	19,386		

Purchases ledger (or creditors ledger) control account

	£		£
Cash paid	14,895	Balance b/d	15,382
Discounts received	107	Purchases	9,175
Returns outwards	67		
Sales ledger – contra			
T. Jones	100		
Balance c/d	9,388		
	24,557		24,557
		Balance b/d	9,388

Any time it is wished to check the accuracy of the total outstanding debtors a list or schedule is made of all the balances on the individual debtor's accounts in the debtors ledger. This is totalled and agreed, after detailed checking if necessary, with the balance on the debtors ledger control account (or sales ledger control account). This agreed balance can be used in the trial balance, and in the balance sheet where the debtors are also aggregated into one figure.

A similar procedure is adopted for the creditors ledger.

It should be noted especially that control accounts do not form part of the double entry system. They are mere memoranda accounts, or total accounts, used as an aid to balancing. They assist in balancing the trial balance. They also assist in balancing the debtors and creditors ledgers, so being a most useful form of internal check on these ledgers. Indeed it is normal practice to agree the control accounts and the ledgers at frequent intervals, rather than just when taking out a trial balance. The control accounts also provide quick total figures of debtors and creditors for management purposes.

Sometimes, in practice, the control accounts are regarded as part of the double entry system. The contents of the debtors' and creditors' ledgers then become subsidiary records. In principle this makes little difference, and examination questions do not normally assume this arrangement.

As indicated previously, it sometimes happens that the control account balance does not agree with the list of balances extracted. The reasons for the non-agreement are given below analysed to show where (a) the control account and (b) the list of balances will need amending.

(a) The control account will need amending where an item is correctly
  (i)   recorded in a book of prime entry and correctly posted to a personal account but not entered in the control account;
  (ii) recorded in a book of prime entry and correctly posted to a personal account but entered incorrectly in the control account;
  (iii) posted to a personal account but not entered in a book of prime entry;
  (iv) posted to a personal account but entered incorrectly in a book of prime entry;
  and where,
  (v)   one or more of the books of prime entry is incorrectly cast, i.e. the total is under-added or over-added.

(b) The list of balances will need amending where
  (i)   an item is correctly recorded in a book of prime entry and entered correctly in the control account but not posted to a personal account;
  (ii) an item is correctly recorded in a book of prime entry and entered correctly in the control account but posted incorrectly to a personal account;
  (iii) a personal account balance is incorrectly calculated;
  (iv) a correct personal account balance is listed incorrectly;
  (v)   a personal account balance is omitted from the list of balances.

An example bringing in several of these types of errors is shown below.

EXAMPLE 9.2

A routine comparison showed that the sales ledger (debtors ledger) control account balance amounted to £5,779 whilst the schedule of debtors extracted from the ledger totalled £5,771.

Detailed checking showed the following errors:

(1) Discounts amounting to £23 had been entered correctly in all accounts other than the control account, where it had been omitted.

(2) The sales returns day book had been overcast (i.e. over-added) by £20.

(3) Smith has been credited with goods returned valued at £17, but no entry made in the sales returns day book.

(4) The account for Jones had been overcast by £27 in the sales ledger, whilst the account for Thompson had been undercast £15.

Show the necessary adjustments to the control account and the schedule of debtors.

Solution:

Adjustment to schedule of debtors

	£
Original balance	5,771
less (4) Jones overcast	27
	5,744
add (4) Thompson undercast	15
Balance c/d	5,759

Sales ledger control account

	£		£
Original balance	5,779	Discounts allowed omitted (1)	23
Sales returns overcast (2)	20	Sales returns omitted (3)	17
		Balance c/d	5,759
	5,799		5,799
Balance b/d	5,759		

It is quite possible to have a credit balance on an individual debtor's account. This may be due to a debtor making an overpayment, for example, or the debtor may have been credited with goods he has returned but has already paid for. When the balances on the debtors' accounts are listed or scheduled, a separate total might be taken of the debit balances and a separate total of the credit balances. The net balance, of course, should agree with the control account. When the control account has been agreed, it is then quite common practice to carry forward the control account as two separate balances, in agreement with the totals determined from the schedules. In the case of the debtors' control account, one would expect a large debit balance and a relatively small credit balance.

In a similar way it is possible to have a debit balance on a creditor's account, and the control account might again be carried forward as two balances.

Examination questions often have two brought forward balances for each control account. The questions following this chapter include examples of this nature. There is not usually enough information to calculate two carried forward balances, but this should be done if it is possible.

In a balance sheet, for strict accuracy if the figures are available, the debtors figure should be the total of the debit balances on the debtors' accounts and the debit balances on the creditors' accounts. In the same way the creditors figure should be the total of the credit balances on both the creditors' accounts and the debtors' accounts.

Questions

9.1S   (a) Give the sources from which a creditors control account would be compiled.

     (b) From the following figures compile a debtors control account at 30 June 19X6.

	£
Total debtors at 1 July 19X5	32,170
Transactions for the year:	
Credit sales	293,220
Cash received from debtors	290,040
Discount allowed	6,740
Debts written off as irrecoverable	3,200
Sales returns	2,640

9.2S   The following details were extracted from the books of S. Oldham & Co. at 30 June 19X8.

	£
Sales ledger balances, 1 January 19X8	
Debit	20,400
Credit	560
Purchase ledger balances, 1 January 19X8	
Debit	120
Credit	14,680
Transactions for the six months:	
Payments to suppliers	93,856
Discounts received	2,580
Cash received from trade debtors	119,390
Discounts allowed	3,840
Purchases on credit	98,550
Credit sales	126,400
Purchase returns	1,630
Sales returns	480
Bad debts written off as irrecoverable	402

During the six month period, debit balances of £834 were transferred to the purchase ledger.

At 30 June 19X8:	£
Sales ledger credit balances were	730
Purchase ledger debit balances were	126

You are required to prepare the sales ledger control account and the purchase ledger control account as at 30 June 19X8.

9.3S   The net total balances extracted from Tipper's purchase ledger on 31 March 19X7 amounted to £12,560, which did not agree with the balance on the purchase ledger control account. The audit revealed the following errors and, when the appropriate adjustments had been made for these, the books balanced.

(1) A debit balance of £40 in the purchase ledger had been listed as a credit balance.

(2) Hector had been debited for goods returned to him, £90, and no other entry had been made.

(3) The purchase day book had been overcast by £100.

(4) Credit balances on the purchase ledger amounting to £480 and debit balances amounting to £24 had been omitted from the list of balances.

(5) A payment of £8 to Tiger for a cash purchase of goods had been recorded in the petty cash book and posted to his account in the purchase ledger, no other entry having been made.

(6) The transfer of £120 from Harrow's account in the sales ledger to the credit of his account in the purchase ledger had not been entered in the control account.

You are required to prepare:

(a) a statement reconciling the original net balances extracted from the purchase ledger with the corrected balance on the purchase ledger control account, and

(b) the purchase ledger control account showing the balance before the correction of the errors and the necessary adjustments thereon.

(Institute of Chartered Accountants in England and Wales)

9.4S   The net total balances extracted from Starling's purchase ledger on 31 March 19X4 amounted to £5,676, which did not agree with the balance on the purchase ledger control account. The audit revealed the following errors and, when the appropriate adjustments had been made for these, the books balanced.

(1) An item of £20, purchases from A. Brown, had been posted from the purchase day book to the credit of B. Brown's account.

(2) On 31 January 19X4, Charles had been debited for goods returned to him, £84, and no other entry had been made.

(3) Credit balances on the purchase ledger amounting to £562 and debit balances amounting to £12 had been omitted from the list of balances.

(4) Returns of £60 allowed by Austin had been correctly recorded and posted in Starling's books. This item was later disallowed, entered in the sales return book, and credited to Austin's account in the sales ledger.

(5) The transfer of £90 from the debit of Cook's account in the sales ledger to the credit of his account in the purchase ledger had not been entered in the journal.

(6) The purchase day book had been undercast by £100.

(7) A payment to Brook of £3 for a cash purchase of goods had been recorded in the cash book and posted to his account in the purchase ledger, no other entry having been made.

You are required to set out:

(a) journal entries, where necessary, to correct these errors, and

(b) the purchase ledger control account showing the balance before the correction of the errors and the necessary adjustments thereon.

(Institute of Chartered Accountants in England and Wales)

9.5S   The following transactions relate to a sales ledger for the year ended 31 December 19X4:

	£
Balance on sales ledger control 1 January 19X4	8,952
Sales as per posting summaries	74,753
Receipts from debtors	69,471
Discounts allowed	1,817

The clerk in charge had prepared from the ledger cards a list of balances outstanding on 31 December 19X4 amounting to £9,663 but this did not agree with the balance of the sales ledger control account. There were no credit balances on the ledger cards.

Investigation of the differences revealed:

(i)   The bank statement showed credit transfers of £198 which had been completely overlooked.

(ii)   Journal entries correctly posted to the ledger cards had been overlooked when posting control account: debts settled by set off against creditors' accounts £2,896, bad debts £640.

(iii) When listing the debtor balances three ledger cards with debit balances of £191 had been incorrectly filed and consequently had not been included in the list of balances.

(iv)   The machine operator when posting a ledger card had incorrectly picked up an old balance of £213.50 as £13.50 and had failed to check her total balance.

(v)   £1,173 entered in the cash book as a receipt from J. Spruce had not been posted as no account under that name could be traced. Later it was discovered it was in payment for a car which had been used by the sales department and sold to him second-hand.

Required:

(a)   Prepare the sales ledger control account for the year ended 31 December 19X4 taking into account the above adjustments.

(b)   Reconcile the clerk's balance of £9,663 with the corrected balance on the sales ledger account.

(c)   Explain the benefits that accrue from operating control accounts.

(Chartered Association of Certified Accountants)

9.6   During the course of the audit of Webster & Co. it was found that the net total balances of £16,460 extracted from the sales ledger on 30 June 19X1 did not agree with the net balance on the sales ledger control account. On checking, the following errors were discovered, after the adjustment of which the books balanced and the corrected net total of sales ledger balances agreed with the amended balance on the control account:

(1)   Sales ledger balances had been omitted from the list of balances as follows:

	£
Debit	760
Credit	80

(2)   A credit balance of £80 in the sales ledger had been listed as a debit balance.

(3)   The sales day book had been undercast by £1,000.

(4)   The list of balances had been overcast by £10.

(5) Smith's account had been credited with £280 for goods returned by him but no other entry had been made in the books.

(6) A transfer of £420 from Howard's account in the purchase ledger to the credit of his account in the sales ledger had not been entered in the control account.

(7) A balance of £60 owing by Hector had been written off as irrecoverable on 30 June 19X1, and debited to bad debts, but no entry had been made in the control account.

(8) A cheque for £260 received from Twist had been dishonoured but the entry recording this fact in the cash book had not been posted to Twist's account although dealt with in the control account.

(9) The debit column of West's account in the sales ledger had been overcast by £100.

You are required to prepare:

(a) a statement reconciling the original net balances extracted from the sales ledger with the adjusted final balance on the sales ledger control account, and

(b) the sales ledger control account showing the necessary adjustments and the balance on the account before these adjustments.

(Institute of Chartered Accountants in England and Wales)

9.7   During the course of the audit of Giles & Co. it was found that the net total balances of £17,780 extracted from the purchase ledger on 30 June 19X9 did not agree with the balance on the purchase ledger control account.

Audit tests revealed the following errors, and when the necessary adjustments had been made the books balanced:

(1) Purchase ledger balances had been omitted from the list of balances as follows:

	£
Credits	270
Debits	20

(2) Discounts received for the month of March, amounting to £15, had been recorded in the cash book and posted to the correct accounts in the purchase ledger, but no entry had been made in the control account.

(3) The purchase returns day book had been overcast by £100.

(4) Credit balances of £35 in the purchase ledger had been incorrectly listed as debit balances.

(5) Payments for rates had been analysed as a purchase and posted to an account in the purchase ledger. The balance on this account, £180, had been transferred to the nominal ledger, but no entry had been made in the control account.

(6) By arrangement, Burton's account on the sales ledger was set off by contra against the credit balance on his account in the purchase ledger. Transfers amounting to £450 had not been entered in the control account.

(7) Johnson had been debited for goods returned to him, £40, and no entry had been made in the purchase returns day book.

(8) An old debit balance on the purchase ledger of £2 had been written off as bad in June 19X9, but no entry had been made in the control account.

(9) In June 19X9, payment of £120 had been correctly entered in the control account but had been posted to the purchase ledger as July 19X9.

(10) The credit column of Taylor's account in the purchase ledger had been undercast by £10.

You are required to prepare:

(a) a statement reconciling the original net balances extracted from the purchase ledger with the adjusted final balance on the purchase ledger control account, and

(b) the purchase ledger control account showing the necessary adjustments and the balance on the account before these adjustments.

(Institute of Chartered Accountants in England and Wales)

9.8   During the course of the audit of Grey & Co. it was found that the net total balances of £28,200 extracted from the sales ledger on 31 December 19X2 did not agree with the net balance on the sales ledger control account. On checking, the following errors were discovered, after the adjustment of which the books balanced and the corrected net total of sales ledger balances agreed with the amended balance on the control account:

(1) A debit balance of £860 and credit balances amounting to £140 had been omitted from the list of balances.

(2) The sales returns book had been undercast by £1,000.

(3) The list of balances had been overcast by £100.

(4) A balance owing by Silver of £180 had been written off as irrecoverable on 31 December 19X2 and debited to bad debts, but no entry had been made in the control account.

(5) A debit balance of £140 in the sales ledger had been listed as a credit balance.

(6) No entries had been made in the control accounts in respect of a transfer of £410 standing to the credit of Green's account in the purchase ledger to his account in the sales ledger.

(7) Black's account had been credited with £340 for goods returned by him but no other entry had been made in the books.

(8) A discount of £50 allowed to Brown had been correctly recorded and posted in the books. This item was subsequently disallowed and a corresponding amount entered in the discounts received in the cash book and posted to Brown's account in the purchase ledger and included in the total of discounts received.

You are required to prepare:

(a) a statement reconciling the original net balances extracted from the sales ledger with the adjusted final balance on the sales ledger control account, and

(b) the sales ledger control account showing the necessary adjustments and the balance on the account before and after these adjustments.

(Institute of Chartered Accountants in England and Wales)

9.9   Wright maintains control accounts in the nominal ledger in respect of both the sales ledger and the purchase ledger. The net total of the balances extracted from the sales ledger as on 30 September 19X8 amounted to £6,438, which did not agree with the balance on the sales ledger control account. On checking the following errors were discovered after the adjustment of which the books balanced and the corrected net total of the sales ledger balances agreed with the amended balance of the control account:

(1) The sales return book had been overcast by £100.

(2) A balance owing by Williams of £239 had been written off as irrecoverable on 30 September 19X8 and debited to bad debts but no entry had been made in the control account.

(3) No entries had been made in the control accounts in respect of a transfer of £180 standing to the credit of Andrew's account in the purchase ledger to his account in the sales ledger.

(4) A debit balance of £735 and credit balances amounting to £23 had been omitted from the list of balances.

(5) A cheque for £127 received from Cox had been dishonoured but the entry recording this fact in the cash book had not been posted to Cox's account although dealt with in the control account.

(6) A discount of £15 allowed to Steel had been correctly recorded and posted in the books. This item was subsequently disallowed and a corresponding amount entered in the discounts received in the cash book and posted to Steel's account in the purchase ledger and included in the total of discounts received.

You are required:

(a) to give the journal entries, where necessary, to correct these errors, or if no journal entry is required, to state how they will be corrected, and

(b) to set out the sales ledger control account showing the balance before and after the correction of the errors.

(Institute of Chartered Accountants in England and Wales)

9.10 Nostla Products Limited includes in its accounting system a purchases ledger control account and a sales ledger control account.

The company's trial balance at 30 November 19X9 included the following entries:

	£	£
Purchases ledger control account	1,242	24,647
Sales ledger control account	39,650	941

The following is a summary of the company's transactions with its suppliers and customers during the year ended 30 November 19X0:

	£
Goods purchased and received from suppliers	
Gross invoice value before trade discounts	210,786
Net invoice price after trade discounts	176,410
Goods returned to suppliers	
Gross invoice value before trade discounts	16,476
Net invoice price after trade discounts	15,113
Amounts due to suppliers	
Total full amount	163,300
Settled by payment of	159,400
Goods sold to customers	
Gross invoice value before trade discounts	344,700
Net invoice price after trade discounts	310,690
Goods returned from customers	
Gross invoice value before trade discounts	7,600
Net invoice price after trade discounts	6,764
Amounts due from customers	
Full amount	307,610
Settled by receipt of	306,540
Customers' debts written off as irrecoverable	970

It has been decided to create a provision for doubtful debts at 30 November 19X0 of $2^1/2$% of the total amount due from customers indebted to the company; there was no provision for doubtful debts in the trial balance at 30 November 19X9.

At 30 November 19X0 both the purchases ledger and the sales ledger included accounts with J. Dyke:

	£
Purchases ledger	1,630 credit
Sales ledger	1,268 debit

It has been decided to set off J. Dyke's balance in the sales ledger against his balance in the purchases ledger.

The purchases ledger at 30 November 19X0 included the following accounts with debit balances:

	£
G. Graham	930
L. Brooke	420

The sales ledger at 30 November 19X0 included the following accounts with credit balances:

	£
P. Hilltop	230
H. Pumpkin	83
K. Bunson	500

Required:

(a) The following accounts for the year ended 30 November 19X0 in the books of Nostla Products Limited:
      Purchases ledger control account,
      Sales ledger control account.
      Note: The balances outstanding on 30 November 19X0 should be brought down.

(b) (i) The journal entry for the creation of the provision for doubtful debts at 30 November 19X0. *Note:* The journal narrative is required.

   (ii) Explain the relationship between the provision for doubtful debts and the sales ledger control account.

10 Bank reconciliation

Aims of the chapter:

To identify the need for a bank reconciliation statement
To show how such statements are prepared

It will be apparent to anyone who has a bank account that the balance in the bank as shown on the bank statement is rarely in agreement with one's own calculations! Of course a well managed firm will keep a detailed cash book, with a bank column along the lines set out in Chapter 6 and so there should be less chance of a disagreement.

Even so, the balance shown on the bank statement rarely agrees precisely with the balance shown in the bank column of the cash book. This is usually due to a difference in timing; it is rarely due to error.

The bank statement records all the firm's transactions through its bank, as shown in the bank's ledger. The bank opens a personal account for each of its customers and this account records all payments into or out of the account. Because it is a personal account, each customer is normally a creditor of the bank unless his account is overdrawn whereupon he becomes a debtor. A credit balance on the bank statement is therefore equivalent to, or reflected as, a debit balance in the cash book (bank column).

The purpose of a bank reconciliation statement is to explain the difference at a given date between the balance of the bank account, as shown in the firm's cash book, and the balance as shown on the bank statement.

There are a number of reasons why the two balances may not agree at a particular date.

1. Payments made by the bank on behalf of the firm (e.g. standing orders or direct debits), or charges levied by the bank (e.g. bank charges, interest on overdraft) have not been recorded in the firm's cash book.
2. Amounts received directly by the bank (e.g. standing orders, direct debits, dividends) have not been recorded in the firm's cash book.
3. Cheques received from debtors and paid into the bank, have subsequently been dishonoured and not yet entered in the firm's cash book.
4. Cheques drawn by the firm in favour of suppliers or other creditors have been correctly credited in the cash book but not yet been presented for payment at the firm's bank.
5. Cheques or cash paid into the bank by the firm and recorded as such in the firm's cash book have not yet been recorded by the bank. For

example, cash received and recorded in the cash book on 30 September and put in the bank's night safe on that date will not appear on the bank statement until 1 October. Cheques received and recorded immediately in the bank column of the cash book will not appear on the bank statement until paid into the bank.

6. An error made by the bank on the bank statement. In practice this is a rare occurrence, except in examination questions.

A detailed examination and comparison of the cash book (bank column) and the bank statement is necessary to identify each individual cause of a difference.

Where a difference is due to explanations 1, 2 or 3 as outlined above, the cash book should be updated with the items omitted from the cash book but shown correctly on the bank statement.

The cash book should then show the correct figure so far as the firm's accounts are concerned. Any remaining differences due to 4, 5 or 6 are explained in the bank reconciliation statement.

The bank reconciliation statement is not, of course, part of the double entry system. Its function is to reassure owners and auditors that the difference between the bank statement and the cash book is explicable and due to legitimate factors.

EXAMPLE 10.1

Bank Statement

D. Bradshaw
39 West Road
Longsight
Manchester M12 8JD

MIDMINSTER BANK LIMITED
Longsight Branch
220 Stockport Road
Manchester M12 5BE

Statement of Account

19X1	Sheet 2 Account No. 04725824		Debit	Credit	Balance	C = Credit D = Debit
Sep. 4	Balance brought forward				5,000	C
5	034851		700			
	034852		2,000		2,300	C
7	034853		100		2,200	C
9	034854		800		1,400	C
16	Cheques			960		
	AA subscription	SO	20			
	034855		390		1,950	C
19	Cheque			820	2,770	C
22	Middleton Building Soc.	CT		60		
	034856		60			
	034857		2,000		770	C
24	Cheques			2,220		
	034858		780		2,210	C
30	013428		80		2,130	C
	Charges		5		2,125	C

Cash book (bank columns)

19X1		£	£	19X1			£
Sep.	1 Balance b/d		5,000	Sep.	2 Shopfittings	034851	700
	14 A. Smith	420			Purchases	034852	2,000
	W.P. Burke	540	960		4 Purchases	034853	100
	17 W. Tree		820		6 J. Rowley	034854	800
	22 J. Carey	480			11 S. Pearson	034855	390
	J. Crompton	360			18 C. Mitton	034856	60
	J. Ashton	860			G. Farm	034857	2,000
	H. Anderson	520	2,220		20 H. Shinwell	034858	780
	28 A. Chilton	510			25 Rent	034859	450
	H. Cockburn	390			Purchases	034860	60
	J. Delaney	890			30 Balance c/d		4,000
	J. Morris	550	2,340				
			11,340				11,340
Oct.	1 Balance b/d		4,000				

It is first necessary to check items in the cash book against items on the bank statement. A suitable method is to tick common items.

Any items remaining unticked on the bank statement should normally represent amounts received or paid by the bank but not recorded in the cash book. The cash book should therefore be updated to include these items. The only exception to this is a bank error, which will appear on the bank reconciliation statement. The cheque payment no. 013428 of £80 does not appear in the cash book, is out of numerical sequence with other cheques, and would appear to be an error. In practice this would be confirmed with the bank, and the bank would make a correcting entry on the date that the error was discovered. In the meantime it must appear on the bank reconciliation statement.

The other three items unticked on the bank statement, i.e. the bank charges, the AA subscription and the interest from the Middleton Building Society, should be entered in the cash book to give the amended and correct balance:

Cash book (bank columns)

19X1		£	19X1		£
Sep.	30 Balance b/d	4,000	Sep.	16 AA subscription	20
	22 Middleton			30 Bank charges	5
	Building Society	60		30 Balance c/d	4,035
		4,060			4,060
Oct.	1 Balance b/d	4,035			

The items unticked on the cash book (plus the error previously mentioned) appear in the bank reconciliation statement below:

Bank Reconciliation Statement as at 30 September 19X1

	£	£	
Balance per cash book		4,035	In hand
add Cheques not yet presented			
Sep. 25 034859 Rent	450		
Sep. 25 034860 Purchases	60	510	
		4,545	In hand
deduct Deposits not yet recorded by bank			
Sep. 30		2,340	
		2,205	In hand
deduct Cheque 013428 charged in error (confirmed with bank)		80	
Balance as per bank statement		2,125	In hand

In the bank reconciliation statement it is recommended that the words 'in hand' or 'overdrawn' be used, as appropriate, to indicate the state of the cash book/bank statement. The use of the words 'credit' and 'debit' can be confusing in this statement as a credit balance at the bank is equivalent to a debit balance in the cash book.

It should be noted that the effect of cheques not presented at the bank is that the bank is holding more money than would appear from the cash book.

The effect of monies unrecorded at the bank is that the bank statement shows less than would appear from the cash book.

A logical, common sense approach to a bank reconciliation statement will cope with all situations whether the balance at the bank is in hand or overdrawn.

An extract of the cash book and bank statement is not always provided in examination questions. Sometimes the question will give the appropriate balances and indicate the total amount of cheques not presented, deposits not entered or recorded, and errors made. The comparison of entries in the cash book with those shown on the bank statement is not therefore required in these circumstances. But once again, the cash book should be amended if necessary first, and the bank reconciliation statement prepared afterwards.

EXAMPLE 10.2

The cash book of J. Jones showed a balance at the bank of £570 in hand on 31 January 19X1. At the same date, the bank statement balance of J. Jones' account was £446 overdrawn. The difference was accounted for as follows:

(i) Cheques for £1,555 sent to creditors on 30 January were not paid by the bank until 8 February.

(ii) Cheques amounting to £2,520 paid into the bank on 31 January were not credited by the bank until 1 February.

(iii) A standing order for a charitable subscription of £60 had been paid by the bank on 21 January but no entry had been made in the cash book.

(iv) A cheque paid by J. Jones for rent on 15 January for £345 had been entered in his cash book as £354.

Solution:

Before the bank reconciliation statement can be prepared, the cash book balance (bank column) must be amended:

Cash book (bank column)

19X1	£	19X1	£
Jan. 31 Balance b/d	570	Jan. 21 Charitable	
31 Correction of error		subscription SO	60
on rent paid 15 January	9	31 Balance c/d	519
	579		579
Feb. 1 Balance b/d	519		

Bank Reconciliation Statement as at 31 January 19X1

	£	
Balance per cash book	519	In hand
add Cheques not yet presented	1,555	
	2,074	In hand
deduct Amounts not yet recorded by the bank	2,520	
Balance per bank statement	446	Overdrawn

Questions

10.1S   From the information given below you are required to prepare a bank reconciliation statement as at 31 December 19X6.

	£
Cash at bank as per bank column of cash book	6,870
Cheques not yet presented for payment	2,560
Lodgements not yet cleared by the bank	1,510
Cash at bank as per bank statement	7,920

10.2S   From the information given below you are required to:

(i)   show the additional entries required in the company's cash book and the amended bank balance at 30 June 19X2;

(ii) prepare a statement reconciling the amended bank balance as shown in (i) above with the balance in the bank pass book.

At 30 June 19X2 a company's cash book showed a balance overdrawn at the bank of £262, whereas the bank pass book showed a balance in hand of £1,046. The difference arose as follows:

1. Cheques drawn by the company in June in favour of C Limited for £727,

D Limited for £641 and E Limited for £218 had not yet been presented for payment.

2. An amount of £184 paid into the bank by the company on 30 June was not credited by the bank until 1 July.

3. The pass book showed an entry on 30 June of £94 for bank charges which had not been entered in the cash book.

(Chartered Association of Certified Accountants)

10.3S   On 30 December 19X1 the bank column of A. Phillips' cash book showed a debit balance of £461. On examination of the cash book and bank statement you find that:

1. Cheques amounting to £630 which were issued to creditors and entered in the cash book before 30 December 19X1 were not presented for payment until after that date.

2. Cheques amounting to £250 had been recorded in the cash book as having been paid into the bank on 30 December 19X1, but were entered in the bank statement on 1 January 19X2.

3. A cheque for £73 had been dishonoured prior to 30 December 19X1, but no record of this fact appeared in the cash book.

4. A dividend of £38 paid direct to the bank had not been recorded in the cash book.

5. Bank interest and charges amounting to £42 had been charged in the bank statement but not entered in the cash book.

6. No entry had been made in the cash book for a trade subscription of £10 paid by banker's order in November 19X1.

7. A cheque for £27 drawn by A. Phillpots had been charged to A. Phillips' bank account in error in December 19X1.

You are required:

(a) to make appropriate adjustments in the cash book bringing down the correct balance, and

(b) to prepare a statement reconciling the adjusted balance in the cash book with the balance shown in the bank statement.

(Institute of Chartered Accountants in England and Wales)

10.4S   From the information of bank transactions given below you are required to prepare a company's bank reconciliation statement at 31 December 19X5.

Company's Cash Book

19X5 December		£	19X5 December		£
2	Balance brought forward from previous page	985	2	D Limited	123
4	G & Company	3,041	2	M Corporation Limited	402
4	P Limited	862	5	Wages	5,371
12	U & Sons	1,749	5	Petty cash	89
12	P & Q	2,680	5	Q & Sons	326
12	N Associates	3,124	8	T Limited	48
15	A Limited	678	9	J & Sons	1,060
16	K & Company	2,413	12	Wages	5,288
16	X Limited	29	12	Petty cash	73
22	J & Sons	1,840	13	Y Limited	145
24	S Limited	1,026	16	G & Company	36
24	XYZ Limited	3,003	19	Wages	5,197
			19	Petty cash	81

	£			£
24 R Electrical Limited	1,156	22	U & Sons	247
30 Z Limited	2,331	22	S Limited	762
31 C & Sons	704	22	B & Company	97
31 V Limited	85	22	W & Sons	431
31 F Sons & Company Ltd	1,598	23	O Limited	158
31 Balance carried forward	347	24	Wages	5,316
		24	Petty cash	78
		29	H Limited	504
		29	N Associates	65
		30	M Corporation Limited	120
		30	P & Q	234
		31	D Limited	1,145
		31	L Limited	93
		31	E Associates	162
	27,651			27,651

Statement of Company's Account from the Bank's Books

			Payments £	Receipts £		Balance £
Dec.	1					1,011
	4	Sundry credit		3,903		
	4	465267	26			
	4	465272	402			4,486
	5	465274	89			
	5	465271	123			
	5	465273	5,371		O/D	1,097
	10	465276	48		O/D	1,145
	12	465279	73			
	12	Sundry credit		7,553		
	12	465278	5,288			1,047
	15	Sundry credit		678		1,725
	16	Sundry credit		2,442		4,167
	17	465275	326			3,841
	19	465282	5,197			
	19	465281	36			
	19	465283	81		O/D	1,473
	22	Sundry credit		1,840		367
	23	465280	145			222
	24	Sundry credit		5,185		
	24	465285	762			
	24	465290	78			
	24	465289	5,316		O/D	749
	30	465286	97		O/D	846
	30	465288	158			
	30	Sundry credit		2,331		1,327
	31	Charges	531			
	31	Sundry credit		2,387		
	31	Dividends on investment		1,608		
	31	465291	504			
	31	465293	120			4,167

(Chartered Institute of Management Accountants)

10.5S The cash book of a business shows a favourable bank balance of £3,856 at 30 June 19X7. After comparing the entries in the cash book with the entries on the related bank statement you find that:

(i) Cheques amounting to £218 entered in the cash book have not yet been presented for payment to the bank.

(ii) An amount of £50 entered on the debit side of the cash book has not been banked.

(iii) An amount of £95 has been credited by the bank to the account in error.

(iv) The bank has credited and then debited the bank statement with an amount of £48, being A. Jones' cheque which it forwarded on 1 July 19X7 marked 'insufficient funds – return to drawer'.

(v) Interest of £10 has been charged by the bank, but not yet entered in the cash book.

(vi) A cheque from a customer entered in the cash book as £88 had been correctly entered by the bank as £188.

Required:

(a) (i) Show the additional entries to be made in the cash book and bring down the corrected balance.

(ii) Prepare a bank reconciliation statement.

(b) Explain the reasons for preparing a bank reconciliation statement.

(Chartered Association of Certified Accountants)

10.6 The summary of the bank column in the cash book of Smith and Jones for the year ending 31 March 19X1 is as follows:

	£	
Opening balance	1,954	In hand
Receipts	361,537	
	363,491	
Payments	343,287	
Closing balance	20,204	In hand

On examination of the cash book and bank statement you find that:

(i) Cheques paid by Smith and Jones totalling £4,135 have not been presented at the bank and a lodgement of £3,230 on 30 March 19X1 has not been recorded by the bank on the bank statement.

(ii) Standing orders entered in the bank statement in respect of hire purchase payments on a machine have been omitted from the cash book – 12 months at £150 per month.

(iii) A cheque drawn for £119 has been entered in the cash book as £191.

(iv) Bank charges of £524 have not been entered in the cash book.

(v) A cheque for £832 has been charged to the company's bank account in error by the bank.

(vi) The bank statement shows a balance as at 31 March 19X1 of £18,025 in the company's favour.

You are required:

(a) to show the necessary adjustments in the cash book of Smith and Jones, and

(b) to prepare a bank reconciliation statement as on 31 March 19X1.

10.7   When Transit Co. Ltd received its bank statement for the period ended 30 June 19X7, this did not agree with the balance shown in the cash book of £2,972 in the company's favour. An examination of the cash book and bank statement disclosed the following:

(1)   A deposit of £492 paid in on 29 June 19X7 had not been credited by the bank until 1 July 19X7.

(2)   Bank charges amounting to £17 had not been entered in the cash book.

(3)   A debit of £42 appeared on the bank statement for an unpaid cheque, which had been returned marked 'out of date'. The cheque had been re-dated by the customer of Transit Co. Ltd and paid into the bank again on 3 July 19X7.

(4)   A standing order for payment of an annual subscription amounting to £10 had not been entered in the cash book.

(5)   On 25 June, the managing director had given the cashier a cheque for £100 to pay into his personal account at the bank. The cashier had paid it into the company's account by mistake.

(6)   On 27 June, two customers of Transit Co. Ltd had paid direct to the company's bank account £499 and £157 respectively in payment for goods supplied. The advices were not received by the company until 1 July and were entered in the cash book under that date.

(7)   On 30 March 19X7 the company had entered into a hire purchase agreement to pay by banker's order a sum of £26 on the tenth day of each month, commencing April. No entries had been made in the cash book.

(8)   £364 paid into the bank had been entered twice in the cash book.

(9)   Cheques issued amounting to £4,672 had not been presented to the bank for payment until after 30 June 19X7.

(10)   A customer of the company, who received a cash discount of $2\frac{1}{2}\%$ on his account of £200, paid the company a cheque on 10 June. The cashier, in error, entered the gross amount in the bank column of the cash book.

After making the adjustments required by the foregoing, the bank statement reconciled with the balance in the cash book.

You are required:

(a)   to show the necessary adjustments in the cash book of Transit Co. Ltd, bringing down the correct balance on 30 June 19X7, and

(b)   to prepare a bank reconciliation statement as on that date.

(Institute of Chartered Accountants in England and Wales)

10.8   According to the cash book of Rex Ltd, the company has an overdrawn balance at the bank of £380 on 30 June 19X5, but this is *not* borne out by the bank statement of the same date. An investigation into the difference yields the following information.

(i)   A standing order for a charitable subscription of £40 had been paid by the bank on 29 June but no entry had been made in the cash book.

(ii)   A cheque paid for advertising on 10 June for £179 had been entered in the cash book as £197.

(iii)   Cheques for £1,037 sent to creditors on 30 June were not paid by the bank until 6 July.

(iv)   Cheques received from customers amounting to £1,680 were paid into the bank on 30 June but were not credited by the bank until 1 July.

(v) On 20 June a cheque for £114 was received from a customer in settlement of an invoice for £120. An entry of £120 had been made in the cash book.

Required:

(a) Prepare a statement reconciling the cash book balance with the bank statement.

(b) Explain how a company may have reduced its bank balance during an accounting period but still have earned a profit for that same period.

(Chartered Association of Certified Accountants)

10.9 On 15 May 19X8, Mr Lakes received his monthly bank statement for the month ended 30 April 19X8. The bank statement contained the following details.

Mr Lakes
Statement of Account with Baroyds Limited
(*Balance indicates account is overdrawn)

Date	Particulars	Payments £	Receipts £	Balance £
1 April	Balance			1,053.29
2 April	236127	210.70		842.59
3 April	Bank Giro Credit		192.35	1,034.94
6 April	236126	15.21		1,019.73
6 April	Charges	12.80		1,006.93
9 April	236129	43.82		963.11
10 April	427519	19.47		943.64
12 April	236128	111.70		831.94
17 April	Standing Order	32.52		799.42
20 April	Sundry Credit		249.50	1,048.92
23 April	236130	77.87		971.05
23 April	236132	59.09		911.96
25 April	Bank Giro Credit		21.47	933.43
27 April	Sundry Credit		304.20	1,237.63
30 April	236133	71.18		1,166.45

For the corresponding period Mr Lakes' own records contained the following bank account:

Date	Detail	£	Date	Detail	Cheque No.	£
1 April	Balance	827.38	5 April	Puchases	128	111.70
2 April	Sales	192.35	10 April	Electricity	129	43.82
18 April	Sales	249.50	16 April	Purchases	130	87.77
24 April	Sales	304.20	18 April	Rent	131	30.00
30 April	Sales	192.80	20 April	Purchases	132	59.09
			25 April	Purchases	133	71.18
			30 April	Wages	134	52.27
			30 April	Balance		1,310.40
		1,766.23				1,766.23

Required:

(a) Prepare a statement reconciling the balance at 30 April as given by the bank statement to the balance at 30 April as stated in the bank account.

(b) Explain briefly which items in your bank reconciliation statement would require further investigation.

(Chartered Association of Certified Accountants)

10.10 You are given the following information extracted from the records of B. Webb.

Bank Account

Dr.	£		Cheque No.	Cr. £
1 Dec. Total b/f	16,491	1 Dec. Alexander	782	857
2 Dec. Able Ltd	962	6 Dec. Burgess	783	221
2 Dec. Baker Ltd	1,103	14 Dec. Barry	784	511
10 Dec. Charlie Ltd	2,312	17 Dec. Cook	785	97
14 Dec. Delta & Co	419	24 Dec. Hay	786	343
21 Dec. Echo Ltd	327	29 Dec. Rent	787	260
23 Dec. Cash sales to bank	529	31 Dec. Balance c/d		19,973
30 Dec. George	119			
	22,262			22,262

Marrods Bank Ltd
Bank Statement – B. Webb

Detail	Payments £	Receipts £	Date	Balance £
Balance forward			1 Dec.	17,478
836780	426		2 Dec.	17,052
Remittance		176	2 Dec.	17,228
836782	857		5 Dec.	16,371
Charges	47		5 Dec.	16,324
836781	737		6 Dec.	15,587
Counter credit		2,065	6 Dec.	17,652
Standing order	137		10 Dec.	17,515
836783	212		11 Dec.	17,303
Remittance		2,312	13 Dec.	19,615
836784	511		17 Dec.	19,104
Counter credit		419	17 Dec.	19,523
Remittance		327	23 Dec.	19,850
Counter credit		528	24 Dec.	20,378
836786	343		28 Dec.	20,035
310923	297		30 Dec.	19,738

Required:
(a) From the above data prepare a bank reconciliation as at 31 December.
(b) List the reasons for preparing such a statement.
(c) Comment briefly upon any aspects of your reconciliation which might require further investigation.

(Chartered Association of Certified Accountants)

11 Partnership

Aims of the chapter:

To outline the accounting requirements of a business partnership

The trading and profit and loss accounts and balance sheets previously illustrated were related to the simplest model of the firm, the sole trader.

The next logical development in the firm is the partnership. The Partnership Act 1890 and the Limited Partnership Act 1907 set out the law, and the 1890 Act defines partnership as 'the relation which subsists between persons carrying on a business in common with a view of profit'.

The maximum number of partners in a firm is twenty, except that there is no maximum limit for professional firms such as accountants and solicitors who have received the approval of the Board of Trade for this purpose. A firm with more than twenty members would normally be registered as a limited company (dealt with later).

Most partnerships are formed by formal agreement. In the absence of an agreement the Partnership Act 1890 provides, amongst other things, that all profits and losses are to be shared equally between the partners, no interest is allowed on capital, no remuneration will be paid to a partner, and any advance or loan made by a partner in excess of his agreed share of capital will receive interest at 5% per annum.

An agreement is most important, therefore, if it is intended that partners should be rewarded according to their differing contributions made to the firm in the form of capital, expertise, experience or effort. Resulting from this an agreement would probably contain provisions regarding the following to ensure, so far as possible, that there is an equitable distribution of profits or losses:

1. The amount of capital to be provided and maintained by each partner.
2. The rate of interest (if any) to be paid on capital.
3. The extent to which drawings are allowed and the rate of interest (if any) to be charged on drawings.
4. The remuneration (if any) to be paid to partners for their services.
5. The proportions in which profits and losses are to be divided after taking account of any adjustments due to items 2–4.
6. The interest to be paid on any advance or loan made to the firm by a partner over and above his agreed capital.

Payments under items 2–5 are regarded as a distribution or *appropriation* of profit. This means that the profit and loss account of a partnership would be precisely the same as it would be if the business were carried on by a sole trader, except that interest on an advance or loan made by a partner above his agreed capital (item 6) would appear as an expense. Note in particular that remuneration or salaries paid to partners are not an expense. They are a form of drawing taken in anticipation of profit.

The appropriation or distribution of profits or losses under items 2–5 are shown in a new section, following the trading and profit and loss account, of the final accounts called a *profit and loss appropriation account*, as illustrated below and also later. Item 6, interest on a loan from a partner, is included in the profit and loss account.

Trading and Profit and Loss Account

	£	£
Sales		X
Cost of sales		X
Gross profit		X
Expenses	X	
Interest on loan from partner(s)	X	X
Net profit		X

Appropriation of Profit
*(This section must appear after 'net profit', though it might not have a
separate heading)*

Salary		
A	X	
B	X	X
Interest on capital		
A	X	
B	X	X
Interest on current account		
A	X	
B	X	X
		X
Share of remaining profits		
A	X	
B	X	X
		X

Decisions regarding the division of profits can be quite complex in practice due to the need for an equitable relationship between partners. If all partners provide equally in all respects, an equal division of profits might adequately represent each interest. But differing amounts of capital, all other contributions to the firm being equal, would usually be compensated for by allowing interest on capitals at an agreed rate. In this way each partner would be given a return on his capital before division of the remaining profit.

Differences in partners' contributions in the form of expertise, experience or effort could be taken into account by salaries and/or differential division of profits.

The problems inherent in determining a just and equitable division of profits are not usually a concern of examination students. A question will normally indicate whether salaries are to be paid, whether interest is to be allowed on capital, whether interest is to be charged on drawings, and how the remaining profit should be divided. The student's problems are usually arithmetical and presentational.

A firm of partners will often decide that each partner should, as previously mentioned, provide and maintain a fixed amount of capital. Under these circumstances it is preferable that only this agreed capital should be credited to a separate *capital account* for each partner. All other transactions involving partners such as share of profits, interest, salary, drawings, should be dealt with in a *current account* rather than through the capital accounts. It is simple in this way to keep a constant check on the current accounts and, providing the current account is not overdrawn, the agreed capital at least must remain with the firm. Of course profits (or losses) accrue over the whole of the year, and not just when the final accounts are prepared. It follows that an overdrawn current account is not necessarily an indication that a partner is not maintaining his agreed capital. It is therefore up to the partners to agree on the extent to which drawings are allowed, and whether the drawings may exceed the current account balance at the beginning of the year.

EXAMPLE 11.1

Snow, Hail and Slush are partners preparing accounts annually to 31 December.

Snow is entitled to a salary of £4,000 per annum for special services he is providing to the firm. It is agreed that any salary taken before the year end will be regarded as a drawing.

Interest is allowed on capital at the rate of 10% per annum. Interest is also allowed or charged on current accounts and charged on drawings at the same rate of 10% per annum.

The remaining profits are divided: Snow one-half, Hail one-quarter, Slush one-quarter.

The partners' capital account balances at 1 January 19X1 were: Snow £20,000, Hail £12,000, Slush £8,000.

Their current account balances, all in credit, at 1 January 19X1 were: Snow £4,000, Hail £2,000, Slush £2,000.

During 19X1 the partners made drawings at the end of each of the first three quarters on account of anticipated earnings for the year: Snow £3,000, Hail £2,000, Slush £1,500. Snow did not make a separate drawing for his salary.

Profits for 19X1 prior to distribution amounted to £27,133.

Prepare the profit and loss appropriation account and the partners' current accounts for the firm for the year ending 31 December 19X1.

Solution:

	£	£
Net profit		27,133
Appropriation of profit		
Salary – Snow		4,000
Interest allowed on capital		
Snow	2,000	
Hail	1,200	
Slush	800	4,000
Interest allowed on current accounts		
Snow	400	
Hail	200	
Slush	200	800
		8,800
less Interest charged on drawings		
Snow	450	
Hail	300	
Slush	225	975
		7,825
Share of remaining profits		
Snow ½	9,654	
Hail ¼	4,827	
Slush ¼	4,827	19,308
		27,133

The current accounts of the partners are shown below in columnar presentation. This columnar presentation is often required and should always be used when preparing current accounts.

Current Accounts for the year ending 31 December 19X1

	Snow £	Hail £	Slush £		Snow £	Hail £	Slush £
Drawings:				Balance b/d	4,000	2,000	2,000
1st quarter	3,000	2,000	1,500	P and L appro-			
2nd quarter	3,000	2,000	1,500	priation:			
3rd quarter	3,000	2,000	1,500	Salary	4,000		
P and L appro-				Interest on			
priation:				capital	2,000	1,200	800
Interest on				Interest on			
drawings	450	300	225	current a/cs	400	200	200
Balance c/d	10,604	1,927	3,102	Profits	9,654	4,827	4,827
	20,054	8,227	7,827		20,054	8,227	7,827
				Balance b/d	10,604	1,927	3,102

The capital account and current account balances would appear in the balance sheet of the firm as follows:

Balance Sheet (extract) of Snow, Hail and Slush as at 31 December 19X1

Financed by

	Snow	Hail	Slush	
	£	£	£	£
Capital	20,000	12,000	8,000	40,000
Current accounts	10,604	1,927	3,102	15,633
				55,633

Alternatively, the calculations on the current accounts can be shown in the balance sheet. This is a perfectly satisfactory presentation unless the current accounts are specifically requested. In these circumstances the balance sheet would read as follows:

Financed by

	Snow	Hail	Slush	
	£	£	£	£
Capital	20,000	12,000	8,000	40,000
Current accounts				
Brought forward	4,000	2,000	2,000	
add Salary	4,000			
Interest on capital	2,000	1,200	800	
Interest on current	400	200	200	
Profit	9,654	4,827	4,827	
	20,054	8,227	7,827	
less Interest on drawings	450	300	225	
	19,604	7,927	7,602	
less Drawings	9,000	6,000	4,500	
	10,604	1,927	3,102	15,633
				55,633

The Limited Partnership Act 1907 mentioned earlier deals with a relatively unusual type of partnership having one or more *general partners* and one or more *limited partners*. These firms have to be registered, and a limited partner's liability for losses is limited to the extent of the capital he has contributed. This contrasts with an unlimited partner, or a partner in a normal partnership, or a sole trader, where the owner(s) can be required to meet deficiencies in capital from their private resources outside the business entity. A limited partner cannot take part in the management of a firm.

Questions

11.1S R. Hayton and D. Webster are in partnership trading as Hayton and Co.
The balances on the partners' accounts at 1 January 19X6 were:

	All credit balances	
	Capital accounts	Current accounts
	£	£
R. Hayton	12,000	1,500
D. Webster	6,000	200

The drawings for the year ended 31 December 19X6 were Hayton £6,000
and Webster £5,000. The net trading profit for the year amounted to
£18,000 and, after charging interest on capital account balances at 5% per
annum, the partners share profits equally. No interest is chargeable on drawings.

You are required to show the profit and loss appropriation account and
the partners' current accounts for the year ended 31 December 19X6.

11.2S Tilson and Hewitt are partners in a retail business sharing profits and losses
equally. Interest on capital is allowed at 5% per annum. The following
balances were extracted from their books at 31 March 19X7.

	£	£
Capital accounts at 1 April 19X6		
Tilson		6,000
Hewitt		3,000
Current accounts at 1 April 19X6		
Tilson		3,000
Hewitt		4,500
Drawings during the year		
Tilson	600	
Hewitt	900	
Partners' salaries		
Tilson	7,500	
Hewitt	10,500	
Shop fittings at cost	15,000	
Provision for depreciation on shop fittings		5,250
Motor vans at cost	11,250	
Provision for depreciation on motor vans		3,750
Stock at 1 April 19X6	4,950	
Debtors and creditors	1,650	1,320
Cash at bank and in hand	1,920	
Purchases and sales	36,750	78,000
Wages	3,300	
Rent and rates	9,300	
Heating and lighting	1,200	
	104,820	104,820

The following matters are to be taken into account:

1. Stock at 31 March 19X7 was £4,050.
2. Rent of £750 has been paid in advance.
3. Depreciate shop fittings at 10% and motor vans at 20% both on cost.

You are required to prepare a trading and profit and loss account for the
year ended 31 March 19X7 and a balance sheet at that date.

11.3S   Hawes and Peters are partners, sharing profits and losses in the ratio 3 : 2. The following is the trial balance in the partnership books at 31 December 19X5.

	£	£
Capital account at 1 January 19X5		
Hawes		16,400
Peters		13,200
Drawings		
Hawes	3,600	
Peters	2,400	
Provision for doubtful debts		480
Purchases	101,640	
Sales		131,860
Vans at cost	11,600	
Fittings at cost	2,400	
Provision for depreciation		
Vans		5,920
Fittings		1,140
Stock at 1 January 19X5	17,360	
Petty cash	40	
Office expenses	6,400	
Vehicle expenses	3,960	
Motor car at cost (1 January 19X5)	1,600	
Debtors and creditors	12,200	4,200
Bank		540
Wages	7,360	
Insurance	620	
Discounts allowed	2,560	
	173,740	173,740

The following additional information is available:
(i)   Stock at 31 December 19X5 was valued at £26,380.
(ii)   Depreciation is to be provided at 10% per annum on the written down value of the fittings and at 20% per annum on the written down value of the vans and car. Hawes is to bear personally £400 of the vehicle expenses and one-half of the depreciation charge on the car.
(iii)   No rent has been paid on the business premises during the year because of a dispute with the landlord. The rental agreement provides for a rent of £928 per year.
(iv)   The partners are entitled to interest on capital at 10% per annum.
(v)   Bad debts of £200 are to be written off, and the provision for doubtful debts to be adjusted to 2½% of the remaining debtors.
(vi)   Insurance, £70, has been paid in advance at 31 December 19X5.
(vii)   Wages, £370, were owing at 31 December 19X5.
(viii) An item of £70 for bank charges appears in the bank statement but has not yet been entered into the partnership bank account.

Required:
Prepare the trading, profit and loss account for the year ended 31 December 19X5 and a balance sheet as at that date. (Ignore taxation.)

(Chartered Association of Certified Accountants)

11.4S Rowe and Martin, partners in a manufacturing business, have prepared from the books of account the following draft balance sheet as on 31 December 19X9:

	Rowe	Martin			Cost	Depre-ciation	
	£	£	£		£	£	£
Capital 1 Jan. 19X9	20,100	10,000		Freehold buildings	12,000	–	12,000
Profit for the year	4,770	4,770		Plant and machinery	15,000	7,000	8,000
	24,870	14,770		Motor vehicles	8,000	2,700	5,300
less Drawings	2,000	3,800		Stocks			5,000
	22,870	10,970	33,840	Debtors			14,000
				Cash in hand			40
Creditors			7,800				
Bank overdraft			2,700				
			44,340				44,340

During the course of your examination of the books you ascertain that adjustments are required for the following items:

(1) Freehold buildings are shown at cost less £3,000 being the proceeds of the sale during the year of premises costing £3,500.

(2) Plant and machinery having a net book value of £215 had been scrapped during the year. The original cost was £615.

(3) Motor vehicle licences for twelve month period costing £100 had been written off, but did not expire until 30 June 19X0.

(4) Debts to the value of £521 were considered to be bad, and a further £270 doubtful requiring 100% provision. Provision had previously been made for £500 doubtful debts.

(5) Stocks included at a value of £1,870 had a net realisable value of only £1,300, and scrap material having a value of £330 had been omitted from the stock valuation.

(6) The cashier had misappropriated £35.

(7) The cash book included payments amounting to £3,462, the cheques having been made out but not mailed to suppliers until 19X0.

(8) Interest is to be allowed on partners' opening capital account balances less drawings during the year at 9%.

You are required to prepare:

(a) a summary of adjustment to the profit and loss account for the year and revised division of profit between the partners, and

(b) a revised balance sheet as on 31 December 19X9.

(Institute of Chartered Accountants in England and Wales)

11.5 Exe, Wye and Zed are in partnership sharing profits and losses: Exe two-fifths, Wye two-fifths and Zed one-fifth. Interest is credited on partners' capital accounts and charged on partners' drawings at 10% per annum. Zed is paid a salary of £1,000 per annum.

During the year ended 31 December 19X0, the net profit of the firm was £16,640 after charging Zed's salary which had been debited to Wages and Salaries Account. The partners' monthly drawings all drawn on the last day of each month were:

Exe	£400
Wye	£350
Zed	£250

The balances on the partners' accounts at 1 January 19X0 were:

All credit balances

	Capital accounts £	Current accounts £
Exe	10,000	2,660
Wye	10,000	1,820
Zed	5,000	940

You are required:

(a) to prepare the profit and loss appropriation account of Exe, Wye and Zed for the year ended 31 December 19X0;

(b) to prepare the partners' capital and current accounts, in columnar form, for the year ended 31 December 19X0;

(c) to state, briefly, the provisions of the Partnership Act, 1890, with regard to interest on partners' capital and drawings, and the payments of partnership salaries where there is no Partnership Deed.

11.6   Sagar and Banyard were in partnership sharing profits and losses $\frac{2}{3}$ and $\frac{1}{3}$ respectively. The trial balance extracted from their books for the year ended 31 December 19X8 was as follows:

	£	£
Freehold shop at cost	12,000	
Fixtures and fittings at cost	2,000	
Provision for depreciation on fixtures and fittings		700
Stock at 1 January 19X8	6,000	
Debtors and creditors	4,900	3,000
Cash at bank	2,500	
Cash in hand	500	
Capital accounts		
Sagar		10,000
Banyard		4,000
Current accounts at 1 January 19X8		
Sagar		300
Banyard		100
Drawings for the year		
Sagar	2,100	
Banyard	3,150	
Purchases and sales	20,000	41,950
Returns inwards and outwards	600	400
Carriage inward	200	
Wages	4,500	
Lighting and heating	800	
Rates	1,200	
	60,450	60,450

The following information is relevant:
1. Stock at 31 December 19X8, £3,050.
2. Interest on capital is charged at 5% per annum.
3. Banyard is entitled to a salary of £4,000.
4. Rates of £200 are prepaid.
5. Depreciation on fixtures and fittings is £100.

You are required to prepare the trading and profit and loss account for the year ended 31 December 19X8 and a balance sheet as at that date.

11.7 Webb and Guy are partners sharing profits and losses in the ratio 3:1 and the partnership agreement provides for Guy to receive a salary of £2,000 per annum, and for interest on capital at 5% per annum. The partners' current accounts for the year ended 31 December 19X8 were as follows:

	Webb £	Guy £		Webb £	Guy £
Drawings	4,280	3,950	Balance at 1		
Goods		100	January 19X8	900	100
Balance at 31			Salary		2,000
December			Interest on		
19X8	1,600		capital	480	300
			Share of profit	4,500	1,500
			Balance at 31		
			December 19X8		150
	5,880	4,050		5,880	4,050

The balance sheet as at 31 December 19X8 was:

	£	£		£	£
Capital accounts			Premises at cost		10,400
Webb	8,000		Equipment at cost	4,000	
Guy	5,000	13,000	less Depreciation	2,400	1,600
					12,000
Current accounts			Stock	2,800	
Webb	1,600		Debtors	1,100	
Guy	(150)	1,450	Cash	200	4,100
Creditors and					
accruals		1,650			
		16,100			16,100

Investigation of the accounts revealed the following information:
(i)   The goods taken by Guy had been charged at selling price rather than at cost (£65).
(ii) The interest on capital had been provided at 6% per annum.
(iii) The closing stock included some items which had been valued at original cost (£550), but which had deteriorated badly while in store and were considered to have a market value of £200.
(iv) The equipment had been depreciated in 19X8 at 10% on original cost, but should have been depreciated at 15% per year of the written down value at 1 January 19X8.
(v)   The partnership agreement had been amended on 1 July 19X8 to

increase Guy's annual salary to £2,700 with effect from 1 July, but this had not been reflected in the accounts.

(vi) No provision had been made for doubtful debts, but a provision of 3% of debtors is now considered desirable.

(vii) £82 owing for electricity had not been accrued.

Required:
Prepare
(a) a statement showing the revised net trading profit for the year ended 31 December 19X8;
(b) the amended current accounts of the partners; and
(c) a revised balance sheet as at 31 December 19X8.

(Chartered Association of Certified Accountants)

11.8   The balance sheet of Jack and Fred as at 31 March 19X6 was as follows:

	£	£		£	£
Capital accounts			Land and build-		
Jack	5,000		ings (cost)	8,000	
Fred	4,000	9,000	Depreciation	1,560	6,440
Current accounts			Machinery (cost)	9,000	
Jack	980		Depreciation	4,300	4,700
Fred	720	1,700			
			Stock		1,180
Loan (made by Jack)		2,000	Debtors		1,350
Trade creditors		830	Prepaid expenses		140
Accrued expenses		90	Cash in hand		80
Bank overdraft		270			
		13,890			13,890

The balance on the current accounts had been reached as shown below:

	Jack	Fred		Jack	Fred
	£	£		£	£
Drawings	3,160	3,960	Opening balance	1,140	780
Closing balance	980	720	Interest on		
			capital	500	400
			Share of profits	2,500	2,000
			Salary	–	1,500
	4,140	4,680		4,140	4,680

An accountant carrying out an audit of the partnership records discovered the following facts:

(i)   The closing stock included items which had cost £220 at that value, but, in fact, the items were damaged and could only be sold for £80.

(ii)   Fred had introduced £2,000 additional capital on 1 October 19X5, but the interest on that capital had been calculated for a full year.

(iii) Bank charges of £70 had not been included in the partnership records.

(iv)   The depreciation on machinery for the year (£450) had been omitted in error.

(v)   A trade creditor for £370 had been omitted from both creditors and purchases, although the items concerned had been included in the closing stock.

(vi)   Rates of £600 had been charged in the profit and loss account but £80 of the sum related to the period after 1 April.

(vii) Jack was entitled to interest on his loan of $7\frac{1}{2}\%$ per annum but this had been omitted from the accounts.

(viii) Fred's salary credited at £1,500 should have been £1,400.

Required:

(a) Prepare a statement to show the net profit (before appropriation) for the year, taking into account the data above.

(b) Prepare the amended current accounts of the partners.

(c) Redraft the balance sheet as at 31 March 19X6.

(d) Explain clearly in the context of a partnership the reason underlying the different treatment of (I) interest on a bank loan as contrasted with interest on a loan by a partner and (II) a salary to an employee as contrasted with a salary to a partner.

(Chartered Association of Certified Accountants)

12 Goodwill, with particular reference to partnership; revaluation of assets

Aims of the chapter:

> To look at the role of goodwill in a partnership
> To consider changes in a partnership

Goodwill

Several attempts have been made in the courts to define goodwill. Possibly the most simplistic definition was that it is 'nothing more than the probability that the old customers will resort to the old place'.

Goodwill is most likely to arise as an accounting entry on the acquisition of a business. If one firm acquires another firm, and the purchase price exceeds the value of the assets acquired, the excess is regarded as being for the asset of *goodwill*.

This situation will arise frequently when a new owner acquires a firm as a going concern. The new owner may be influenced into paying more than just the asset value for a firm because of its profit record coupled with the firm's general overall reputation, or the strength of its products, or its monopoly position, or the situation of its premises.

Goodwill normally remains unrecorded until evidenced by such a transaction, although it must implicitly be in existence in any business which is operating successfully. But as goodwill is intangible and constantly changing as the reputation of the firm changes, there is little point in trying to determine or record a value.

When a potential new owner is considering the acquisition of a firm, he will presumably make some calculations as to the amount, if any, he is prepared to pay for goodwill. There are several theoretical ways in which the value of goodwill can be calculated, some of which are relatively crude and some of which are quite sophisticated. However, the potential new owner will require information to proceed with his calculations. The extent to which this information will be provided voluntarily depends upon whether the existing owner is a willing or unwilling seller. And even with a willing seller, the information is likely to be presented in the manner most favourable to the seller.

On the acquisition of any business, therefore, it is highly likely that normal market rules will apply, i.e. the purchaser will try to acquire the business as cheaply as possible, and the seller will try to obtain the highest possible price. The value of goodwill results from a willing buyer meeting a willing seller, and a price being agreed.

The above introductory remarks apply to all businesses, including partnerships, when the business is either purchased or sold in total as a business entity and a going concern.

Additional complications arise, however, with a partnership when:

(1) a partner retires or dies
(2) a new partner is admitted
(3) there is a change in the profit sharing ratio.

In any of the above circumstances the normal market rules cannot apply in determining the value of goodwill, but it is nevertheless necessary that a value should be placed on goodwill for reasons that will soon become apparent.

Valuation of goodwill in partnership

The valuation of goodwill is often a rule of thumb method based on the custom of the trade or profession. The method adopted must be agreed by the partners and it may be incorporated in the partnership agreement.

Possible agreed bases are:

(a) Average profits × agreed number of years (possibly three to five years).
(b) Super profits × agreed number of years. Super profits are profits in excess of an agreed return on capital employed in the business. The capital employed in a business might amount to, say, £200,000 (calculated by an agreed method) and the agreed rate of return (comparable to a normal commercial yield) be 10%. Profits in excess of £20,000 per annum would be regarded as super profits.
(c) Gross annual fees × agreed number of years. This is sometimes adopted by professional firms.
(d) Present value of an annuity equivalent to average profits for an agreed number of years at an agreed rate of interest; e.g. average profits £20,000, agreed number of years = 5, agreed rate of interest = 10%. Thus present value of annuity of £20,000 over five years = £75,816.

Goodwill in partnership accounts

1 *A partner retires or dies*

When a partner retires he would expect his capital to be returned (i.e. the balance on both his capital and current accounts) plus a share of the goodwill that he has helped to build up. If a partner dies, his executors would expect to receive a similar amount. The goodwill of the firm has to be valued in an agreed manner so that the departing partner can receive his share.

EXAMPLE 12.1

A, B and C are partners sharing profits and losses in the ratio 3:2:2. B retires and the goodwill is valued at £28,000. The goodwill would be divided as follows:

		Dr. £	Cr. £
Goodwill		28,000	
	Capital accounts		
	A		12,000
	B		8,000
	C		8,000

Division of agreed valuation of goodwill on retirement of B.

The capital account of B has thus been increased by £8,000 to take account of his share of goodwill. The final balance on B's capital account might be paid to him immediately, or a proportion is sometimes left with the firm as a loan at an agreed rate of interest for an agreed time so as not to impose a difficult cash problem on the firm.

Goodwill by its nature is constantly changing. The remaining partners (A and C) might decide that it should not remain in the books of account as an asset but should only be calculated as the need arises. In these circumstances the goodwill account would be closed by charging it to the remaining partners in the new profit sharing ratio. If, for example, the partners A and C decide that in future they will share profits equally, the entries are:

		Dr. £	Cr. £
Capital accounts			
A		14,000	
C		14,000	
	Goodwill		28,000

Elimination of goodwill account.

On any further change in the partnership a new value will be ascribed to goodwill and it will again be shared in profit sharing ratios.

In the above example a goodwill account has been both opened and closed. Examination questions sometimes ask that the capital accounts be adjusted for goodwill without the creation of a goodwill account. This can easily be done by tabulating the workings to net off the adjustments:

Adjustments to Capital Accounts for Goodwill

	Old ratio Cr. £	New ratio Dr. £	Net £
Capital accounts			
A	12,000	14,000	2,000 Dr.
B	8,000		8,000 Cr.
C	8,000	14,000	6,000 Dr.
	28,000	28,000	–

The entries in the accounts would now be:

	Dr. £	Cr. £
Capital accounts		
A	2,000	
C	6,000	
Capital accounts		
B		8,000

Division of agreed valuation of goodwill on retirement of B.

This is just a different way of arriving at exactly the same net result as previously.

2 *A new partner is admitted*

There are several ways of dealing with goodwill on the admission of a new partner. In practice the partnership agreement would be followed; in an examination the criteria set out in a question must be carefully adhered to.

The two most popular methods appear to be as described below.

(a) The new partner pays the old partners for the share of the goodwill which he is acquiring. No goodwill account is opened.

EXAMPLE 12.2

Partners L and M sharing profits 7:5 decide to admit a new partner S to the firm. The value of goodwill is agreed by all parties to be £30,000. The profit sharing ratio for the new partnership of L, M and S is to be 3:3:2 respectively. S is to purchase in cash his share of the goodwill from the other partners, and he is also required to introduce cash into the business amounting to £10,000 which will be credited to his capital account.

S is therefore purchasing two-eighths of the goodwill (i.e. his share of profits), and for this share pays L and M a quarter (i.e. two-eighths) of £30,000 = £7,500.

L and M divide the £7,500 in their old profit sharing ratio of 7:5, and so L receives £4,375 and M receives £3,125.

This payment of £7,500 may be made as a private transaction, completely outside the accounts of the partnership, or it may be paid into the partnership as a matter of record. If it is paid into the partnership the accounting entries for the purchase of the goodwill would be:

		Dr. £	Cr. £
Cash		7,500	
	Capital accounts		
	L		4,375
	M		3,125

Cash payment by S in purchase of share of goodwill.

The cash could then be withdrawn by L and M, in which case their capital accounts would be debited, or alternatively it might by agreement be retained in the business to improve the cash resources.

There is also the payment made by S of £10,000 as capital which would be recorded as:

		Dr. £	Cr. £
Cash		10,000	
	Capital account		
	S		10,000

Cash introduced by S as capital.

(b) By this method the new partner does not make a separate payment for goodwill. A goodwill account may be required.

EXAMPLE 12.3

X, Y and Z are in partnership sharing profits in the ratio 5:4:3. A new partner, W, is to be admitted; it is agreed that goodwill should be valued at £24,000 and a goodwill account is to be raised. W is to introduce £10,000 cash which will be credited in full to his capital account. The new partnership X, Y, Z, W will share profits in the ratio 5:4:3:3.

The goodwill is credited to the old partners in the old profit sharing ratios, i.e. 5:4:3. In this way their capital accounts are increased by their respective shares of the goodwill. The accounting entries are as follows:

		Dr. £	Cr. £
Goodwill		24,000	
	Capital accounts		
	X		10,000
	Y		8,000
	Z		6,000

Creation of goodwill account on introduction of new partner W.

	£	£
Cash	10,000	
Capital account		
W		10,000

Introduction of capital by W.

As a further development of the above, the new partnership of X, Y, Z, W may decide that the goodwill account should not remain in the firm's books. This is dealt with very simply by debiting each partner's capital account with a share of goodwill apportioned in the new profit sharing ratio 5:4:3:3, i.e.

	Dr. £	Cr. £
Capital accounts		
X	8,000	
Y	6,400	
Z	4,800	
W	4,800	
Goodwill		24,000

Elimination of goodwill account.

Of course all these adjustments could be made, without first opening and then closing a goodwill account, by using a simple tabulation as before:

Adjustments to Capital Accounts for Goodwill

	Old ratio Cr. £	New ratio Dr. £	Net £
Capital accounts			
X	10,000	8,000	2,000 Cr.
Y	8,000	6,400	1,600 Cr.
Z	6,000	4,800	1,200 Cr.
W		4,800	4,800 Dr.
	24,000	24,000	–

The book-keeping entries would now be:

	Dr. £	Cr. £
Capital account		
W	4,800	
Capital accounts		
X		2,000
Y		1,600
Z		1,200

Adjustment of capital accounts on introduction of new partner, W, to take account of goodwill.

	£	£
Cash	10,000	
Capital account		
W		10,000

Introduction of capital by W.

Examination questions sometimes ask that answers should be produced as above, without the creation of a goodwill account. How then does this differ from method (a) outlined previously? The essential difference is that in method (a) the new partner was required to pay an amount for goodwill, and a further separate amount as capital. In method (b) no separate amount is specifically identified as being required in payment for goodwill.

3 A change in profit sharing ratio

A change in the proportions in which profits are shared often occurs when there is some alteration in the relative contributions that the partners make to a business. It is usual, under these circumstances, to value goodwill, and to credit each partner with his appropriate share. In this way each partner is rewarded for the goodwill he has helped to create up to the date of the change.

EXAMPLE 12.4

E, F, G and H are sharing profits in the ratio 5:4:3:3. E finds that he cannot devote as much time as previously to the business, and it is decided that future profits will be divided 4:4:3:3. The value of goodwill at this time is agreed by the partners at £29,400.

The accounting entries for goodwill in the old profit sharing ratio are:

	Dr.	Cr.
	£	£
Goodwill	29,400	
Capital accounts		
E		9,800
F		7,840
G		5,880
H		5,880

Creation of goodwill account on a change in profit sharing ratios.

As mentioned before in this chapter, the partners may decide that they do not wish that goodwill should remain in the books of account, and the following entries can be made using the new profit sharing ratios:

	Dr.	Cr.
	£	£
Capital accounts		
E	8,400	
F	8,400	
G	6,300	
H	6,300	
Goodwill		29,400

Elimination of goodwill account.

Again, as described previously, all these adjustments could be made without first opening and then closing a goodwill account by using a simple tabulation thus:

Adjustments to Capital Accounts for Goodwill

	Old ratio	New ratio	Net
	Cr.	Dr.	
	£	£	£
Capital accounts			
E	9,800	8,400	1,400 Cr.
F	7,840	8,400	560 Dr.
G	5,880	6,300	420 Dr.
H	5,880	6,300	420 Dr.
	29,400	29,400	–

The entries would then be:

	Dr.	Cr.
	£	£
Capital accounts		
F	560	
G	420	
H	420	
Capital account		
E		1,400

Adjustment to capital accounts in respect of goodwill on change in profit sharing ratio.

It may appear strange that the above adjustments, whichever method of book-keeping is adopted, only increase E's capital by £1,400, though his share of goodwill is reckoned to be £9,800. It must be remembered that his capital relative to the other partners has also been increased as their capitals have all been reduced. Also, the goodwill still exists; it has merely been eliminated from the accounts for the time being. On the retirement of a partner, or on his death, or on the sale of the business goodwill will be re-introduced at its then current value and the partner appropriately compensated.

Revaluation of assets

So far this chapter has been devoted to demonstrating the necessity for amending partners' capital accounts to reflect the value of goodwill when a change takes place in the structure of the firm.

It is also necessary under these circumstances that other assets and liabilities should be correctly valued. As

$$Capital = Assets - Liabilities$$

an incorrect valuation will result in incorrect balances on the partners' capital accounts.

Fixed assets could be valued incorrectly due to over- or under-depreciation; premises could have appreciated substantially due to being in a particularly favourable position; stock might be over-valued; and some debts might need to be written off as bad. There is also a slight, if unlikely, chance that creditors might require amendment.

To adjust the accounts a *revaluation account* is used. Goodwill can also be conveniently adjusted through the revaluation account, particularly if it is to remain in the accounts.

The entries in the firm's books would be:

(a)　Asset account(s)	Debit	
Revaluation account		Credit
With the increase in value over the book value shown.		
(b)　Revaluation account	Debit	
Asset account(s)		Credit
With the decrease in value below the book value shown.		
(c)　Where (a) exceeds (b):		
Revaluation account	Debit	
Partners' capital accounts		Credit
With the profit on revaluation credited to the partners' capital accounts in their OLD profit sharing ratio.		
Where (b) exceeds (a):		
Partners' capital accounts	Debit	
Revaluation account		Credit
With the loss on revaluation debited to the partners' capital accounts in their OLD profit sharing ratio.		

EXAMPLE 12.5

Lawton, Toshack and Smith were in partnership, sharing profits and losses as follows: Lawton 40%, Toshack 35% and Smith 25%.

The draft balance sheet of the partnership on 30 September 19X9 was as follows:

Assets

Fixed assets	Cost	Depreciation	Net
	£	£	£
Leasehold premises	15,000	–	15,000
Plant and machinery	16,000	5,600	10,400
	31,000	5,600	25,400

Current assets		
Stock	8,400	
Debtors	5,600	
Cash at bank	6,600	
	20,600	
less Current liabilities		
Creditors	3,800	
Net current assets		16,800
		42,200

Financed by		
Capital accounts		
Lawton	18,000	
Toshack	10,000	
Smith	6,000	34,000
Current accounts		
Lawton	2,400	
Toshack	1,600	
Smith	1,200	5,200
Loan – Toshack		3,000
		42,200

Toshack retired on 30 September 19X9 and Lawton and Smith continued in partnership, sharing profits and losses as follows: Lawton 60%, Smith 40%.

It was agreed that adjustments were to be made to the balance sheet as on 30 September 19X9, in respect of the following:

1. The value of the goodwill was agreed at £18,000.
2. The leasehold premises were to be valued at £13,000.
3. The plant and machinery was to be revalued at £11,600.
4. Stock was to be written down to £7,600.

Show the adjusted balance sheet of the firm and the amount to which Toshack would be entitled on retirement.

Solution:
In journal form, the accounting entries would be:

	Dr. £	Cr. £
Asset accounts		
Goodwill	18,000	
Plant and machinery	1,200	
Revaluation account		19,200
Introduction into the books of goodwill, and revaluation of plant and machinery as agreed on the retirement of Toshack.		
Revaluation account	2,800	
Asset accounts		
Leasehold premises		2,000
Stock		800
Revaluation of leasehold premises and stock, as agreed, on the retirement of Toshack.		
Revaluation account	16,400	
Partners' capital accounts		
Lawton		6,560
Toshack		5,740
Smith		4,100
Profit on revaluation on the retirement of Toshack.		

The revaluation account and the adjusted balance sheet would be:

Revaluation account

		£		£
Leasehold premises		2,000	Goodwill	18,000
Stock		800	Plant and machinery	1,200
Capital accounts				
Lawton	6,560			
Toshack	5,740			
Smith	4,100	16,400		
		19,200		19,200

Lawton and Smith
Balance Sheet as at 30 September 19X9 (after adjustment)

Assets	Cost or valuation	Depreciation	Net
Fixed assets	£	£	£
Goodwill	18,000	–	18,000
Leasehold premises	13,000	–	13,000
Plant and machinery	16,000	4,400	11,600
	47,000	4,400	42,600

	£	£
Current assets		
Stock	7,600	
Debtors	5,600	
Cash at bank	6,600	
	19,800	
less Current liabilities		
Creditors	3,800	
Net current assets		16,000
		58,600
Financed by		
Capital accounts		
Lawton	24,560	
Smith	10,100	34,660
Current accounts		
Lawton	2,400	
Smith	1,200	3,600
Loan – Toshack		20,340
		58,600

Note: When a partner retires or dies, the balances on his capital and current accounts are normally transferred to a loan account in his name to show clearly how much is due to him from the partnership.

The capital and current accounts of the partners would be:

Capital accounts

	Lawton £	Toshack £	Smith £		Lawton £	Toshack £	Smith £
Loan account		15,740		Balance b/d	18,000	10,000	6,000
Balance c/d	24,560		10,100	Revaluation	6,560	5,740	4,100
	24,560	15,740	10,100		24,560	15,740	10,100
				Balance b/d	24,560		10,100

Current accounts

	Lawton £	Toshack £	Smith £		Lawton £	Toshack £	Smith £
Loan account		1,600		Balance b/d	2,400	1,600	1,200
Balance c/d	2,400		1,200				
	2,400	1,600	1,200		2,400	1,600	1,200
				Balance b/d	2,400		1,200

Toshack's loan account is shown below:

Loan account – Toshack

	£		£
Balance c/d	20,340	Balance b/d	3,000
		Capital account	15,740
		Current account	1,600
	20,340		20,340
		Balance b/d	20,340

Questions

12.1S Edwards and Coleman were in partnership sharing profits and losses equally. Their balance sheet at 31 December 19X6 was as follows:

Edwards and Coleman
Balance sheet as at 31 December 19X6

	£	£
Assets		
Fixed assets		21,000
Current assets	12,000	
less Current liabilities	8,000	
Net current assets		4,000
		25,000

Financed by	Edwards	Coleman	
	£	£	£
Capital accounts	7,500	7,500	15,000
Current accounts	7,500	2,500	10,000
			25,000

The partners agreed that from 1 January 19X7, they would share profits and losses: Edwards three-fifths, Coleman two-fifths. The goodwill was valued at £5,000 and all the other assets at their balance sheet value.

You are required to prepare a balance sheet as at 1 January 19X7 to record the change in profit sharing ratio. No goodwill account is to be shown in the books (i.e. the adjustments for goodwill are to be made direct to the partners' capital accounts).

12.2S On 31 March 19X6 the balance sheet of Exe and Wye, who shared profits and losses in the ratio of 2:1, was as follows:

	£	£
Assets		
Fixed assets		24,000
Current assets (excluding cash)	54,000	
Cash at bank	6,000	
	60,000	
less Current liabilities	48,000	

	£	£
Net current assets		12,000
		36,000

Financed by		
Capital accounts		
Exe	24,000	
Wye	12,000	36,000
		36,000

On 1 April 19X6 Exe and Wye agreed to admit Zed as a partner who brought in £18,000, one-half of which was for his share of goodwill and the balance as his capital. It was agreed that Exe and Wye would immediately withdraw the cash credited to their respective capital accounts for the goodwill purchased by Zed.

You are required to show:

(a) the partners' capital accounts, and
(b) the opening balance sheet of the new firm.

12.3S Doohan, Buckley and Mannion were in partnership sharing profits and losses 2:2:1 respectively. The balance sheet as at 31 December 19X3 was as follows:

	£	£
Assets		
Fixed assets		40,800
Current assets (excluding bank)	31,300	
Cash at bank	9,600	
	40,900	
less Current liabilities	26,800	
Net current assets		14,100
		54,900

Financed by	Doohan	Buckley	Mannion	
	£	£	£	£
Capital accounts	20,000	20,000	10,000	50,000
Current accounts	1,850	1,600	1,450	4,900
				54,900

Doohan retired on 31 December 19X3 and Buckley and Mannion continued in partnership sharing profits and losses 2:1 respectively. The balance on Doohan's current account was repaid on 1 January 19X4, and it was agreed that the remaining balance due to him should remain on loan to the partnership.

The value of the firm's goodwill as on 31 December 19X3 was agreed to be £15,000.

No account for goodwill was to be maintained in the partnership books, adjusting entries for transactions between the parties being made in their capital accounts.

You are required to prepare:

(a) the partners' capital accounts, and

(b) the balance sheet of Buckley and Mannion as on 1 January 19X4.

12.4S Leech, Luff and Lee were in partnership, sharing profits and losses: Leech six-tenths, Luff three-tenths and Lee one-tenth. The partnership deed provided:

(1) Interest at the rate of 6% per annum shall be allowed on fixed capital accounts. No interest shall be allowed on current accounts but 8% per annum is to be charged on any debit balance at the commencement of the year.

(2) Goodwill shall be valued at 80% of the average annual profits of the previous three or four years, whichever is the lower.

The following are particulars of partners' accounts:

	Fixed capitals as on 31 December 19X6 £	Balances on current account as on 31 December 19X6 £
Leech	18,000	5,000 *Cr.*
Luff	9,000	1,000 *Cr.*
Lee	3,000	1,200 *Cr.*

The partners agreed to take Windward into partnership as on 1 January 19X7, and on that day he introduced £3,500 in cash which included his fixed capital of £3,000. He is to receive a salary of £1,500 per annum in addition to his share of the profits. Leech personally guaranteed that the aggregate of Windward's salary and share of profit shall be not less than £3,000 per annum.

Profit sharing ratios are to be: Leech three-tenths, Luff three-tenths, Lee three-tenths, and Windward one-tenth. Agreed profits for goodwill purposes for the past four years are as follows:

	£
19X6	16,337
19X5	10,255
19X4	10,758
19X3	14,164

No account for goodwill is to be maintained in the books, adjusting entries for transactions between the partners being made in their current accounts.

The draft accounts for the year ended 31 December 19X7, before taking into account Windward's salary or interest on partners' accounts, show a profit of £17,640. Partners' drawings during the year are: Leech £6,320, Luff £4,900, Lee £4,900 and Windward (including salary) £2,193.

You are required to prepare:

(a) a statement showing the division of profit for the year ended 31 December, 19X7, and

(b) the partners' current accounts for the year ended 31 December 19X7, recording therein the entries necessary upon Windward's admission as a partner.

(Institute of Chartered Accountants in England and Wales)

12.5S Brown and Green, who make up their accounts to 30 September in each year, carried on business in partnership under the firm name of Colours.

Their partnership agreement provided:

(1) Profits and losses should be shared Brown two-thirds and Green one-third.

(2) Interest on capital accounts should be allowed at the rate of 6% per annum but no interest should be allowed or charged on current accounts.

(3) On the retirement or admission of a partner:

    (i)   If the change takes place during any accounting year, such partner's share of profits or losses for the period up to retirement or from admission is to be arrived at by apportionment on a time basis except where otherwise agreed.

    (ii)   No account for goodwill is to be maintained in the firm's books, any adjusting entries for transactions between the partners being made in their capital accounts.

    (iii)   Any balance due to an outgoing partner is to carry interest at 8% per annum from the date of his retirement to the date of payment.

Brown retired from the firm on 31 March 19X2 and, on the same day, Green took into partnership Black, an employee of the firm. It was agreed that the terms of the previous partnership agreement should apply in all respects except that, as from that date, profits or losses are to be shared Green three-fifths, Black two-fifths.

The trial balance extracted from the books of the firm as on 30 September 19X2 was as follows:

	£	£
Capital accounts – 30 September 19X1		
Brown		8,000
Green		6,000
Current accounts – 30 September 19X1		
Brown		2,400
Green		1,600
Black – Cash introduced 31 March 19X2		3,000
Plant and machinery at cost	14,000	
Plant and machinery: provision for depreciation 30 September 19X1		2,800
Motor vehicles at cost	6,200	
Motor vehicles: provision for depreciation 30 September 19X1		3,400
Purchases	62,000	
Stock 30 September 19X1	12,400	
Wages	14,600	
Salaries	10,800	
Debtors	4,600	
Sales		96,000
Trade expenses	1,600	
Creditors		6,200
Rent and rates	1,400	
Bad debts	600	
Balance at bank	1,200	
	129,400	129,400

You are given the following further information:

(1) The value of the firm's goodwill as on 31 March 19X2 was agreed to be £12,000.

(2) On 31 March 19X2 Black had paid Brown £5,000 on account of the balance due to him on retirement. No entries had been made in the books in respect of this payment. The balance due to Brown after taking into account this payment remained unpaid as on 30 September 19X2.

(3) Brown on retirement had taken over one of the firm's motor vehicles and it was agreed that he should be charged for it at its written down value at the date of his retirement. The vehicle had cost £1,400 and up to 30 September 19X1 depreciation of £625 had been provided on it.

(4) The stock as on 30 September 19X2 was valued at £14,200.

(5) Partners' drawings which are included in salaries were as follows:
Brown £1,800   Green £2,400   Black £900

(6) Salaries also included £1,200 paid to Black prior to his being admitted as a partner and which amount is to be charged against the profits of the first half-year.

(7) Professional charges of £250 included in trade expenses are specifically attributable to the second half of the year.

(8) The whole of the charge of £600 for bad debts related to the period to 31 March 19X2.

(9) A bad debts provision specifically attributable to the second half of the year of 5% of the total debtors is to be made as on 30 September 19X2.

(10) As on 30 September 19X2, rent paid in advance amounted to £400 and trade expenses accrued amounted to £180.

(11) Provision is to be made for depreciation on plant and machinery and on motor vehicles at the rates of 10% and 25% per annum respectively, calculated on cost.

You are required to prepare:

(a) the trading and profit and loss account for the year ended 30 September 19X2,

(b) Partners' capital and current accounts covering the year ended 30 September 19X2, and

(c) the balance sheet as on that date.

(Institute of Chartered Accountants in England and Wales)

12.6S   Lock, Stock and Barrel were in partnership sharing profits and losses: Lock 50% Stock 30% and Barrel 20%. The draft balance sheet of the partnership as on 30 June 19X3 was as follows:

	£	£		£	£
Capital accounts			Freehold premises		8,000
Lock	12,000		Plant and equipment		4,200
Stock	6,000		Motor vehicles		2,100
Barrel	4,000		Stock		3,600
		22,000	Debtors	5,200	
Loan – Lock		3,000	*less* Provision for		
Provision for			doubtful debts	400	
repainting of					4,800
premises		1,400	Balance at bank		8,300
Creditors		4,600			
		31,000			31,000

Lock retired on 30 June 19X3 and Stock and Barrel continued in partnership, sharing profits and losses: Stock 60% Barrel 40%.

Lock's loan was repaid on 1 July 19X3 and it was agreed that 10% of the outstanding balance due to him should be paid as soon as the amount was computed, the remaining balance remaining on loan to the partnership.

It was agreed that the following adjustments should be made to the balance sheet as on 30 June 19X3:

(1) The freehold premises to be revalued at £15,000 and the plant and equipment at £3,500.

(2) Lock to be charged £400 for one of the motor vehicles taken over by him, this vehicle having a book value of £450.

(3) The provision for doubtful debts to be increased by £200.

(4) The provision for repainting of the premises to be increased to £2,000.

(5) £400 to be written off the stock in respect of damaged and obsolete items included therein.

(6) A provision of £250 included in creditors to be written back.

The partnership agreement provided that on the retirement of a partner, goodwill was to be valued at an amount equal to the lower of the average annual profits of either the three or five years expiring on the date of retirement.

The relevant profits were:

	£
Year ended 30 June 19X9	6,420
Year ended 30 June 19X0	5,360
Year ended 30 June 19X1	8,180
Year ended 30 June 19X2	7,840
Year ended 30 June 19X3	8,150 (as shown by draft accounts)

It was agreed that, for the purposes of valuing goodwill, only the adjustments in respect of the provisions for repainting and doubtful debts, creditors and stock should be regarded as affecting the profits.

No account for goodwill was to be maintained in the books, adjusting entries for the transactions between the partners being made in the capital accounts.

You are required to prepare:

(a) the revaluation account,
(b) the partners' capital accounts,
(c) Lock's account, showing the outstanding balance due to him, and
(d) the balance sheet of Stock and Barrel as on 1 July 19X3.

(Institute of Chartered Accountants in England and Wales)

12.7   The balance sheet of Neal, Thompson, Watson and Mills is shown below as at 30 June 19X1. The partners agree that from 1 July 19X1 they will share profits and losses in the ratio of 3:3:2:2, instead of equally. The goodwill of the firm at 30 June 19X1 is to be valued at £20,000.

Neal, Thompson, Watson and Mills
Balance Sheet as at 30 June 19X1

	£	£
Assets		
Fixed assets		50,000
Current assets	46,000	
less Current liabilities	28,000	
Net current assets		18,000
		68,000
Financed by		
Capital accounts		
Neal	20,000	
Thompson	20,000	
Watson	14,000	
Mills	14,000	68,000
		68,000

You are required to prepare a balance sheet as at 1 July 19X1, to record the change in profit sharing ratios. No goodwill account is to remain in the books.

12.8   The firm of Bradshaw and Co. consisted at 30 June 19X2 of two partners, S. Bradshaw and M. Pearson, sharing profits in the ratio of 4:3 respectively. The balance sheet at that date was as follows:

	£	£
Assets		
Fixed assets		38,200
Current assets (excluding cash)	49,200	
Cash	4,200	
	53,400	
less Current liabilities	30,000	
Net current assets		23,400
		61,600
Financed by		

	S. Bradshaw	M. Pearson	
	£	£	£
Capital accounts	32,000	24,000	56,000
Current accounts	3,200	2,400	5,600
			61,600

It was agreed to admit D. Dyson into partnership on 1 July 19X2 on payment of £8,400 to the existing partners for a share of goodwill; the cash is to remain in the partnership. Dyson also introduced £16,000 capital. One-half of the balance on the current accounts of Bradshaw and Pearson was to be withdrawn in cash and the balances to be transferred to their capital accounts.

You are required to show:

(a) the capital accounts of the three partners as at 1 July 19X2, after making the entries for the above adjustments, and

(b) a balance sheet of the new firm as at that date.

12.9 Taylor and Best were in partnership sharing profits and losses: Taylor two-thirds, Best one-third. The partnership deed provided:

(1) Interest at the rate of 8% per annum is to be allowed on fixed capital accounts. No interest is to be allowed on current accounts but 10% per annum is to be charged on any debit balance at the commencement of the year.

(2) Goodwill is to be valued at 1¹/₂ times the average annual profits of the previous four or five years whichever is the lower.

The partners agreed to take Watson into partnership as on 1 January 19X0, and he introduced £5,000 into the business. It was agreed that the fixed capital of the business should be £20,000 contributed by the partners in their profit sharing ratio, any surplus or deficiency being transferred to their current accounts. Taylor was to be entitled to a prior share of the profits of £500 and the balance was to be shared: Taylor two-fifths, Best two-fifths, and Watson one-fifth. In addition it was agreed that Watson's share of the profits should be not less than £3,500 per annum.

Agreed profits for goodwill purposes of the past five years are as follows:

	£
19X5	10,420
19X6	11,760
19X7	9,400
19X8	13,820
19X9	14,600

No account for goodwill is maintained in the books, adjusting entries for transactions between the partners being made in their current accounts.

Partners' accounts as on 31 December 19X9 were as follows:

	Fixed capital £	Current £
Taylor	10,000	3,400 (Credit)
Best	6,000	1,200 (Credit)

The draft accounts for the year ended 31 December 19X0, before taking into account interest on partners' accounts, show a profit of £16,400. Partners' drawings during the year are: Taylor £5,000, Best £2,500 and Watson £1,500.

You are required to prepare:

(a) a statement showing the division of profits for the year ended 31 December 19X0, and

(b) the partners' current accounts for the year ended 31 December 19X0, recording therein the entries necessary upon Watson's admission as a partner.

(Institute of Chartered Accountants in England and Wales)

12.10 On 30 June 19X6, Campbell was admitted as a partner to the firm of Brown and Allen. He introduced £4,000 by way of capital, and as he could not immediately find additional monies to pay for his share of goodwill, it was agreed to create a goodwill account for £12,000. Prior to his admission,

Brown and Allen shared profits and losses in the ratio of 3:1, but the new partnership profit sharing ratio was agreed at 3:2:1. Interest was allowed on capital at 8% per year.

At the year ended 31 December 19X6 the trial balance was:

	£	£
Capital – Brown		15,000
– Allen		12,000
Current accounts – Brown		900
– Allen	259	
– Campbell		700
Suspense account – Campbell		4,000
5% loan – Brown		4,000
Interest on loan	200	
Sales		50,630
Purchases	47,300	
Stock at 1 January 19X6	9,250	
Discounts allowed and received	650	950
Wages	2,120	
Lighting and heating	860	
Rates	870	
Depreciation – Buildings		3,100
– Vehicles		4,000
Buildings (cost)	23,000	
Vehicles (cost)	9,000	
Debtors and creditors	5,300	5,300
Provision for doubtful debts		130
Bad debts	150	
Vehicle running expenses	680	
Miscellaneous expenses	471	
Bank	600	
	100,710	100,710

The following data is to be taken into account:

(i)   Stock at 31 December 19X6 was valued at £14,200.
(ii)   Wages owing at 31 December 19X6 amounted to £80.
(iii) Rates include £80 in respect of the period 1 January 19X7–31 January 19X7.
(iv)   Depreciation is to be provided on buildings at 2% on cost, and on vehicles at 10% on cost. No new vehicles have been acquired during the year.
(v)   The provision for doubtful debts is to be increased to 3% of debtors.
(vi)   All revenues and expenses can be deemed to accrue evenly through the year.

Required:
(a) Prepare the journal entries in relation to Campbell's admission as a partner.
(b) Prepare the trading, profit and loss and appropriation account for the period ended 31 December 19X6, and a balance sheet as at that date.

(Chartered Association of Certified Accountants)

12.11 Birch, Rose and Larch were in partnership sharing profits and losses: Birch one-half, Rose one-third, Larch one-sixth.

The draft balance sheet as on 31st March, 19X7, was as follows:

	£	£		£	£
Capital accounts			Freehold premises		6,000
Birch	12,000		Plant and equipment		9,400
Rose	6,000		Stock		4,600
Larch	3,000		Debtors	6,200	
		21,000	less Provision for		
Current accounts			doubtful debts	600	
Birch	960				5,600
Rose	840		Balance at bank		8,060
Larch	560				
		2,360			
Loan – Birch		2,500			
Provision for					
staff pensions		3,000			
Creditors		4,800			
		33,660			33,660

Birch retired on 31 March 19X7 and Rose and Larch continued in partnership, sharing profits and losses: Rose two-thirds, Larch one-third. Birch's loan was repaid on 1 April 19X7 and it was agreed that the remaining balance due to him, other than that on his current account, should remain on loan to the partnership.

It was agreed that the following adjustments were to be made to the balance sheet as on 31 March 19X7:

(1) The freehold premises were to be revalued at £12,000 and the plant and equipment at £7,900.
(2) The provision for bad debts was to be increased by £200.
(3) A provision of £250 included in creditors was no longer required.
(4) The provision for staff pensions was to be increased by £2,000.
(5) £600 was to be written off the stock in respect of damaged and obsolete items included therein.
(6) Provision of £120 was to be made for professional charges in connection with the revaluations.

The partnership agreement provided that on the retirement of a partner, goodwill was to be valued at an amount equal to the average annual profits of the three years expiring on the date of the retirement. The relevant profits were:

	£
Year ended 31 March 19X5	6,520
Year ended 31 March 19X6	8,420
Year ended 31 March 19X7	7,210 (as shown by the draft accounts).

It was agreed that, for the purpose of valuing goodwill, the revaluation of the fixed assets, the adjustment to the provision for staff pensions and the professional charges should not be regarded as affecting the profits.

No account for goodwill was to be maintained in the books, adjusting entries for transactions between the parties being made in their capital accounts.

You are required to prepare:

(a) the revaluation account,
(b) Birch's account, showing the balance due to him, and
(c) the balance sheet of Rose and Larch as on 1 April 19X7.

(Institute of Chartered Accountants in England and Wales)

13 Partnership dissolution

Aims of the chapter:

To show how the partners' accounts are finalised on dissolution of a partnership

A partnership may be dissolved, subject to anything to the contrary in the partnership agreement, under circumstances laid down by the Partnership Act 1890.
These circumstances include amongst others:

(a) the expiration of the partnership term, if fixed
(b) a partner giving notice of his intention to dissolve the partnership
(c) the death of a partner
(d) the bankruptcy of a partner.

In certain cases the court may order dissolution, e.g. insanity of a partner, misconduct of a partner, wilful or persistent breach of the partnership agreement.
Section 44 of the Partnership Act provides that on dissolution the assets of the partnership shall be applied in the following manner and order:

(1) In paying the debts and liabilities of the firm to persons who are not partners therein.
(2) In paying to each partner rateably what is due to him for advances as distinguished from capital.
(3) In paying to each partner rateably what is due to him in respect of capital.
(4) The ultimate residue, if any, shall be divided among the partners in the proportion in which profits are divisible.

Much of the accounting for the dissolution of a partnership is done through a *realisation account*. The entries in a firm's books necessary to record its dissolution and realisation would be:

Realisation account	Debit
Asset account	Credit
With the book values of assets except cash.	

After the above entries have been made the assets are represented by the realisation account, not the individual asset accounts.

Cash account   Debit
      Realisation account   Credit
      With the actual amounts realised on the sale of the
      assets.

As the assets are converted into cash, the cash account is debited. If any assets are taken over by a partner, that partner's capital account should be debited with the agreed value.

Realisation account   Debit
      Cash   Credit
      With any expenses of dissolving the firm.

Creditors   Debit
      Cash   Credit
      With the cash paid to creditors. (Any discount
      received is credited to realisation account.)

The balance now left on the realisation account represents the profit or loss on realisation. It is divided between the partners in the ratio in which they share profits and losses, and transferred to their individual capital accounts.

If any capital account at this stage has a debit balance, the partner concerned should introduce cash to that extent, or he may set the debit balance off against his loan account, if there is one.

Partners' loan account balances (if any) can now be repaid.

Finally the credit balances on the capital accounts can be repaid.

EXAMPLE 13.1

Horne, Ball and Toohey, partners sharing profits and losses in the ratio 3 : 2 : 1, dissolved their partnership on 31 December 19XX when their accounts showed the following balances:

	Dr. £	Cr. £
Capital accounts		
Horne		6,500
Ball		3,500
Toohey		1,000
Loan – Ball		9,500
Creditors		19,700
Premises	15,000	
Fixtures and fittings	4,200	
Stock	7,200	
Debtors	12,300	
Cash	1,500	
	40,200	40,200

Part of the stock was sold for £3,200, the remainder being taken over by Ball at an agreed valuation of £2,100.

The premises were sold for £15,500 whilst the fixtures and fittings realised £500.

Creditors were settled less £60 discount, and debtors paid £11,700. Winding up expenses amounted to £960.

Prepare the appropriate accounts to show the realisation of the firm.

Solution:

The accounting entries would be made in the following order. The solution should be worked through carefully stage by stage.

	Dr. £	Cr. £
Realisation (in individual items as below)	38,700	
Premises		15,000
Fixtures and fittings		4,200
Stock		7,200
Debtors		12,300
	38,700	38,700
Transfer of assets to realisation account.		
Cash (in individual items as below)	30,900	
Realisation – stock		3,200
– premises		15,500
– fixtures and fittings		500
– debtors		11,700
	30,900	30,900
Amounts realised on the sale of assets.		
Capital – Ball	2,100	
Realisation – stock		2,100
Asset taken over by partner at agreed value.		
Creditors	19,640	
Cash		19,640
Payment of creditors.		
Creditors	60	
Realisation		60
Discount on creditors transferred to realisation account.		
Realisation	960	
Cash		960
Cost of winding up firm.		

Capital	£	£
Horne	3,300	
Ball	2,200	
Toohey	1,100	
Realisation		6,600
	6,600	6,600

Loss on realisation shared 3 : 2 : 1.

Cash	100	
Capital – Toohey		100
Introduction of cash by Toohey to meet deficit.		

Loan – Ball	800	
Capital – Ball		800
Deficit on Ball's capital transferred to his loan account.		

Loan – Ball	8,700	
Cash		8,700
Balance on Ball's loan account paid in cash.		

Capital – Horne	3,200	
Cash		3,200
Surplus on Horne's capital account paid in cash.		

Note: Should there be any balances on partners' current accounts, they would be transferred to the partners' capital accounts.

The closing entries would appear in the accounts as follows:

Realisation account

	£			£
Premises	15,000	Cash (sale of stock)		3,200
Fixtures and fittings	4,200	Ball – Capital (sale of stock)		2,100
Stock	7,200	Cash (sale of premises)		15,500
Debtors	12,300	Cash (fixtures and fittings)		500
Cash (winding up expenses)	960	Cash (debtors)		11,700
		Creditors (discount)		60
		Loss on realisation:		
		Horne	3,300	
		Ball	2,200	
		Toohey	1,100	6,600
	39,660			39,660

Cash account

	£		£
Brought forward	1,500	Creditors	19,640
Realisation (sale of stock)	3,200	Realisation (winding up	
Realisation (sale of		expenses)	960
premises)	15,500	Ball – Loan	8,700
Realisation (fixtures and		Capital – Horne	3,200
fittings)	500		
Realisation (debtors)	11,700		
Capital – Toohey	100		
	32,500		32,500

Creditors account

	£		£
Cash	19,640	Brought forward	19,700
Realisation – discounts	60		
	19,700		19,700

Ball – Loan account

	£		£
Capital – Ball	800	Brought forward	9,500
Cash	8,700		
	9,500		9,500

Partners' capital accounts

	Horne £	Ball £	Toohey £		Horne £	Ball £	Toohey £
Realisation (stock)		2,100		b/f	6,500	3,500	1,000
Realisation (losses)	3,300	2,200	1,100	c/d		800	100
c/d	3,200						
	6,500	4,300	1,100		6,500	4,300	1,100
b/d		800	100	b/d	3,200		
Cash	3,200			Loan – Ball		800	
				Cash			100
	3,200	800	100		3,200	800	100

Garner v. Murray

In 1903 the case of *Garner v. Murray* caused great controversy amongst accountants, and its repercussions are still being felt by present day students.

The partnership of Garner, Murray and Wilkins was dissolved and

Wilkins finished up with a debit balance on his capital account (as did Toohey in Example 13.1). But Wilkins was insolvent and could not contribute anything. It was held that this debit balance should be shared amongst Garner and Murray in proportion to their capitals, and not in their profit sharing ratios. There have been complex arguments as to precisely how this should be done, and whether the solvent partners should introduce further cash in respect of their share of the loss.

However, it would appear generally acceptable, certainly for examination purposes, if the following rules are adhered to:

1. *Garner v. Murray* only applies if there is no agreement to the contrary. In examinations there rarely is an agreement to the contrary as the case is a traditional favourite with examiners.
2. Any loss on realisation should be divided in profit sharing ratios. *Garner v. Murray* only applies to the final balances on the partners' capital accounts immediately prior to capital being repaid.
3. The loss caused by the default of a partner (i.e. the debit balance on his capital account after sharing losses on realisation) should be shared amongst the remaining partners in proportion to their last agreed capitals. The capital account balances at the end of the last accounting period should be used as the basis. For this purpose current account balances should be ignored.

In Example 13.1 Toohey had to contribute £100 to make good the debit balance on his capital account. Ball also had a debit balance (of £800) on his capital account, but this was met from his loan account. Of course the debit balance on Ball's account was due to a very large extent to his taking over stock valued at £2,100, and this would not have been allowed if Ball was unable to show that he had sufficient resources either within or outside the firm.

It is worth examining for comparison the situation in Example 13.1 if Toohey were not able to contribute £100 to make good his indebtedness, due to his insolvency.

The balances on the capital accounts after division of the losses on realisation would be brought down just as before, i.e.

Partners' capital accounts

	Horne £	Ball £	Toohey £		Horne £	Ball £	Toohey £
b/d		800	100	b/d	3,200		

The debit balance on Toohey's capital account would now be transferred to Horne and Ball in the ratio of last agreed capitals, i.e. 6500 : 3500 or £65 to Horne and £35 to Ball. (*Not* profit sharing ratios of 3 : 2, i.e. £60 : £40.) As previously, the debit on Ball's capital account is transferred to his loan account.

Partners' capital accounts

	Horne £	Ball £	Toohey £		Horne £	Ball £	Toohey £
b/d		800	100	b/d	3,200		
Toohey – deficiency	65	35		Horne and			
Cash	3,135			Ball –			
				deficiency			
				of			
				Toohey			
				capital			100
				Loan – Ball		835	
	3,200	835	100		3,200	835	100

Ball's loan account would now appear as follows:

Ball – loan account

	£		£
Capital – Ball	835	b/d	9,500
Cash	8,665		
	9,500		9,500

Piecemeal realisation

In a dissolution of partnership it may take a considerable time to realise all the assets. Initial receipts of cash should be used to discharge liabilities of the firm in accordance with the requirements of the Partnership Act. Subsequent receipts of cash should be applied rateably to repay advances or loans from partners as distinct from capital.

When all the above have been discharged or repaid in full, the partners might naturally wish to have some of their capital repaid as and when cash becomes available, rather than wait until all the assets have been sold.

This partial repayment of capital should be done in such a way that no partner might subsequently be required to return any cash to the partnership. The most cautious approach is to regard any unrealised assets as valueless, and to apply the *Garner v. Murray* rule to any distribution.

The accounts are written up in the same way as before. The realisation account is not balanced off until all assets that can be realised have been disposed of. But at each interim distribution stage, a separate calculation is required to determine how much can be repaid to each partner.

EXAMPLE 13.2

Three partners, Goodwin, Jackson and Castle, sharing profits and losses in the ratio 4 : 2 : 1 agree to a dissolution. The balance sheet at the date of dissolution was

	£		£
Capital		Sundry assets	16,000
Goodwin	9,000		
Jackson	3,000		
Castle	2,000		
Creditors	1,000		
Bank overdrawn	1,000		
	16,000		16,000

The assets were realised in three stages, i.e. £3,400, £2,030, £8,400. It is agreed that any distribution should assume that none of the partners is able to provide additional capital.

Prepare a statement showing the distributions to the partners.

Solution:

	Loss £	Goodwin £	Jackson £	Castle £
First distribution				
Opening capital		9,000	3,000	2,000
First realisation	3,400			
Loss in profit sharing ratios	12,600	7,200	3,600	1,800
	16,000			
		1,800	−600	200
Jackson's deficiency divided 9 : 2		491		109
First distribution		1,309		91
Second distribution				
Opening capital		9,000	3,000	2,000
First and second realisations	5,430			
Loss in profit sharing ratios	10,570	6,040	3,020	1,510
	16,000			
		2,960	−20	490
Jackson's deficiency divided 9 : 2		16		4
		2,944		486
less First distribution		1,309		91
Second distribution		1,635		395
Third distribution				
Opening capital		9,000	3,000	2,000
First, second and third realisations	13,830			
Loss in profit sharing ratios	2,170	1,240	620	310
	16,000			

	£	£	£	£
		7,760	2,380	1,690
less First and second distributions		2,944		486
Third distribution		4,816	2,380	1,204

The accounts would be closed as under:

Realisation account

	£			£
Sundry assets	16,000	Cash (1st realisation)		3,400
		Cash (2nd realisation)		2,030
		Cash (3rd realisation)		8,400
		Loss – capital		
		Goodwin	1,240	
		Jackson	620	
		Castle	310	2,170
	16,000			16,000

Cash account

	£		£
Realisation:		Bank	1,000
(1st realisation)	3,400	Creditors	1,000
(2nd realisation)	2,030	Capital – Goodwin, 1st distribution	1,309
(3rd realisation)	8,400	Capital – Castle, 1st distribution	91
		Capital – Goodwin, 2nd distribution	1,635
		Capital – Castle, 2nd distribution	395
		Capital – Goodwin, 3rd distribution	4,816
		Capital – Jackson, 3rd distribution	2,380
		Capital – Castle, 3rd distribution	1,204
	13,830		13,830

Partners' capital accounts

	Goodwin	Jackson	Castle		Goodwin	Jackson	Castle
	£	£	£		£	£	£
Cash – 1st distribution	1,309		91	b/f	9,000	3,000	2,000
Cash – 2nd distribution	1,635		395				
Cash – 3rd distribution	4,816	2,380	1,204				
Realisation – Loss	1,240	620	310				
	9,000	3,000	2,000		9,000	3,000	2,000

Questions

13.1S Anderson and Birch, equal partners, dissolved their partnership on 31 December 19X1, when their balance sheet was as follows:

Balance Sheet as at 31 December 19X1

Assets

Fixed assets	Cost	Depre-ciation	Net
	£	£	£
Plant and machinery	20,000	11,500	8,500

Current assets		
Stock at cost	4,900	
Debtors	4,100	
Cash at bank	1,600	
	10,600	
less Current liabilities		
Creditors	3,100	
Net current assets		7,500
		16,000

Financed by		
Capital accounts		
Anderson	8,000	
Birch	8,000	16,000
		16,000

The assets realised £14,000 and the creditors were paid less a discount of 4%. The costs of realisation were £300.

You are required to prepare:
(a) the realisation account
(b) the cash account
(c) the partners' capital accounts.

13.2S   Old and Young who had been trading in partnership sharing profits and losses in the ratio of 2 : 1 respectively, decided to dissolve their partnership on 31 May 19X3, when their balance sheet showed the following position:

Assets

Fixed assets at net book value	£	£
Warehouse		50,000
Retail shops		75,000
Fixtures		15,000
Motor vehicles		8,400
		148,400
Current assets		
Stocks – Warehouse	30,000	
– Retail shops	45,000	
Debtors	2,400	
Cash at bank	2,700	
	80,100	
less Current liabilities		
Creditors	17,800	62,300
		210,700

Financed by	£	£
Capital accounts – Old	75,000	
– Young	50,000	125,000
Current accounts – Old	25,260	
– Young	20,440	45,700
Loan account – Old		40,000
		210,700

It was agreed that Old should take over the warehouse and the warehouse stock and that Young should take over the retail shops and shops' stock at the book values, and that Young should take over the fixtures at £16,500. The motor vehicles were sold for £8,000 and the debtors realised their book value. The creditors were paid in full and the costs of dissolution amounted to £1,200.

You are required to prepare the accounts showing the winding up of the firm.

13.3S   Smart and Swift were in partnership as hotel proprietors sharing profits and losses: Smart three-fifths, Swift two-fifths. No interest was charged on drawings or credited on capital. The following was a summary of their trial balance as on 31 December 19X8:

	£	£		£	£
Debtors		600	Bank overdraft		4,590
Fittings and fixtures		1,800	Loan – Smart at 6%		3,000
Foodstuffs – stock			Partners capital accounts		
31 December 19X7		420	Smart	3,000	
Foodstuffs purchased		2,600	Swift	500	3,500
Freehold premises		6,000			
General expenses		810	Sundry creditors		210
Partners drawings			Takings		5,100
Smart	520				
Swift	750	1,270			
Motor vehicle	—	700			
Wages		2,200			
		16,400			16,400

For the purposes of accounts as on 31 December 19X8, the stock of foodstuffs was valued at £300, and £200 was to be written off the book value of the motor vehicle and £100 off fittings and fixtures. A provision of £60 was required for accrued general expenses and Smart was to be credited with a year's interest on his loan account.

The partnership was dissolved on 31 December 19X8, it being agreed that:

(1) Smart should take over the stock of foodstuffs for £250 and part of the fittings and fixtures for £600.
(2) Swift should take over the motor vehicle for £400.
(3) Interest on Smart's loan should cease as on 31 December 19X8.
    During January 19X9:
    (i) The freehold premises were sold, realising a net amount of £6,800.

(ii) £480 was collected from debtors (the balance proving irrecoverable).

(iii) The net proceeds from an auction of the balance of fittings and fixtures was received amounting to £1,400. It was agreed that the few unsold items should be taken over partly by Smart for £40 and the rest by Swift for £20.

(iv) Creditors were paid in full together with incidental realisation and dissolution expenses of £120.

(v) All amounts receivable or payable by Smart and Swift were settled.

You are required to prepare:

(a) the profit and loss account for the year ended 31 December 19X8, excluding any profit or loss arising on dissolution,
(b) the realisation account,
(c) the cash account for January 19X9, and
(d) partners' capital accounts (in columnar form) showing the final settlement on dissolution.

(Institute of Chartered Accountants in England and Wales)

13.4S Clark, Hibbert and Thomas were in partnership sharing profits and losses equally. On 31 October 19X2, they decided to dissolve their partnership and wind up their business. Hibbert was insolvent and unable to contribute towards any loss on the winding up. The balance sheet of the firm at the above date was as follows:

Balance Sheet as at 31 October 19X2

Assets	£	£
Fixed assets		
Fixtures and fittings		2,000
Current assets		
Stock	9,000	
Debtors	5,000	
Cash at bank	2,500	
	16,500	
less Current liabilities		
Creditors	7,250	
Net current assets		9,250
Hibbert – capital account		750
		12,000
Financed by		
Capital accounts		
Clark	7,000	
Thomas	5,000	12,000
		12,000

The assets realised – stock £6,800; debtors £4,650; fixtures and fittings £1,700. Creditors were paid less a discount of £100.

Realisation expenses were £400.

You are required to prepare accounts showing the effect of the realisation, and the partners' capital accounts.

13.5   Louis and Edmonds, who shared profits and losses equally, decided to dissolve their partnership and to retire on 31 March 19X2, on which date their balance sheet was as follows:

Balance Sheet as at 31 March 19X2

Assets

Fixed assets	Cost	Depre-ciation	Net
	£	£	£
Fixtures and fittings	6,000	4,800	1,200
Motor vehicles	9,200	4,600	4,600
	15,200	9,400	5,800

Current assets		
Stock at cost	8,750	
Debtors	5,870	
Cash at bank	1,600	
	16,220	
less Current liabilities		
Creditors	3,820	
Net current assets		12,400
		18,200

Financed by		
Capital accounts		
Louis	5,000	
Edmonds	5,000	10,000
Current accounts		
Louis	2,200	
Edmonds	2,000	4,200
Loan – Louis		4,000
		18,200

The debtors realised £5,600; stock £8,400; fixtures and fittings £1,400; and motor vehicles £5,400. Creditors were discharged less £90 discount and winding up expenses amounted to £460.

You are required to prepare:

(a) the realisation account
(b) the cash account
(c) the partners' capital accounts.

13.6   Black and White, who make up their accounts annually to 31 March, were in partnership as restaurateurs sharing profits and losses, Black two-thirds and White one-third. No interest was charged on drawings or credited on capital.

The following was a summary of the balances as on 31 March 19X1:

	£		£
Fixtures and fittings	2,200	Partners' capital accounts:	
Leasehold premises	5,000	Black	3,100
Foodstuffs – stock		White	1,000
31 March 19X0	760	Loan – Black at 8% p.a.	2,000
Debtors	180	Creditors	640
Foodstuffs purchased	4,800	Charges for meals	10,400
General expenses	1,600	Motor vehicle:	
Partners drawings:		Provision for	
Black	600	depreciation	
White	480	31 March 19X0	360
Motor vehicle at cost	900	Bank overdraft	2,620
Wages	3,600		
	20,120		20,120

For the purpose of the accounts at 31 March 19X1, the stock of food-stuffs was valued at £620 and the fixtures and fittings at £1,800. Provisions are to be made for depreciation of the motor vehicle at 20% per annum calculated on cost and for accrued general expenses of £120. In addition, Black is to be credited with a year's interest on his loan account.

The partnership was dissolved on 31 March 19X1, it being agreed that:

(1) Black should take over the stock for £500.
(2) White should take over the motor vehicle for £270 and part of the fittings and fixtures for £750.
(3) Interest on Black's loan should cease on 31 March 19X1.

During April 19X1:

(1) The leasehold premises were sold, realising a net amount of £6,500.
(2) £140 was collected from debtors, the balance being taken over by Black.
(3) The net proceeds from an auction of the balance of the fittings and fixtures was received amounting to £800. It was agreed that the few remaining unsold items should be taken over by White for £50.
(4) Creditors and accrued expenses were paid in full together with realisation and dissolution expenses of £190.
(5) All amounts receivable or payable by Black and White were settled.

You are required to prepare:

(a) Profit and loss account for the year ended 31 March 19X1, excluding any profit or loss arising on dissolution,
(b) Realisation account,
(c) Cash account for April 19X1, and
(d) Partners' capital accounts (in columnar form) showing the final settlement on dissolution.

(Institute of Chartered Accountants in England and Wales)

13.7   Hill, Stone and Rock were in partnership owning a riding school and livery stables. Profits and losses were shared: Hill three-fifths, Stone one-fifth, Rock one-fifth. No interest was charged on drawings or credited on capital. The firm provided an instructor to the equitation classes of the local agricultural college.

The following was a summary of the balances as on 31 December 19X5:

	£	£		£	£
Drawings:			Capital:		
Hill	1,500		Hill	6,000	
Stone	1,200		Stone	4,400	
Rock	1,000	3,700	Rock	1,690	12,090
Freehold land and			Loan: Stone	3,000	
buildings		8,000	Interest at 6% to		
Hay and fodder,			30 June 19X5	90	3,090
balance on					
1 January 19X5		250	Agricultural college		
Hay and fodder			equitation fees		150
purchased		1,500	Sundry creditors		130
Harness, equipment			Hire of horses and		
and fittings		250	riding lessons		2,905
Horses valued on			Receipts from		
1 January 19X5		1,600	horses at livery		870
Horses purchased		100	Prize money		75
Motor vehicles		2,500	Sale of horses		60
Debtors		600	Bank overdraft		2,500
Salaries and wages		2,500			
Veterinary and					
other fees		180			
General expenses		600			
Loan interest		90			
		21,870			21,870

On 31 December 19X5, hay and fodder were valued at £50, motor vehicles at £2,000, harness, equipment and fittings at £200, and horses at £1,400. Provision was needed for veterinary fees, £50. With the exception of loan interest no further provisions were considered necessary.

The partnership was dissolved on 31 December 19X5, on the following terms:

(1) Rock was appointed instructor to the local agricultural college, and for this privilege, he paid into the partnership £200 which is to be divided between Hill and Stone.

(2) He also took over assets at the following valuation:
    (i)   six horses £600
    (ii) the hay and fodder, £40
    (iii) part of the harness and equipment, £75
    (iv) a horse-box, £800.

(3) Hill took over a motor car at a valuation of £450.

(4) Net receipts from the sale of the freehold land and buildings amounted to £8,750.

(5) The debtors realised £530 and the remaining assets were sold by auction, the net receipts being £1,765.

(6) The loan, with interest accrued to date, was repaid on 1 January 19X6.

(7) The creditors were paid and a contingent liability, not brought into the accounts, was settled early in January for £250.

(8) Cups and plate, not brought into the accounts, were distributed among the partners at the following valuation: Hill £20, Stone £10, Rock £60.

All transactions were completed and all amounts receivable or payable by the partners were settled before the end of January 19X6.

You are required to prepare:
(a) the profit and loss account for the year ended 31 December 19X5, excluding any profits or losses arising on dissolution,
(b) the realisation account,
(c) the cash account, and
(d) partners' capital accounts showing the final settlement on dissolution.

(Institute of Chartered Accountants in England and Wales)

13.8   Smith, Jones and Brown were in partnership, sharing profits in the ratio of 3 : 2 : 1 respectively. They decided to dissolve the partnership at 31 July 19X6, at which date their balance sheet was as follows:

Balance Sheet as at 31 July 19X6

Assets	£	£
Fixed assets at net book value		21,000
Current assets (excluding cash)	22,500	
Cash at bank	12,000	
	34,500	
less Current liabilities		
Creditors	9,000	
Net current assets		25,500
		46,500
Financed by		
Capital accounts		
Smith	18,000	
Jones	13,500	
Brown	9,000	40,500
Loan – Smith		6,000
		46,500

The assets were realised 'piecemeal' during the following year:

	£		£
1st realisation	6,000	Final realisation	19,500
2nd realisation	13,500		

The cash was distributed as and when it was available.
You are required to prepare:
(a) a statement showing the cash distribution
(b) the realisation account
(c) the cash account
(d) the partners' capital accounts.

14 Incomplete records

Aims of the chapter:

> To emphasise the importance of the accounting equation and the necessity of recognising the dual nature of every transaction

Accounting records which have not been maintained according to strict double entry principles are usually referred to as *incomplete records*. This does not necessarily mean that the records are unsatisfactory. Very few small cash traders will keep a full double entry ledger system. An analytical cash book entered up regularly and accurately together with neatly filed invoices and other relevant vouchers will prove quite adequate for most small traders since their accountant will be able to compile a trading and profit and loss account and balance sheet from those records.

The expression 'incomplete records' therefore covers a wide range of accounting records varying from the abysmal and incomplete to the very good though still incomplete.

The problem, both in practice and in examinations, is to use the information in the incomplete records to form a conventionally presented trading and profit and loss account and balance sheet. In practice this may not be too difficult if well organised records have been maintained. At the other extreme, a few notes on the back of an envelope are not conducive to good relations between accountant, client and tax inspector. In examinations the degree of difficulty is related to the examiner's intentions when he sets the question.

Where records are at their most disorganised level it may be necessary to use the capital computation method of determining profit for the period. This method is based on the accounting equation, i.e.

$$\text{Capital} = \text{Assets} - \text{Liabilities}.$$

A statement of the assets and liabilities (often described as *a statement of affairs*) at the beginning of the relevant period is built up. From this is derived the opening capital. The statement of affairs is of course equivalent to a balance sheet, but as it is not a list of ledger balances it is more accurate to describe it as a statement of assets and liabilities or a statement of affairs. A similar statement is also prepared for the end of the period, so providing the closing capital. The closing capital − opening capital = increase in capital. And increase in capital + withdrawals during the year = profit.

Formulae:

Capital = Assets − Liabilities,

Opening capital + Profit − Drawings = Closing capital,

Profit = $(A - L)_2 - (A - L)_1$ + Drawings in the year,

Where A = assets, L = liabilities, 2 refers to the end of the accounting period, and 1 refers to the start of the accounting period.

In practice, the above can be a most difficult and sometimes unsatisfactory exercise. All withdrawals from the business must be traced because they represent an increase in assets generated during the period. The value of any additional assets provided from outside the business during the period should by similar reasoning be omitted when the profit is deduced as above.

Perhaps the greatest problem can be that a business owner with such poor records will have little knowledge of the business entity concept. His personal affairs might be hopelessly and inextricably mixed up with his business affairs. In this case his personal increase in capital has to be examined, as well as that of the business. In any case this method of computation cannot be used effectively without the private affairs of the owner being carefully investigated to identify movements of funds in and out of the business.

EXAMPLE 14.1

J. Barton is running a butcher's business from rented premises. It is his second year in business. During the first year he was assisted by his nephew who kept reasonably acceptable records in addition to helping in the shop. However, the nephew left early in the second year. The records are now in a very poor state. You have been able to ascertain the following:

	1 Jan. 19X1 £	31 Dec. 19X1 £
Debtors	150	275
Creditors	360	590
Stock	420	570
Cash	115	123
Bank	785	60 Overdrawn
Van	3,600	
Fixtures and fittings	2,000	

The van is now valued at £2,700 and the fixtures and fittings at £1,500. Barton has been withdrawing £125 per week in cash and £10 in meat for his own use.

Prepare a statement showing the profit for the year and a balance sheet at 31 December 19X1.

Solution:

Statement of Assets and Liabilities

	1 Jan. 19X1	31 Dec. 19X1
Assets	£	£
Van	3,600	2,700
Fixtures and fittings	2,000	1,500
Stock	420	570
Debtors	150	275
Bank	785	–
Cash	115	123
	7,070	5,168
Liabilities		
Creditors	360	590
Bank	–	60
	360	650
Capital	6,710	4,518

Profit:		
Capital 31 December 19X1	4,518	
less 1 January 19X1	6,710	
	−2,192	
Drawings, 52 × £125	6,500	
Meat, 52 × £10	520	
Profit for year	4,828	

J. Barton
Balance Sheet as at 31 December 19X1

Assets	£	£	£
Fixed assets			
Van			2,700
Fixtures and fittings			1,500
			4,200
Current assets			
Stock		570	
Debtors		275	
Cash		123	
		968	
less Current liabilities			
Creditors	590		
Bank overdrawn	60	650	
Net current assets (working capital)			318
			4,518

Financed by	£
Capital 1 January 19X1	6,710
add Profit for year	4,828
	11,538
less Drawings	7,020
	4,518

Note that the butcher is taking more from the business than he is making in profit. This can easily occur when there are inadequate records and controls. If this continues the capital will be eroded. In the early years of a business it is usually more appropriate to build up the capital by leaving in some of the profit.

Most examination examples of incomplete records provide summarised or analysed details of cash and/or bank transactions. Additionally there are provided details of assets and liabilities, sometimes in a somewhat obscure manner. The student is usually required to make further computations and adjustments and present a conventional trading and profit and loss account and a balance sheet.

EXAMPLE 14.2

Prepare for Mr J. Lewthwaite, who is a retail trader, a trading and profit and loss account for the year ended 31 December 19X5 and a balance sheet at that date. Mr Lewthwaite has been trading since 1 January 19X4 but has not kept full books of account and does not operate a normal bank account, using a savings bank for money in reserve and paying suppliers in cash. He has kept receipts for payments and a daily record of takings.

Gross takings for 19X5 amounted to £40,782. An analysis of the payments shows:

	£
Suppliers	30,926
Rent	2,100
Rates and water	1,400
Electricity	350
Repairs	238
Miscellaneous business expenses	196
Household and personal expenses	434

He states that he always takes £60 a week out of the takings for himself, pays his wife £20 a week for part-time assistance, and also takes goods out of stock which he values at £20 per week at cost price.

The savings bank account showed a balance at 1 January 19X5 of £3,703 and this had grown to £4,730 by 31 December 19X5 including interest for the year of £119.

When Mr Lewthwaite started he paid £42,000 for a lease which then had 15 years to run.

Stock was valued at £3,682 on 31 December 19X4 and £4,095 on 31 December 19X5.

Further information available shows:

1. Rates and water charges for year to 31 March 19X5 were £1,260 and for year to 31 March 19X6, £1,400. These are paid half-yearly in advance.
2. Amounts owing to suppliers at 31 December 19X4 amounted to £2,548 and at 31 December 19X5, £2,604.
3. Cash in hand at 31 December 19X4 was £350 and 31 December 19X5 was £420.

Solution:
The first step in creating order out of this chaos of facts is to prepare a statement of affairs (or statement of assets and liabilities). This would not have been necessary if it were the first year for Lewthwaite; the analysis of bank/cash (which appears later in this exercise) would have provided all the information required. Very careful scrutiny of the information is necessary to prepare the following statement accurately.

Statement of Affairs at 1 January 19X5

	£
Lease (£42,000 *less* amortisation, one year £2,800)	39,200
Stock	3,682
Prepayments (rates and water, ¼ year × £1,260)	315
Bank	3,703
Cash	350
	47,250
Creditors (suppliers)	2,548
Capital 1 January 19X5 (balancing figure)	44,702

Note that the term *amortisation* is normally used, rather than *depreciation*, to describe the writing down of leaseholds, patents and other assets which become exhausted due to the passing of time.

Next a comprehensive cash/bank analysis should be built up:

Cash/bank transaction for 19X5

	£		£
Bank b/f	3,703	Payments – Suppliers	30,926
Cash b/f	350	Rent	2,100
Takings	40,782	Rates and water	1,400
Bank interest	119	Electricity	350
		Repairs	238
		Business expenses	196
		Private expenses	434

£		£
	Drawings – Self	3,120
	Wages – Wife	1,040
		£
	Bank c/d	4,730
	Cash c/d	420 5,150
44,954		44,954

The cash/bank transactions have now been listed in a cash/bank account formed from the information provided. The following procedure should now be adopted:

1. Open T accounts commencing with all balances in the statement of affairs, except for cash/bank where this account is given or has already been built up.
2. Post cash/bank transactions to T accounts, opening new T accounts where necessary.
3. Bring other adjustments required (e.g. drawings in form of food, creditors and debtors at year end) into T accounts.
4. Calculate sales and purchases for the period.[1]
5. Prepare trial balance.
6. List adjustments to be made to the trial balance to allow the final accounts to be prepared.
7. Prepare final accounts.

J. Lewthwaite – T accounts

Lease – cost		Amortisation of lease	
Balance b/d 42,000			Balance b/d 2,800

Stock		Rates and water	
Balance b/d 3,682		Prepayment b/d 315	
		Cash 1,400	

Capital		Creditors control	
	Balance b/d 44,702	Cash 30,926	Balance b/d 2,548
		Balance c/d 2,604	Purchases 30,982
		33,530	33,530
			Balance b/d 2,604

[1] The method suggested is that sales are calculated by using a *debtors control account* and purchases are calculated by using a *creditors control account*. All cash received for sales is credited to the debtors control account and all cash paid for purchases is debited to the creditors control account. When the opening and closing debtors and creditors are taken into account, the balances on the debtors control account and creditors control account will represent respectively the sales and purchases for the period since

Sales = Cash received during the period + Closing debtors − Opening debtors
Purchases = Cash paid during the period + Closing creditors − Opening creditors

Debtors control			
Sales	40,782	Cash	40,782

Bank interest		
	Bank	119

Rent	
Cash	2,100

Electricity	
Cash	350

Repairs	
Cash	238

Expenses	
Cash	196

Drawings	
Cash	434
Cash	3,120
Purchases	1,040

Wages	
Cash	1,040

Purchases			
Creditors control	30,982	Drawings	1,040

Sales		
	Debtors control	40,782

Note: It is not necessary to balance off the accounts before preparing the trial balance.

Trial Balance at 31 December 19X5

	£	£
Lease	42,000	
Amortisation of lease		2,800
Stock	3,682	
Rates and water	1,715	
Capital		44,702
Creditors		2,604
Bank interest		119
Rent	2,100	
Electricity	350	
Repairs	238	
Expenses	196	
Drawings	4,594	
Wages	1,040	
Purchases	29,942	
Sales		40,782
Bank	4,730	
Cash	420	
	91,007	91,007

Adjustments to trial balance:
1. Closing stock £4,095
2. Rates and water prepaid ($1/4 \times £1,400$) £350
3. Amortisation of lease £2,800.

J. Lewthwaite
Trading and Profit and Loss Account
for the year ended 31 December 19X5

	£	£
Sales		40,782
Cost of sales		
Opening stock	3,682	
Purchases	29,942	
	33,624	
less Closing stock	4,095	29,529
Gross profit		11,253
add Bank interest		119
		11,372
less Expenses		
Wages – wife	1,040	
Rent	2,100	
Rates and water	1,365	
Electricity	350	
Repairs	238	
Business expenses	196	
Amortisation of lease	2,800	8,089
Net profit		3,283

J. Lewthwaite
Balance Sheet as at 31 December 19X5

Assets	Cost	Depreciation	Net
Fixed asset	£	£	£
Lease	42,000	5,600	36,400
Current assets			
Stock		4,095	
Prepayment (rates and water)		350	
Bank		4,730	
Cash		420	
		9,595	
less Current liabilities			
Creditors		2,604	
Net current assets			6,991
			43,391
Financed by			
Capital			44,702
add Profit for year			3,283
			47,985
less Drawings			4,594
			43,391

It is recommended that T accounts are opened for all transactions until familiarity is gained. For most examinations, however, this method of working would take too long. Most students find that, once they are familiar with the problems presented by incomplete records, they are able to proceed directly to the trading and profit and loss account using the information provided by the cash/bank account and only opening T accounts in their working papers when the cash/bank transactions require adjustment. Working papers prepared in this manner for the J. Lewthwaite example are shown below.

Working Papers – J. Lewthwaite
(recommended minimum)

Purchases

	£		£
Cash – suppliers	30,926	Owing to suppliers	
Owing to suppliers		1 Jan. 19X5	2,548
31 Dec. 19X5 c/d	2,604	Drawings (in goods)	1,040
		Trading account	29,942
	33,530		33,530
		Owing to suppliers	
		1 Jan. 19X6 b/d	2,604

Rates and water

Prepayment b/f	315	Prepayment 31 Dec. 19X5 c/d	350
Cash	1,400	Profit and loss	1,365
	1,715		1,715
Prepayment 1 Jan. 19X6 b/d	350		

Drawings

Cash	3,120	Capital account	4,594
Purchases (in goods)	1,040		
Cash (private expenses)	434		
	4,594		4,594

Questions

14.1S On 31 December 19X2, P. Jennings' shop was burned down before he had been able to make his annual stock-taking. All his stock was lost. Jennings wishes to make an insurance claim as quickly as possible and has asked you to calculate his stock loss from the following information:

1. All his sales were made at a uniform gross profit on selling price of 33⅓%.
2. Stock on hand at 1 January 19X2 was £6,933.

3. Purchases for the year to 31 December 19X2 were £16,711 and sales £24,696.

14.2S G. Holt has asked you to calculate his profit for 19X2 and has given you the following information:

Balance Sheet as at 31 December 19X1

Capital employed			£
Capital account: balance at 31 December 19X1			17,246

Represented by Assets	Cost	Depre-ciation	Net
	£	£	£
Fixed assets	20,000	7,500	12,500
Current assets			
Stock		4,092	
Debtors		2,984	
Bank		1,386	
		8,462	
Deduct current liabilities			
Trade creditors	3,338		
Expense creditors	378	3,716	
Net current assets			4,746
			17,246

Holt's assets and liabilities at 31 December 19X2 were:

	£
Stock	4,838
Debtor	2,856
Bank	2,221
Creditors: Trade	1,568
Expense	382

During the year ended 31 December 19X2, Holt withdrew £3,120 from the business for private use.

Depreciation in the past has been charged at 12½% per annum on cost and Holt does not see any reason why this rate should be changed.

14.3S Reel Limited, a company with a chain of retail drapery shops, decided to dispose of some of its smaller branches in the interests of economy.

Bobbin agreed to purchase from the company the goodwill, fixtures and fittings at its Seaport branch for £2,500, plus stock at valuation. Fixtures and fittings included in the price had an agreed value of £500. The landlord of the premises agreed to grant Bobbin a new lease for seven years at £400 per annum, payable quarterly in arrears.

Bobbin opened a bank account for the business with £6,000, paid Reel Limited the amount due for the business including the stock, and commenced business on 1 April 19X6.

The only record he kept was a notebook in which he recorded cash payments made out of takings, before paying them into the bank. The following payments were extracted from the book for the year ended 31 March 19X7: wages and National Insurance £597; cash purchases for resale £158; sundry shop expenses £104, and his drawings £624.

A summary of his bank account for the year ended 31 March 19X7 showed the following:

Deposits	£
Cash introduced	6,000
Shop bankings	12,050
Withdrawals	
Reel Limited	3,750
Purchases for resale	10,000
Rent	300
Rates	196
Electricity	49
Additional fixtures (purchased	
1 April 19X6)	100

On 31 March 19X7, stock on hand (at cost) was valued at £1,456, cash on hand amounted to £112, and amounts were outstanding for trade creditors £268 and electricity £17. Depreciation on fixtures and fittings is to be provided at a rate of 10% p.a.

You are required to prepare Bobbin's trading and profit and loss accounts for the year ended 31 March 19X7 and balance sheet as on that date.

(Institute of Chartered Accountants in England and Wales)

14.4S I. Patchett was a small contractor, making up his accounts to 30 June in each year. On 30 November 19X7 he fell off a roof he was repairing and died the same day.

His balance sheet on 30 June 19X7 showed the following position:

	£	£		£	£
Capital account:			Fixed assets:		
I. Patchett		2,654	Motor van, at cost	450	
Current liabilities:			*less* Depreciation	150	300
Trade creditors	256				
Expenses accrued:			Plant and equip-		
Rates	21		ment, at cost	250	
Electricity	14	291	*less* Depreciation	150	100
					400
			Current assets:		
			Stock of materials	185	
			Debtors	75	
			Balance at bank	2,270	
			Cash in hand	15	2,545
		2,945			2,945

He had not written up his books since the date of the last balance sheet, but an analysis of his bank account for the period to the date of death showed the following:

	£		£
Balance as on		Materials purchased	1,023
30 June 19X7	2,270	Rent of office and yard for	
Deposits	4,162	quarter to 30	
		September 19X7	51
		Rates for year to 31 March	
		19X8	84
		Electricity	41
		Van expenses	74
		Cash withdrawn	
		(including drawings)	1,402
		Balance as on 30	
		November 19X7	3,757
	6,432		6,432

You also obtain the following information:

(1) Bank deposits represent receipts from customers for work done, with the exception of one deposit of £500 being the proceeds of an endowment insurance policy.

(2) Patchett kept a petty cash box in his office which was replenished each week out of the cash withdrawn from the bank. He kept a record of cash payments in a notebook and a summary of the entries to 30 November 19X7 was as follows:

	£
Wages and National Insurance	748
Materials	156
Sundry expenses	49

The balance of cash in the box on 30 November 19X7 was £12.

(3) On the date of death, debtors amounted to £176 and £349 was owed to suppliers for materials. There was £11 outstanding for electricity.

(4) An employee of the deceased agreed to purchase the trading assets from the executors for £525, based on the following valuations, which are to be reflected in the accounts:

	£
Motor van	250
Plant and equipment	75
Stock of materials	200
	525

You are required to prepare I. Patchett's profit and loss account for the period 1 July 19X7 to 30 November 19X7, and balance sheet as on that date.

(Institute of Chartered Accountants in England and Wales)

14.5S Angus, a tenant farmer, has failed to keep books of account for the year ended 31 March 19X6.

A summary of his bank account for the past year shows the following:

	£		£	£
Balance on 31 March 19X5	492	New tractor	700	
Receipts from Milk		less Allowance on		
Marketing Board	3,084	old tractor in		
Ploughing grant	145	part exchange	360	340
Cereal deficiency payment	217	Seeds and fertilizers	——	728
Cattle auctions	570	Feeding stuffs		1,296
Cash bankings	1,724	Tractor and machinery		
		expenses		537
		Veterinary fees		55
		Additional machinery		125
		Rent and rates		483
		Transfer to private		
		bank account		2,000
		Balance on 31 March 19X6		668
	6,232			6,232

You also obtain the following information:

(1) The amount received from cattle auctions is the net figure after taking into account purchases of £426.

(2) A neighbouring farmer did threshing and baling work for Angus in exchange for hay valued at £273, and the feeding stuffs merchant had accepted produce to the value of £730 in part payment of his account.

(3) Angus has sold crops and produce for cash, and has banked the balance of the proceeds after paying:

	£
Electricity	79
Wages and National Insurance	1,109
Own drawings	624
Sundry expenses	29

(4) Outstanding amounts on 31 March were:

	19X5	19X6
	£	£
Milk Marketing Board	267	294
Electricity	23	21

(5) The part exchange allowance on the old tractor was equivalent to its written down value in the balance sheet as on 31 March 19X5. The new tractor is to be written down to £600, and other machinery which was valued at £1,500 on 31 March 19X5, together with the additional machinery purchased during the year, is to be written down to £1,300.

(6) Stocks on hand on 31 March have been valued as follows:

	19X5	19X6
	£	£
Livestock	1,825	1,700
Crops, produce and fertilizers	200	240
	2,025	1,940

You are required to prepare a profit and loss account for the year ended 31 March 19X6 and a balance sheet as on that date.

(Institute of Chartered Accountants in England and Wales)

14.6   A. Neal, a haulage contractor, seeks your assistance in calculating his profit for the year ended 30 June 19X5 and also requires a balance sheet as at that date. He submits the following data:

	£
Cash balance at 1 July 19X4	3,740
Cash balance at 30 June 19X5	2,950
Drawings for the year	1,780
Receipts from debtors	10,354
Debtors at 1 July 19X4	2,511
Debtors at 30 June 19X5	3,114
Drivers' wages (including £200 owing)	4,111
Rent of business premises (£1,600 per year)	1,200
Miscellaneous payments	2,134

Required:
(a)   Ascertain the profit for the year ended 30 June 19X5, and draw up a balance sheet as at that date making any assumptions you think reasonable. List the additional data you would require from Mr Neal in order to undertake the task more completely.
(b)   Explain to Mr Neal the benefits which would accrue if his accounts were kept in a 'double entry' form.

(Chartered Association of Certified Accountants)

14.7   Sparrow retired from his employment abroad and returned to this country, where he purchased a small retail business. He took over the business on 1 July 19X9, acquiring the existing stock at a valuation of £1,142 and the rest of the purchase consideration was apportioned as to £1,500 for fixtures and fittings and the balance for goodwill.

He used his existing bank account and, other than bank statements and vouchers, the only record available was a till book recording cash payments from the till. Surplus cash was banked periodically during the year.

A summary of his bank account for the year ended 30 June 19X0 shows:

	£		£
Balance 1 July 19X9	3,646	Purchase of business	3,192
Pension from former		Rent, 15 months to 30	
employment	975	September 19X0	500
Bankings from shop	16,427	Rates, 9 months to 31	
		March 19X0	84
		Electricity	92
		Hire of frozen food	
		cabinet	80
		Purchases for resale	14,700
		Private cheques	1,122
		Balance 30 June 19X0	1,278
	21,048		21,048

A summary of the till book for the year ended 30 June 19X0, shows:

	£
Cash purchases for resale	1,606
Staff wages	742
Sundry shop expenses	156
Cash drawings	520

On 30 June 19X0, stock, valued at cost, amounted to £1,542, amounts due from customers £74, and cash in hand amounted to £54. Depreciation is to be provided on fixtures and fittings at a rate of 10%.

Accounts outstanding on 30 June 19X0, were purchases £470 and rates for the year ending 31 March 19X1, £120.

You are required to prepare Sparrow's trading and profit and loss account for the year ended 30 June 19X0 and a balance sheet as on that date.

(Institute of Chartered Accountants in England and Wales)

14.8   On 30 September 19X7, Alexander and Arnold completed their first year of trading in partnership. They shared profits and losses in the ratio Alexander ²/₃, Arnold ¹/₃, and were entitled to 5% per annum interest on capital. Arnold was also entitled to a salary of £1,490 per annum. They kept a debtors ledger, a creditors ledger for goods purchased, and a single entry record of all other transactions.

A summary of their cash transactions for the year ended 30 September 19X7 is given below:

		£
Receipts		
	Cash float for till	20
	Cash sales	12,800
	Receipts from debtors	44,900
Payments:		
	Creditors – goods purchased	2,600
	Drawings – Alexander	1,400
	– Arnold	1,200
	Lodgements with bank	52,190

A summary of the partnership bank account for the year ended 30 September 19X7 is also available.

		£
Bankings:		
	Capital paid in – Alexander	8,400
	– Arnold	7,200
	Banked from business	52,190
Cheques drawn:		
	Premises	11,000
	Cash float	20
	Creditors for goods	50,200
	Van	1,600
	Sundry expenses	4,720

The partners also supplied the following details:

		£
(i)	Stock in hand at 30 September 19X7	6,000
(ii)	Debtors at 30 September 19X7	5,400
(iii)	Bad debts written off (already excluded from debtors balance)	200
(iv)	Creditors at 30 September 19X7	3,000
(v)	Depreciation is to be provided for the van at 10% on cost	
(vi)	Sundry expenses accrued	150

Required:
Prepare the trading, profit and loss and appropriation account for the period ended 30 September 19X7 and a balance sheet as at that date.

(Chartered Association of Certified Accountants)

14.9   On 1 April 19X5 Edward Watson bought the Prime Butchers Company for a cash price of £4,000, acquiring the following assets and liabilities.

	£
Buildings	3,000
Plant and fittings	200
Debtors	400
Stock of meat	200
Creditors (for purchases)	600

He opened a bank account, depositing a further £800 as working capital, and in addition borrowed £2,000 from Roger Mitchell at 10% per annum.

He did not bank all proceeds, but made a number of payments out of cash which, during his first year of trading, he summarised as:

	£
Stock purchased	9,728
Slaughtering charges	504
Sundry expenses	872
Heating and lighting	152
Wages (to delivery boy)	164

In addition to the above cash payments, a summary of his cheque stubs discloses the following payments:

	£
Stock purchases	11,304
Shop wages	864
Personal drawings	1,048
Rates	780
Interest on loan	100

Watson advises that each week he pays into the bank all cash on hand (after meeting cash payments above) except a till float of £20. The total monies paid into the bank are revealed by the paying-in book to be £16,140 (exclusive of capital and loan). At 31 March 19X6 Watson was owed £296 by debtors, and owed £860 to trade creditors and £35 for wages. He considered that he wished to make a provision of 2% per annum for depreciation on buildings, and 10% per annum for depreciation on plant and equipment. The stock at 31 March 19X6 was valued at £580.

Required:
(a) Prepare bank and cash accounts for the year ended 31 March 19X6.
(b) Prepare a trading, profit and loss account for the year ended 31 March 19X6 and a balance sheet as at that date. (Ignore taxation.)

(Chartered Association of Certified Accountants)

15 Income and expenditure accounts

Aims of the chapter:

To consider the accounts of simple non-trading organisations

A conventional trading and profit and loss account is not an appropriate form in which to present the final accounts of a non-trading entity. Clubs, institutions, societies, professional bodies and similar concerns not formed with the intention of profit making will usually prepare an *income and expenditure account*. Occasionally it may be called a *revenue account*.

A correctly presented income and expenditure account differs little in principle and concept from a trading and profit and loss account. The income and expenditure account will show either a *surplus* or a *deficit* on the year's (or period's) activities, rather than a gross profit and a net profit. A separate account will often be presented for the bar or any other identifiable activity on which it is intended that a profit should be made. The profit (or loss) on the bar, or dances, or whatever, will then be transferred to the main income and expenditure account.

Many small clubs and similar organisations present a *receipts and payments account* rather than an income and expenditure account. This is nothing more than a summary of the cash transactions of the organisation. A receipts and payments account may be quite adequate for a small club, though it does suffer from the disadvantage that accruals and prepayments will not be reflected in the presented receipts and payments account. Some of the cash transactions may also be for fixed assets (i.e. capital expenditure). In such a case, an increase or decrease in cash as shown in the receipts and payments account would not be equivalent to a *surplus* or *deficit* on the year's activities, though it may be presented ostensibly as such. Another disadvantage of a simple receipts and payments account is that there is no balance sheet to show the assets and liabilities of the organisation. The information provided to members and interested parties is therefore of a very limited nature. Some very small clubs will in fact quite inaccurately describe a receipts and payments account as a 'balance sheet'.

Examination questions often require the conversion of a receipts and payments account into an income and expenditure account and the preparation of a balance sheet. In many respects, therefore, this chapter is a continuation of the previous one. An opening statement of affairs is required if it is not the first year of the concern and there is no opening balance sheet. The cash/bank transactions plus other adjustments have then to be converted into an income and expenditure account and balance sheet. Indeed the cash/bank transactions are often available in a less obscure form than is sometimes found in an 'incomplete records' question of the type illustrated in the previous chapter. To be strictly accurate these questions also involve converting incomplete records into conventional double entry, albeit into an income and expenditure account rather than a trading and profit and loss account.

There are a few points in particular that should be noted when attempting an income and expenditure question in an examination.

1. The capital account is sometimes described as an *accumulated fund.* A surplus of income over expenditure for the period is added to this fund, and a deficit is deducted.

2. A gift to the concern in the form of an asset should be added directly to the accumulated fund (or capital if described as such) in the balance sheet and listed as an asset if a value is stated. It should not appear in the income and expenditure account.

3. A gift in the form of money should be added directly to the accumulated fund and not shown in the income and expenditure account if it is a large and non-recurring amount. Small gifts of money may be shown as income in the income and expenditure account if they are of little individual significance and are a regular and recurring form of income. The principle to follow is that the income and expenditure account should reflect the normal operations of the year.

4. If receipts are described as 'bar receipts' or 'dance receipts' or other 'special effort receipts', careful scrutiny is recommended to see if expenses are similarly identified. It is quite probable that the examiner is looking for a separate 'bar account' or 'dance account', the profit or loss on which should be transferred to the main income and expenditure account. Marks will be lost if the individual items are simply merged into the income and expenditure account. In the case of a bar account, stocks at the beginning and the end of the year should of course be included, as should items such as barman's wages.

5. Subscriptions in arrears in practice may not be brought in as income by clubs and societies as their eventual recovery can be very uncertain. However, if an examination question indicates an amount of subscriptions in arrears, the examiner obviously expects this amount to be brought into the accounts. An adjustment should always be made for advance payment of subscriptions.

6. Depreciation of fixed assets may or may not be required. If depreciation is required there will be some indication of this, though it may be implicit rather than explicit.

EXAMPLE 15.1

From the following information relating to the WX Club you are required to prepare:
(a) an income and expenditure account (including any profit or loss on the bar) for the year ended 31 December 19X9;
(b) a balance sheet at that date.

(i)   A summary of the cash book for the year 19X9 is as follows:

	£		£
Bank balance at			
1 January 19X9	836	Bar supplies	13,461
Annual subscriptions	3,668	Bar wages	1,099
Bar takings	15,392	Salaries and wages	1,365
Hire of rooms	146	Office expenses	424
Income from investments	315	Lighting and heating	372
Sales of investments		Rates and insurance	287
(original cost £263)	328	Miscellaneous expenses	303
		Investments	1,400
		Furniture (purchased	
		30 June 19X9)	900
		Bank balance at	
		31 December 19X9	1,074

(ii)   The balance at bank on 1 January 19X9 represented £336 on current account and £500 on deposit account. All the receipts shown in the above summary were paid into the current account except for £51 deposit account interest (included in income from investments) and all payments were made from the current account. During 19X9 £300 was transferred from the current account to the deposit account.

(iii)   The following items were outstanding at 31 December:

	19X8	19X9
	£	£
Subscriptions in arrears	79	98
Salaries and wages accrued	33	41
Creditors for bar supplies	1,217	1,325
Stock of stationery	56	65
Subscriptions in advance	14	26
Telephone account outstanding	29	37
Electricity account outstanding	31	44
Debtors for bar sales	12	49
Repairs account outstanding	9	53
Bar wages accrued	21	23
Stock of coke	40	57
Rates and insurance prepaid	62	73
Stock of bar supplies	1,422	1,989

(iv)   At 31 December 19X8 the club owned the following assets which are shown at the amounts they cost on purchase. At 31 December 19X8 they had been in the ownership of the club for the number of years indicated.

	£	
Freehold premises	6,000	12 years
Furniture	1,000	12 years
Furniture	800	5 years
Investments	3,000	4 years

(v)   The club is providing for the depreciation of freehold premises at 2½% per annum and of furniture at 10% per annum both rates being calculated on original cost.

(Adapted from a question originally set by the *Chartered Institute of Management Accountants.*)

Solution:

WX Club
Opening Statement of Affairs at 31 December 19X8

Assets			
Fixed assets	Cost	Depre-ciation	Net
	£	£	£
Freehold premises	6,000	1,800	4,200
Furniture	1,800	1,400	400
	7,800	3,200	4,600
Investments[1]			3,000
Current assets			
Stocks: Stationery		56	
Bar supplies		1,422	
Coke		40	
Debtors and prepayments[2]		153	
Bank: Deposit		500	
Current		336	
		2,507	
Current liabilities			
Creditors[2]		1,354	1,153
Capital (i.e. assets – liabilities)			8,753

Notes: 1. Investments are usually shown under a separate heading between fixed assets and current assets as above.

2.

Debtors	£	Creditors	£
Subscriptions	79	Salaries, etc.	33
Bar sales	12	Bar supplies	1,217
Rates, etc., prepaid	62	Subscriptions	14
	—	Telephone	29
	153	Electricity	31
		Repairs	9
		Bar wages	21
			1,354

WX Club
Bar Trading Account for the year ended 31 December 19X9

	£	£
Sales		15,429
Cost of sales		
Stock b/f	1,422	
Purchases	13,569	
	14,991	
less Stock c/f	1,989	13,002
Gross profit		2,427
Bar wages		1,101
Bar profit		1,326

WX Club
*Income and Expenditure Account for the
year ended 31 December 19X9*

	£	£
Income		
Subscriptions		3,675
Hire of rooms		146
Income from investments		315
Profit on sale of investments		65
Profit on bar		1,326
		5,527
Expenditure		
Salaries and wages	1,373	
Office expenses	423	
Light and heating	368	
Rates and insurance	276	
Repairs	44	
Miscellaneous expenses	303	
Depreciation – Premises	150	
Furniture[1]	125	3,062
Surplus of income		2,465

Note: 1. Calculated as full year on £800 and half year on new furniture of
£900.

WX Club
Balance Sheet as at 31 December 19X9

Assets	Cost	Depre-ciation	Net
Fixed assets			
	£	£	£
Freehold premises	6,000	1,950	4,050
Furniture	2,700	1,525	1,175
	8,700	3,475	5,225
Investments			4,137

	£	£
Current assets		
Stocks: Stationery	65	
Bar supplies	1,989	
Coke	57	
Debtors and prepayments[1]	220	
Bank: Deposit[2]	851	
Current	223	
	3,405	
Current liabilities		
Creditors[1]	1,549	1,856
		11,218

		£
Financed by		
Capital (or Accumulated Fund) balance b/f		8,753
add Surplus for year		2,465
		11,218

Notes: 1.

Debtors	£	Creditors	£
Subscriptions	98	Salaries, etc.	41
Bar sales	49	Bar supplies	1,325
Rates, etc., prepaid	73	Subscriptions	26
	——	Telephone	37
	220	Electricity	44
	====	Repairs	53
		Bar wages	23
			1,549

2. *Bank*

	£
Balance at 1 Jan. 19X9	500
add Transfer during year	300
Interest	51
	851

WX Club
Working Papers

Bar purchases

				Bar sales			
Cash	13,461	Creditors b/d	1,217	Debtors b/d	12	Cash	15,392
Creditors c/d	1,325	Bar a/c	13,569	Bar a/c	15,429	Debtors c/d	49
	14,786		14,786		15,441		15,441
		Creditors b/d	1,325	Debtors b/d	49		

Bar wages

				Subscriptions			
Cash	1,099	Accrued b/d	21	Arrears b/d	79	Prepaid b/d	14
Accrued c/d	23	Bar a/c	1,101	Prepaid c/d	26	Cash	3,668
				I and E a/c	3,675	Arrears c/d	98
	1,122		1,122		3,780		3,780
		Accrued b/d	23	Arrears b/d	98	Prepaid b/d	26

Salaries and wages

Cash	1,365	Accrued b/d	33
Accrued c/d	41	I and E a/c	1,373
	1,406		1,406
		Accrued b/d	41

Office expenses

Stock of stationery b/d	56	Phone b/d	29
Cash	424	Stock of stationery c/d	65
Phone c/d	37	I and E a/c	423
	517		517
Stock of stationery b/d	65	Phone b/d	37

Light and heat

Stock of coke b/d	40	Electricity b/d	31
Cash	372	Stock of coke c/d	57
Electricity c/d	44	I and E a/c	368
	456		456
Stock of coke b/d	57	Electricity b/d	44

Rates and insurance

Prepaid b/d	62	Prepaid c/d	73
Cash	287	I and E a/c	276
	349		349
Prepaid b/d	73		

Repairs

Accrued c/d	53	Accrued b/d	9
		I and E a/c	44
	53		53
		Accrued b/d	53

Investments

Balance b/d	3,000	Disposal	263
Cash	1,400	Balance c/d	4,137
	4,400		4,400
Balance b/d	4,137		

Profit on sale of investments

Investments	263	Cash	328
I and E a/c	65		
	328		328

Questions

15.1S   The Darset Old Comrades club makes up its accounts to 31 December in each year. On 31 December 19X8 the treasurer left the club premises and has not been seen since. An examination of the records showed that the books had not been written up for a considerable time, and it was decided to reconstruct the figures from 1 January 19X8.

A summary of the bank account for the year showed the following:

	£		£
Balance as on 1 Jan. 19X8	416	Rent and rates	460
Bank deposits	42,610	Insurance	39
		Light and heat	156
		Bar purchases	35,067
		Telephone	59
		Cash withdrawn	5,848
		Balance as on 31 Dec. 19X8	1,397
	43,026		43,026

The following information is also obtained:

(1) The barman places the takings in the bank night safe on his way home for crediting to the club account. The duplicate paying-in slips total £40,612 for the year. The treasurer had no access to bar takings or stock.

(2) The receipt counterfoils for members' subscriptions total £3,050 for the year.

(3) A summary of expenditure for petty cash and wages was as follows:

	£
Glasses, crockery and maintenance	1,310
Wages	2,658
National Insurance	210
Sundry expenses	257

(4) Outstanding amounts and prepayments at 31 December were:

	19X7	19X8
	£	£
Rates prepaid	26	28
Rent outstanding	41	82
Electricity outstanding	22	18

(5) The bar stock on 1 January 19X8 was £3,607, and on 31 December 19X8, £2,916.

You are required to prepare:

(a) A summary of the cash position for the year ended 31 December 19X8, indicating the amount, if any, to be claimed under the club's fidelity insurance policy, and

(b) an income and expenditure account for the year.

(Institute of Chartered Accountants in England and Wales)

15.2S The treasurer of the Seaside Golf Club has prepared the following receipts and payments account for the year ended 30 September, 19X0

	£		£
Balance at bank, 1 Oct. 19X9	2,548	Bar purchases	21,814
Cash in hand, 1 Oct. 19X9	65	Rent and rates	1,652
Subscriptions	6,000	Telephone	154
Entrance fees	580	Light and heat	367
Green fees	4,012	Postage and stationery	182
Bar receipts	28,805	Wages and National Insurance	5,585
		Professional's retainer	1,500
		Fertilizers and seed	1,122
		General expenses	362
		New mower	2,200
		Cash at bank, 30 Sep. 19X0	7,041
		Cash in hand, 30 Sep. 19X0	31
	42,010		42,010

You are given the following additional information:

(1) Outstanding amounts and prepayments as on 30 September were:

	19X9	19X0
	£	£
Subscriptions due but not received	150	175
Rent owing	120	140

	£	£
Rates prepaid	160	180
Bar purchases owing	250	410

You ascertain that all the 19X8/X9 outstanding subscriptions were received with the exception of those due from one member amounting to £50. This amount, together with the amount due from the same member for the year to 30 September 19X0, £55, has been included in the total of £175 subscriptions outstanding for 19X9/X0. The balance of the 19X9/X0 outstanding subscriptions was received in October 19X0.

(2) The bar stock on 30 September 19X9 was £414 and on 30 September 19X0 £355.

(3) On 30 September 19X9 the club house was valued at £30,000, fixtures and fittings were valued at £7,500 and equipment at £5,600. The new mower purchased during the year ended 30 September 19X0 actually cost £2,500; the difference between the cost and the amount shown in the receipts and payments account represents a trade-in allowance of £300 received on the old mower which had been included in the equipment at 30 September 19X9 at a value of £200.

(4) Depreciation is charged for a full year irrespective of the date of acquisition of the asset at a rate of 2% on the club house, 10% on fixtures and fittings and 20% on equipment on the reducing balance.

You are required:

(a) to prepare an income and expenditure account for the year ended 30 September 19X0 and a balance sheet as on that date, and

(b) to state why the receipts and payments account prepared by the treasurer would not be acceptable as an account of the transactions of the Seaside Golf Club.

15.3S The following bank and cash summary has been prepared from the records of the Midon Cricket Club, for the year ended 31 December 19X6.

	£		£
Balance at bank,		Bar purchases	4,129
31 December 19X5	997	Wages and National	
Cash in hand,		Insurance	741
31 December 19X5	21	Heating and lighting	110
Joining fees	56	Rent and rates	230
Subscriptions	412	Postage and stationery	75
Bar sales	5,200	Ground expenses	56
Receipts from cricket		Expenses of cricket	
festival	310	festival	114
Interest on Wessex Loan		New mowing machine	76
Stock (gross)	35	General expenses	102
		Purchase of £1,000 7%	
		Wessex Loan Stock	1,000
		Balance at bank	
		31 December 19X6	362
		Cash in hand 31 December	
		19X6	36
	7,031		7,031

You are also given the following additional information:

(1) The bar stock, at cost, on 31 December 19X6, amounted to £426, which was £29 higher than the value of stock on 1 January 19X6.

(2) On 31 December 19X6 amounts outstanding for rent, and heating and lighting, amounted to £35 and £12 respectively, whilst rates paid in advance amounted to £21. On 31 December 19X5 the corresponding amounts had been: rent £20, heating and lighting £14, and rates paid in advance £19.

(3) Fixtures and fittings on 31 December 19X5, were valued at £504. Depreciation is to be provided at a rate of 12$\frac{1}{2}$% per annum.

(4) The amount paid for the new mowing machine, purchased on 1 May 19X6, represented the net payment after taking into account a trade-in allowance of £14 on the old machine. Machines and equipment were valued at £200 on 31 December 19X5, including the old mowing machine valued at £20. Depreciation on machines and equipment is to be provided at a rate of 20% per annum.

You are required to prepare:

(a) a receipts and expenditure account for the year ended 31 December 19X6, including the net receipts from the bar and cricket festival, and

(b) a balance sheet as on that date.

(Institute of Chartered Accountants in England and Wales)

15.4S   The Alway Social Club had the following assets and liabilities as at 31 March 19X5.

		£
Assets		
	Clubhouse (at cost)	8,400
	Equipment (cost £2,300)	1,200
	Bar stocks	400
	Rates prepaid	100
	Insurance prepaid	35
	Subscriptions in arrears	16
	Cash at bank	980
	Cash in hand	10
Liabilities		
	Creditors for bar purchases	800
	Subscriptions in advance	8
	Electricity account owing	30

The treasurer seeks your assistance in preparing a forecast income and expenditure account for the period ending 31 March 19X6 and a balance sheet as at that date, and supplies you with the following information.

(i) The club has 300 members, and it is intended to raise the subscriptions from the current £4 per annum to £5 per annum. The members who have paid in advance will be allowed subscriptions at the old rates. It is anticipated that the members currently in arrears with their subscriptions will pay the arrears during the coming year.

(ii) Extensions to the clubhouse are planned which will cost an estimated £1,500. Of this sum it is anticipated that £1,000 will be paid during the year.

(iii) Some of the club's sports equipment (which cost £250 and has a written down value of £100) will be sold for an estimated £50, and replaced with new equipment costing £340. All equipment is depreciated on a straight line basis over four years, and none of the equipment is more than three years old.

(iv) Bar purchases are made monthly on credit and paid for in the month following delivery. It is anticipated that the same volume of business – which is fairly constant on a monthly basis – will be done during the coming year, but that costs will rise by 25% from 1 April 19X5. Bar stocks are normally held at the level of one-half of one month's purchases. The bar makes a gross profit margin of 20% on all sales. Bar sales are for cash which is banked daily. The bar steward, who is paid £100 per month, receives a commission of 5% of the gross profit for the year. This is paid with his final wage cheque.

(v) The club runs monthly social evenings, and charges members £1 per head admission. An average of 200 members attend each of these evenings. Expenses usually amount to 70 pence per head.

(vi) Other expenditure is estimated at:

	£
Insurance	80
Bar licence	50
Rates	500
Heat and light	250
Miscellaneous	70

The rates are paid on 1 July in respect of the following 12 months, and the insurance payment is for the period 1 October 19X5 to 30 September 19X6. All payments are made by cheque, except for the miscellaneous expenses which are paid from the imprest cash fund, which is reimbursed immediately.

Required:

(a) Prepare the estimated bank account for the year ending 31 March 19X6.

(b) Construct an estimated bar trading and profit and loss account for the year ending 31 March 19X6.

(c) Prepare an income and expenditure account for the year ending 31 March 19X6, and a balance sheet as at that date.

(Chartered Association of Certified Accountants)

15.5   The following is a summary of the Ilkton Social Club's cash book for the year ended 30 June 19X7:

Payments	£	Receipts	£
Rent	625	Bar sales	583
Rates	200	Entrance fees	60
Lighting	182	Members' subscriptions	2,220
Wages	760	Donations	350
Printing, stationery	126		
General expenses	79		
Creditors for bar purchases	430		
Improvements to club house	388		
Repairs	310		

Additional information available from the records is as follows:

	30 June 19X6	30 June 19X7
	£	£
Creditors for – Wines and spirits	190	130
Printing	12	16
Wages	27	38
Lighting	21	37
Arrears of subscriptions	89	97
Subscriptions paid in advance	45	38
Bar stock	148	123
Cash in hand	60	72
Cash at bank	210	
Premises	7,500	
Fittings (net of depreciation)	1,740	

Depreciation on fittings is to be provided at 10% on the reducing balance.

Required:
(a) A combined cash/bank account for the year ended 30 June 19X7, and
(b) An income and expenditure account for the year ended 30 June 19X7, and a balance sheet as at that date.

(Chartered Association of Certified Accountants)

15.6 The treasurer of the Walkover Cricket Club has prepared the following receipts and payments account for the year ended 31 December 19X8.

Receipts	£	Payments	£
19X8		19X8	
Jan. 1 Cash in hand	7	Dec. 31 Groundsman's wages	
Balances at bank		(including PAYE,	
Current account	159	National Insurance,	
Deposit account	617	etc.)	641
Dec. 31 Members' subscrip-		Rent of ground	100
tions	453	Repairs to pavilion	69
Bar takings	1,828	Cricket equipment	34
Surplus on dances	193	New mower (*less*	
Bank deposit		proceeds of sale of	
account interest	28	old mower £45)	155
Donation	10	Bar purchases	1,524
		Secretarial	
		expenses	47
		Insurance	48
		Cash in hand	15
		Balances at bank	
		Current account	111
		Deposit account	551
	3,295		3,295

You are given the following additional information:

(1) As on 31 December 19X7 the book values of the fixed assets were pavilion £1,450 (cost £3,200) and mower £15 (cost £135).
(2) The other current assets and liabilities were as follows:

	On 31 Dec. 19X7	On 31 Dec. 19X8
Value of bar stock at cost	131	110
Subscriptions due but not received	57	43
Creditors for bar purchases	40	33
Creditors for secretarial expenses	15	17
Insurance paid in advance	12	8
PAYE payable to Inland Revenue	5	6

(3) £150 is to be provided for depreciation of the pavilion for the year but no depreciation is to be provided on the new mower. Expenditure on cricket equipment is to be written off in the year in which it is incurred.

You are required to prepare:

(a) a statement showing the accumulated fund of the club as on 31 December 19X7,
(b) the income and expenditure account for the year ended 31 December 19X8 (showing separately the excess of bar sales over their cost), and
(c) the balance sheet as on 31 December 19X8.

(Institute of Chartered Accountants in England and Wales)

15.7   On 1 April 19X6 Homer commenced to run a small preparatory school for boys.

A separate bank account was opened for the school and the following was a summary prepared from the bank statements for the year ended 31 March 19X7:

Receipts	£	*Payments*	£
Cash paid in by Homer,		Salaries and wages	6,400
1 April 19X6	3,000	Food	3,740
Loan from Ovid,		Heating and lighting	420
30 September 19X6	1,000	Rent and rates	1,220
Fees and extras	13,420	Stationery and books	480
		Fittings and sports	
		equipment purchased	
		1 April 19X6	860
		Laundry	545
		Petty cash	620
		Balance at bank 31 March	
		19X7	2,055
		Drawings	1,080
	17,420		17,420

You are given the following information:

(1) At 31 March 19X7, cheques amounting to £300 for fees and extras had not been credited by the bank and a cheque for £60 for food had not been presented to the bank.

(2) Accounts are sent out at the beginning of each term and include fees for that term and extras incurred for the previous term. Term ended on 25 March 19X7 and on 31 March 19X7 accounts unpaid for that term amounted to £280, of which £50 is to be written off. Extras still to be charged for the term amounted to £310.

(3) The petty cash book showed the following:

Payments	£
Food	460
Stationery and books	80
Sundries	40
Cash in hand 31 March 19X7	25

Any difference is to be written off to sundries.

(4) Stocks on 31 March 19X7 amounted to: food £80, fuel £40 and stationery £60.

(5) Provision is to be made for the following amounts owing on 31 March 19X7: food £50, fuel £25.

(6) The rent paid for the premises is £800 per annum, payable half-yearly, and has been paid up to 30 June 19X7.

(7) Depreciation is to be provided on fittings and sports equipment at the rate of 10% per annum on cost.

(8) Homer is to be charged £10 per week for his personal living expenses and is to be credited with £12 per month for the use made by the school of his private motor car.

(9) Ovid's loan is to bear interest at the rate of 6% per annum. No interest had been paid up to 31 March 19X7.

(10) Simpson, the senior master, is entitled to a commission of 5% of the net profits after charging such commission.

You are required to prepare:

(a) Income and expenditure account for the year ended 31 March 19X7 and

(b) Balance sheet as on 31 March 19X7.

(Institute of Chartered Accountants in England and Wales)

15.8 The treasurer of the Bamford Country Dancing and Rambling Society has prepared the following receipts and payments account for the year ended 31 December 19X8:

Receipts	£	Payments	£
Opening balance	1,760	Purchase of amplifier	
Subscriptions (*see note* (i)):		(bought 1 July 19X8)	700
Country dancing	2,410	Country dancing:	
Rambling	1,690	Musicians' fees	900
Annual dinner – ticket sales	340	Coaching fees	820
Sale of hut	670	Hall – Rent	330
Country dancing festival –		Rates for year to	
admissions	940	31 December 19X8	800
Sales – Clothes	2,100	Decorating	110
Refreshments	8,300	Cleaning	160
		Annual rambling	
		expedition	1,320
		Annual dinner – hotel and	
		catering	410
		Country dancing festival:	
		Prizes	170
		Adjudicator's fee	90
		Purchases – Clothes	1,800
		Refreshments	7,000
		Closing balance	3,600
	18,210		18,210

Additional information:

(i) (*a*) Subscriptions

	Country dancing £	Rambling £
Received in 19X7 for 19X8	130	60
Received in 19X8 for 19X7	10	140
for 19X8	2,300	1,520
for 19X9	100	30
	2,410	1,690

(*b*) It is not the policy of the Society to take into account subscriptions in arrears until they are paid.
(ii) The hut which was sold during 19X8 had been valued at £800 on 31 December 19X7, and was used for the Society's activities until sold on 30 June 19X8.
(iii) Immediately after the sale of the hut, the Society rented a new hall at £330 per annum.
(iv) The above receipts and payments account is a summary of the Society's bank account for the year ended 31 December 19X8; the opening and closing balances shown above were the balances shown in the bank statement on 31 December 19X7 and 19X8 respectively.
(v) All cash is banked immediately and all payments are made by cheque.
(vi) A cheque for £200 drawn by the Society on 28 December 19X8, for stationery was not paid by the bank until 4 January 19X9.
(vii) The Society's assets and liabilities at 31 December 19X7 and 19X8, in addition to those mentioned earlier, were as follows:

	31 December 19X7 £	31 December 19X8 £
Stocks of goods for resale, at cost:		
Clothes	1,300	1,100
Refreshments	310	600
Sundry creditors –		
Annual dinner (catering)	–	70
Purchases – Clothes	600	400
Refreshments	300	500

The Society has now instructed its treasurer to prepare an income and expenditure account for the year ended 31 December 19X8, and a balance sheet at that date.

It is proposed to provide for depreciation on the amplifier at the rate of 20% per annum on cost, pro rata to time.

Required:
(a) The Society's income and expenditure account for the year ended 31 December 19X8, and balance sheet as at that date. Comparative figures are not required.
(b) Outline the advantages of income and expenditure accounts as compared with receipts and payments accounts.

(Chartered Association of Certified Accountants)

16 Manufacturing accounts

Aims of the chapter:

To explain how cost of production is calculated
To show how the cost of a product is built up in the final accounts of a manufacturing company

The trading and profit and loss account, together with the balance sheet, is the appropriate form of final accounts for a firm in business with the intention of buying and selling goods at a profit. In Chapter 4, mention was made of a firm making a minor modification to the goods that it is selling, and the trading and profit and loss account was again considered to be the appropriate account in which to bring together the income and expenses of the business.

The complete manufacture of goods does, however, require more comprehensive final accounts and in these circumstances a firm will prepare a *manufacturing account* in addition to the trading and profit and loss account.

In practice a manufacturing account is usually a summary of any costing records which the firm may use. The costing system should be designed around the product and the factory to suit the particular needs and objectives of management.

In general four elements of manufacturing cost are recognised in a manufacturing account. These are:

1. Direct materials		Manufacturing
2. Direct labour	Prime cost	or
3. Other direct expenses		factory
4. Factory overhead expenses		cost

Direct indicates the relationship of the cost element to the actual goods being produced. Direct materials are materials which become a physical part of the goods produced. Direct labour is the cost of labour actually working on the goods produced and excludes costs of supervision and other labour costs which cannot be associated with actual work on the product. There are rarely any other direct expenses which can be related directly to the goods produced, though a royalty calculated per unit of goods produced would be an example of this type of expense.

Factory overhead includes all factory costs which are not direct. These cover indirect labour costs (such as the wages of foremen, cleaners, maintenance men), indirect materials (such as factory cleaning materials, lubricants) and general factory overheads (such as depreciation, rent, rates, insurance, electricity).

Another way of classifying costs is by behaviour. By classifying costs in this way, patterns and trends in future situations can be forecast since costs tend to vary either with volume or with time. Costs which vary in direct proportion to output are known as variable costs, e.g. materials used. Those which vary with time and tend to be unaffected by fluctuations in volume of output are known as fixed costs, e.g. rent.

In practice many costs are semi-variable in that although they vary with output they do not do so in direct proportion, e.g. fuel costs.

In a manufacturing account as illustrated in this chapter the direct costs are largely variable while the factory overhead expenses will tend to be either fixed or semi-variable.

Texts on cost and management accounting examine cost behaviour patterns in considerable detail.

An example format of a conventional manufacturing account is as follows:

Manufacturing Account for the year ended 31 December 19X1

		£	£
	Direct materials		
	Opening stock	X	
	Purchases (net of returns)	X	
	Carriage inwards	X	
		X	
(3)	*less* Closing stock	X	
	Materials consumed		X
	Direct labour		X
	Other direct expenses (if any)		X
	Prime cost		X
(2)	Factory overhead expenses		
	Indirect labour	X	
	Lubricants	X	
	Cleaning materials	X	
	Power, light and heat	X	
	Factory rates	X	
	Plant repairs	X	
	Plant depreciation	X	
			X
			X
(1) (3)	*add* Work in progress at start		X
(1) (3)	*less* Work in progress at end		X
	Manufacturing (or factory or production) cost of goods produced		X

Notes:

(1) *Work in progress.* If the 'work in progress' is valued at 'prime cost', the adjustment for the different values of the work in progress at the beginning and at the end of the accounting period should be shown after all the direct expenses have been totalled, and before factory overhead expenses are added.

(2) *Factory overhead expenses.* Care should be taken that only factory overhead expenses are included under this heading. Expenses other than those relating to the factory are included in the profit and loss account in the usual way.

(3) *Stock.* It should be noted particularly that there are three levels of stock in a manufacturing firm. Raw material stocks and work in progress are shown in the manufacturing account; stocks of finished goods are shown in the trading account.

The trading and profit and loss account of a manufacturing concern is very similar to those described in previous chapters. An attempt is often made, however, to distinguish between *selling and distribution* expenses, *administration* expenses, and *other* or *financial* expenses in the profit and loss account.

A firm which is simply buying and selling goods, as distinct from one which is also manufacturing, might similarly arrange its profit and loss account expenses under appropriate groupings. Examination questions do seem to require this subdivision of expenses more frequently in the case of manufacturing firms.

A suggested format is shown overleaf:

Trading and Profit and Loss Account
for the year ended 31 December 19X1

	£	£	£
Sales			X
Cost of sales			
Manufacturing cost of goods		X	
Purchases from outside suppliers (if any)		X	
add Opening stock of finished goods		X	
		X	
less Closing stock of finished goods		X	X
Gross profit			X
add Discounts received			X
			X
less:			
Selling and distribution expenses			
Commission	X		
Salaries	X		
Motor expenses	X	X	
Administration expenses			
Salaries	X		
Rent, rates, insurance	X		
Heat and light	X		
Postage and stationery	X		
Depreciation of furniture and fittings	X	X	
Other expenses			
Discount allowed	X		
Bad debts	X		
Accountancy and legal fees	X	X	X
Net profit for year			X

Occasionally, in examination questions, a 'profit' is calculated on the manufacture of goods. This is sometimes done by comparing the actual production costs with the hypothetical cost of purchase from an outside supplier. Under these circumstances the manufacturing account is concluded thus:

	£
Manufacturing cost of goods produced	X
Manufacturing profit	X
Market value of goods produced	X

The manufacturing profit is then transferred to the profit and loss account. A suggested format for the trading and profit and loss account under these circumstances is shown below:

Trading and Profit and Loss Account
for the year ended 31 December 19X1

	£	£	£
Sales			X
Cost of sales			
Market value of goods produced		X	
Purchases from outside suppliers (if any)		X	
add Opening stock of finished goods[1]		X	
		X	
less Closing stock of finished goods[1]		X	X
Gross profit			X
add Profit on manufacture			X
Discounts received			X
			X
less:			
Selling and distribution expenses			
Commission	X		
Salaries	X		
Motor expenses	X	X	
Administration expenses			
Salaries	X		
Rent, rates, insurance	X		
Heat and light	X		
Postage and stationery	X		
Depreciation of furniture and fittings	X	X	
Other expenses			
Discount allowed	X		
Bad debts	X		
Accountancy and legal fees	X	X	X
Net profit for year			X

1. Stock of finished goods will include goods manufactured by the firm. These should be shown at cost, not at market value. This is sometimes done by creating a *provision for unrealised profit* on manufactured goods.

The manufacturing, trading and profit and loss account can be shown as one continuous account. This is probably the best presentation. But most students seem to find it easier at first to build up the manufacturing costs separately in the manufacturing account. It is suggested that students should prepare a separate manufacturing account unless they are completely confident of their ability to produce a continuous presentation.

An outline of a continuous presentation is given below.

Manufacturing, Trading and Profit and Loss Account
for the year ended 31 December 19X1

	£	£
Sales		X
Cost of sales		
Direct materials consumed	X	
Direct labour	X	
Direct expenses	X	
Prime cost	X	
Factory overheads	X	
	X	
add Work in progress at start	X	
	X	
less Work in progress at end	X	
Manufacturing cost	X	
Purchases (if any)	X	
	X	
add Opening stock of finished goods	X	
	X	
less Closing stock of finished goods	X	X
Gross profit		X
Selling and distribution expenses	X	
Administration expenses	X	
Other expenses	X	X
Net profit		X

EXAMPLE 16.1

From the following information prepare the manufacturing, trading and profit and loss accounts for the year ending 31 December 19X6 and the balance sheet as at 31 December 19X6 for the firm of J. Jones.

	£	£
Purchase of raw materials	258,000	
Fuel and light	21,000	
Administration salaries	17,000	
Factory wages	59,000	
Carriage outwards	4,000	
Rent and rates	21,000	
Sales		482,000
Returns inward	7,000	
General office expenses	9,000	
Repairs to plant and machinery	9,000	
Stock at 1 January 19X6		
Raw materials	21,000	
Work in progress	14,000	
Finished goods	23,000	
Sundry creditors		37,000
Capital account		457,000
Freehold premises	410,000	
Plant and machinery	80,000	
Debtors	20,000	
Provision for depreciation on plant and machinery at 1 January 19X6		8,000
Cash in hand	11,000	
	984,000	984,000

Make provision for the following:

(a) Stock in hand at 31 December 19X6

	£
Raw materials	25,000
Work in progress	11,000
Finished goods	26,000

(b) Depreciation of 10% on plant and machinery – straight line method
(c) 80% of fuel and light and 75% of rent and rates to be charged to manufacturing
(d) Doubtful debts provision – 5% of sundry debtors
(e) £4,000 outstanding for fuel and light
(f) Rent and rates paid in advance – £5,000
(g) Market value of finished goods – £382,000.

Solution:

J. Jones
Manufacturing Account for the year ended
31 December 19X6

	£	£
Direct materials		
Stock at 1 January 19X6	21,000	
Purchases	258,000	
	279,000	
less Stock at 31 December 19X6	25,000	254,000
Direct labour		59,000
Prime cost		313,000
Factory overhead expenses		
Fuel and light	20,000	
Rent and rates	12,000	
Repairs to plant and machinery	9,000	
Depreciation on plant and machinery	8,000	49,000
		362,000
add Work in progress 1 January 19X6		14,000
		376,000
less Work in progress 31 December 19X6		11,000
Manufacturing cost of goods produced		365,000
Manufacturing profit		17,000
Market value of goods produced		382,000

J. Jones
Trading and Profit and Loss Account
for the year ended 31 December 19X6

	£	£
Sales		482,000
less Returns		7,000
		475,000
Cost of sales		
Market value of goods produced	382,000	
add Stock of finished goods 1 January 19X6	23,000	
	405,000	
less Stock of finished goods 31 December 19X6	26,000	
		379,000
Gross profit		96,000
add Profit on manufacturer		17,000
		113,000

	£		
less:			
Selling and distribution expenses			
Carriage outwards	4,000	4,000	
Administration expenses			
Salaries	17,000		
Office expenses	9,000		
Fuel and light	5,000		
Rent and rates	4,000	35,000	
Other expenses			
Doubtful debts provision	1,000	1,000	40,000
Net profit			73,000

Note: Wages described as 'factory wages' or 'productive wages' or 'manufacturing wages' should be regarded as 'direct' labour costs unless otherwise indicated. 'Factory salaries' (as distinct from 'administrative' or 'office salaries') should be regarded as factory overheads.

It has been assumed that stocks of finished goods have been valued at cost, rather than market value.

J. Jones
Balance Sheet as at 31 December 19X6

Assets	Cost	Depre-ciation	Net
Fixed assets			
	£	£	£
Freehold premises	410,000	–	410,000
Plant and machinery	80,000	16,000	64,000
	490,000	16,000	474,000
Current assets			
Stock			
Raw materials	25,000		
Work in progress	11,000		
Finished goods	26,000	62,000	
Debtors	20,000		
less provision	1,000	19,000	
Prepayment		5,000	
Cash		11,000	
		97,000	
less Current liabilities			
Creditors		41,000	
Net current assets			56,000
			530,000
Financed by			
Capital			457,000
add Profit for year			73,000
			530,000

Questions

16.1S   N. Jones manufactures one product. His trial balance at 30 April 19X1 was as follows:

	£	£
Capital account – balance at 1 May 19X0		105,000
Current account – balance at 1 May 19X0		21,800
Drawings	10,000	
Fixed assets at cost	120,000	
Depreciation on fixed assets		48,000
Stocks at 1 May 19X0		
Materials	8,000	
Work in progress	6,300	
Finished goods	43,000	
Debtors and creditors	30,600	9,000
Provision for doubtful debts at 1 May 19X0		1,250
Sales		220,000
Purchases of materials	82,000	
Manufacturing wages	40,000	
Manufacturing expenses	20,800	
Administration expenses	13,950	
Selling and distribution expenses	21,400	
Cash at bank and in hand	9,000	
	405,050	405,050

Notes:
1. Stocks at 30 April 19X1 were: materials £10,000, work in progress £6,300, finished goods £39,000.
2. Depreciation is to be provided on fixed assets at the rate of 10% per annum on cost. The annual depreciation charge is to be apportioned among manufacturing, administration, and selling and distribution in the proportions of 8:1:1.
3. Bad debts of £600 are to be written off and the provision for doubtful debts is to be increased to £1,500. These items are a selling and distribution expense.
4. Accruals and prepayments at 30 April 19X1 were:

	Accruals	Prepayments
	£	£
Administration expenses	200	100
Selling and distribution expenses	700	100

You are required:
(a) to prepare a manufacturing, trading and profit and loss account for the year to 30 April 19X1, and a balance sheet as at that date;
(b) to state what is meant by the term 'direct' in each of the elements of prime cost.

16.2S Black and White are in partnership as flowerpot manufacturers, Black being responsible for the factory and White for the sales department.

Finished goods are transferred immediately from the factory to the sales department at cost plus two-sevenths. Black and White are credited with two-thirds of the factory and sales department profits respectively, the balance of the firm's profit being shared equally. No interest is credited or charged on capital accounts or drawings.

The following trial balance was extracted as on 31 December 19X5:

	£	£
Capital accounts		
Black		3,460
White		4,150
Drawings		
Black	1,700	
White	2,100	
Freehold factory at cost (including site £6,000)	8,500	
Provision for depreciation thereon to 31 December 19X4		500
Gas ovens and factory equipment at cost	750	
Provision for depreciation thereon to 31 December 19X4		300
Delivery vans, at cost	1,250	
Provision for depreciation thereon to 31 December 19X4		500
Stocks at cost, 31 December 19X4:		
Raw materials	750	
Finished goods	2,000	
Trade debtors and creditors	2,300	1,800
Provision for doubtful debts		150
Bank	475	
Purchases of raw materials	2,750	
Wages	6,200	
Gas	700	
Rates and insurance (factory)	225	
Sundry expenses (factory)	700	
Advertising	225	
Delivery van running expenses	485	
Sales		20,250
	31,110	31,110

Stocks held on 31 December 19X5, cost £2,000, including raw materials, £500. On that date there were accrued expenses: gas £300 and advertising £75. Rates, £50, and van licences, £35, were prepaid.

The two men employed in the sales department had been paid £600 each during the year.

Of the trade debtors £50, for which provision had previously been made, is to be written off. The provision otherwise is considered adequate.

Provision for depreciation is to be made at the following rates per annum, calculated on cost:

Factory building	2%
Gas ovens and factory equipment	10%
Delivery vans	20%

You are required to prepare:

(a) accounts for the year ended 31 December 19X5, showing:

    (i) prime cost,

    (ii) factory cost of goods produced,

    (iii) profit of the factory and of the sales department, and

    (iv) appropriation of profits, and

(b) the balance sheet as on that date.

(Institute of Chartered Accountants in England and Wales)

16.3S Field, Meadow and Park are partners in a manufacturing business sharing profits and losses: Field four-sevenths, Meadow two-sevenths and Park one-seventh. Park's annual share of the net profit is to be a minimum of £5,000, any deficiency being borne by the other two partners in their profit sharing ratios. No interest is allowed or charged on partners' current accounts but fixed capitals carry interest at 10% per annum.

The firm's trial balance as on 31 December 19X2 was as follows:

	£		£	£
Freehold premises at cost	22,000	Capital accounts:		
Plant and machinery at		Field	10,000	
cost	16,000	Meadow	7,000	
Motor vehicles at cost	3,400	Park	3,000	20,000
Purchases	46,000	Current accounts		
Stock 1 January 19X2	12,400	Field	2,400	
Manufacturing wages	14,400	Meadow	1,100	3,500
Carriage inwards	840	Sales		104,000
Discounts allowed	980	Motor vehicle –		
Salaries	6,100	proceeds of sale		600
Office expenses	2,450	Creditors		4,600
Repairs	1,210	Provision for doubtful		
Debtors	9,400	debts 1 January 19X2		840
Balance at bank	2,360	Provision for depreci-		
Current account – Park	600	ation 1 January 19X2:		
		Plant and machinery		3,200
		Motor vehicles		1,400
	138,140			138,140

You are given the following information:

(1) Stock on hand on 31 December 19X2 amounted to £13,600.

(2) Sales included £1,800 for goods sent out on sale or return, charged to customers at cost plus 25% and which remained in their hands unsold as on 31 December 19X2.

(3) The following amounts, included in salaries, had been drawn each month by the partners:

    Field £100   Meadow £60   Park £40.

(4) Repairs included an amount of £600 for the reconditioning of a machine which it is agreed should be capitalised.

(5) Provision is to be made for bonuses as follows:

    Factory £800   Office £1,400.

(6) Depreciation on plant and machinery and on motor vehicles is to be

provided at the rate of 10% and 25% per annum, respectively, calculated on cost at the end of the year.

(7) A debt of £210 is to be written off and the provision for doubtful debts increased to £1,000.

(8) The motor vehicle sold during the year for £600 had cost £1,400 and had been written down to £400. Any profit or loss on the sale is to be credited or charged in the profit and loss account.

You are required to prepare:

(a) trading and profit and loss account for the year ended 31 December 19X2,

(b) balance sheet as on that date, and

(c) partners' current accounts for the year.

(Institute of Chartered Accountants in England and Wales)

16.4   Rock was the sole proprietor of a sweet manufacturing business and the following trial balance was extracted from his books as on 31 December 19X7:

	Dr. £	Cr. £
Capital account: Rock		20,400
Freehold land and buildings at cost	15,000	
Plant and machinery at cost	14,500	
Plant and machinery, provision for depreciation		7,000
Travellers' cars at cost	4,000	
Travellers' cars, provision for depreciation		2,800
Loose tools and utensils at valuation on 1 January 19X7	1,200	
Stocks, 1 January 19X7		
Raw materials	3,300	
Finished goods (25 tons)	6,000	
Purchases		
Raw materials	18,500	
Tools and utensils	800	
Sales 210 tons		66,000
Wages		
Factory	13,640	
Administration	5,400	
Sales department	3,000	
Rates and insurance	1,600	
Repairs to buildings	1,000	
Sales expenses including vehicle running costs	1,440	
Electricity and power	6,000	
Administration expenses	2,810	
Provision for doubtful debts		1,000
Sales ledger balances	6,100	
Purchase ledger balances		3,580
Bank		3,610
Cash in hand	100	
	104,390	104,390

You are given the following information:
(1) Closing stocks on 31 December 19X7: raw materials £2,800; finished goods (15 tons) £3,900; loose tools and utensils, £1,600.
(2) Provision is to be made for the following amounts owing on 31 December 19X7: electricity and power £800, new machinery £500.
(3) Payments in advance on 31 December 19X7, were as follows: rates £300, vehicle licences £40.
(4) Annual depreciation on plant and machinery and travellers' cars is to be provided at the rate of 15% and 20% respectively on cost at the end of the year.
(5) Bad debts amounting to £500 are to be written off and the provision for doubtful debts reduced to £600.
(6) Expenses are to be allotted as follows:

	Works	Administration
Rates and insurance	7/10	3/10
Repairs	4/5	1/5
Electricity and power	9/10	1/10

Adjustments for bad debts and the provision for doubtful debts are attributable to selling and delivery expenses.

You are required to prepare:

(a) the manufacturing, trading and profit and loss accounts for the year ended 31 December 19X7, showing the works cost and administration cost per ton produced, and
(b) the balance sheet as on that date.

(Institute of Chartered Accountants in England and Wales)

16.5   Green, Hill and Smith are partners in a manufacturing business sharing profits and losses: Green two-fifths, Hill two-fifths and Smith one-fifth. Smith's annual share of profit is to be a minimum of £2,000, any deficiency being borne by the other two partners in their profit sharing ratios. No interest is allowed or charged on partners' current accounts but fixed capital accounts carry interest at 6% per annum.

The firm's trial balance as on 31 March 19X6 was as follows:

	£		£	£
Freehold premises at cost	9,000	Capital accounts:		
Plant and machinery at		Green	8,000	
cost	8,000	Hill	6,000	
Motor vehicles	2,400	Smith	3,000	17,000
Purchases	38,000			
Stock 1 April 19X5	7,200	Current accounts,		
Manufacturing wages	8,200	1 April 19X5:		
Trade expenses	600	Green	1,800	
Salaries	5,400	Hill	600	2,400
Repairs	1,200			
Cash discounts	240	Sales		67,800
Office expenses	3,600	Creditors		4,200
Carriage inwards	620	Provision for		
Carriage outward	800	doubtful debts,		
Rates and insurance	1,400	1 April 19X5		340
Professional charges	400	Cash discounts		420
Debtors	6,800	Provision for		
Balance at bank	800	depreciation on		
Current account 1 April		1 April 19X5:		
19X5:		Plant and		
Smith	1,100	machinery		2,400
		Motor vehicles		1,200
	95,760			95,760

You are given the following information:

(1) Stock on hand on 31 March 19X6 amounted to £6,480.
(2) Sales included £2,400 for goods sent out on sale or return, charged to customers at cost plus 20% and which remained in their hands unsold on 31 March 19X6.
(3) The following amounts, included in salaries, have been drawn each month by the partners:

> Green £50   Hill £40   Smith £25.

(4) It was agreed that a charge of £250 should be made to Hill for goods supplied to him from stock during the year.
(5) Green, who acted as traveller, is to be credited with an expenses allowance of £200.
(6) Repairs include an item of £750 for alterations to the offices, which amount it is agreed should be capitalised.
(7) Rates and insurance paid in advance amounted to £500 and office expenses accrued amounted to £120.
(8) A motor vehicle costing £900 had been purchased during the year against which £600 had been allowed on the sale of an old vehicle, the net amount only being debited to motor vehicles account. The vehicle sold had cost £750 and had been written down to £250. Any profit or loss on sale of this vehicle is to be credited or charged in the profit and loss account.
(9) Depreciation on plant and machinery and motor vehicles is to be provided at the rate of 10% and 20% per annum respectively on the cost at the end of the year.
(10) A debt of £60 is to be written off and the provision for doubtful debts increased to £450.

You are required to prepare:

(a) the trading and profit and loss account for the year ended 31 March 19X6.
(b) the balance sheet as on that date, and
(c) the partners' current accounts, in columnar form, for the year.

(Institute of Chartered Accountants in England and Wales)

Note: Although this question does not ask for a manufacturing account to be prepared, students must give careful thought when dealing with manufacturing businesses.

Further questions requiring the preparation of manufacturing accounts can be found amongst those at the end of the chapter on limited companies (Ch. 17).

17 Limited companies

Aims of the chapter:

To consider the nature of limited liability
To explain the capital structure of a company
To discuss taxation in company accounts
To look at the accounting requirements

Introduction

So far in our studies we have been considering businesses with unlimited liability. This means that in the event of a business closing down any creditors can sue for the full amount they are owed, regardless of the net worth of the business. In other words, the courts can go behind the business and seize the personal assets of the owners if necessary.

From an accounting point of view the business and the owner(s) should always be kept separate – hence the very nature of capital being a debt owed by the business to the owner. This is the business entity concept. However, legally, for sole traders and partnerships the owners (other than limited partners) do not have a separate identity from the business and do not enjoy limited liability.

During the period of rapid business expansion during the reign of Queen Victoria unlimited liability was seen as a severe disincentive for the smaller investor, who stood to lose almost everything in the event of a business failure. To overcome this problem in order to encourage investment in the large new undertakings such as railways and electricity, the Limited Liability Act 1855 and the first Companies Act of 1862 were passed. These Acts recognised the principles of limited liability and the separate legal identity of a limited liability company – the corporate body.

Companies Acts

Since the original Act many changes and additions have been made. The 1948 Companies Act was a very important one as it consolidated all the previous ones. This was then superseded by the Companies Act 1985 which again consolidated all the legislation and came into effect on 1 July 1985. Almost every year a further Companies Act is passed which either amends points already covered or extends the provisions. In order to comply with the accounting requirements of these Acts most limited companies adapt their systems to provide the necessary details.

Types of company

Limited companies can be either public or private. Section 1 of the Companies Act 1985 defines a *public company* as one which, amongst other things,

(a) has a minimum authorised share capital of £50,000;
(b) publishes its accounts (usually on an annual basis);
(c) includes in its name 'plc' or 'public limited company', or the Welsh equivalent (ccc) if registered in Wales.

Any company which does not meet all the requirements is therefore by definition a *private limited company*, although it must still include 'limited' or 'Ltd' in its name to protect the public and creditors.

The essential difference between the two types is that a private company may not offer shares and debentures to the general public, i.e. invite the public to subscribe.

Forming a company

The promoters, of which there must be at least two, who wish to float a new company must submit a *memorandum of association* and *articles of association* to the Registrar of Companies.

The memorandum of association gives details of the way in which the company will relate to the outside world, defining its powers, constitution and objects. These may only be altered within limits contained in the Companies Acts. The articles of association contain the internal regulations for the way the company is managed. Table A of the Companies Act gives a model set of articles for those companies who do not wish to submit their own. In most cases the articles contained in Table A are adopted.

Once the memorandum and articles have been accepted by the registrar, together with a statutory declaration that all the requirements of the Acts have been met, a certificate of incorporation is issued. This gives the company a separate legal status. This legal entity is not affected by changes in the membership (shareholders). From this point the company can enter into contracts, sue or be sued in its own name.

In the case of a trading company sufficient capital must then be raised before the registrar will grant a trading certificate to allow the business to begin operations. To do this it is necessary to issue a prospectus giving details of the company and its objects, together with an application form for prospective investors.

Company law

Under the terms of the Companies Acts the following additional points apply:

1. The liability of each individual shareholder (member) is limited to the amount paid or agreed to be paid for the shares held;

2. The number of members is limited only by the total authorised share capital, although there must be a minimum of two;
3. Management of the company is in the hands of elected or delegated directors;
4. Accounts in one of the prescribed formats must be filed annually with the registrar and be available for inspection by the public;
5. Proper books of accounts must be maintained and audited annually;
6. Company profits are subject to corporation tax;
7. Recognised accounting principles must be followed – see the Appendix for details;
8. The powers of the company as set out in the memorandum of association can only be altered within certain limits.

Accounting standards

In addition to the legal requirements, accountants (and limited companies) are expected to follow certain guidelines. The Accounting Standards Board (ASB), in consultation with the profession and other interested bodies, formulates and revises financial reporting standards (FRSs) which cover many aspects. The Companies Act 1985 makes it a legal requirement for all medium- to large-sized companies to comply with the standards. Furthermore, any member of a professional accounting body may be subject to the institute's own disciplinary procedures if standards are not followed. As an additional safeguard the Financial Reporting Council was set up as a result of the Companies Act 1989. The FRC is independent of the profession and oversees the work of the ASB.

There are also International Accounting Standards which attempt to rationalise accounting practices between countries, and European Directives to harmonise accounting within the Community. For example the required lay-out for published accounts as shown in the Companies Acts complies with the fourth directive of the EEC, and the Companies Act 1989 incorporates the seventh and eighth directives, which deal with consolidated accounts and regulation of auditors. Statements of Recommended Practice (SORPs) cover what is considered to be the best practice in other areas of accounting, charities for example.

Capital

Unlike a sole trader or partnership the capital of a company is usually made up of several elements comprising subscribed capital, reserves and long-term borrowings. The following example will illustrate this.

EXAMPLE 17.1

XYZ PLC Balance Sheet (extract) on 31 December 19XX

	£	£
Capital and reserves		
Authorised		
100,000 £1 ordinary shares		100,000
50,000 5% £1 preference shares		50,000
		150,000
Allotted		
50,000 £1 ordinary shares, 50p paid		25,000
25,000 5% £1 preference shares		25,000
		50,000
Reserves		
Share premium	20,000	
Capital redemption	10,000	
General	5,000	
Profit and loss	15,000	50,000
Shareholders' equity		100,000
Long-term liabilities		
7% Debentures		20,000
Capital employed		120,000

We will now consider each of these and other items which do not appear in Example 17.1 but are relevant and may appear in a company balance sheet.

Authorised capital

This is the maximum amount which a company can issue as specified in the memorandum. It is also known as the *nominal* capital because it is divided into shares of a fixed face, nominal or par value. The authorised capital is always shown in accounts at the nominal value regardless of the actual market value.

Shares

Shares can be of various types, the two main ones being *ordinary* and *preference*. Holding shares in a company gives the shareholder part ownership of the company, the share of ownership being in proportion to the number and value of shares held.

Ordinary shares

These shares carry most of the risk associated with capital investment, but stand to earn higher dividends when profits are good. Voting rights are usually *pro rata* to the number of shares held, although some companies restrict votes to certain classes of shares to retain control in the hands of the original promoters.

Preference shares

The rights of preference shareholders are set out in the memorandum and articles of association. These shares usually give priority to payment of dividends at a fixed rate (based on the nominal value) and repayment of capital in the event of a winding-up of the company.

Unless specifically stated preference shares are cumulative. This means that any arrears of dividend arising from insufficient profits are carried forward until there are adequate profits available to pay the amount outstanding.

In order to compensate preference shareholders when there are high profits such shares can also be participating, and carry an entitlement to additional dividends when profits exceed a certain level.

Preference shares usually carry restricted or no voting rights in decisions about the way the company is run since action could be sanctioned which was detrimental to the ordinary shareholders.

Stocks and shares

Some companies refer to their ordinary shares as ordinary stock. This term is used to denote a block of share capital. Shares can only be converted to stock after they have been issued and fully paid.

Allotted (issued) share capital

A company does not necessarily *allot* all its shares at once, but will raise as much capital as it requires for the foreseeable future. Shares not allotted can be offered to the public through a prospectus as and when necessary, although some of the authorised capital may never be allotted.

Both authorised and allotted shares must be detailed in the balance sheet but if they are the same they can be shown under one heading.

Allotted shares are sometimes referred to as *issued* shares.

Partly paid shares

In order to encourage shareholders to invest, or to phase receipts of capital over a longer period, shares may be issued in such a way that they are paid for by way of an initial deposit on application, a further instalment when they are allotted and subsequent calls as and when decided.

Until such time as the full value of the share has been paid the shares must be shown on the balance sheet as partly paid with a note of the total paid to date. Any outstanding balance is a liability of the shareholder and can be called in when required. This allows a company to obtain extra funding without the expense of a new issue which involves the costs of preparing a prospectus and advertising the offer.

A more detailed explanation of shares and partly paid shares will be found in Chapter 19.

Reserves

Reserves are sums set aside from profits or income for a specific or general purpose. Certain reserves, often referred to as capital reserves, cannot be distributed to the shareholders.

The two main capital reserves are *share premium* and *capital redemption*.

Share premium reserve

This arises when shares are issued by a company for more than their face value. For example, a £1 share is offered for sale at £2.50. In this case £1 will be shown on the balance sheet as share capital and £1.50 will appear as the share premium. This amount has been subscribed by the shareholder as part of the capital and so cannot be distributed as a dividend, although it can be used for an issue of bonus shares, or to provide the premium payable on redemption of debentures, or to write off the preliminary expenses of forming the company.

Capital redemption reserve

This reserve is created when issued shares are bought back or redeemed by the company out of profits. The Companies Act 1985 requires a sum equal to the nominal value of any purchased or redeemed shares to be transferred to reserves to protect the creditors. If this were not done profits could be distributed with the effect of reducing the capital. This reserve may also be used for bonus shares but otherwise it must be treated as paid-up share capital.

Other reserves

The directors are normally empowered to set aside sums from profits for general or specific purposes, e.g. fixed asset replacement. This retains profits in the company to increase the overall capital invested. Any balance shown on the profit and loss account after all distributions have been made together with the balance brought forward from previous years is included as the final reserve. The issued capital and all reserves form the total capital invested by the shareholders – the shareholders' equity.

Debentures

Where a company is empowered by the memorandum to raise loans it may do so by issuing debentures which carry a fixed rate of interest. They do not form part of the shareholders' capital nor do they carry any voting rights. The interest is a normal business expense in the profit and loss account and must be paid whether or not a profit is made.

To distinguish debentures from shares such capital is sometimes referred to as loan capital.

Provisions

It is important to distinguish provisions from reserves, both of which are sums set aside from profits. However, a provision is an amount written off or retained to provide for some known expense or liability such as depreciation, renewals or reduction in value of an asset, the exact amount of which cannot be accurately determined. Any charge for an increase in a provision will appear as an expense in the profit and loss account, whereas transfers to reserves are made in the appropriation section after the profit or loss for the period has been calculated. In the balance sheet, provisions are generally deducted from the asset to which they relate.

Annual general meeting

Every limited company must convene at least one meeting each year, the AGM. At this meeting the shareholders (the owners) consider the annual accounts and chairman's report, as well as electing directors and auditors for the following year. Any amendments to the articles which are felt appropriate will also be voted on at this meeting. If a matter is felt to be so urgent that the directors or the members do not think it appropriate to wait until the next AGM an extraordinary meeting can be arranged.

Company taxation

Company profits are subject to corporation tax, although the profit and loss figure is not necessarily the profit figure upon which tax is payable. Adjustments have to be made to assess the taxable profit. These adjustments include writing back expenses which are disallowed, such as certain entertaining and legal expenses; the treatment of depreciation on fixed assets which is operated by the Inland Revenue as capital allowances; and adjustments to stock valuation figures if the particular methods used by a company are not allowed for tax purposes.

Note that tax is never allowed as an expense and cannot therefore be included in the profit and loss account as such.

In addition to payment of corporation tax a company is also responsible for collecting the income tax element of debenture interest and royalties. Payments of debenture interest and royalties are therefore made net of income tax at the basic rate. There is no further obligation on the recipient unless the recipient is a higher rate tax payer. If a company itself receives net debenture interest or royalties the tax so deducted can be set off against the corporation tax due. The income must be shown gross in the profit and loss account and is referred to as unfranked investment income.

Advance corporation tax

When dividends are paid out no distinct tax deductions are made. However, dividends are paid out of the balance of profits after corporation tax has been deducted. Shareholders therefore receive a tax credit equal to

$$\frac{\text{basic rate of income tax}}{100 - \text{basic rate of income tax}}$$

of the dividend received. Assuming basic rate to be 25% this gives a tax credit equal to one-third of the dividend.

When dividends are actually paid out, as opposed to declared, a company is required to make an advance payment of corporation tax (ACT) at the above rate (i.e. equal to the total of tax credits). ACT is payable within three months of the dividend payment. The balance of corporation tax after deducting ACT is called mainstream corporation tax (MCT). The amount of ACT which can be deducted or recovered is limited to an amount equal to the basic rate of income tax applied to the profits. The following example will explain this last point.

EXAMPLE 17.2

A company pays total dividends in a year of £420,000. Assessed taxable profits are £500,000. Corporation tax and basic rate of income tax are 35% and 25% respectively.

	£	£
ACT (25/75 of £420,000)		140,000
Corporation tax due		
35% × £500,000	175,000	
Less ACT limit		
25% × £500,000	125,000	
Mainstream tax due		50,000
Total corporation tax paid		190,000

Payment of corporation tax

Mainstream corporation tax is due nine months after the end of the company's year-end. At the balance sheet date any corporation tax liability will be shown as a short-term liability payable within twelve months, as will any proposed dividends which have not yet been paid.

Deferred tax

As indicated previously, the corporation tax liability is not based simply on the accounting profit. Where the amount of tax due is substantially less than indicated by the profit, and there is good reason to believe that the difference will be due at some time in the future, an additional transfer can be made to a deferred taxation account. This usually arises as a result of timing differences in the treatment of capital allowances relating to acquisition and disposal of fixed assets.

When the tax does eventually fall due a corresponding sum can be transferred back to the appropriation account.

Company accounts

The format and contents of the accounts to be deposited at Companies House are detailed in Schedule 4 of the Companies Act 1985. Full disclosure of all profit and loss items are not required as this would give competitors an unfair advantage. However, for internal purposes a company must clearly draft a full set of accounts. Example 17.3 illustrates this.

EXAMPLE 17.3

E. Maycock and Company Limited
Trading and Profit and Loss Account
for the year to 31 December 19XX

	£	£	£
Sales			X
less Cost of sales			X
Gross profit			X
Selling and distribution:			
Carriage outwards	X		
Motor expenses	X		
Depreciation of motor vehicles	X	X	
Administration:			
Directors' emoluments (Note 1)	X		
Salaries	X		
Rent	X		
Rates	X		
Insurance	X		
Heating and lighting	X		
Repairs	X		
Telephone	X		
Postages and stationery	X		
Depreciation:			
Freehold land and buildings	X		
Leasehold land and buildings	X		
Furniture and fittings	X		
Legal and professional charges	X	X	
Finance:			
Interest on debentures (Note 1)	X		
Bank interest	X		
Discount allowed	X		
Bad debts	X		
Provision for doubtful debts	X	X	X
Net profit before taxation			X
Taxation on profits for the year:			
Corporation tax at % (Note 2)			X
Net profit for the year after taxation			X
Appropriation of profit: (Note 3)			
Transfer to general reserve		X	
Dividends: (Note 3)			
Paid: Half-year's preference dividend %	X		
Interim dividend on ordinary shares %	X		
Proposed: Half-year's preference dividend %	X		
Final dividend on ordinary shares %	X	X	X
Unappropriated profit for the year (Note 3)			X
Add retained profit brought forward			X
Retained profit carried forward			X

E. Maycock and Company Limited
Balance Sheet as at 31 December 19XX

Assets

Fixed assets	Cost	Depre-ciation	Net
	£	£	£
Freehold land and buildings	X	X	X
Leasehold land and buildings	X	X	X
Furniture and fittings	X	X	X
Motor vehicles	X	X	X
	X	X	X

Current assets		
Stock		X
Debtors		X
Cash at bank and in hand		X
		X

less Current liabilities		
Creditors	X	
Corporation tax	X	
Proposed dividends	X	X
Net current assets		X
		X

Financed by

Share capital	Author-ised	Allotted and fully paid
	£	£
% Preference shares of £ each	X	X
Ordinary shares of £ each	X	X
	X	X

Reserves		
Share premium account	X	
General reserve	X	
Profit and loss account	X	X
Shareholders' funds		X
% Debentures		X
		X

Some of the items shown in the specimen accounts of E. Maycock and Company Limited will not have been met with previously. Detailed comments on those items are now given.

Notes:

1. *Profit and loss account*

Two items of expense peculiar to limited companies are:

(a) Directors' emoluments
(b) Interest on debentures.

Directors' emoluments refers to the total salaries, fees, etc., paid to the directors for managing the business. In this respect they are employees of the company, and their salaries, etc., are a normal charge against the profits.

Unlike a shareholder who is part owner of the company, a debenture holder is a creditor of the company. Any interest paid to debenture holders is chargeable against the company's profits before corporation tax is assessed. Debenture interest must always be shown *gross* (i.e. before the deduction of income tax) in the profit and loss account.

2. *Taxation on profits for the year*

Corporation tax based on the profits of the year is a first charge against a company's net profit and is shown in the profit and loss account as a deduction from that figure. Although corporation tax is shown as a percentage, it does not mean that the tax payable is a percentage of the net profit as shown in the accounts.

3. *Appropriation of profit*

Profit after taxation belongs to the company's shareholders but the articles of association generally contain clauses to the following effects:

(a) The directors may, before recommending any dividend, set aside profits as a reserve or carry forward the whole of the profits to the following year.
(b) The company (i.e. the shareholders) in general meeting may declare dividends but no dividend shall exceed the amount recommended by the directors.
(c) The directors may pay interim dividends to the shareholders.

An interim dividend is one which is paid on account of the full year's dividend at any time between two annual general meetings.

Distributable profits

The Companies Act 1985 defines the amount of profit which may be legally distributed by a company. Whilst students should be aware of the existence of a legal definition of distributable profits, the complex calculations are beyond the scope of this book. But it should again be noted that certain reserves are classed as undistributable reserves. The more usual reserves so classified are:

(a) the share premium account
(b) the capital redemption reserve

Those reserves not classed as undistributable reserves are, of course, distributable by the company. Examples of distributable reserves are the credit balance on the profit and loss account or a general reserve account.

Proposed dividends

Proposed dividends are subject to ratification by the members in general meeting which will of necessity take place some time after the end of the accounting period. Proposed dividends must, therefore, always be debited to profit and loss appropriation account and shown in the balance sheet as a current liability.

Unappropriated profit or retained profit

As previously mentioned, a limited company does not necessarily, and indeed does not usually, distribute all its profits. The amount unappropriated is carried forward as a credit balance on the profit and loss account and shown in the balance sheet as a *reserve*.

A further worked example illustrates the previous points.

EXAMPLE 17.4

The following trial balance has been prepared at 31 December 19X0, from the books of account of S. Bradshaw Limited, traders:

	£	£
8% Preference share capital – shares £1 each		100,000
Ordinary share capital – shares £1 each		200,000
Share premium account		40,000
Profit and loss account – balance at 31 December 19X9		138,300
10% Debentures 19X6–19X7		100,000
Bank overdraft		72,400
Leasehold property: at cost	210,000	
amortisation of leasehold (Note)		20,000
Fixtures and fittings: at cost	300,000	
provision for depreciation		90,000
Motor vehicles: at cost	64,000	
provision for depreciation		16,000
Trade debtors and creditors	192,000	49,000
Sales		2,350,000

	£	£
Cost of goods sold	1,565,000	
Directors' emoluments	45,000	
Wages and salaries	322,000	
Rates and insurance	43,800	
Motor expenses	53,000	
Heating and lighting	40,600	
Telephone	16,400	
Debenture interest – six months to 30 June 19X0	5,000	
Bank overdraft interest	8,900	
Discounts allowed and received	17,000	12,000
Preference dividend – half-year to 30 June 19X0	4,000	
Interim dividend on ordinary shares at 5%	10,000	
Stock of goods at cost	250,000	
Advertising	41,000	
	3,187,700	3,187,700

Note: Amortisation is the term used for the allocation of the cost of a lease over its life. It is treated in the same way as depreciation.

Additional information:
The authorised share capital of the company is:

> 100,000 8% Preference shares of £1 each
> 400,000 Ordinary shares of £1 each.

Accruals and prepayments at 31 December 19X0 were:

	Accruals £	Prepayments £
Directors' emoluments	5,000	
Heating and lighting	3,200	
Telephone	1,300	
Advertising	4,000	
Rates and insurance		5,200
Motor expenses		4,200

Depreciation is to be provided as follows:

> Amortisation of leasehold property – £10,000
> Fixtures and fittings – 10% on cost
> Motor vehicles – 25% on cost

The debenture interest for the six months to 31 December 19X0 was paid on 5 January 19X1.

Corporation tax at 35%, based on the year's profit, is estimated at £52,000.

The directors have decided to transfer £30,000 to a general reserve and are recommending that the preference dividend for the half-year to 31

December 19X0 should be paid together with a final dividend of 10% on the ordinary share capital for the year ended 31 December 19X0.

Solution

S. Bradshaw Limited
Trading and Profit and Loss Account
for the year to 31 December 19X0

	£	£	£
Sales			2,350,000
less Cost of sales			1,565,000
Gross profit			785,000
add Discount received			12,000
			797,000
Selling and distribution			
Advertising	45,000		
Motor expenses	48,800		
Depreciation of motor vehicles	16,000	109,800	
Administration:			
Directors' emoluments	50,000		
Wages and salaries	322,000		
Rates and insurance	38,600		
Heating and lighting	43,800		
Telephone	17,700		
Depreciation: Leasehold property	10,000		
Fixtures and fittings	30,000	512,100	
Finance:			
Interest on debentures	10,000		
Bank interest	8,900		
Discount allowed	17,000	35,900	657,800
Net profit before taxation			139,200
Taxation on profits for the year:			
Corporation tax at 35%			52,000
Net profit for the year after taxation			87,200
Appropriation of profit:			
Transfer to general reserve		30,000	
Dividends:			
Paid: Half-year's preference			
dividend 4%	4,000		
Interim dividend on			
ordinary shares 5%	10,000		
Proposed: Half-year's preference			
dividend 4%	4,000		
Final dividend on			
ordinary shares 10%	20,000	38,000	68,000
Unappropriated profit for the year			19,200

S. Bradshaw Limited
Balance Sheet as at 31 December 19X0

Assets

Fixed assets	Cost	Depreciation	Net
	£	£	£
Leasehold property	210,000	30,000	180,000
Fixtures and fittings	300,000	120,000	180,000
Motor vehicles	64,000	32,000	32,000
	574,000	182,000	392,000

Current assets			
Stock at cost		250,000	
Debtors	1.	201,400	
		451,400	
less Current liabilities			
Creditors	2.	67,500	
Bank overdrafts		72,400	
Corporation tax /		52,000	
Proposed dividends		24,000	215,900
Net current assets			235,500
			627,500

Financed by

Share capital

	Authorised	Allotted and fully paid
	£	£
8% Preference shares of £1 each	100,000	100,000
Ordinary shares of £1 each	400,000	200,000
	500,000	300,000

Reserves			
Share premium account		40,000	
General reserve		30,000	
Profit and loss account	3.	157,500	227,500
Shareholders funds			527,500
10% Debentures 19X6–19X7	4.		100,000
			627,500

Notes:

1. Debtors

	£
Trade debtors per trial balance	192,000
Prepaid expenses:	
Rates and insurance	5,200
Motor expenses	4,200
	201,400

2. Creditors

	£
Trade creditors per trial balance	49,000
Debenture interest owing	5,000
Accrued expenses:	
Directors' emoluments	5,000
Heating and lighting	3,200
Telephone	1,300
Advertising	4,000
	67,500

3. Profit and loss account

	£
Balance at 31 December 19X9	138,300
Unappropriated profit for the year	19,200
	157,500

4. 10% Debentures 19X6–19X7. The description shows that the debentures are redeemable by the company not earlier than 19X6 and not later than 19X7.

Questions

17.1S   Using the information below, prepare a full set of final accounts.

Trial Balance of Derby Dale plc
at 31 December 19X7

	£	£
Authorised Capital (issued and paid up)		
£1 Ordinary shares		40,000
£1 9% Preference shares		20,000
5% Debentures (£100 each)		30,000
Purchases and sales	100,400	175,600
Returns inwards and outwards	325	475
Bad debts provision		3,000
Rent and rates	2,800	
Lighting and heating	840	
Salaries	15,480	
General expenses	4,700	
Provision for depreciation on furniture and fittings		1,500
Debtors and creditors	42,520	20,180
Furniture and fittings (at cost)	13,320	
Building (at cost)	80,000	
Stock	20,520	
Profit and loss		2,000
Balance at bank	11,850	
	292,755	292,755

The following information is also available:

(a) Lighting and heating accrued £142
(b) Rent and rates paid in advance £150
(c) Closing stock £19,242
(d) Dividend declared: ordinary shares 30%; preference shares
(e) Transfer to reserve £10,000
(f) Debenture interest has not been paid for the year
(g) Depreciation on furniture and fittings at 10% per annum on cost.

Note: Tax has been ignored.

17.2S   Using the information given below, which relates to a manufacturing company VHR Limited, you are required to prepare a statement to show clearly:

(a) cost of raw materials used or consumed
(b) prime cost
(c) cost of the finished goods produced
(d) cost of the finished goods sold (manufactured internally and purchased externally)
(e) gross profit
(f) net profit before taxation

for the year ended 31 December 19X6.

	£
Raw materials: Stock at 1 January 19X6	39,000
Purchases	152,000
Stock at 31 December 19X6	41,000
Finished goods: Stock at 1 January 19X6	51,000
Purchases	9,000
Stock at 31 December 19X6	57,000
Work in progress: at 1 January 19X6	16,000
at 31 December 19X6	18,200
Sales	400,000
Manufacturing wages	60,000
Manufacturing expenses	25,300
Repairs and maintenance of plant and machinery	13,500
Depreciation: Factory	38,000
General offices	5,000
Sales warehouse and offices	7,000
Carriage outwards	6,600
Power	10,000
Light and heat: Factory	2,400
General offices	800
Sales warehouse and offices	1,300
Administration expenses	16,200
Selling and distribution expenses	26,100

(Chartered Institute of Management Accountants)

17.3S   The following balances remained in the books of D. Yorke Ltd at 30 June 19X5 after the preparation of the trading account:

	£
Share capital, authorised and issued	
60,000 £1 Ordinary shares	60,000
20,000 8% £1 Preference shares	20,000
Stock at 30 June 19X5	41,926
Debtors and prepayments	13,600
Creditors and accruals	6,861
Bank balance	3,898
10% Debentures	8,000
General reserve	14,000
Bad debts	170
Gross profit for the period	40,754
Wages and salaries	14,100
Rates and insurances	705
Postage and telephone	310
Light and heat	608
Debenture interest ($\frac{1}{2}$ year to 31 Dec. 19X4)	400
Directors' fees	1,250
General expenses	1,554
Vehicles (cost £9,700)	3,400
Office fittings and equipment (cost £22,320)	13,720
Land and buildings at cost	66,100
Profit and loss account at 1 July 19X4	12,126

The following information is also available:

(i) Office fittings and equipment are to be depreciated at 15% of cost, and vehicles at 20% of cost.

(ii) A bill for £274 in respect of electricity consumed up to 30 June 19X5 has not been entered in the ledger.

(iii) The amount for insurance includes a premium of £150 paid in December 19X4 to cover the company against fire loss for the year 31 December 19X4 to 31 December 19X5.

(iv) Provisions are to be made for:

Directors' fees	£2,500
Audit fee	£600
The outstanding debenture interest.	

(v) The Directors have recommended that:
(1) £6,000 be transferred to general reserve
(2) The preference dividend be paid
(3) A 10% ordinary dividend be paid.

Required:

(a) Prepare the profit and loss and appropriation accounts for the period ended 30 June 19X5 and a balance sheet as at that date. (Ignore taxation.)

(b) Explain briefly why 'directors' fees' are treated as an expense when measuring profit, but 'partnership salaries' are treated as an appropriation.

(Chartered Association of Certified Accountants)

17.4S The following list of balances at 31 October 19X0 has been extracted from the books of account of Skyblue Limited, traders:

	£
Ordinary share capital – shares of £1.00 each, fully paid	400,000
Share premium account	30,000
Retained earnings at 31 October 19X9	158,300
8% Debentures, 19X9-X0 (i.e. 9/10 years after the balance sheet date)	80,000
Bank overdraft (Downley Bank Limited)	89,000
Balance at bank (Crownside Bank Limited)	3,600
Freehold property: at cost	280,000
provision for depreciation	91,000
Fixtures and fittings: at cost	410,000
provision for depreciation	153,000
Trade debtors	182,000
Trade creditors	38,000
Cost of goods sold	1,210,000
Sales	1,830,000
Wages and salaries	340,000
Directors' emoluments	41,000
Repairs and renewals	60,000
Advertising	92,000
Debenture interest, six months to 30 April 19X0	3,200
Bank overdraft interest	4,300
Discounts allowed	1,700
Discounts received	8,500
Interim dividend	20,000
Stock of goods, at cost	230,000

Additional information:

(i) A cheque for £9,000 received from K. Bone, trade debtor, on 10 October 19X0 has been credited to sales.
Note: Trade debtors at 31 October 19X0 includes 'K. Bone £20,000'.

(ii) The debenture interest for the six months to 31 October 19X0 was paid on 14 November 19X0.

(iii) The charge for advertising includes £60,000 paid for advertising materials and displays for a new product being introduced by the company for the first time in February 19X1.
The forecast of profit in this new venture is adequate to cover the advertising expense.

(iv) Trade creditors at 31 October 19X0 includes £13,000 received in August 19X0 being the proceeds from the sale of certain fixtures and fittings bought in January 19X7 at a cost of £40,000; no other accounting entries have been made for the sale of these fixed assets.

(v) Repairs and renewals includes £16,000 expended on the acquisition of additional fixtures and fittings in June 19X0.

(vi) Directors' emoluments accrued due on 31 October 19X0 amounted to £4,000.

(vii) The company's long established policy provides for depreciation at the following percentages of the cost of fixed assets held at the end of each financial year:

> Freehold property   5%
> Fixtures and fittings   10%

(viii) The directors are recommending that a final dividend of $2\frac{1}{2}\%$ be paid on the ordinary share capital for the year ended 31 October 19X0.
Note: Ignore Advance Corporation Tax.

Required:
(a) The trading, profit and loss account for the year ended 31 October 19X0 and a balance sheet at that date of Skyblue Limited.
(b) Define 'working capital' and briefly explain its importance.

(Chartered Association of Certified Accountants)

17.5S The following list of balances at 31 March 19X0 was extracted from the books of Greater Bargains Limited:

	£
Ordinary share capital – ordinary shares of £1 each, fully paid	200,000
Share premium account	20,000
Retained earnings at 31 March 19X9	15,000
Cost of goods sold	350,000
Rates, light and heat	11,400
Telephone and postages	5,600
Salaries	21,000
Directors' emoluments	12,000
Motor vehicle expenses	24,100
Sales	500,000
Debtors	21,700
Stock in trade, at cost	38,000
Freehold property, at cost	140,000
Fixtures and fittings: at cost	120,000
provision for depreciation	72,000
Motor vehicles: at cost	80,000
provision for depreciation	16,000
Balance at bank	7,000
Creditors	7,800

Additional information:
(*a*) The authorised capital of Greater Bargains Limited is £250,000.
(*b*) The company's freehold property was valued at £190,000 on 31 March 19X0; the company's board of directors has decided that this valuation should be reflected in the accounts.
(*c*) (i) Rates, light and heat charges prepaid at 31 March 19X0 amounted to £2,300.
(ii) Accrued charges at 31 March 19X0, were:

	£
Telephone and postages	900
Motor vehicle expenses	300

(*d*) Depreciation is provided annually on the cost of fixed assets held at the end of the accounting year as follows:

Fixtures and fittings	5%
Motor vehicles	20%

(*e*) In February 19X0 the company sold a motor vehicle which had been bought for £8,000 in January 19X7. The only entry in the company's books of account relating to the sale concerns the receipt of the sale proceeds of £1,500 which have been credited to motor vehicle expenses.
(*f*) The directors are recommending that a dividend of 15% be paid on the ordinary shares for the year ended 31 March 19X0.

Note: Ignore Advance Corporation Tax.

Required:
(a) The trading and profit and loss account for the year ended 31 March 19X0 and a balance sheet as at that date of Greater Bargains Limited.
(b) Outline the functions of the profit and loss appropriation account in limited company accounts.

(Chartered Association of Certified Accountants)

17.6 From the information given below you are required to prepare the manufacturing, trading and profit and loss account of ABC Limited for the year ended 31 December 19X5 and a balance sheet on that date.

Balances at 31 December 19X4	£
Authorised and issued share capital:	
Ordinary shares of £1 each, fully paid	100,000
Reserves	1,000
Creditors	57,400
Fixed assets (cost £60,000)	39,000
Stocks: Raw materials	25,000
Work in progress, valued at prime cost	5,800
Finished goods	51,000
Debtors	35,000
Cash at bank	2,000
Administration expenses prepaid	600

The following transactions occurred during 19X5:

Invoiced sales, *less* returns	243,000
Cash received from debtors	234,700
Discount allowed	5,400
Bad debt written off	1,100
Invoiced purchases of raw materials, *less* returns	80,000
Payments to creditors	82,500
Discount received	1,700
Factory wages paid	33,300
Manufacturing expenses paid	61,900
Administration expenses paid	16,200
Selling and distribution expenses paid	16,800
Payment for purchase of fixed assets	30,000

Balances at 31 December 19X5	
Fixed assets (cost £90,000)	60,000
Stocks: Raw materials	24,000
Work in progress	5,000
Finished goods	52,000
Administration expenses accrued	1,100
Factory wages accrued	700
Selling and distribution expenses prepaid	1,200

The following information is given:
(i) Depreciation of fixed assets is to be apportioned between manufacturing, administration, and selling and distribution in the proportions of 7 : 2 : 1.
(ii) Discount allowed and bad debt written off are to be regarded as selling and distribution expenses.
(iii) Discount received is to be credited to administration expenses.
(iv) Taxation is to be ignored.

(Chartered Institute of Management Accountants)

17.7   Xerces Ltd, a manufacturing company, acquired the business of Jack Jones on 30 June 19X6 and took over the following assets and liabilities:

	£
Buildings	16,000
Machinery	9,500
Stock	2,600
Debtors	1,800
Creditors	1,900

The agreed purchase price was £36,000, and this was fully discharged by the issue to Mr Jones of 30,000 £1 ordinary shares in Xerces Ltd which will not qualify for dividend for the year ended 30 June 19X6.

On 30 June 19X6 the other balances in the ledgers of Xerces Ltd (excluding all items relating to the acquisition of the business of Jack Jones) were as follows:

	£	£
Net trading profit for the year ended 30 June 19X6		57,460
Ordinary shares (£1)		120,000
6% £1 Preference shares		50,000
10% Debentures		40,000
Stock at 30 June 19X6	19,500	
Interim dividends paid		
5% Ordinary	6,000	
3% Preference	1,500	
Debenture interest accrued		2,000
Undistributed profit, 1 July 19X5		84,680
General reserve, 1 July 19X5		52,000
Land (cost)	254,180	
Building (cost)	73,210	
Depreciation on buildings		5,950
Plant and machinery (cost)	68,900	
Depreciation on plant and machinery		14,470
Debtors and creditors	10,850	6,110
Accruals and prepayments	1,230	840
Bank overdraft		2,240
Cash in hand	380	
	435,750	435,750

The directors propose to pay a final ordinary dividend of 10%, the final preference dividend, and to transfer £25,000 to general reserve.

Required:

(a) Prepare the appropriation account for the year ended 30 June 19X6, and a balance sheet as at that date, incorporating the acquisition of the business of Jack Jones.

(b) Explain carefully the extent to which you consider the balance sheet you have prepared discloses the 'value' of Xerces Ltd. (Ignore taxation.)

(Chartered Association of Certified Accountants)

17.8   (a) Indicate three ways in which each of the following arise in accounting:
(i) reserves;   (ii) provisions.

(b) Distinguish between reserves and provisions in accounting.

(Chartered Association of Certified Accountants)

17.9   A summary of the final accounts of Burlay Ltd for the year ended 31 December 19X6 is as follows:

Balance Sheet as at 31 December 19X6

	£		£
£1 Ordinary shares	150,000	Buildings (revalued	
£1 8% Preference shares	50,000	in 19X6)	139,000
Share premium	20,000	Fixtures at cost	
Revaluation reserve	9,000	*less* Depreciation	40,000
General reserve	19,000	Investments	33,000
Undistributed profit	21,000	Stock	50,000
10% Debentures	30,000	Debtors	60,000
		Bank	44,750
	299,000		
Creditors	48,000		
Accruals			
Debenture interest	1,500		
Wages	250		
Audit	1,000		
Dividends proposed	17,000		
	366,750		366,750

Trading, Profit and Loss Account for the year ended 31 December 19X6

	£		£
Opening stock	40,000	Credit sales	500,000
Credit purchases	440,000	Closing stock	50,000
Gross profit	70,000		
	550,000		550,000
Wages (accrued £250)	18,250	Gross profit	70,000
Heating	750	Investment income	2,000
Debenture interest	3,000		
Depreciation of fixtures	4,000		
Directors' fees	8,000		
Audit fee	1,000		
Net profit	37,000		
	72,000		72,000
Dividends paid:		Net profit	37,000
5% Ordinary	7,500		
4% Preference	2,000		
Dividends proposed:			
10% Ordinary	15,000		
4% Preference	2,000		
Transfer to general			
reserve	5,500		
Balance	5,000		
	37,000		37,000

A summary of the receipts and payments for the year ended 31 December 19X6 showed:

Receipts	£
Issue of 50,000 £1 ordinary shares	70,000
Collected from debtors	480,000
Investment income	2,000
Payments	
Dividends	16,500
Wages	18,300
Heating	750
Debenture interest	1,500
Directors' fees	8,000
Payment to creditors	460,000
Audit fee	800

Required:
Prepare a balance sheet in good form as at 31 December 19X5 from the above data. Show your workings clearly.

(Chartered Association of Certified Accountants)

18 Suspense accounts and the correction of errors

Aims of the chapter:

To show the uses of suspense accounts, and how the errors giving rise to those accounts are corrected

Suspense accounts can be used for a variety of purposes. The type of suspense account most frequently found in examination questions is where the debit side of the trial balance does not agree with the credit side. If the error or errors which have caused this cannot easily be found, a suspense account is opened as a temporary measure to balance the trial balance pending the discovery of the errors.

A typical examination question might show a trial balance or a balance sheet which includes a suspense account. Following the trial balance or balance sheet, there would be a list of errors discovered after the trial balance or balance sheet date.

The student is usually asked to provide journal entries to make the necessary corrections to the accounts which are in error and to amend or close the suspense account.

The question might also require:

1. the suspense account
2. the corrected trial balance
3. the corrected balance sheet
4. the corrected net profit to be calculated.

It should be particularly noted that some of the errors may not affect the suspense account. There may be corresponding errors affecting two existing accounts and they should also be corrected through the journal.

EXAMPLE 18.1

Balance Sheet of J. Craig as at 31 December 19X1

	£		£
Capital	10,000	Fixtures and fittings	12,500
Net profit for year	8,650	Stock	5,000
	———	Debtors	2,100
	18,650	Cash	50
Drawings	3,930		
	———		
	14,720		
Creditors	4,350		
Suspense account	580		
	———		———
	19,650		19,650
	═══		═══

When the above balance sheet was prepared there was a difference in the trial balance, and it was necessary to open a suspense account for the amount shown.

Subsequently the following errors were discovered:

(a) The balance of £140 on E. Jackson's account in the sales ledger had been brought forward as £14.

(b) The sales day book had been undercast by £210.

(c) A new cash register costing £310 had been debited to purchases account instead of fixtures and fittings.

(d) Depreciation of equipment had been entered in the profit and loss account as £1,724 instead of £1,274.

(e) Discounts allowed of £65 had been posted to the credit of discounts received account.

You are required:

(i) to provide journal entries necessary to correct the errors;

(ii) to produce a corrected balance sheet showing the amended balance of the suspense account.

Solution:

(i)   Journal

		Dr. £	Cr. £
(a)	E. Jackson (sales ledger)	126	
	Suspense		126
	Balance on E. Jackson's account brought forward as £14 instead of £140.		
(b)	Suspense	210	
	Sales		210
	Sales day book undercast by £210.		
(c)	Fixtures and fittings	310	
	Purchases		310
	Cash register wrongly debited to purchases account. (*Note*: This journal entry does not affect the suspense account.)		
(d)	Suspense	450	
	Profit and loss (depreciation)		450
	Depreciation incorrectly entered in the profit and loss account as £1,724 rather than £1,274.		
(e)	Discounts allowed	65	
	Discounts received	65	
	Suspense		130
	Discount allowed of £65 wrongly credited to discounts received.		

A suspense account as such is not requested by this question. But the question is unusual in that the suspense account is not cleared as it would be if all the errors had been discovered. A suspense account to calculate the amended balance is therefore most useful:

Suspense account

	£		£
(b) Sales	210	Opening balance	580
(d) Profit and loss		(a) E. Jackson (sales	
(depreciation)	450	ledger)	126
Balance c/f	176	(e) Discounts allowed	65
		(e) Discounts received	65
	836		836

Similarly a corrected net profit is not requested, but is nevertheless necessary to complete the balance sheet. It is calculated as below:

	Deduct	Add	£
Net profit as shown on balance sheet			8,650
	£	£	
(b) Sales understated		210	
(c) Cash register wrongly charged to purchases		310	
(d) Depreciation overstated		450	
(e) Discounts allowed not charged	65		
Discounts received wrongly credited	65		
	130	970	840
Amended net profit			9,490

(ii) The balance sheet is shown below in the same format as in the question, but in narrative style.

Amended Balance Sheet of J. Craig as at 31 December 19X1

	£	£
Assets		
Fixtures and fittings		12,810
Stock	5,000	
Debtors	2,226	
Cash	50	7,276
		20,086
Financed by		
Capital		10,000
Net profit for year		9,490
		19,490
Drawings		3,930
		15,560
Creditors		4,350
Suspense account		176
		20,086

The correction of errors

The errors previously described in Example 18.1 were all discovered and corrected at the year end. Most of the errors, though not all, affected a suspense account opened as a temporary measure to balance a trial balance.

Errors may, of course, be discovered during the course of the year, before a trial balance is prepared. Some of these errors may be corrected by simply altering the relevant account(s) (e.g. if an incorrect figure has been inserted). Where the error affects more than one account, the correction will usually be made through a journal entry. In any event it is good practice to record any amendments that might have to be made.

Examples of errors which would not of themselves create an imbalance in the trial balance are as follows:

1. Omission, where a transaction is completely omitted and neither the debit nor credit entry is made.
2. Commission, where both a debit and credit entry are made but a wrong account is used. A receipt of cash from debtor C. Wilson is credited to the account of C. Wisden. A purchase of goods from R. Slater is credited to S. Slater's account.
3. Principle, where both a debit and credit entry are made but one of the entries is wrong in principle. A purchase of machinery for use in the firm (i.e. an asset and therefore capital expenditure) debited to purchases account is an error of principle.
4. Original entry, where a figure shown in the day book is wrong, and so postings to both debit and credit show the wrong figure.

Examples of errors which would normally affect the trial balance, if they were not discovered prior to trial balance stage, are

1. An incorrect posting on one side of the transaction
2. An error in addition
3. A balance wrongly brought forward.

It is possible that errors of the type listed above might compensate each other to some extent (e.g. a credit over-posting of £100 to an account might be matched by an error of £100 in the calculation of a debit balance).

Other uses of a suspense account

A suspense account can also be used for temporarily holding transactions until the correct account is known. For example a debtor might make a payment in cash, but the debtor's name in the receipt book is illegible. The amount could be posted to a suspense account until the correct source of the cash was discovered.

Another use of suspense accounts is to defer income or expenditure until a subsequent accounting period.

Neither of the types of suspense account referred to above is raised due to a difference in the trial balance, and they are unlikely to appear in foundation level examinations.

Questions

18.1S   After the preparation of a trial balance, an unexplained difference of *Dr.* £218 remains, and a suspense account is opened for that amount. Subsequent investigations reveal:

(i)   £35 received from A. Jones and credited to his account has not been entered in the bank account.

(ii)   The owner of the business has taken goods which cost £69 for his own use. No entries have been made for this at all.

(iii) A payment of £47 to M. Smith has been credited to that account.

(iv)   Discounts allowed (£198) and discounts received (£213) have been posted to the discount accounts as credits and debits respectively.

(v)   Bank interest received of £111 has not been entered in the bank account.

(vi)   £211 owing by A. Able has been debited incorrectly to B. Able.

(vii) The carriage outwards (£98) has been treated as a revenue.

Required:

(a)   Prepare the suspense account making the entries necessary to eliminate the debit balance there is. Indicate clearly how you would deal with *all* of the errors discovered.

(b)   To what extent is the balancing of a trial balance evidence of absence of error?

(Chartered Association of Certified Accountants)

18.2S   Misbal Co. has produced a trial balance for the year ended 31 March 19X0, which does not balance. An examination of the company's books discloses the following errors:

(1)   An invoice from J. Smith amounting to £100, for goods purchased, has been omitted from the purchase day book and posted direct to purchases account in the nominal ledger and J. Smith's account in the purchase ledger, but has not been included in the creditors control account in the trial balance.

(2)   The sales day book has been undercast by £240 and posted to the debtors control account accordingly.

(3)   Discount allowed for the month of March amounting to £489 has not been posted to the nominal ledger.

(4)   Goods received from Why Ltd on 31 March 19X0, costing £2,410, have been included in stock, but the invoice has not yet been received.

(5)   A cheque for £192 received from J. Jones, a debtor, has been posted direct to the sales account in the nominal ledger.

(6)   Sales account in the nominal ledger has been credited with a credit note for £250 being trade in allowance given on a company van. This amount had already been taken into account when dealing with the replacement in the motor van account.

You are required:

(a)   to give the journal entries, where necessary, to correct these errors, or if no journal entry is required, state how they will be corrected,

(b) to prepare a statement showing the effect the corrections would have on the company's profit for the year, and

(c) to prepare a statement showing the net adjustment to the trial balance.

(Institute of Chartered Accountants in England and Wales)

18.3S After completing a draft profit and loss account for the year ended 30 April 19X0 of ABC Limited the following balances remained and a suspense account entry was required for the difference which had arisen:

	£	£
Fixed assets: at cost	60,000	
provision for depreciation		31,000
Ordinary share capital		35,000
Retained earnings		12,000
Stock in trade, at cost	14,000	
Sales ledger control account	9,600	
Purchases ledger control account		6,500
Balance at bank	1,640	
Difference on balances suspense account		740
	85,240	85,240

After investigation the following discoveries were made:

(*a*) A rent payment of £350 in March 19X0 had been debited in the sales ledger control account.

(*b*) Although instructed to do so, the accounts clerk had not set a debt due from B. Bell of £1,560 in the sales ledger control account against an amount due to B. Bell in the purchases ledger control account.

(*c*) Discounts allowed of £500 during the year ended 30 April 19X0 had not been recorded in the company's accounts.

(*d*) No entry had been made for the refund of £2,620 made by cheque to L. Green in March, 19X0, in respect of defective goods returned to the company. *Note*: The correct entries had been made previously for the return of the goods to ABC Limited.

(*e*) The purchases day book for February 19X0 had been undercast by £300.

(*f*) A payment of £1,000 to K. Bloom in January 19X0 for cash purchases had been debited in the purchases ledger control account. *Note*: The company does not maintain a credit account with K. Bloom.

(*g*) No entries had been made in the company's books for cash sales of £2,450 on 30 April 19X0 and banked on that date.

(*h*) No entries had been made in the company's books for bank charges of £910 debited in the company's bank account in December 19X9.

(*i*) The company's cash book (bank debit column) had been overcast by £1,900 in March 19X0.

(*j*) A cheque payment of £8,640 for new fixtures and fittings in April 19X0 had not been recorded in the company's books.

(*k*) A payment by cheque of £1,460 in June 19X9 for stationery had not been posted to the appropriate nominal account.

Required:

(a) The journal entries for items (*a*), (*f*) and (*i*) above. *Note*: Narratives are required.

(b) The corrected list of balances at 30 April 19X0.

(c) Explain briefly the reasons for preparing bank reconciliation statements.

(Chartered Association of Certified Accountants)

18.4S The balances extracted from the records of Perrod and Company at 31 December 19X8 were as follows:

	£
Premises (cost)	7,000
Capital	8,440
Drawings	1,935
Provision for depreciation of office equipment at 1 January 19X8	480
Debtors control account	1,891
Creditors control account	2,130
Stock at 1 January 19X8	1,200
Purchases	9,480
Sales	14,003
Returns inwards	310
Office equipment (cost) (balance at 1 January 19X8)	1,600
Wages	1,540
Commission	160
Discount allowed	210
Discount received	121
Bank (credit balance)	980
Cash in hand	56
Heating and lighting	375
Postage and stationery	224
Bad debts	68

A preliminary trial balance was prepared, but, although no arithmetical errors were made, the trial balance did not balance. In seeking the reasons for the difference, the following facts emerged.

(i) *Debtors control account*

(a) No entry had been made in the control account in respect of the debts written off as bad.

(b) A cheque paid by a debtor for £110 had been returned on 31 December 19X8 by the bank marked 'return to drawer'. An entry had been made in both the bank account and the debtor's account for this, but no entry had been made in the control account.

(c) Sales on credit of £97 to A. Jones had been correctly entered in his account but nothing had been entered in the control account.

(d) M. Smith had been allowed a cash discount of £43, but no corresponding entry had appeared in the control account.

(ii) *Creditors control account*

This exceeded the balance of the individual creditors' accounts by £12. The difference was caused by:

(a) Goods returned to R. Hardy costing £69 had been entered correctly in the control account, but no entry had been made in Mr Hardy's account.

(b) An invoice for £56 had been incorrectly entered in the control account as £65.

(c) Two credit balances of £45 and £27 had been omitted from the list extracted from the creditors ledger.

(iii) Some office equipment which had cost £240 had been debited to the purchase account.

(iv) The wages (£1,540) included £320 of personal drawings by the owner of the business.

(v) The provision for depreciation of office equipment had been credited in 19X7 with straight line depreciation of 10%, i.e. £160, but the depreciation should have been charged at 12½% per annum.

(vi) The account for stationery (£224) included £45 of personal notepaper for the owner.

(vii) The returns inwards account had been credited with £90 for some goods returned to a creditor.

Required:

(a) Prepare the debtors and creditors control accounts, taking into account where appropriate the facts ascertained in (i) and (ii) above.

(b) Prepare journal entries to correct the errors and omissions enumerated in (iii) to (vii) above.

(c) Given that Perrod and Company's stock at 31 December 19X8 was valued at £1,400 and the depreciation on office equipment for the year was £230, prepare a balance sheet as at 31 December 19X8, showing clearly the net profit for the year. (*Note*: A trading profit and loss account is *NOT* required.)

(Chartered Association of Certified Accountants)

18.5   Chi Knitwear Ltd is an old fashioned firm with a hand-written set of books. A trial balance is extracted at the end of each month, and a profit and loss account and balance sheet are computed. This month, however, the trial balance will not balance, the credits exceeding debits by £1,536.

You are asked to help and, after inspection of the ledgers, discover the following errors:

1. A balance of £87 on a debtor's account has been omitted from the schedule of debtors, the total of which was entered as debtors in the trial balance.

2. A small piece of machinery purchased for £1,200 had been written off to repairs.

3. The receipts side of the cash book had been undercast by £720.

4. The total of one page of the sales day book had been carried forward as £8,154, whereas the correct amount was £8,514.

5. A credit note for £179 received from a supplier had been posted to the wrong side of his account.

6. An electricity bill in the sum of £152, not yet accrued for, is discovered in a filing tray.

7. Mr Smith, whose past debts to the company had been the subject of a provision, at last paid £731 to clear his account. His personal account has been credited but the cheque has not yet passed through the cash book.

You are required to:

(a) write up the suspense account to clear the difference, and

(b) state the effect on the accounts of correcting each error.

(Chartered Association of Certified Accountants)

18.6 (*a*) An inexperienced book-keeper has drawn up a trial balance for the year ended 30 June 19X7:

	Dr. £	Cr. £
Provision for doubtful debts	200	
Bank overdraft	1,654	
Capital		4,591
Creditors		1,637
Debtors	2,983	
Discount received	252	
Discount allowed		733
Drawings	1,200	
Office furniture	2,155	
General expenses		829
Purchases	10,923	
Returns inwards		330
Rent and rates	314	
Salaries	2,520	
Sales		16,882
Stock	2,418	
Provision for depreciation of furniture	364	
	24,983	25,002

Required:
Draw up a 'corrected' trial balance, debiting or crediting any residual error to a suspense account.

(*b*) Further investigation of the suspense account, ascertained in (*a*) above, reveals the following errors:

(i) Goods bought from J. Jones amounting to £13 had been posted to his account as £33.

(ii) Furniture which had cost £173 had been debited to the general expense account.

(iii) An invoice from Suppliers Ltd for £370 had been omitted from the purchase account, but credited to Suppliers Ltd's account.

(iv) Sales on credit to A. Hope Ltd for £450 had been posted to the sales account, but not to the debtors ledger.

(v) The balance on the capital account had been incorrectly brought forward in the ledger, and should have been £4,291.

(vi) An amount of £86 received from A. Blunt, a debtor, in settlement of his account had been treated as a cash sale.

(vii) Discount allowed has been undertotalled by £35.

Required:
Prepare journal entries correcting each of the above errors and write up the suspense account.

(*c*) There are several types of error which will not affect the balancing of a trial balance; these include errors of omission, commission and principle.

Required:
Explain what is meant by these terms and give an example of each.

(Chartered Association of Certified Accountants)

18.7 The accountant of a small company, J.A. Doube Ltd, has made a preliminary attempt to calculate the profit for the year to 31 December 19X7. His original trial balance did not balance and he transferred the difference to the profit and loss account for 19X7. After doing so, the balances are as follows:

Trial Balance at 31 December 19X7

	Dr. £	Cr. £
Ordinary share capital		10,000
Profit and loss account balance at 1 January 19X7		12,310
Net profit for 19X7		19,360
Fittings and equipment (at cost)	18,400	
Provision for depreciation on fittings and equipment (including charge for 19X7)		9,400
Stock of goods for resale	22,160	
Debtors and creditors	13,420	8,310
Bank balance	5,400	
	59,380	59,380

(Fittings and equipment are depreciated by 12½% of cost per annum and it is the practice to make a full year's charge in the year of purchase. None of the items is more than eight years old.)

A number of matters are subsequently noted which may affect these figures. They are:

(i) The total debtors figure in the trial balance does not agree with a listing of the debtors ledger balances and a thorough check reveals that cash discounts of £310 allowed to customers in December have been correctly entered in the individual accounts but nowhere else; bad debts of £165 written off individual accounts and debited to the bad debts account have not been entered in the total debtors account.

(ii) J.A. Doube Ltd has recently agreed to act as a selling agent for Konsines Ltd at a commission of 15% of gross sales. Any associated expenses are chargeable against the principal. So far, goods with a retail value of £12,500 have been received and £8,000 of them sold. No information about the sales has yet been notified to the principal and no settlement made. The sales proceeds were credited to the sales account and relevant expenses of £320 included with selling and distribution expenses. The balance of goods unsold was included in the closing stock figure at £4,500.

(iii) During December some goods costing £240 were sent to a potential customer on approval. When the accounts were closed off they were forgotten and no entry had been made. Since 31 December the customer notified J.A. Doube Ltd that he would be retaining two-thirds of the goods at the selling price of £220 and would be sending the remainder back.

(iv) During the year, some fittings which originally cost £1,600 in 19X2 were sold for £240 and the proceeds credited to sales account, no other adjustment being made.

(v) Some goods, cost value £480, had been damaged by fire. They had no scrap value and nothing was included in the closing stock in respect of them. A claim of £400 has since been agreed with the insurers.

(vi) A cheque for £90 received from a debtor and banked on 31 December has subsequently been returned from the bank as unpaid. No adjusting entries have yet been made and it has not yet been possible to discover the circumstances.

Required:
Show all the journal entries necessary to deal with the above. Calculate the revised net profit for 19X7 and prepare a balance sheet at 31 December 19X7.

(Chartered Association of Certified Accountants)

19 Issue and forfeit of shares

Aims of the chapter:

To explain how a company's share capital is built up
To illustrate the stages involved

General background

Shares in a public company may be acquired as follows:

(a) direct from the company by subscribing the memorandum
(b) by receiving an allotment of shares from the company
(c) from another person by transfer through the stock market.

Under (a), the subscribers of the memorandum are limited to the founder members of the company. The normal way of acquiring shares direct from the company is under (b), i.e. by receiving an allotment from the company. The presence of an offer to purchase shares (i.e. the application to the company) and the acceptance of that offer (i.e. the allotment by the company) constitutes a contract between the member and the company.

An acquisition of shares under (c) has no effect on the share capital of the company; such transfers are simply recorded in the company's register of members.

The directors of a company, whether the company is public or private, may not allot relevant securities in the company unless they are given the authority to do so either by the company in general meeting or by the articles of the company. The term relevant securities means

(a) shares in the company *except* those that are
   (i) shown in the memorandum as subscribers of the memorandum shares
   (ii) allotted in pursuance of an employees' share scheme;
(b) any right to subscribe for, or to convert any security into, shares in the company except shares allotted under an employees' share scheme.

The authority to allot

(i) must state the maximum amount of relevant securities that may be allotted under it;

(ii) must be renewed at least every five years;
(iii) may be revoked at any time in general meeting.

Shares can be offered for subscription payable either in full on application, or by instalments. But shares so offered in a public company may not be allotted unless the full number of shares offered are applied for, or the offer states that the shares will be allotted even if the shares are not fully applied for. In addition, the Companies Act 1985 prohibits a first allotment of shares offered to the public for subscription unless the minimum subscription stated in the prospectus has been received. The minimum subscription is the minimum amount which, in the opinion of the directors, must be raised in cash by the allotment of those shares to provide for

(i)   the purchase price of any property to be acquired;
(ii)   any preliminary expenses, including commissions, payable by the company;
(iii) the repayment of any monies borrowed for the above expenditure;
(iv)   working capital.

A further restriction on the allotment of shares offered for subscription by a public company is that at least 25% of the nominal value and the whole of any premium relating to each share must have been received on application.

Before a newly incorporated public company can commence business or exercise borrowing powers the Registrar of Companies must have issued a certificate entitling it to do business. To obtain this certificate, the company must demonstrate, *inter alia*, that it has allotted the minimum share capital as may be specified by statutory instrument.

The issue of shares

Shares may be offered for subscription by a public company at a price which is termed either

(i)   at par, i.e. the price required to be paid to the company for the share is the nominal value of that share (e.g. a £1 ordinary share issued at a price of £1)

       or

(ii)   at a premium, i.e. the price required to be paid to the company for the share is in excess of the nominal value of that share (e.g. a £1 ordinary share issued at a price of, say, £2).

The shares, whether offered for subscription at par or at a premium, may be payable either in full on application or by instalments.

Shares payable in full on application

The accounting entries where shares are payable in full on application are:

Bank account	Debit
Application account	Credit

With the amount of the application money
(including premium, if any,) received.

Application account	Debit
Share capital account	Credit

With the *nominal* value of the shares allotted.

Note: No entries should be made in the share capital account until the shares are *allotted.*

Where shares are issued at a premium a further entry is required:

Application account	Debit
Share premium account	Credit

With the amount of the *premium* on the shares allotted.

Where applications are oversubscribed and the applicants are not allotted any shares, or only a proportion of the shares applied for, a refund is made:

Application account	Debit
Bank account	Credit

With the amount of the application money
(including premium, if any) refunded.

EXAMPLE 19.1

A.V. Perry and Co. Ltd has an authorised capital of £2 million divided into ordinary shares of £1 each. One-quarter of the authorised capital was offered to the public at par, payable in full on application. Applications were received on 12 January 19X1, for 800,000 shares. Applicants for 50,000 shares received no allotment and the shares were allotted to the remaining applicants on the basis of two shares for every three applied for. The shares were allotted on 26 January 19X1, and the excess cash returned to applicants on the same day.

(Both the journal entries and the ledger accounts are shown for this illustration; for future illustrations only ledger accounts will be shown. In answering examination questions, students should take careful note of what is required by the question.)

Journal

19X1		£	£
Jan. 12	Bank	800,000	
	Ordinary share application account		800,000
	Amounts received on applications for 800,000 ordinary shares of £1 each.		
Jan. 26	Ordinary share application account	500,000	
	Ordinary share capital account		500,000
	Allotment of 500,000 ordinary shares of £1 each to sundry applicants.		
Jan. 26	Ordinary share application account	300,000	
	Bank		300,000
	Refund of excess money received on application for 500,000 ordinary shares of £1 each.		

Ledger

Bank

19X1		£	19X1		£
Jan. 12	Ordinary share application	800,000	Jan. 26	Ordinary share application	300,000
			26	Balance c/d	500,000
		800,000			800,000
Jan. 27	Balance b/d	500,000			

Ordinary share application

19X1		£	19X1		£
Jan. 26	Ordinary share capital	500,000	Jan. 12	Bank	800,000
26	Bank	300,000			
		800,000			800,000

Ordinary share capital

			19X1		£
			Jan. 26	Ordinary share application	500,000

EXAMPLE 19.2

The directors of A.V. Perry and Co. Ltd decided to increase the allotted share capital of the company by offering for subscription a further 500,000 ordinary shares of £1 each at a price of £1.50 per share payable in full on application.

Applications were received on 12 July 19X3, for 700,000 shares. The directors decided to allot the shares on the basis of five for every seven applied for. The shares were allotted on 26 July 19X3, and the excess cash returned to applicants on the same day.

Bank

19X3	£	19X3	£
Jul. 12 Ordinary share		Jul. 26 Ordinary share	
application	1,050,000	application	300,000
		26 Balance c/d	750,000
	1,050,000		1,050,000
Jul. 27 Balance b/d	750,000		

Ordinary share application

19X3	£	19X3	£
Jul. 26 Ordinary share		Jul. 12 Bank	1,050,000
capital	500,000		
26 Share premium	250,000		
26 Bank	300,000		
	1,050,000		1,050,000

Ordinary share capital

19X3	£	19X3	£
Jul. 26 c/d	1,000,000	Jul. 1 Balance b/d	500,000
		26 Ordinary share	
		application	500,000
	1,000,000		1,000,000
		Jul. 27 b/d	1,000,000

Share premium

		19X3	£
		Jul. 26 Ordinary share	
		application	250,000

Shares payable by instalments

Where shares are payable by instalments, the dates on which the instalments are due are usually specified in the prospectus giving details of the offer. Other than the amounts due on application and allotment, Table A (see Ch. 17) regulates subsequent *calls* where dates are not specified. Where a company does not require the immediate use of all the cash to be raised by an issue of shares, the request to have shares payable by instalments is sensible.

Accounting entries:

Bank account   Debit
    Application and allotment account   Credit
With the amount of the application money
(including premium, if any) received.

Application and allotment account   Debit
    Share capital account   Credit
With the amount due on application and
allotment on the shares allotted (excluding premium,
if any).

Note: No entries should be made in the share capital account until the shares are allotted.

Application and allotment account   Debit
    Share premium account   Credit
With any premium received from applicants
to whom shares have been allotted.

Application and allotment account   Debit
    Bank account   Credit
With the money refunded to unsuccessful applicants.

Bank account   Debit
    Application and allotment account   Credit
With the money received on allotment.

When a *call* is made by the directors, the entries are

Call account   Debit
    Share capital account   Credit
With the amount due on the call.

Bank account   Debit
    Call account   Credit
With the money received from the shareholders
in respect of the call.

Note: The share capital account is credited when the 'call' is made by the directors and not when the cash is received. Separate *call accounts* are opened for each call made by the directors and numbered accordingly (i.e. 1st call account, 2nd call account, and so on).

EXAMPLE 19.3

On 1 July 19X5 the directors of A.V. Perry and Co. Ltd decided to increase the allotted share capital of the company again, by offering for subscription a further 500,000 ordinary shares of £1 each at a price of £2 per share payable as follows:

	Per share
On application including premium	£1.25
On allotment	£0.35
On first call on 1 October 19X5	£0.20
On second and final call on 1 April 19X6	£0.20

The application lists were closed on 15 July 19X5, by which date applications for 1,250,000 shares had been received. The directors decided to allot the shares to the applicants for the first 600,000 shares *pro rata* to their original application, the balance of the money received on application being applied to the amounts due on allotment. The shares were allotted on 22 July 19X5, and the cash paid by unsuccessful applicants was returned to them on the same date. The balance of the allotment money was received by 31 July 19X5 and the 'call' monies were received on the due dates.

Bank

19X5		£	19X5		£
Jul. 15	Application and allotment – application money received	1,562,500	Jul. 22	Application and allotment – money refunded	812,500
31	Application and allotment – balance of allotment money	50,000	19X6 Apr. 1	Balance c/d	1,000,000
Oct. 1	1st call A/c	100,000			
19X6 Apr. 1	2nd call A/c	100,000			
		1,812,500			1,812,500
Apr. 1	Balance b/d	1,000,000			

Application and allotment

19X5		£	19X5		£
Jul. 22	Share capital	300,000	Jul. 15	Bank – application money received	1,562,500
22	Share premium	500,000	31	Bank – balance of allotment money	50,000[1]
22	Bank – money refunded	812,500			
		1,612,500			1,612,500

Note 1:

	£
Amount due on application and allotment from successful applicants – 500,000 × £1.60	800,000
Amount received from those applicants on application – 600,000 × £1.25	750,000
Amount due on allotment	50,000

Share capital

19X6		£	19X5		£
Apr.	1 Balance c/d	1,500,000	Jul.	1 b/d	1,000,000
				22 Application and	
				allotment	300,000
			Oct.	1 1st call	100,000
			19X6		
			Apr.	1 2nd call	100,000
		1,500,000			1,500,000
			Apr.	1 Balance b/d	1,500,000

Share premium

19X6		£	19X5		£
Apr.	1 Balance c/d	750,000	Jul.	1 b/d	250,000
			Jul.	22 Application and	
				allotment	500,000
		750,000			750,000
			19X6		
			Apr.	1 Balance b/d	750,000

1st call

19X5		£	19X5		£
Oct.	1 Share capital	100,000	Oct.	1 Bank	100,000

2nd call

19X6		£	19X6		£
Apr.	1 Share capital	100,000	Apr.	1 Bank	100,000

Note: Where more than one class of capital is being issued, e.g. both preference shares and ordinary shares, separate application and allotment accounts, call accounts and share capital accounts must be opened for each class.

Forfeiture of shares

The balance unpaid on any call account is described as *called up share capital not paid,* and should be shown as such in a balance sheet under current assets in a similar way to other debtors.

Where calls on shares remain unpaid after the due dates, the directors are usually given power by the articles of association to forfeit those shares after giving proper notice to the defaulting shareholders. After forfeiture the unpaid calls become *investment-own shares.* For convenience it is likely that a transfer will be made as follows:

Investment-own shares   Debit
   Call   Credit
   With the amount unpaid and forefeited on the call
   (i.e. the balance outstanding on the call account).

Forfeited shares can be re-issued at any price so long as the total amount received for those shares (excluding any premium) is not less than their nominal value. For example, a £1 nominal share issued at £1.25 on which £0.75 (including the premium) has been paid, and which is forfeited, can be re-allotted as fully paid at £0.50 or more. Any excess amount (i.e. over £0.50 per share in the example) would be transferred to share premium account.

Assuming just one share as above had been forfeited, and it was re-allotted at £0.75, the accounting entries would be:

	Dr.	Cr.
	£	£
Bank	0.75	
Investment–own shares		0.50
Share premium		0.25
Amount received on forfeited share re-allotted.		

Share capital remains intact in the balance sheet unaffected by unpaid calls or forfeited shares, except that forfeited shares must be cancelled if they are not re-allotted within three years of forfeiture. In this case the shares must be cancelled and the share capital reduced.

EXAMPLE 19.4

C. Doohan and Co. Ltd has a nominal capital of £500,000 divided into 500,000 ordinary shares of £1 each. The allotted capital at 1 July 19X6 was £300,000 which was fully paid. On that date the directors of the company, being authorised so to do in accordance with Section 80 of the Companies Act 1985, decided to increase the share capital of the company by offering a further 100,000 ordinary shares of £1 each at a price of £1.50 per share payable on the following terms.

	Per share
Payable on application (including the premium)	£0.75
Payable on allotment	£0.25
First call – payable three months after allotment	£0.25
Second call – payable three months after date of	
first call	£0.25

On 12 July 19X6, applications had been received for 150,000 shares and it was decided to allot the shares to applicants for 125,000 shares on the basis of four shares for every five for which applications had been received, the balance of the money received on application being applied to the amounts due on allotment.

The shares were allotted on 1 August 19X6, and the cash paid by unsuccessful applicants was returned to them on that same date. The balance of the allotment money was received in full by 15 August 19X6.

Calls were made and paid in full by the members within two weeks of the call being made with the exception of one member who failed to pay either of the calls on the 1,000 shares allotted to him.

After giving the notice required by the articles of association, the directors resolved to forfeit the shares on 1 March 19X7. The forfeited shares were re-allotted on 31 March 19X7, to another member at £1.25 each.

Bank

19X6	£	19X6	£
Jul. 12 Application and allotment – application money received	112,500	Aug. 1 Application and allotment – money refunded	18,750
Aug. 15 Application and allotment – balance of allotment money	6,250	19X7 Mar. 31 Balance c/d	150,750
Nov. 15 1st call	24,750		
19X7			
Feb. 15 2nd call	24,750		
Mar. 31 Investment-own shares	500		
Share premium	750		
	169,500		169,500
Apr. 1 Balance b/d	150,750		

Application and allotment

19X6	£	19X6	£
Aug. 1 Share capital	50,000	Jul. 12 Bank – application money received	112,500
1 Share premium	50,000	Aug. 15 Bank – balance of allotment money received	6,250[1]
1 Bank – money refunded	18,750		
	118,750		118,750

Note 1:

	£
Amount due on application and allotment from successful applicants – 100,000 × £1	100,000
Amount received from those applicants on application – 125,000 × £0.75	93,750
Amount due on allotment	6,250

Share capital

19X7	£	19X6	£
Mar. 31 Balance c/d	400,000	Jul. 1 Balance b/d	300,000[2]
		Aug. 1 Application and allotment	50,000
		Nov. 1 1st call	25,000
		19X7	
		Feb. 1 2nd call	25,000
	400,000		400,000
		Apr. 1 Balance b/d	400,000

Note 2: The opening balance is shown since the shares allotted on 1 August 19X6, being of the same class, would be credited to the same share capital account.

Share premium

19X7	£	19X6	£
Mar. 31 Balance c/d	50,750	Aug. 1 Application and allotment	50,000
		19X7	
		Mar. 31 Bank	750
	50,750		50,750
		Apr. 1 Balance b/d	50,750

1st call

19X6	£	19X6	£
Nov. 1 Share capital	25,000	Nov. 15 Bank	24,750
		19X7	
		Mar. 1 Investment-own shares	250
	25,000		25,000

2nd call

19X7	£	19X7	£
Feb. 1 Share capital	25,000	Feb. 15 Bank	24,750
		Mar. 1 Investment-own shares	250
	25,000		25,000

Investment-own shares

19X7		£	19X7	£
Mar. 1	1st Call	250	Mar. 31 Bank	500
	2nd Call	250		
		500		500

Calls in advance

There is nothing to prohibit a company receiving money for calls before the due date. An applicant for, say, 1,000 shares who is allotted only 500 shares may have paid sufficient money on application to satisfy the full purchase price of the shares allotted to him. Assuming the shares were payable so much on application, so much on allotment, and the balance on call, a transfer would be made debiting the application and allotment account and crediting the call account with the amount of the call. If the articles of association so provide, interest may be paid on calls received in advance.

At the balance sheet date, amounts received in advance should be described as such and included with share capital.

Rights issues

Where a company needs extra capital, the directors may decide to make a rights issue of shares rather than make a general offer to the public. Under a rights issue of shares, existing shareholders are informed of the number of extra shares which they are entitled to buy, calculated generally as a proportion of their existing holding. The price of the shares so offered is usually slightly lower than the current stock market price. An existing shareholder who does not wish to increase his holding can renounce his rights in favour of a third party on terms beneficial to both of them. Conditions of issue usually provide that any shares not taken up may be disposed of by the directors. The accounting entries to record a rights issue are the same as those required for a new issue, except that applicants will know in advance the number of shares to which they will be entitled and will therefore subscribe the correct amount.

Bonus issues

Most articles of association contain authority for the company to capitalise reserves by allotting as fully paid any shares or debentures of the company. It should be noted, however, that a share premium account may only be applied in the paying up of fully paid bonus shares and not in the paying up of fully paid bonus debentures.

Bonus issues are usually made when a company has substantial undistributed profits, which really represent investments in the company made by the shareholders.

An advantage to the company of making a bonus issue is that the cash resources of the company are conserved since the reserves capitalised cease to be legally and theoretically available for the payment of dividends. The accounting entries on a bonus issue of shares are:

	Debit	
Reserve account(s)		
Share capital account		Credit

With the nominal value of the shares allotted as fully paid bonus shares.

Questions

19.1S On 10 May B. Booth Ltd offered for subscription 300,000 shares of £1 each at a premium of £0.25 per share payable as follows:

On application	£0.50 per share, including the premium
On allotment 31 May	£0.50 per share
On 31 July	£0.25 per share.

Applications were received for 424,000 shares. Applicants for 24,000 shares were refused and the shares were allotted *pro rata* to the remaining applicants. Excess money paid on application was treated as part payment of the amount due on allotment. All money was received on the due dates.

You are required to give the entries in the company's journal and cash book to record the above transactions.

19.2S The authorised share capital of K. Boydell Ltd was £200,000 divided into 200,000 ordinary shares of £1 each. The directors of the company issued 100,000 shares and called up the full amount. A subscriber for 1,200 shares failed to pay the first call of £0.25 per share and the final call of £0.25 per share and the shares were forfeited.

You are required:

(a) to draft the journal entries recording the forfeiture, and
(b) to show how the share capital will subsequently appear in the company's balance sheet.

19.3S Applications were invited by the directors of Grobigg Ltd for 150,000 of its ordinary shares at £1.15 per share payable as follows:

	Per share
On application on 1 April 19X8 (including the premium of £0.15 per share)	£0.75
On allotment on 30 April 19X8	£0.20
On first and final call on 31 May 19X8	£0.20

Applications were received for 180,000 shares and it was decided to deal with these as follows:

1. To refuse allotment to applicants for 8,000 shares.
2. To give full allotment to applicants for 22,000 shares.
3. To allot the remainder of the available shares *pro rata* among the other applicants.
4. To utilise the surplus received on applications in part payment of amounts due on allotment.

An applicant, to whom 400 shares had been allotted, failed to pay the amount due on the first and final call and his shares were declared forfeit on

31 July 19X8. These shares were re-issued on 3 September 19X8, as fully paid at £0.90 per share.

Show how the transactions would be recorded in the company's books.

(Adapted from a question originally set by the *Chartered Institute of Management Accountants*)

19.4   From the information given below you are required:

(a) to prepare balance sheets of HFW Limited as at 1 January 19X6 and 31 December 19X6;

(b) to calculate the net profit or loss, before taxation, for the year.

	1 Jan. £	31 Dec. £
Land and buildings: at cost	50,000	50,000
provision for depreciation	7,000	8,000
Plant and machinery: at cost	60,000	70,000
provision for depreciation	24,000	30,000
Stock of materials	18,600	19,400
Work in progress	2,200	3,100
Stock of finished products	20,900	21,300
Sundry debtors	23,000	25,000
Provision for bad debts	1,200	1,800
Prepaid expenses	900	1,300
Cash at bank and in hand	9,100	10,700
Sundry creditors	12,000	13,000
Accrued expenses	2,500	3,000
Liability for taxation	9,000	11,000
Recommended dividends	8,000	7,000
10% debentures	20,000	Nil
Ordinary share capital issued	80,000	
Share premium	3,000	

During 19X6 the company issued a further 20,000 ordinary shares of £1 each at a price of £1.25 each. During the year cash payments of £11,000 for dividends and £9,000 for taxation were made.

(Chartered Institute of Management Accountants)

19.5   The directors of Yewtree Ltd invited applications for 200,000 of its £1 ordinary shares to be issued at £1.12½ pence per share payable as follows:

	Per share
On application on 31 July 19X1 (including the premium of 12½ pence per share)	£0.62½
On allotment on 31 August 19X1	£0.25
On first and final call on 29 September 19X1	£0.25

Applications for 250,000 shares were received and the directors decided

1. to refuse allotment to the applicants for 10,000 shares
2. to allot in full to the applicants for 40,000 shares
3. to allot the balance of the available shares *pro rata* among the other applicants
4. to utilise excess application monies in part payment of allotment monies.

One applicant, to whom shares had been allotted in full, did not pay the call due, on 29 September 19X1, and his 500 shares were forfeited on 30

November 19X1. These shares were re-issued as fully paid at £0.95 pence per share on 29 December 19X1.

You are required to draft the journal entries, including those relating to cash, to record the above transactions.

(Institute of Chartered Accountants in England and Wales)

19.6   You are required for HST Limited to show:

(a)   the journal entries for the transactions given below
(b)   the balance sheet as at 30 June 19X7.

The summarised balance sheet of HST Limited on 30 June 19X6 was as follows:

	Authorised	Issued and fully paid
	£	£
Share capital:		
Ordinary shares of £1 each	2,000,000	800,000
Reserves: Retained profit		207,000
		1,007,000
Cash at bank, overdrawn		(550,000)
Other net assets		1,557,000
		1,007,000

On 1 July 19X6 the company made a bonus issue of one ordinary share, fully paid, for every four held.

On 1 January 19X7 the company issued a prospectus inviting the general public to apply for 500,000 of the company's £1 ordinary shares at a price of £1.20 per share, payable £0.50 (including the premium) on application, and £0.70 on allotment.

Applications were received for 900,000 shares by 7 January 19X7 and the directors dealt with these as follows:

(i)   Applicants for 200,000 shares were allotted the full number of shares applied for.
(ii)   Applicants for 600,000 shares were allotted half of the number of shares applied for; no money was returned to applicants, but the surplus on applications was set off against the amount due on allotment.
(iii) The remaining applicants received no allotment and their money was returned.

The full amount due on allotment was received on 31 January 19X7.

During the year to 30 June 19X7 the company made a net profit of £230,000. An improved cash at bank position arose, not only from the share transactions, but from trading results to the extent of £60,000.

No fixed assets were purchased or sold and no dividends were paid. Taxation is to be ignored.

(Adapted from a question originally set by the
Chartered Institute of Management Accountants)

20 Redemption of shares and the purchase by a company of its own shares

Aims of the chapter:

> To consider the legal requirements when a company redeems or purchases its own shares
> To show the necessary accounting entries

Issue of redeemable shares

The Companies Act 1985 permits a company so authorised by its articles to issue redeemable shares under the following conditions:

(a) There are other shares in issue which are not redeemable.
(b) The shares may not be redeemed unless they are fully paid.
(c) The terms of redemption provide for the company to make payment at the time the shares are redeemed. The redemption may be effected on such terms and in such manner as may be provided by the articles as long as the provisions of the Act are complied with.
(d) Except in the case of a private company which takes advantage of the facility to redeem shares out of capital, the shares may be redeemed only
    (i) out of distributable profits of the company, or
    (ii) out of the proceeds of a fresh issue of shares made for the purposes of the redemption.
(e) Any premium payable on redemption is payable out of the company's distributable profits except:
    (1) the premium payable on the redemption of redeemable *preference* shares which were issued before 15 June 1982 may be paid out of the share premium account or partly out of that account and partly out of distributable profits.
    (2) Where the redemption is made out of the proceeds of a fresh issue of shares made for the purposes of the redemption *and* the shares to be redeemed were originally issued at a premium, any premium payable on their redemption *shall* be payable out of the share premium account up to an amount equal to the lesser of:
        (i) the aggregate of the premiums received by the company on the issue of the shares redeemed, or
        (ii) the current amount of the company's share premium account (including any sum transferred to that account in respect of premiums on the new shares).

Purchase of own shares

The Companies Act 1985 allows a company so authorised by its articles to purchase its own shares (including any redeemable shares) subject to the same terms and conditions as apply to the redemption of redeemable shares except that the terms and manner of purchase need not be determined by the articles. But a company may not purchase any of its shares unless, after the purchase, there would be at least one member holding non-redeemable shares. In addition, after the purchase, the allotted share capital of a public company must not be less than the authorised minimum.

A public company's purchase of its own shares may be either an 'off-market' purchase or a 'market' purchase as defined by the Companies Act 1985. A private company's purchase of its own shares will be an 'off-market' purchase.

A company must treat redeemed or purchased shares as being cancelled. The redemption or purchase of shares will thus reduce the allotted share capital by the nominal amount of the shares redeemed or purchased but the authorised share capital will not be reduced in either case.

Capital redemption reserve

The Companies Act 1985 provides that where any shares are redeemed or purchased out of the profits of the company a sum equal to the nominal amount of the shares so redeemed or purchased must be transferred to a reserve to be called the *capital redemption reserve*. The capital redemption reserve may be applied by the company in paying up unissued shares of the company to be allotted to members of the company as fully paid bonus shares. Other than this one use, the capital redemption reserve shall be capable of reduction only as if it were paid-up share capital of the company.

The reason for the creation of a capital redemption reserve where the shares are redeemed out of the profits of the company is for the protection of the company's creditors, since a company's directors may normally distribute retained profits by way of dividend. Consider the following:

A. Griffiths & Co. Ltd
Balance Sheet as at 31 December 19X1

	£	£
Assets		
Fixed assets		84,000
Current assets (excluding cash)	40,000	
less Creditors	16,000	24,000
Cash		76,000
		184,000

	£
Financed by	
Share capital – authorised, allotted and fully paid	
25,000 7% redeemable shares of £1 each	25,000
100,000 ordinary shares of £1 each	100,000
	125,000
Profit and loss account	59,000
	184,000

The redeemable shares were redeemable at a premium of 20% on 1 January 19X2.

If a capital redemption reserve were not created, the balance sheet at 1 January 19X2, following the redemption of the redeemable shares, would be:

A. Griffiths & Co. Ltd
Balance Sheet as at 1 January 19X2

	£	£
Assets		
Fixed assets		84,000
Current assets (excluding cash)	40,000	
less Creditors	16,000	24,000
Cash		46,000
		154,000
Financed by		
Share capital – authorised, allotted and fully paid		
100,000 ordinary shares of £1 each		100,000
Profit and loss account		54,000
		154,000

It is clear that the share capital has been reduced by the amount of the redeemed shares, and the cash balance has been reduced by the cash paid out. The balance on the profit and loss account has also been reduced by the amount of the premium payable on redemption (i.e. £5,000). However, the interests of the creditors were originally protected by £125,000 of share capital, but they are now only protected by £100,000 of share capital.

By transferring a sum equal to the nominal amount of the shares redeemed out of the profits of the company to a capital redemption reserve, which is not distributable, the fixed capital is maintained at £125,000, i.e. share capital £100,000 plus capital redemption reserve £25,000, as shown below.

A. Griffiths & Co. Ltd
Balance Sheet as at 1 January 19X2

	£	£
Assets		
Fixed assets		84,000
Current assets (excluding cash)	40,000	
less Creditors	16,000	24,000
Cash		46,000
		154,000
Financed by		
Share capital – authorised, allotted and fully paid		
100,000 ordinary shares of £1 each		100,000
Capital redemption reserve		25,000
		125,000
Profit and loss		29,000
		154,000

Redemption of redeemable shares

It frequently happens, particularly in examination questions, that a premium is payable on the redemption of redeemable shares (i.e. a £1 share is to be redeemed at, say, £1.20). In order to ascertain the full amount payable by the company to the redeemable shareholders, it is good practice to transfer the nominal value of the shares to be redeemed plus the premium payable on redemption to a single account called a *share redemption account*.

The accounting entries to do this are

Redeemable share capital	Debit	
Share redemption		Credit

With the nominal value of the shares to be redeemed.

Premium on redemption of shares	Debit	
Share redemption		Credit

With the amount of any premium payable on redemption of the shares.

Where the shares are to be redeemed, or partly redeemed, out of the proceeds of a new issue of shares, the accounting entries to record the issue of shares will be exactly the same as those described in Chapter 19.

The additional accounting entry where the shares are to be redeemed, or partly redeemed, out of the company's distributable profits is

Profit and loss	Debit
Capital redemption reserve	Credit

With an amount equal to the nominal value of
the shares redeemed otherwise than out of the
proceeds of a new issue.

Whichever method of redemption is used (i.e. either out of the proceeds
of a new issue of shares or out of the profits of the company), the following
accounting entries will then be made to finalise the redemption:

Share redemption	Debit
Bank	Credit

With the amount paid on the redemption of the
redeemable shares including any premium.

Where there is a premium payable on the redemption of the shares,
either

Share premium	Debit
Premium on redemption of shares	Credit

With the premium payable on redemption.

or

Profit and loss	Debit
Premium on redemption of shares	Credit

With the premium payable on redemption.

Whether the premium on redemption is debited to the share premium
account or to the profit and loss account will depend on the facts of the
particular case (see Note (e) at the beginning of this chapter).

EXAMPLE 20.1

The balance sheet of J. Goddard & Co. Ltd on 30 June 19X2 was as
follows:

Assets	£	£
Fixed assets		160,000
Current assets (excluding cash)	112,000	
Bank	30,000	
	142,000	
less Current liabilities	54,000	88,000
		248,000

Financed by

Share capital	Authorised	Allotted and fully paid
	£	£
7% redeemable preference shares of £1 each	50,000	50,000
Ordinary shares of £1 each	250,000	150,000
	300,000	200,000

Reserves		
Profit and loss		48,000
Shareholders' funds		248,000

The preference shares, which were issued before the appointed day, are redeemable at a premium of 5% on 1 August 19X2.

In order to finance the redemption of the preference shares, it was decided:

1. To redeem half of the shares from company funds.
2. To issue 25,000 ordinary shares at a premium of $7\frac{1}{2}$ pence per share, payable in full on application to raise the balance of funds required.

The ordinary shares were issued on 15 July 19X2 and the issue was fully subscribed. The preference shares were then redeemed on the due date.

For illustration purposes, both the journal entries and the ledger accounts are shown below:

Journal

19X2		£	£
Jul. 15	Bank	26,875	
	Ordinary share application		26,875
	Amount received on application for 25,000 ordinary shares of £1 each at a premium of $7\frac{1}{2}$ pence per share.		
	Ordinary share application	26,875	
	Ordinary share capital		25,000
	Share premium		1,875
	Allotment of 25,000 ordinary shares in accordance with minute no. . . . . dated . . . . 19X2.		
Aug. 1	7% redeemable preference share capital	50,000	
	Premium on redemption of preference shares	2,500	
	Preference shares redemption		52,500
	Transfer of the nominal value of the redeemable preference shares plus the premium payable on redemption.		

	£	£
Profit and loss	25,000	
Capital redemption reserve		25,000

Transfer of an amount equal to the nominal
value of shares redeemed other than out of
the proceeds of the new issue.

	£	£
Preference shares redemption	52,500	
Bank		52,500

Redemption of 50,000 7% redeemable
preference shares of £1 each at a premium
of 5%.

	£	£
Share premium	1,875	
Profit and loss	625	
Premium on redemption of preference shares		2,500

Transfer of the premium payable on the
redemption of the redeemable preference
shares.

Ledger

(Only those accounts affected by the above journal entries are shown
below. The opening balance in each case has been taken from the balance
sheet at 30 June 19X2.)

Bank

19X2			£	19X2			£
Jul. 1	Balance b/d		30,000	Aug. 1	Preference shares redemption		52,500
15	Ordinary share application		26,875	1	Balance c/d		4,375
			56,875				56,875
Aug. 1	Balance b/d		4,375				

Ordinary share application

19X2		£	19X2		£
Aug. 1	Ordinary share capital	25,000	Jul. 15	Bank – application money received	26,875
Aug. 1	Share premium	1,875			
		26,875			26,875

7% redeemable preference shares

19X2		£	19X2		£
Aug. 1	Preference share redemption	50,000	Jul. 1	Balance b/d	50,000

Premium on redemption of preference shares

19X2			£	19X2			£
Aug.	1	Preference shares redemption	2,500	Aug.	1	Share premium	1,875
					1	Profit and loss	625
			2,500				2,500

Preference shares redemption

19X2			£	19X2			£
Aug.	1	Bank	52,500	Aug.	1	7% redeemable preference share capital	50,000
					1	Premium on redemption of preference shares	2,500
			52,500				52,500

Ordinary shares

19X2			£	19X2			£
Aug.	1	Balance c/d	175,000	Jul.	1	Balance b/d	150,000
				Aug.	1	Ordinary share application	25,000
			175,000				175,000
				Aug.	1	Balance b/d	175,000

Share premium

19X2			£	19X2			£
Aug.	1	Premium on redemption of preference shares	1,875	Aug.	1	Ordinary share application	1,875
			1,875				1,875

Profit and loss

19X2			£	19X2			£
Aug.	1	Capital redemption reserve	25,000	Jul.	1	Balance b/d	48,000
	1	Premium on redemption of preference shares	625				
	1	Balance c/d	22,375				
			48,000				48,000
				Aug.	1	Balance b/d	22,375

Capital redemption reserve

	19X2		£
	Aug. 1	Profit and loss	25,000

The balance sheet of J. Goddard & Co. Ltd on 1 August 19X2, after the redemption of the preference shares and the issue of the ordinary shares would be:

	£	£
Assets		
Fixed assets		160,000
Current assets (excluding cash)	112,000	
Bank	4,375	
	116,375	
less Current liabilities	54,000	
Net current assets		62,375
		222,375

	Authorised	Allotted and fully paid
Financed by		
Share capital		
	£	£
Ordinary shares of £1 each	250,000	175,000
Unclassified shares of £1 each	50,000	
	300,000	
Reserves		
Capital redemption reserve	25,000	
Profit and loss	22,375	47,375
		222,375

The following points should be noted carefully:

1. The redemption of shares by a company does not reduce the amount of the company's authorised share capital. But the Companies Act 1985 requires any part of the allotted capital that consists of redeemable shares to be specified and the earliest and latest dates, *inter alia*, on which the company has power to redeem those shares to be stated. Once the redeemable shares have been redeemed the authorised share capital can no longer be described as consisting partly of redeemable shares. Since the redemption does not reduce the company's authorised share capital, it is suggested that the former redeemable shares should be described as *unclassified shares* in future balance sheets.
2. The transfer to the capital redemption reserve is of an amount equal to

the nominal value of the shares redeemed other than out of the proceeds of the new issue of ordinary shares.

3. The premium payable on redemption of the redeemable preference shares was first charged to the share premium account because *those shares were preference shares and they were issued before the appointed day.*

The purchase by a company of its own shares

Where a company purchases its own shares the price paid may be above, below or at par value.

Where shares are purchased by a company at a price above par, the accounting entries to record the purchase will be the same as those given earlier in this chapter for the redemption of shares but substituting the word 'purchase' for the word 'redemption'.

Where the shares are acquired for less than the nominal value, i.e. at a discount, the discount should be transferred to the credit of the capital redemption reserve.

Thus, the accounting entries to be made where a company purchases its own shares at a figure below par are:

Share capital   Debit
    Share purchase   Credit
With the nominal value of the shares purchased.

Share purchase   Debit
    Capital redemption reserve   Credit
With the discount on purchase.

Share purchase   Debit
    Bank   Credit
With the purchase price of the shares.

Where the purchase is made wholly or partly out of the distributable profits of the company, an additional accounting entry must be made:

Profit and loss   Debit
    Capital redemption reserve   Credit
With an amount equal to the nominal value of the shares purchased otherwise than out of the proceeds of a new issue, less any discount on purchase.

EXAMPLE 20.2

The following extract is given from the balance sheet of Jowetts PLC as at 31 December 19X2.

Financed by

Share capital	Authorised	Allotted and fully paid
	£	£
Ordinary shares of £1 each	200,000	150,000
'A' ordinary shares of £1 each	50,000	50,000
	250,000	200,000
Profit and loss		150,000
		350,000

On 1 January 19X3, the company purchased half of the 'A' ordinary share capital for £20,000. The whole of this purchase was made out of the distributable profits.

The journal entries to record the purchase are:

	£	£
'A' ordinary share capital	25,000	
Share purchase		25,000
Nominal value of shares purchased.		
Share purchase	5,000	
Capital redemption reserve		5,000
Discount on purchase.		
Share purchase	20,000	
Bank		20,000
Purchase price of shares acquired.		
Profit and loss	20,000	
Capital redemption reserve		20,000
Nominal value of shares purchased out of distributable profits, less discount on purchase.		

The balance sheet extract of the company's share capital and reserves, after the purchase, would show:

Financed by

Share capital	Authorised	Allotted and fully paid
	£	£
Ordinary shares of £1 each	200,000	150,000
'A' ordinary shares of £1 each	50,000	25,000
	250,000	175,000
Capital redemption reserve		25,000
Profit and loss		130,000
		330,000

Where the shares are acquired at par, the entries will be the same as those above except, of course, there will be no discount on purchase.

Questions

20.1S The summarised balance sheet of F. Davies Ltd at 30 June 19X3 was as follows:

Assets	£	£
Fixed assets		105,000
Current assets (excluding cash)	95,000	
Cash at bank	85,000	
	180,000	
less Current liabilities	75,000	
Net current assets		105,000
		210,000
Financed by		
Share capital – authorised and allotted		
Redeemable preference shares of £1 each		50,000
Ordinary shares of £1 each		100,000
		150,000
Profit and loss account		60,000
		210,000

The preference shares which were issued before the appointed day were redeemed at a premium of 10p per share on 1 July 19X3.
    You are required to prepare:
(a) the necessary ledger accounts to record the transactions
(b) a summarised balance sheet after the shares have been redeemed.

20.2S What is the *main* difference between a redemption of shares:
(a) out of distributable profits, and
(b) out of the proceeds of a new issue of shares?

20.3S Traders Limited has an authorised capital of £250,000 comprising 50,000 6% redeemable cumulative preference shares of £1 each and 200,000 ordinary shares of £1 each. The preference shares are redeemable on 1 July 19X3 at £1.05 per share.

The summarised balance sheet of the company as on 31 December 19X2 was

	£	£
Sundry assets	196,700	
Investments	14,000	
Balance at bank	28,000	238,700
less Creditors		16,700
Total net assets		222,000
Representing:		
Share capital issued and fully paid up:		
Preference		50,000
Ordinary		100,000
		150,000
Share premium		9,500
General reserve		20,000
Profit and loss account		42,500
		222,000

The necessary resolutions were duly passed and the following transactions carried through on the dates stated:

(1) On 31 May 19X3, in order to provide cash towards the redemption of the preference shares, (i) all the investments were sold for £18,000 and (ii) 20,000 ordinary shares of £1 each were issued, to existing shareholders, at £1.25 per share payable in full forthwith, and duly paid;

(2) On 1 July 19X3 the preference shares were duly redeemed; and

(3) On 30 September 19X3, a bonus issue of ordinary shares was made at the rate of one new share for every ten then held.

You are required to prepare the necessary journal entries to record these transactions (including those relating to cash) having regard to the directors' wishes that only the minimum reduction should be made in revenue reserves.

(Institute of Chartered Accountants in England and Wales)

Note: The preference shares were issued before the appointed day.

20.4S The summarised balance sheet of Barrows PLC at 31 December 19X2 was as follows:

	£	£
Assets		
Fixed assets		155,000
Current assets (excluding cash)	130,000	
Cash at bank	105,000	
	235,000	
Less Current liabilities	120,000	
Net current assets		115,000
		270,000

Financed by

Share capital	Authorised	Allotted and fully paid
Ordinary shares of £1 each	400,000	100,000
Redeemable shares of £1 each	100,000	100,000
	500,000	200,000
Share premium		5,000
Profit and loss account		65,000
		270,000

The redeemable shares, which had been issued at par, were redeemable at a premium of £0.10 per share on 31 March 19X3. To provide part of the funds for the redemption, it was decided to issue 75,000 ordinary shares of £1 each at £1.20 payable in full on application on 31 January 19X3. This issue was fully subscribed.

You are required to prepare the necessary journal entries including those relating to cash.

20.5S The facts are the same as those given for Question 20.4S except that the redeemable shares had been issued at a premium of 5p per share.

(a) Prepare the journal entries relating to the redemption of the shares.
(b) Show the different journal entries, if any, if the redeemable shares had been issued at a premium of 10p per share.

20.6S Vincent Ganley PLC has an authorised share capital of £1 million comprising 800,000 ordinary shares of £1 each and 200,000 'A' ordinary shares of £1 each. The summarised balance sheet of the company as at 31 March 19X5 was:

Assets	£	£
Fixed assets		421,400
Current assets (excluding cash)	370,720	
Cash at bank	112,000	
	482,720	
Less current liabilities	260,120	222,600
		644,000

Financed by
Share capital – allotted and fully paid

Ordinary shares	300,000
'A' ordinary shares	100,000
	400,000
Share premium	100,000
Profit and loss account	144,000
	644,000

On 1 April 19X5, the company purchased half of the allotted 'A' ordinary

shares on the stock market at a price of £1.80 pence per share. These shares had been issued at a premium of £0.50 per share.

You are required to prepare a summarised balance sheet after the shares have been purchased in each of the following cases:

(a) out of the distributable profits of the company, and
(b) out of the proceeds of a fresh issue of 50,000 ordinary shares at a price of £2.00 per share.

20.7   J. Simmons Ltd had in issue 100,000 8% redeemable preference shares of £1 each fully paid which were issued before the appointed day. The company decided to exercise its option to redeem these shares at a premium of 5% on 1 July 19X6. In order to provide some of the money required, 40,000 ordinary shares of £1 each were issued at £1.50 per share payable in full on application. The issue was fully subscribed.

The preference shares were redeemed on the above date; the balance of money required was provided out of distributable profits.

You are required to show by journal entries how the above transactions should be recorded in the books of J. Simmons Ltd.

20.8   Change Limited has an issued share capital of 65,000 7% redeemable cumulative preference shares of £1 each and 450,000 ordinary shares of £0.50 each. The preference shares are redeemable at a premium of 7½% on 1 August 19X7.

As on 31 July 19X7, the company's balance sheet showed the following position:

	£		£
Issued share capital		Sundry assets	346,000
65,000 7% redeemable		Investments	17,500
cumulative preference		Balance at bank	30,000
shares of £1 each,			
fully paid	65,000		
450,000 ordinary			
shares of £0.50 each,			
fully paid	225,000		
Profit and loss account	46,000		
Sundry creditors	57,500		
	393,500		393,500

In order to facilitate the redemption of the preference shares, it was decided:

(1) to sell the investments for £15,000;
(2) to finance part of the redemption from company funds, subject to leaving a balance on profit and loss account of £10,000; and
(3) to issue sufficient ordinary shares at a premium of 12½ pence per share to raise the balance of funds required.

The preference shares were redeemed on the due date, and the issue of ordinary shares was fully subscribed.

You are required to prepare:

(a)   the necessary journal entries to record the above transactions (including cash), and

(b)   the balance sheet as on completion.

(Institute of Chartered Accountants in England and Wales)

Note: The preference shares were issued before the appointed day.

20.9   Nonsum Limited has an authorised share capital of £400,000, consisting of 50,000 7% redeemable preference shares of £1 each and 700,000 ordinary shares of 50p each. The issued capital on 30 June 19X4 consisted of:

40,000 7% redeemable preference shares of £1 each, fully paid, and 200,000 ordinary shares of 50p each, fully paid.

The preference shares are redeemable on or after 1 January 19X4, at a premium of 12½ pence per share. The company had a credit balance on profit and loss account of £60,000 and a balance on general reserve of £50,000.

On 30 June 19X4, the company resolved:

(1)   to make from general reserve a bonus issue of one share for every two held by the existing ordinary shareholders,

(2)   to redeem the preference shares, and

(3)   to issue 40,000 ordinary shares of 50 pence each at 57½ pence per share in order to provide part of the funds for the redemption of the preference shares.

These resolutions were carried into effect.

You are required to show:

(a)   the journal entries in the company's books necessary to record the above transactions, including those relating to cash, and

(b)   the share capital and reserves of the company as they would appear in its balance sheet after their completion.

(Institute of Chartered Accountants in England and Wales)

Note: The preference shares were issued before the appointed day.

20.10   The directors of James Manock PLC resolved to purchase on the stock market up to 20% of the company's own ordinary share capital. The necessary resolution authorising the purchase was passed and, before the authority expired, 100,000 £0.50 ordinary shares were bought at a price of £1.10 each. At that date, the balances on the relevant accounts were as follows:

	Authorised	Allotted and fully paid
	£	£
Share capital		
Ordinary shares of £0.50 each	1,000,000	500,000
'A' shares of £1 each	200,000	50,000
Share premium		10,000
Profit and loss		279,000

The shares purchased had been issued at a premium of £1 per share.

You are required to prepare the necessary journal entries recording the purchase and to show the balances on *all* the relevant accounts after the purchase where:

(a) the purchase is made wholly out of the company's distributable profits, and

(b) the purchase is made partly out of the issue of 25,000 'A' ordinary shares at a price of £1.40 per share.

21 The issue and redemption of debentures

Aims of the chapter:

To describe how a company may borrow money by the issue of debentures
To show the accounting entries

A limited company may borrow money by issuing debentures provided that it is authorised to do so by its memorandum of association. The debentures may be either redeemable or perpetual.

The amount of money borrowed by an issue of debentures is usually considerable and the company may:

(1) issue a series of debentures, each debenture being of the same nominal amount, or
(2) issue debenture stock.

The distinction between individual debentures and debenture stock is similar to the distinction between stocks and shares, but unlike capital stock, debenture stock can be issued initially in the form of stock.

The accounting entries in a company's books on an issue of debentures are similar to those on an issue of shares. The debenture account is credited when the debentures are allotted and, where payment is by instalments, when the calls are made.

Debentures issued at par

The accounting entries on an issue of debentures at par are shown by the following examples.

EXAMPLE 21.1

T. Smith & Co. Ltd issued £100,000 9% debentures at par on 1 May 19X6, payable on the following terms:

	£
On application	0.40
On allotment	0.30
On call on 1 August 19X6	0.30

The issue was fully subscribed and all the application money was received by 10 May 19X6. Allotment was made two weeks later and the cash payable on allotment was received in full by 31 May 19X6. The call was made on the due date and fully paid one week later.

Both the journal entries and ledger accounts are shown below for this illustration; for future illustrations only ledger accounts will be shown.

Journal

19X6		£	£
May 10	Bank	40,000	
	9% debentures application and allotment		40,000
	Amount received on application for £100,000 9% debentures issued at par.		
May 24	9% debentures application and allotment	70,000	
	9% debentures		70,000
	Allotment of £100,000 9% debentures in bonds of £100 to sundry applicants.		
May 31	Bank	30,000	
	9% debentures application and allotment		30,000
	Amount received on allotment of £100,000 9% debentures.		
Aug. 1	9% debentures call	30,000	
	9% debentures		30,000
	Call made on holders of 9% debentures in accordance with the terms of issue.		
Aug. 8	Bank	30,000	
	9% debentures call		30,000
	Amount received on call to holders of 9% debentures.		

Ledger

Bank

19X6		£	19X6		£
May 10	9% debentures application and allotment – cash received on application	40,000	Aug. 8	Balance c/d	100,000
31	9% debentures application and allotment – cash received on allotment	30,000			
Aug. 8	9% debenture call – cash received on call	30,000			
		100,000			100,000
Aug. 9	Balance b/d	100,000			

9% debentures application and allotment

19X6		£	19X6		£
May 24	9% debentures – amount due on application and allotment	70,000	May 10	Bank – cash received on application	40,000
			31	Bank – cash received on allotment	30,000
		70,000			70,000

9% debentures

19X6		£	19X6		£
Aug. 1	Balance c/d	100,000	May 24	9% debentures application and allotment	70,000
			Aug. 1	9% debentures call	30,000
		100,000			100,000
			Aug. 1	Balance b/d	100,000

9% debentures call

19X6		£	19X6		£
Aug. 1	9% debentures	30,000	Aug. 8	Bank	30,000

Debentures issued at a premium

Where debentures are issued at a premium and assuming the full amount including the premium is payable on application, the accounting entries would be as follows:

When the cash is received:

Bank	Debit	
Application		Credit

With the full amount of cash received.

When the debentures are allotted:

	Debit	Credit
Application	With the total of the nominal amount and the premium	
Debenture		With the nominal value
Debenture premium		With the premium on the debentures

The uses of the debenture premium account are not specified in the Companies Acts, but since such gains are not made by trading it is suggested that the debenture premium account should not be used for distribution by way of dividend. It should be limited in the uses to which it is put to such things as writing off debenture issue expenses and, where debentures are redeemable, forming part of a debenture redemption fund.

EXAMPLE 21.2

R. Cropper & Co. Ltd issued £100,000 9% debentures at a premium of 5% payable in full on application by 1 April 19X3. The issue was fully subscribed and the debentures were allotted on 15 April 19X3.

Bank

19X3		£			
Apr. 1	9% debenture application – cash received on application	105,000			

9% debentures application

19X3		£	19X3		£
Apr. 15	9% debentures	100,000	Apr. 1	Bank – cash received on application	105,000
15	Debenture premium	5,000			
		105,000			105,000

9% debentures

			19X3		£
			Apr. 15	9% debentures application	100,000

Debenture premium

			19X3		£
			Apr. 15	9% debentures application	5,000

Balance Sheet (extract) as at 15 April 19X3

	Authorised	Allotted and fully paid
Financed by	£	£
Share capital		
. . . ordinary shares of £1 each	X	X
Reserves		
Share premium	X	
Debenture premium	5,000	
Profit and loss	X	X
Shareholders' funds		X
9% debentures		100,000
		X

Debentures issued at a discount

Debentures, not being part of the capital of the company, may be issued at a discount. The amount of such discount should be shown separately in every balance sheet of the company until the whole is written off. The debentures will be shown in the balance sheet at their nominal value.

Assuming the discounted amount to be payable on application, the accounting entries would be as follows:

When the cash is received:

Bank	Debit	
Application		Credit
With the full amount of cash received.		

When the debentures are allotted:

	Debit	Credit
Application	With the amount of cash received	
Discount on debentures	With the discount allowed on the debentures	
Debenture		With the nominal value of the debentures

EXAMPLE 21.3

B. Woods & Co. Ltd issued £100,000 9% debentures in bonds of £100 each, at £90 per bond, payable in full on application by 1 May 19X2. The issue was fully subscribed and the debentures were allotted on 15 May 19X2.

Bank

19X2	£	
May 1 9% debentures application – cash received on application	90,000	

9% debentures application

19X2	£	19X2	£
May 15 9% debentures	90,000	May 1 Bank – cash received on application	90,000
	90,000		90,000

Discount on debentures

19X2	£	
May 15 9% debentures	10,000	

9% debentures

19X2	£	19X2	£
May 15 Balance c/d	100,000	May 15 9% debenture application	90,000
		15 Discount on debentures	10,000
	100,000		100,000
		May 15 Balance b/d	100,000

Balance Sheet (extract) as at 15 May 19X2

Assets	£	£
Fixed assets		X
Current assets	X	
less Current liabilities	X	
Net current assets		X
Discount on debentures not yet written off[1]		10,000
		X

Note 1: This could be shown as an item under the heading of 'current assets'.

Financed by

	Authorised	Allotted and fully paid
Share capital	£	£
. . . ordinary shares of £1 each	X	X

Reserves
Profit and loss	X
Shareholders' funds	X
9% debentures	100,000
	X

If the debentures are not redeemable, the discount on issue could be written off gradually over a long period. Where the debentures are redeemable, the discount should be written off over the period of the debenture loan.

It should be noted that although debentures may be issued at a discount, such debentures cannot be exchanged for fully paid shares as this would amount to an issue of shares at a discount. If the debentures are redeemable at par or at a premium, however, they can be exchanged for fully paid shares of an equal amount on the redemption date as this is equivalent to paying for the shares in full.

Unlike shares, debentures are not subject to forfeiture for non-payment of calls due. This is because under the Companies Act 1985 a contract with a company to take up and pay for any debentures may be enforced by an order for specific performance.

Redemption of debentures

The Companies Act 1985 gives a company power to re-issue any redeemed debentures unless the articles or a contract entered into by the company (e.g. with the existing debenture holders) forbids re-issue, or the company has by resolution or by some other act made clear its intention that the debentures shall be cancelled.

The Act requires particulars of any redeemed debentures which the company has power to re-issue to be given in the balance sheet.

The accounting entries to record the redemption of the debentures are similar to those on the redemption of shares:

	Debit	
Debenture	Debit	
Debenture redemption		Credit

With the nominal value of the debentures to be redeemed.

	Debit	
Premium on redemption of debenture	Debit	
Debenture redemption		Credit

With the amount of any premium payable on redemption of the debentures.

Debenture redemption	Debit	
Bank		Credit

With the amount paid on the redemption of the debentures, including the premium if any.

Where the debentures are redeemed at a premium, the balance on the premium on redemption of debentures account must be written off, usually by transfer to the following accounts in the order given:

(i) debenture premium account, and/or
(ii) share premium account, and/or
(iii) profit and loss account.

Redeemable debentures are redeemed according to the terms of issue which are usually:

1. redemption at a fixed date; or
2. redemption by annual instalments; or
3. redemption by purchase in the open market.

The main difference between the three methods is the availability of funds with which to purchase the debentures.

Where debentures are redeemed at a fixed date, it is usual for the company to create a special fund (called a sinking fund). The money received on the sale of the fund investments is used to repay the debentures. Where no sinking fund is created (i.e. where redemption is by means of annual instalments or by purchase in the open market), an amount equal to the cash used in redemption might be transferred to a debenture redemption reserve fund from the profit and loss account. Unless this is done, working capital may be depleted since the balance on profit and loss account is often regarded as indicating the amount available for distribution by way of dividend.

When all the debentures have been redeemed, the balance on the debenture redemption reserve fund should be transferred to a general reserve account as it represents an accumulation of undistributed profits.

The three more usual ways of redeeming debentures are now illustrated.

1   *Redemption at a fixed date*

EXAMPLE 21.4

A. Lawton & Co. Ltd issued £100,000 debentures, at par, on 1 January 19X1, repayable at $102\frac{1}{2}\%$ at the end of ten years. A sinking fund was created and the investments in that fund were sold in November 19X0 (i.e. almost ten years later). The money realised was sufficient to repay the debentures. The premium on redemption was written off to profit and loss account.

Debentures

19X0		£	19X0		£
Dec. 31	Debenture redemption	100,000	Jan. 1	Balance b/d	100,000

Debenture redemption

19X0		£	19X0		£
Dec. 31	Bank	102,500	Dec. 31	Debentures	100,000
			31	Premium on redemption of debentures	2,500
		102,500			102,500

Premium on redemption of debentures

19X0		£	19X0		£
Dec. 31	Debenture redemption	2,500	Dec. 31	Profit and loss	2,500

Sinking fund

19X0		£	19X0		£
Dec. 31	Balance c/d	102,500	Jan. 1	Balance b/d	92,250
			Dec. 31	Sinking fund investments	10,250
		102,500			102,500
			19X1		
			Jan. 1	Balance b/d	102,500

Sinking fund investment

19X0		£	19X0		£
Jan. 1	Balance b/d	92,250	Nov.	Bank	102,500
Nov.	Sinking fund – profit on sale of investments	10,250			
		102,500			102,500

2   Redemption by annual instalments

The accounting entries where debentures are redeemed in this way are shown by the following example:

EXAMPLE 21.5

On 1 July 19X2, M. Dixon & Co. Ltd issued £50,000 debentures at a discount of 5%, repayable at par by annual instalments of £5,000. The entries in the company's books for the first year are given below.

Debentures

19X3		£	19X2		£
Jun. 30	Debenture redemption	5,000	Jul. 1	Balance b/d	50,000
30	Balance c/d	45,000			
		50,000			50,000
			19X3		
			Jul. 1	Balance b/d	45,000

Debenture discount

19X2		£	19X3		£
Jul. 1	Debentures	2,500	Jun. 30	Profit and loss appropriation	250
			30	Balance c/d	2,250
		2,500			2,500
19X3					
Jul. 1	Balance b/d	2,250			

Debenture redemption

19X3		£	19X3		£
Jun. 30	Bank	5,000	Jun. 30	Debentures	5,000

Debenture redemption reserve

			19X3		£
			Jun. 30	Profit and loss appropriation	5,000

Assuming the above debentures to be available for re-issue, a footnote to the balance sheet would state that the company has redeemed £5,000 debentures which it has power to re-issue.

Since the debentures are redeemable over a period of ten years, the discount on the issue of the debentures will be written off over the same period by annual charges to the profit and loss account of £250.

3   Redemption by purchase in the open market

Where the articles of association contain the power, a company limited by shares may redeem its own debentures by purchase in the open market. Unless debentures are redeemed at par, there will be either a profit (where the debentures are redeemed at a discount) or a loss (where the debentures are redeemed at a premium). Any profits should be transferred to the debenture redemption reserve account thus reducing the amount to be transferred from the profit and loss appropriation account in that year. Losses on purchase will be written off as shown earlier in this chapter against (i) the debenture premium account and/or (ii) the share premium account and/or (iii) the profit and loss account.

Where a company purchases its own debentures in the open market, strict accounting demands that appropriate adjustments are made for accrued interest in the purchase price.

In Example 21.6, following, the debentures have been purchased on the day after the interest due on them has been paid, (in technical terms – ex interest) so that the accounting entries on redemption in this way will not be obscured by other points.

EXAMPLE 21.6

P. Gale & Co. Ltd had outstanding £100,000 9% debentures at 1 January 19X5, interest on which was payable on 30 June and 31 December. On 1 July 19X5, £20,000 nominal debentures were purchased in the open market for £19,200 ex interest.

The debentures were cancelled immediately.

Debentures

19X5			£	19X5			£
Jul.	1	Debenture		Jan.	1	Balance b/d	100,000
		redemption	20,000				
	1	Balance c/d	80,000				
			100,000				100,000
				Jul.	1	Balance b/d	80,000

Debenture redemption

19X5			£	19X5			£
Jul.	1	Bank	19,200	Jul.	1	Debentures	20,000
	1	Debenture re-					
		demption reserve	800				
			20,000				20,000

Debenture redemption reserve

19X5		£	19X5			£
Jul.	1 Balance c/d	20,000	Jul.	1	Debenture redemption – profit on redemption	800
				1	Profit and loss appropriation	19,200
		20,000				20,000
			Jul.	1	Balance b/d	20,000

Where a company purchases its own debentures and does not cancel them immediately, the debentures so purchased should be shown as an asset in the balance sheet.

EXAMPLE 21.7

Assume that the debentures purchased by P. Gale & Co. Ltd were not cancelled until July 19X6, and the company's year end was 31 December.

Balance Sheet (extract) as at 31 December 19X5

	£	£
Assets		
Fixed assets		X
Investments		
Company's own debentures (nominal £20,000) at cost		19,200

When the purchase of a company's own debentures in the open market is made between interest dates, the price paid for the debentures will include accrued interest (in technical terms the debentures have been purchased *cum* interest). As stated earlier, an adjustment would then be necessary for the accrued interest included in the purchase price, viz.

Debenture interest receivable account	Debit
Profit and loss account	Credit

Date of redemption of debentures

Where debentures are redeemable, the date of redemption is often indicated by their description in the balance sheet. For example, '9% debentures 19X9' would indicate that those debentures would be redeemed during that year or on a fixed date in that year. Debentures shown as, say, '9% debentures 19X4–19X9' would be redeemed by the company not earlier than 19X4 and not later than 19X9.

Questions

21.1S On 1 July 19X2, J. Pilling & Co. Ltd issued £100,000 9% debentures at a discount of 5% repayable in 20 years time at par. These debentures were all taken up.

The discount is to be written off equally over the term of the debentures.

You are required to show:

(a) the ledger accounts to record the issue
(b) an extract of the company's balance sheet as at 30 June 19X3.

21.2S On 30 April 19X6 the summarised balance sheet of Craft Limited showed the following position:

	£	£		£
Share capital:			Fixed assets	429,000
7% redeemable			Current assets	200,000
preference shares			Balance at bank	204,000
of £1 each	120,000			
Ordinary shares of				
£1 each	280,000	400,000		
General reserve		80,000		
Profit and loss account		226,000		
		706,000		
Current liabilities		127,000		
		833,000		833,000

On 1 May 19X6, the following transactions took place:

(1) The redeemable preference shares were repaid at a premium of 10p per share, and
(2) £150,000 7½% debentures 19X0/X2 were issued at £98 *per centum*.

You are required to show:

(a) the necessary ledger accounts (including cash) to record the above transactions, and
(b) the summarised balance sheet of the company as it would appear immediately after completion.

(Institute of Chartered Accountants in England and Wales)

21.3S On 30 June 19X1, the summarised balance sheet of Switch Ltd showed the following position:

	£		£
Issued share capital:		Sundry assets	562,850
175,000 6½% redeemable			
preference shares of			
£1 each, fully paid	175,000		
500,000 ordinary shares			
of 50p each, fully paid	250,000		
Profit and loss account	95,000		
Sundry creditors	19,600		
Bank overdraft	23,250		
	562,850		562,850

The preference shares are redeemable at a premium of 5% on 1 July 19X1, and in order to facilitate the redemption the following procedure was adopted:

(1) 200,000 ordinary shares were issued at a premium of 10p per share.

(2) £150,000 9% unsecured loan stock, 19X5/19X4 was issued at 97.

Both issues were fully subscribed and the preference shares were redeemed on the due date.

You are required to prepare:

(a) the journal entries necessary to record the above transactions (including cash), and

(b) a balance sheet showing the position after completion.

(Institute of Chartered Accountants in England and Wales)

21.4S Tapical Ltd has the following balances included in its books at 31 December 19X6 year end:

	£
Ordinary share capital in 25p fully paid shares	
(authorised capital is £2,500,000)	1,500,000
Share premium account	90,000
Unappropriated profits	2,830,000
7½% redeemable loan stock 19X7/X2 (interest	
payable 30 June and 31 December)	520,000

The following transactions took place at 30 April 19X7, the necessary authorisations having been made at the annual general meeting:

(i) Part of the reserves were capitalised by a one-for-three bonus issue of fully paid shares.

(ii) Additional funds were raised by a one-for-four rights issue at 52p per share (based on the number held after the bonus issue). Members holding 90% of the shares accepted by the specified date. The remainder of the shares were sold by the company, on behalf of the shareholders renouncing their rights, at a price of 60p per share. The underwriting and other expenses amounted to £53,000.

(iii) In accordance with its powers in the trust deed, the company bought £60,000 (nominal) of its loan stock for cancellation at a price of £51,220.

Required:

(a) Show all of the journal entries resulting from these transactions, assuming that they were all completed (including cash items) on 30 April.

(b) Briefly explain your treatment of the difference between 52p and 60p in (ii), and what this represents.

(Chartered Association of Certified Accountants)

21.5 Resale Ltd a retail trading company decided that the value of its freehold properties could be used to provide additional working capital.

The summarised balance sheet of the company as on 31 March 19X9 showed the following:

	£		£	£
50,000 6% redeemable preference shares of £1 each	50,000	Freehold properties at cost Depreciation	175,000 35,000	140,000
80,000 ordinary shares of £1 each	80,000	Furniture and equipment at cost	90,000	
Share premium account	3,000			
Profit and loss account	69,000	Depreciation	30,000	60,000
	202,000			200,000
8% debentures (secured on freehold properties)	70,000	Stocks Debtors	30,000 72,000	
Creditors	35,000	Balance at bank	5,000	107,000
	307,000			307,000

Note: Depreciation on the freehold properties has been provided at 2% per annum on cost.

The following action was taken:

(1) The freehold properties were sold for £200,000 to an insurance company, who leased them back to Resale Ltd for 21 years at an annual rental of £15,000, Resale Ltd continuing to be responsible for all repairs and insurance.
(2) The 8% debentures were discharged at par.
(3) The 50,000 6% redeemable preference shares were redeemed at a premium of 10%.

The directors estimate that, in addition to the effect of the above transactions, the increased working capital available will enable the company to improve profits by £11,000 per annum.

You are required:

(a) to show the journal entries necessary to record the above transactions (including cash) in the company's books, and
(b) to calculate the effect on the future annual profits (before taxation) available for distribution to ordinary shareholders.

(Institute of Chartered Accountants in England and Wales)

21.6 Revise Ltd has an authorised capital of £150,000 in ordinary shares of £1 each and its summarised balance sheet as on 31 December 19X2 was

	£	£
Sundry assets	186,300	
Investment in own debentures (nominal amount £10,000)	8,500	
Balance at bank	6,000	200,800
less		
Creditors	22,800	
5% debentures 19X3	40,000	62,800
Total net assets		138,000

Representing:

Share capital issued and fully paid	50,000
Capital reserve	15,000
General reserve	25,000
Profit and loss account	48,000
	138,000

The 5% debentures were due for redemption on 30 September 19X3, at a premium of 10%.

The company resolved:

(1) To make an issue of 50,000 ordinary shares of £1 each at £1.20 per share. This was done on 31 May 19X3 and all monies were received on that date.

(2) On 30 September 19X3, to pay the debenture interest for the nine months then ended.

(3) To give the debenture holders the option of repayment in cash or the issue to them of new 6% debentures 19X0/X5 at par, in satisfaction of the full amount due to them on the old debentures. The holders (other than the company itself) of £20,000 of the old debentures applied the sum due to them on redemption in taking up the new debentures. The debentures which the company held as an investment were cancelled. The whole transaction was completed on 30 September 19X3, when a transfer was made from profit and loss account to general reserve equivalent to the cash sum applied in redemption.

(4) Following the completion of the above, to apply all capital reserves then standing in the company's books in making a bonus issue of shares to the ordinary shareholders. The bonus shares were issued on 31 October 19X3.

You are required to show the ledger accounts necessary to record the above transactions. Ignore taxation.

(Institute of Chartered Accountants in England and Wales)

22 Stock valuation

Aims of the chapter:

To consider the valuation of stock

In all the examples of trading and profit and loss accounts shown in this book the value of *purchases* has been adjusted by the value of *stock*[1] to arrive at the *cost of goods sold.* The adjustment has usually been shown as follows:

	£	£
Cost of sales		
Opening stock	X	
Purchases	X	
	X	
less Closing stock	X	X

The reason for this adjustment was first explained in Chapter 3, and will now appear obvious. The determination of profit requires the matching of costs with related revenues. Therefore the value of unsold stocks which it is anticipated will be sold in a future period should be carried forward to be matched against revenue in that future period.

It was also mentioned previously that there was unlikely to be any continuous control of stock at the local newsagent or corner shop, and stock would likely be valued only at the end of the accounting period (usually a year).

In questions and examples the value of stock has always been quoted at *cost.* The reason for using *cost* when valuing stock is quite simple. If stock is carried forward at more than cost, a profit is being taken in the year in which the cost is incurred, rather than in the year in which the sale is made and in which the related revenues and profits arise.

Statement of Standard Accounting Practice 9 (SSAP 9) states that stocks should be stated at cost or, if lower, at net realisable value. Net realisable value is the amount for which items of stock can be sold, less all further costs prior to sale.

Therefore if it is believed that the net realisable value of any goods is less than their cost, those goods should be included in stock at their net realis-

---

[1] In American textbooks stock is described as *inventory.*

able value. This ensures that the matching convention is being adhered to. Any reduction in the value of goods, carried forward as stock, will be reflected in the profit (or loss) of the year in which the loss occurred and was recognised, rather than in the year in which the goods are sold.

The local newsagent or corner shop referred to earlier will very probably make an end of the year effort at listing all the goods that are in stock. It could, to some extent, be a rather hit or miss affair. The schedule or lists of goods that are in stock will then be valued by reference to the cost prices that are shown on the most recent invoices.

Goods that are not selling will probably be omitted from the schedule, and goods that can only be sold at a loss (i.e. a selling price lower than cost) will be included at selling price. In this way the newsagent or corner shop will be adhering, albeit somewhat crudely, to the accounting standard. A further check will be imposed by the small trader's accountant in that he will probably query any substantial increase or reduction in stock compared with previous years. In the case of a substantial company the testing of the value placed on the closing stock will be an important part of the audit programme.

In many firms, however, an annual valuation of the goods in stock is just not sufficient. There is a need for a continuous control of stock. This need is probably greatest in the case of manufacturing firms.

Most manufacturing firms hold their stocks of raw materials and parts in a limited number of stores. All the goods received by a store will be recorded, and all goods issued from that store will be recorded and charged against the particular job or process for which they are being used. The method of recording the receipts and issues of stocks will be very similar to one of those described later, and the various methods are studied in some detail by students of costing.

There are also trading firms where there is a need for a continuous control of stock. Until recently this continuous control was really only feasible for a trading concern selling relatively few highly valued articles. The control of every single small article sold by, say, a multiple store or supermarket was not a realistic proposition, nor was it economically viable.

But now even supermarkets are able to record the sale of each individual item of stock by using a computerised system. This is done by a *bar code* being printed on, or attached to, each package of goods or groceries or other item of sale. A scanner, or light pen, at the check-out point reads the bar code, and a priced list of the sales is issued and totalled for the customer and the cashier. At the same time the data collected can be used to update the stock position. In this way the supermarket has a continuous check on stock in hand, and also of goods that require re-ordering. The system used will be very similar, if not identical, to one of those outlined below, except that the information will be prepared by computer rather than manually.

The word *cost* has figured prominently so far in this chapter. But it is not always easy to relate expenditure (i.e. cost) to specific units of stock. Two of the best known and most widely accepted methods of recording and valuing stock are the *first in, first out* (FIFO) and *average cost* (AVCO) methods.

First in, First out (FIFO)

By this method stock which is received first is regarded as being issued first. This method relates nearest to the physical movement of goods in most firms. As most goods deteriorate with age, the physical movement of goods will probably be organised so that, so far as possible, goods received first are issued or sold first. It should be noted that this physical order of movement is likely to be followed by the majority of firms, whatever method they use for valuing stock.

EXAMPLE 22.1

W. Little and Co. stock and sell a portable gas stove. During the first week of trading in the stove the following transactions took place:

Purchases
Jan. 1	40 stoves at a cost of £50
3	20 stoves at a cost of £53
5	20 stoves at a cost of £55

Sales
Jan. 2	30 stoves were sold
4	20 stoves were sold
6	25 stoves were sold

The firm's stock records based on FIFO would be as follows:

FIFO

	Purchases			Issues			Balance		
	Quan-tity	Price £	Value £	Quan-tity	Price £	Value £	Quan-tity	Price £	Value £
Jan. 1	40	50	2,000				40	50	2,000
Jan. 2				30	50	1,500	10	50	500
Jan. 3	20	53	1,060				10	50	500
							20	53	1,060
Jan. 4				10	50	500			
				10	53	530	10	53	530
Jan. 5	20	55	1,100				10	53	530
							20	55	1,100
Jan. 6				10	53	530			
				15	55	825	5	55	275

The value of stock at the end of the period by this method is therefore £275. The value is the same as would be arrived at by the end of period method of stocktaking adopted by the local shop referred to earlier: however, if the number of units in the stock at the end of the period had exceeded twenty, it would have been necessary to refer to the cost prices on more than one invoice to arrive at a correct valuation. If units in excess of twenty were valued at £55, it would result in a profit being taken which had not been realised.

Average cost (AVCO)

By this method the average unit cost of stock is calculated whenever there is a receipt of goods. Issues are priced at this unit cost until there is a further receipt.

The same details as shown in the FIFO illustration would be recorded as follows using AVCO:

AVCO

	Purchases			Issues			Balance		
	Quan-tity	Price £	Value £	Quan-tity	Price £	Value £	Quan-tity	Price £	Value £
Jan. 1	40	50	2,000				40	50	2,000
Jan. 2				30	50	1,500	10	50	500
Jan. 3	20	53	1,060				30	52	1,560[1]
Jan. 4				20	52	1,040	10	52	520
Jan. 5	20	55	1,100				30	54	1,620[2]
Jan. 6				25	54	1,350	5	54	270

Note: Average unit cost price is calculated as follows:

$$1. \quad \begin{array}{ll} 10 \times 50 = & 500 \\ 20 \times 53 = & 1,060 \\ \hline 30 & 1,560 \\ \hline \end{array} \qquad 2. \quad \begin{array}{ll} 10 \times 52 = & 520 \\ 20 \times 55 = & 1,100 \\ \hline 30 & 1,620 \\ \hline \end{array}$$

$$\text{Price} = \frac{1,560}{30} = £52 \qquad\qquad \frac{1,620}{30} = £54$$

The value of stock at the end of the period by this method is £270. The value of the stock carried forward therefore differs from that calculated using FIFO. Both values have been on the basis of cost, but a different interpretation has been put on *cost*.

Last in, First out (LIFO)

This is another variation on the cost theme. For valuation purposes only, stock is regarded as being issued firstly from the last batch of goods received, secondly from the penultimate batch, and so on.

The same details as shown in the FIFO and AVCO illustrations would be recorded as follows under LIFO:

LIFO

	Purchases			Issues			Balance		
	Quan-tity	Price £	Value £	Quan-tity	Price £	Value £	Quan-tity	Price £	Value £
Jan. 1	40	50	2,000				40	50	2,000
Jan. 2				30	50	1,500	10	50	500
Jan. 3	20	53	1,060				10	50	500
							20	53	1,060
Jan. 4				20	53	1,060	10	50	500
Jan. 5	20	55	1,100				10	50	500
							20	55	1,100
Jan. 6				20	55	1,100			
				5	50	250	5	50	250

The value of stock at the end of the period using LIFO is £250 and differs from both FIFO and AVCO. In times of rising prices stock valued by LIFO will usually result in a lower figure of profits being determined than if either the FIFO or AVCO method were used. The LIFO method, however, is not normally regarded as an appropriate method and is unlikely to be accepted by the Inland Revenue. It is accepted in the United States. Students may be required to use this method in addition to FIFO and AVCO.

Comparison of cost and net realisable value

The comparison of cost and net realisable value should be made separately in respect of each item of stock. Where this is impracticable groups or categories of stock which are similar may be taken together.

The effect this might have on stock value is shown below.

Stock item	Cost	Net realisable value (NRV)	Lower of cost or NRV
	£	£	£
A	20	25	20
B	23	29	23
C	56	53	53
D	12	15	12
E	10	8	8
F	7	10	7
G	15	16	15
	143	156	138

The total value at cost of £143 is clearly below the total of net realisable value of £156. But when each item is considered separately the value to be placed on stock is £138, as this is the total of the lower of cost or net realisable value.

Summary of other methods of valuing stock

1 Adjusted selling price

The use of selling price less an estimated profit margin. This is acceptable only if it gives a reasonable approximation of actual cost.

2 Base stock

This is based on the assumption that some businesses require a fixed or predetermined amount of stock without which they cannot operate. This stock is treated almost as if it were a fixed asset and carried forward at its original cost.

3 Replacement cost

The stock is valued at the cost at which it could be replaced. There are sound arguments for using this basis in times of inflation. The concept will be met again in more advanced studies.

4 Standard cost

Stocks are valued on the basis of predetermined budgeted unit costs. This is a method suitable for costing purposes. It may provide an acceptable value of stock at the end of the year if the standard cost is a reasonable approximation of actual costs.

Questions

22.1S Smith commenced business as a sugar importer on 1 July 19X0. Purchases of sugar were made by him as follows:

	Tons	Price per ton £
1 July	20	38
5 August	30	40
12 September	25	35
20 October	40	42
11 November	15	43
10 December	10	44

On 20 December 19X0 100 tons were sold, the net proceeds being £4,600.
You are required:
(a) to explain the following methods of computing the cost of stock on hand at the end of the period:
(i) first in, first out,

(ii) last in, first out,
(iii) average cost; and
(b) using the above figures, to show the effect of each on Smith's results for the six months and to comment thereon.

(Institute of Chartered Accountants in England and Wales)

22.2S A retailer commenced business on 1 January 19X5 with a capital of £500. He decided to specialise in a single product line and, by the end of June 19X5, his purchases and sales of this product were as follows:

Date	Purchases		Sales	
	Units	Unit price (£)	Units	Unit price (£)
Jan.	30	5.00	20	7.00
Feb.	–	–	5	7.20
Apr.	40	6.00	25	8.00
May	25	6.50	30	8.50
Jun.	20	7.00	20	9.00
	115		100	

Required:
(a) Ascertain the retailer's gross profit for the period assuming that:
  (1) stock is valued on a last in, first out (LIFO) basis, and
  (2) stock is valued on a first in, first out (FIFO) basis.
(b) Assuming that all purchases and sales are made for cash and that there are no other transactions for the period, draw up balance sheets as at 30 June 19X5 showing (1) stock valued on a FIFO basis and (2) stock valued on a LIFO basis. Comment briefly on the significance of these balance sheets.

(Chartered Association of Certified Accountants)

22.3S For the six months ended 31 October, an importer and distributor of one type of washing machine has the following transactions in his records. There was an opening balance of 100 units which had a value of £3,900.

	Bought	
Date	Quantity in units	Cost per unit £
May	100	41
June	200	50
August	400	51.875

The price of £51.875 each for the August receipts was £6.125 per unit less than the normal price because of the large quantity ordered.

	Sold	
Date	Quantity in units	Price each £
July	250	64
September	350	70
October	100	74

From the information given above, and using weighted average, FIFO and LIFO methods for pricing issues, you are required for each method to:

(a) show the stores ledger records including the closing stock balance and stock valuation;

(b) prepare in columnar format, trading accounts for the period to show the gross profit using each of the three methods of pricing issues;

(c) comment on which method, in the situation depicted, is regarded as the best measure of profit, and why.

(Chartered Institute of Management Accountants)

22.4S   You are required to calculate for each product and for the company as a whole

(a) the values of stock at 31 December 19X7, at cost;

(b) the amounts of gross profit, as they would appear in the company's trading account.

The company sells three products A, B and C on which it earns gross profit percentages, calculated on normal selling prices, of 20, 25 and $33^{1}/_{3}$ respectively. The value of its stock at 1 January 19X7, valued at cost, was

Product	£
A	24,000
B	36,000
C	12,000

During the year ended 31 December 19X7 the actual purchases and sales were

Product	Purchases £	Sales £
A	146,000	172,500
B	124,000	159,400
C	48,000	74,600

However, certain items were sold during the year at a discount on the normal selling price, and these discounts were reflected in the values of sales shown above. The items sold at a discount were

Product	Sales At normal prices £	At actual prices £
A	10,000	7,500
B	3,000	2,400
C	1,000	600

These discounts were not provided for in the cost values of stock at 1 January 19X7 given above.

(Chartered Institute of Management Accountants)

22.5   A business sells, *inter alia*, two items of stock – X and Y. During one trading period, the sales and purchases of those two commodities were:

Commodity	Purchases	Sales on credit
X	10 units at £4 each	
	15 units at £4.50 each	30 units at £6 each
	20 units at £5 each	
Y	15 units at £2 each	20 units at £4 each
	10 units at £3 each	

At the end of the trading period, it was known that the purchase price of further stocks of X would be at £6 per unit, and of Y at £2.50 per unit. The sales of Y were discovered to have been made to a customer where there was a high risk of default, and no payment has been received during the period.

Required:
(a) Draw up a table showing the gross and net profit on X and Y, and the value of the closing stock of each commodity.
(b) Explain clearly the basis for your answer to (a), stating what accounting principles you have applied.

(Chartered Association of Certified Accountants)

22.6   The annual stocktaking of Ringers Limited did not take place on the company's year end on 30 April 19X0 owing to staff illness. However, stock was taken at the close of business on 8 May 19X0 and the resultant valuation of £23,850 was used in the preparation of the company's draft accounts for the year ended 30 April 19X0 which showed a gross profit of £158,000, a net profit of £31,640 and net current assets at 30 April 19X0 of £24,600.

Subsequent investigations indicated that during the period from 30 April to 8 May 19X0 sales were £2,900, sales returns £340, purchases £4,200 and purchases returns £500.

In addition it was discovered that:

(a) A quantity of stock bought in 19X6 and included in the stock valuation at 8 May 19X0 at cost of £700 was, in fact, worthless. Instructions have now been given for the destruction of this stock.
(b) Two of the stock sheets prepared on 8 May 19X0 had been overcast by £100 and £40 respectively.
(c) The stock valuation of 8 May 19X0 included the company's office stationery stock of £1,400. (*Note*: It can be assumed that the stationery stock did not change between 30 April and 8 May 19X0.)
(d) The valuation at 8 May 19X0 had not included goods, which had cost Ringers Limited £400, sent on a sale or return basis to John Winters Limited in February 19X0. Half of these goods, in value, were bought by John Winters Limited on 29 April 19X0, but the sale has not been recorded in the company's draft accounts for the year ended 30 April 19X0.

Note: Ringers Limited achieves a uniform rate of gross profit of 20% on all sales revenue.

Required:
(a) A computation of Ringers Limited's corrected stock valuation at 30 April 19X0.
(b) A computation of Ringers Limited's corrected gross profit and net profit for the year ended 30 April 19X0, and the corrected net current assets at 30 April 19X0.

(Chartered Association of Certified Accountants)

22.7   Shortly after the end of the accounting year on 30 November 19X9, the following relevant information was obtained from the records of Greystone Limited:

	£
Capital: Authorised	35,000
Issued and fully paid – Ordinary shares of	
£1 each	25,000
8% redeemable preference	
shares of £1 each	6,000
Loan capital – 9% debentures	8,000
Retained earnings at 30 November 19X8	19,900
Land and buildings: at 30 November 19X9: at cost	20,000
at 30 November 19X8: provision	
for depreciation	6,000
Fixtures and fittings: at 30 November 19X9: at cost	40,000
at 30 November 19X8: provision	
for depreciation	8,000
Sales	50,600
Stock in trade – at 30 November 19X8	9,000
Purchases	30,500
Establishment expenses	2,700
Administrative expenses	6,000
Discounts allowed	600
Discounts received	400
Trade debtors	12,900
Provision for doubtful debts	400
Trade creditors	5,000
Balance in hand at bank	7,600

Additional information:

(i)   Depreciation is provided at the following annual rates on the cost of fixed assets held at the relevant accounting year end:

Land and buildings	2½%
Fixtures and fittings	10%

(ii) It is now estimated that 5% of the amount due from trade debtors at 30 November 19X9, will never be paid; it is proposed that the provision for doubtful debts should be adjusted accordingly.

(iii) The interest on the debentures for the year ended 30 November 19X9, has been paid and recorded correctly in the cash book, but it was debited to various personal accounts in the debtors ledger. In every case, the debenture interest paid was the only entry in the personal account.

(iv) The following information is given concerning the value of the company's stock in trade at 30 November 19X9:

	£
At net realisable value it was	13,800
At cost to the company it was	13,000
At selling price it was	19,000

(v)   During the year under review, certain fixtures and fittings, which had cost £2,000 and whose written down value at 30 November 19X8, was £1,600, were sold for £600. The only entry concerning the sale of these fixtures and fittings related to the sale proceeds which had been paid into the company's bank account and credited to sales.

(vi) The directors propose to pay the dividend on the preference shares and a dividend on the ordinary shares of 10% for the year ended 30 November 19X9.

Note: Ignore ACT.

Required:
(a) The trading and profit and loss account for the year ended 30 November 19X9, and a balance sheet as at that date.
(b) Explain briefly the reasons determining your choice of stock valuation at 30 November 19X9.

(Chartered Association of Certified Accountants)

23 Cash flow statements

Aims of the chapter:

To explain the need for cash flow statements
To illustrate a cash flow statement

The profit and loss account of a business shows the amount of profit it has made during a period (normally a year), and the balance sheet tabulates its assets and liabilities at the end of that period. However, users of such financial statements are also interested in the liquidity, viability and financial adaptability of the business. It is important that a business should be profitable, but it is also important that it is able to generate enough cash to ensure its success. Without cash a business will eventually fail, even though it may continue to report profits.

In 1975 a standard statement of accounting practice (SSAP 10) was issued. This required most companies to provide a *statement of source and application of funds* as part of a set of audited financial statements. Some companies had provided such a statement prior to this requirement. There have been many definitions of what is meant by the word *funds* in the expression *statement of source and application of funds* or *funds statement* or *funds flow statement,* but the tendency before and after SSAP 10 was to interpret funds in terms of working capital rather than cash.

Current opinion is that the information provided by a *cash flow statement* has advantages over that provided by a funds flow statement of the type described above. It is said, for example, that a cash flow statement is more relevant. Cash and cash flow is a normal feature of business life and not a specialised accounting concept, and is easier to understand than changes in working capital.

In late 1991 a financial reporting standard (FRS 1) was issued, and this replaced SSAP 10. Following FRS 1 larger companies and other larger reporting entities are now required to provide a cash flow statement with their annual accounts.

FRS 1 requires that individual cash flows should be classified under standard headings. The five standard headings are *operating activities, returns on investments and servicing of finance, taxation, investing activities,* and *financing.* Additionally a total of the cash flow before financing should be shown. The cash flow statement also includes 'cash equivalents' such as short-term highly liquid investments which are readily convertible into cash without loss.

There are two different and acceptable methods of calculating the cash flow from operating activities. These can be described as the *direct* and the *indirect* methods. The direct method shows the major classes of cash receipts and cash payments, including receipts from customers and payments to suppliers and employees. It can be likened to going back to the cash book and analysing all cash receipts and payments under appropriate headings. The direct method is encouraged but not required.

The indirect method works from the operating profit, showing the adjustments necessary for non-cash items such as depreciation and changes in working capital. The principal advantage of the indirect method is that it highlights the differences between operating profit and net cash flow from operating activities. The FRS requires the cash flow statement to show the net cash flow from operating activities, and this has to be supplemented by a note reconciling it to the operating profit. The result is that the information required by the indirect method must be given, but that required by the direct method may also be given.

It is probable therefore, under examination conditions, that the indirect method will be asked for or implied. The information required can be deduced from the profit and loss account and balance sheet, with some additional information. The direct method would be likely to require much more detailed information.

An example of a cash flow statement would now be appropriate, so shown below is the summarised trading and profit and loss account and balance sheet of F. Lomas and Co. Ltd at the completion of its first year of operations.

F. Lomas and Co. Ltd
Trading and Profit and Loss Account
for the year ending 31 December 19X1

	£
Sales	150,000
Cost of sales	120,000
Gross profit	30,000
Expenses	18,000
Net profit	12,000
Corporation tax	4,000
Net profit after tax	8,000
Proposed dividends	4,000
Retained income c/f	4,000

Balance Sheet as at 31 December 19X1

	£	£
Assets		
Fixed assets		50,000
less Depreciation		5,000
		45,000
Current assets		
Stock	15,000	
Debtors	4,000	
Bank/cash	5,000	
	24,000	
less Current liabilities		
Creditors	3,000	
Proposed dividends	4,000	
Corporation tax	4,000	
	11,000	
Working capital (net current assets)		13,000
		58,000
Financed by		
Ordinary share capital		50,000
Retained income		4,000
Shareholders' funds		54,000
Debentures (10%)		4,000
		58,000

As this is the first year of operations for F. Lomas, all the transactions represented in the balance sheet, as well as in the profit and loss account, must have taken place during the year. From the information provided it is relatively easy to prepare a cash flow statement. It is convenient to calculate first the net cash flow from operating activities. This has been done by the indirect method, and it would normally be presented as a footnote to the cash flow statement. Outflows of cash are shown in brackets.

Reconciliation of operating profit to net cash flow from operating activities

	£
Net profit before tax	12,000
Depreciation charged	5,000
Increase in stock	(15,000)
Increase in debtors	(4,000)
Increase in creditors	3,000
Net cash flow from operating activities	1,000

The logic of the indirect approach is as follows. It is first assumed that the net profit shown in the trading and profit and loss account of £12,000 (before tax) is realised in cash, and that cash therefore has been increased during the year by that amount. This would be perfectly true if the business only traded for cash. But there are debtors of £4,000, which means that cash has not been received for sales amounting to £4,000, and the cash flow is reduced by that amount. However, payment for some of the year's purchases has not yet been made (i.e. creditors of £3,000), and the cash flow will benefit to that extent. Depreciation has been charged as an expense against profits, but it is not a cash expense and has to be added back. The purchase of stock has reduced the amount of cash.

The cash flow statement below has been prepared under the required standard headings. Also included for reference purposes are examples of sub-headings which would usually be required (e.g. interest, dividend, corporation tax) but which could be omitted as they are not applicable in this first year of trading.

F. Lomas and Co. Ltd
Cash Flow Statement for the year ending 31 December 19X1

	£	£
Net cash flow from operating activities		1,000
Returns on investments and servicing of finance		
Interest received		
Interest paid	( )	
Dividends paid	( )	
Net cash flow from returns on investments and servicing of finance		( )
Taxation		
Corporation tax paid		( )
Investing activities		
Payments to acquire fixed assets	(50,000)	
Receipts from sales of fixed assets		
Net cash flow from investing activities		(50,000)
Net cash flow before financing		(49,000)
Financing		
Issue of share capital	50,000	
Issue of debentures	4,000	
Expenses of share issue	( )	
Cash flow from financing		54,000
Increase (decrease) in cash (and cash equivalent)		5,000

The preparation of a cash flow statement at the end of the second year is a somewhat more difficult exercise than that just completed for the first year. The balance sheet now represents the position after two years of operation.

Shown below is the trading and profit and loss account and balance sheet of F. Lomas and Co. Ltd for year 2.

F. Lomas and Co. Ltd
Trading and Profit and Loss Account
for the year ending 31 December 19X2

	£
Sales	170,000
Cost of sales	135,000
Gross profit	35,000
Expenses	20,000
Profit from operations	15,000
add Profit on sale of fixtures	500
Net profit	15,500
Corporation tax	5,000
Net profit after tax	10,500
Proposed dividends	6,000
Increase in retained income	4,500

Note: During the year some fixtures originally costing £5,000 on which depreciation of £1,000 had been provided were sold for £4,500. The increase in fixed assets in the balance sheet was due to the replacement of these fixtures.

Balance Sheets

	at 31 Dec. 19X2		at 31 Dec. 19X1	
	£	£	£	£
Fixed assets		55,000		50,000
less Depreciation		10,000		5,000
		45,000		45,000
Current assets				
Stock	19,000		15,000	
Debtors	6,500		4,000	
Bank/cash	13,000		5,000	
	38,500		24,000	
less Current liabilities				
Creditors	4,000		3,000	
Proposed dividends	6,000		4,000	
Corporation tax	5,000		4,000	
	15,000		11,000	
Working capital (net current assets)		23,500		13,000
		68,500		58,000

Financed by		
Ordinary share capital	55,000	50,000
Share premium account	1,000	
Retained income	8,500	4,000
Shareholders' funds	64,500	54,000
Debentures (10%)	4,000	4,000
	68,500	58,000

Notes:
1. Fixed assets

	£	Cost £	£	Depre-ciation £
Balances at 31 Dec. 19X2		55,000		10,000
Deduct balance at 1 Jan. 19X2	50,000		5,000	
less Sales	5,000	45,000	1,000	4,000
Fixtures purchased		10,000		
Depreciation for year				6,000

The cash flow statement from the information now given is as follows. The reconciliation of operating profit to net cash flow from operating activities is now provided as a footnote.

F. Lomas and Co. Ltd
Cash Flow Statement for the year ending 31 December 19X2

	£	£
Net cash flow from operating activities		15,500
Returns on investments and servicing of finance		
Dividends paid	(4,000)	
Net cash flow from returns on investments and servicing of finance		(4,000)
Taxation		
Corporation tax paid		(4,000)
Investing activities		
Payments to acquire fixed assets	(10,000)	
Receipts from sales of fixed assets	4,500	
Net cash flow from investing activities		(5,500)
Net cash flow before financing		2,000
Financing		
Issue of share capital	5,000	
Receipts from share premium	1,000	
Cash flow from financing		6,000
Increase in cash (and cash equivalent)		8,000

Notes to the cash flow statement:
Reconciliation of operating profit to net cash flow from operating activities

	£
Profit before tax	15,000
Depreciation charged	6,000
Increase in debtors	(2,500)
Increase in creditors	1,000
Increase in stock	(4,000)
Net cash flow from operating activities	15,500

In preparing the above reconciliation of operating profit to net cash flow from operating activities, it is now only the increase in debtors and in stock over the year which has to be deducted from profit before tax, and the increase in creditors which has to be added back. A reduction in debtors, stock or creditors would, of course, have the opposite effect to an increase.

Some further footnotes to the cash flow statement are required by the standard. The two most likely to affect students at this stage of study are as follows. The analysis of changes in cash will certainly be required.

Analysis of changes in cash and cash equivalents during the year

	£
Balance at 1 January 19X2	5,000
Net cash inflow	8,000
Balance at 31 December 19X2	13,000

Analysis of changes in financing during the year

	Share capital £	Debentures £
Balance at 1 January 19X2	50,000	4,000
Cash inflow from financing	5,000	–
Balance at 31 December 19X2	55,000	4,000

The preparation of a cash flow statement such as the above does require both practice and thought. One method might be to prepare a pro forma showing the standard headings, leaving ample space for sub-headings.

A table has been prepared below comparing the two balance sheets of F. Lomas. Column 1 shows the difference between the amounts shown in the two balance sheets. Some of these differences indicate a probable cash inflow, and some a probable outflow. Column 2 shows the adjustments that are necessary to the amounts in column 1, after reference to the profit and loss account and any notes. Column 3 gives the amounts which actually appear in the cash flow statement and in the reconciliation of operating profit to net cash flow from operating activities.

	Column 1 From balances £	Column 2 Adjustments £	Column 3 Cash flow £	
Cash flow statement				
Fixed assets		(10,000)[1]	(10,000)	Purchase of fixed asset
		6,000 [1]	6,000	Depreciation
		4,500 [2]	4,500	Sale of fixed asset
Dividends	2,000	(6,000)[3]	(4,000)	Payment of dividend
Corporation tax	1,000	(5,000)[4]	(4,000)	Payment of corporation tax
Share capital	5,000		5,000	Issue of shares
Premium	1,000		1,000	
Retained income	4,500	(500)[2]		
		6,000 [3]		
		5,000 [4]	15,000	Profit before tax (now agrees with P and L a/c)
Reconciliation				
Stock	(4,000)		(4,000)	Increase in stock
Debtors	(2,500)		(2,500)	Increase in debtors
Creditors	1,000		1,000	Increase in creditors
Cash increase	8,000	–	8,000	

Notes:
1. The calculation to show the cost of assets purchased and the depreciation charge for the year are shown in a footnote to the final accounts.
2. The actual sale price of the fixed asset is shown as a cash inflow, not the book value. The 'profit' on the sale of the asset must therefore be deducted from retained income.
3. Proposed dividends are added back to retained income as part of profit before tax. The previous year's dividend is an outflow.
4. Corporation tax charged against the current year's profit is added back to retained income as part of profit before tax. The tax owing at the end of the previous year is a cash outflow.

In a cash flow statement prepared by the direct method the calculation of cash flow from operating activities would probably appear rather similar to the following. It would still require reconciling by the indirect method to the operating profit shown in the profit and loss account.

	£	£
Operating activities		
Cash received from customers	X	
Interest and dividends received	X	
Cash payments to suppliers	(X)	
Cash paid to and for employees (e.g. wages)	(X)	
Interest paid	(X)	
Payments to Customs and Excise (VAT)	(X)	
Corporation tax	(X)	
Cash flow from operating activities		X

Questions

23.1S   The balance sheets of J. Cook's business at 31 December 19X1 and 31 December 19X2 were as below:

	19X1		19X2	
	£	£	£	£
Assets				
Fixed assets		19,000		20,500
less Depreciation		2,000		3,150
		17,000		17,350
Current assets				
Stocks	2,100		2,200	
Debtors	370		400	
Bank	1,200		1,100	
Cash	140		130	
	3,810		3,830	
less Current liabilities				
Creditors	430		490	
Net current assets		3,380		3,340
		20,380		20,690
Financed by				
Capital at 1 January		19,300		20,380
Profit for year		8,100		9,200
		27,400		29,580
Drawings		7,020		8,890
		20,380		20,690

Prepare a cash flow statement for the year ending 31 December 19X2.

23.2S   Mr D. Riggs is in business as a retail greengrocer with three shops. During 19X3 his profits increased significantly and he only increased his drawings by a relatively small amount. He cannot understand why it has been necessary to arrange an overdraft with his bank. From the balance sheets provided below, draw up a cash flow statement in such a way as to show why the bank account is now overdrawn.

	19X2		19X3	
	£	£	£	£
Assets				
Fixed assets		64,300		78,700
less Depreciation		22,100		28,300
		42,200		50,400
Current assets				
Stocks	1,100		1,950	
Debtors	270		1,290	
Bank	1,320		–	
Cash	370		430	
	3,060		3,670	

	£	£	£	£
less Current liabilities				
Creditors	793		851	
Bank	–		4,322	
	793		5,173	
Net current assets		2,267		(1,503)
		44,467		48,897
Financed by				
Capital b/f		42,412		44,467
Profit for year		12,132		16,225
		54,544		60,692
Drawings		10,077		11,795
		44,467		48,897

23.3S Given below are the condensed balance sheets of MacDonalds Ltd for 19X3 and 19X4 and profit and loss account for 19X4.

19X3			19X4	
£000s	£000s		£000s	£000s
		CAPITAL EMPLOYED		
1,500		Ordinary share capital		1,500
100		Share premium account		100
350		General reserve		400
400		Profit and loss account		550
2,350		SHAREHOLDERS' FUNDS		2,550
350		10% debentures		500
2,700				3,050
		EMPLOYMENT OF CAPITAL		
		FIXED ASSETS		
	600	Freehold land and buildings	600	
525	75	*less* Depreciation	100	500
	655	Plant and machinery	1,735	
550	105	*less* Depreciation	210	1,525
	150	Motor vehicles	150	
75	75	*less* Depreciation	85	65
1,150				2,090
		CURRENT ASSETS		
	510	Stock	585	
	900	Debtors	1,080	
	690	Bank	25	
	2,100		1,690	

£000s	£000s		£000s	£000s
		less CURRENT LIABILITIES		
	150	Taxation	200	
	40	Proposed dividend	50	
	360	Creditors	480	
1,550	550		730	960
2,700				3,050

Summarised Profit and Loss Account 19X4

	£000s	£000s
Trading profit		970
less Expenses	327	
Depreciation	170	
Loss on sale of assets	23	520
		450
Corporation tax		200
		250
Transfer to general reserve	50	
Ordinary dividend proposed	50	100
		150
Retained balance, brought forward		400
Retained balance, carried forward		550

During the year, plant and machinery which had cost £70,000 and which was shown in the books at a written down value of £40,000 was sold for £17,000.

You are required to:

(a) prepare a cash flow statement for 19X4, and

(b) comment on the need for the use of these statements.

23.4S From the information shown below relating to F. Jones Ltd, prepare a cash flow statement for 19X7.

Balance Sheets

	19X7 £	19X6 £		19X7 £	19X6 £
Ordinary			Fixed assets		
shares	600,000	550,000	(at cost)	1,279,300	1,058,700
Preference			*less* Depre-		
shares	50,000	50,000	ciation	283,100	201,400
Share premiums	100,000	75,000			
Profit and loss				996,200	857,300
account	140,000	90,000	Stock	57,400	58,900
Debentures	100,000	100,000	Debtors	36,100	33,800
Creditors	43,200	39,300	Bank	43,800	39,300
Proposed			Cash	400	300
dividends	65,000	55,000			
Corporation tax					
19X6		30,300			
19X7	35,700				
	1,133,900	989,600		1,133,900	989,600

During 19X7 equipment costing £73,250 (accumulated depreciation £54,750) was sold for £17,000.

23.5   Set out below are the condensed balance sheets for Glazings Limited for 19X1 and 19X2 and profit and loss account for 19X2.

	19X1		19X2	
	£000s	£000s	£000s	£000s
Ordinary share capital		600		600
Share premium account		100		100
General reserve		80		100
Profit and loss account		160		220
7% debentures		140		200
Current taxation		60		80
Proposed dividend		16		20
Sundry creditors		144		192
		1,300		1,512
Freehold land and buildings	240		240	
Depreciation	30	210	40	200
Plant and machinery	262		694	
Depreciation	42	220	84	610
Motor vehicles	60		60	
Depreciation	30	30	34	26
Stock		204		234
Debtors		360		432
Bank		276		10
		1,300		1,512

Summarised Profit and Loss Account 19X2

	£000	£000
Trading profit		388
less Expenses	131	
Depreciation	68	
Loss on sale of assets	9	208
		180
Corporation tax		80
		100
Ordinary dividend proposed	20	
Transfer to general reserve	20	40
		60
Balance of profit and loss account b/f		160
Carried forward		220

Plant which cost £28,000 and which was in the books at a written down value of £16,000, was sold for £7,000.

You are required to prepare a flow statement for 19X2 presented in a form in which it explains the change in the bank position.

23.6 This is the balance sheet of Sheltin Ltd at 31 December 19X9:

£ 19X8		£	£	£ 19X8		£	£
	Share capital and reserves:				*Fixed assets:*		
100,000	Ordinary shares	150,000		207,000	Plant at cost		219,000
	Redeemable preference				*Less*		
20,000	shares		–	66,000	Depreciation		53,000
6,000	Capital reserve		–	141,000			166,000
	Share premium				Land and		
10,000	a/c		–	23,000	buildings		37,000
	Profit and						
17,000	loss a/c		34,300	164,000			203,000
153,000			184,300		*Current assets:*		
	Reserve for			22,200	Stocks		49,000
22,000	future taxation		24,000	13,200	Debtors		16,800
–	6% debentures		25,000	2,600	Cash		14,450
					Discount on		
	Current liabilities:				issue of		
9,069	Creditors		19,700		debentures		750
	Provision for						
16,400	current taxation		28,700				
	Provision for proposed						
1,531	dividends		2,300				
202,000			284,000	202,000			284,000

The skeleton profit and loss account for the year ended on that date was

	£	£
Trading profit after deducting depreciation		84,087
less Loss on sale of fixed assets		1,400
		82,687
less Taxation		30,700
		51,987
add Balance brought forward		17,000
		68,987
less Discount on debentures written off	500	
Amounts capitalised	25,000	
Dividends	9,187	34,687
		34,300

(a) The land and buildings were revalued at 1 January 19X9; there were no purchases or sales during the period.
(b) Plant costing £27,500, on which the accrued depreciation amounted to £24,300, was sold during the year for £1,800.
(c) A bonus share issue of one for two was made on 31 January 19X9 to the ordinary shareholders.

(d) On the same date, the redeemable preference shares were redeemed at a premium of 25p per £1 share.

You are required to prepare a cash flow statement for the period.

23.7 From the following balance sheet prepare a funds flow statement for Y Ltd reconciling the opening and closing balances of working capital, and comment on the information revealed by the statement.

	At 31 May 19X1	19X2
	£	£
Issued share capital – £1 ordinary shares	18,000	23,000
Retained profits	7,500	9,200
10% debentures	6,000	7,500
Taxation payable 1 January following	2,900	3,200
Trade and expense creditors	3,200	3,400
Proposed dividends (gross)	500	600
	38,100	46,900
Fixed assets at cost	23,000	25,000
less Depreciation	5,650	6,200
	17,350	18,800
Stocks	12,000	14,695
Debtors	4,200	4,150
Balance at bank	4,550	9,255
	38,100	46,900

Note: During the year fixed assets were purchased at a cost of £5,600. Fixed assets which cost £3,600 were disposed of for £2,500. The book value of these assets was £1,500, and the profit has been included in retained profits.

(Institute of Chartered Accountants in England and Wales)

Note: The above wording is as in the original question. The answer should be prepared as a cash flow statement in line with current practice.

24 Cash budgeting

Aims of the chapter:

To examine the function of a cash budget

A cash budget is in many ways the opposite of a cash flow statement as described in the previous chapter. A cash flow statement (or funds flow statement) analyses what has happened in the past. A cash budget forecasts what is thought likely to occur in the future.

Virtually all types of business or organisation are interested in forecasting their future cash positions. Even a profitable business may experience a temporary shortage of cash. Indeed, many famous companies have experienced cash shortages from time to time and have required the assistance of their banks.

Profitable businesses can experience shortages of cash for several reasons. For example, an expanding firm could well find that the cash generated from profits is insufficient to finance the new capital projects and/or the increase in stocks which the expansion requires. A decision is therefore required as to how this shortfall can be met. Possible solutions might include a further injection of permanent capital, long-term borrowing (possibly by the issue of debentures), or a bank overdraft. Another possible cause of cash shortage could occur in periods of high interest rates when debtors are sometimes loath to pay their debts until absolutely necessary. In this way they can either reduce their own cost of borrowing or profitably invest any surplus funds, and shift the burden on to their suppliers.

It should not be forgotten that banks are in the business of lending, and investors are in the business of investing. But sophisticated lenders and investors, such as banks and institutional investors, look for both security and evidence of good management before providing funds. The necessity for temporary borrowing, or more permanent capital, should be foreseen and planned for. A cash budget, well in advance of the event, showing the reasons why extra cash is required is much more likely to receive a favourable response than is a sudden panic request. Additionally, a cash budget allows a business sufficient time to consider the alternative forms of finance available to it.

Of course, cash budgets are not only of use to foresee temporary cash flow problems. Profitable organisations without cash flow problems can plan in advance how they might utilise their surplus cash. And those meeting difficulties in terms of both profit and cash flow can look for ways of ameliorating their problems.

CASH FLOW FORECAST

FOR: _____

(Name of Company, Partnership)

FOR PERIOD FROM: _____ TO: _____

HOW TO COMPLETE THE FORM:
1. Insert the date in the month when your cash position is likely to be at its lowest (A).
2. Enter the Opening Bank Balance on that date in (B). This is the balance at the Bank – not in the Company's/Firm's etc., books. Receipts paid in but not credited to the Bank Account or Cheques issued, but not debited to the Bank Account should be included in the Income/Expenditure column.
3. Income/Expenditure includes all items which pass

	Projected	Actual	Projected	Actual	Projected	Actual	Projected	Actual	Projected	Actual
ENTER THE DATES CHOSEN (A)										
OPENING BANK BALANCE CREDIT/DEBIT (B)										
INCOME Cash Sales										
Debtors										
OTHER INCOME (Please Specify)										
TOTAL INCOME (C)										
EXPENDITURE Cash Purchases										
Creditors										
Wages and Salaries										
P.A.Y.E.										
Heat, Light & Power										
Rent										
Rates										
Bank Charges (Quarterly)										
Interest Charges (Quarterly)										
H.P. Payments										
Loan Repayments										
V.A.T. (Payments)										
Tax										
Dividends										
OTHER EXPENDITURE (Please Specify)										
TOTAL EXPENDITURE (D)										
CASH INCREASE/DECREASE (E)										
CLOSING BANK BALANCE CREDIT/DEBIT (F)										
ACTUAL BANK BALANCE IN QUESTION										
VARIATION FROM FORECAST FAVOURABLE/ADVERSE										

Figure 24.1 An extract from a cash flow forecast form of The Royal Bank of Scotland plc.

Many banks provide a 'cash flow forecast' form for the use of their smaller customers. The completion of this form will doubtless be required should the customer request overdraft facilities. A form produced by, for example, The Royal Bank of Scotland, bears a close resemblance to the format used later in this chapter. Most of the more usual items of expenditure are printed on this form so that they will not be inadvertently overlooked. There is also provision on the form for actual cash figures to be inserted as they become available so that a comparison can be made with the original projections. In this way forecasting errors are brought to light, and the system can be modified and improved where necessary. An extract from the form designed by The Royal Bank of Scotland plc is reproduced as Figure 24.1 by kind permission of the bank.

Examination questions usually provide the student with all the information required to prepare a cash budget, though not necessarily in a straight-forward manner. In practice, cash budgets are often prepared on a monthly basis as it is difficult to achieve a greater degree of precision. Similarly, most examination questions require an answer on a monthly basis, though this may be implicit in the question rather than explicit.

An examination question may also require a projected trading and profit and loss account and balance sheet. This latter part of the question, if required, may be regarded as an 'incomplete records' type question. The cash budget is, in effect, the cash book and requires converting to income and expenditure rather than receipts and payments.

Additionally the question may require some comment on the projected figures.

EXAMPLE

Tom Booth proposes to purchase a firm dealing in the wholesale supply of rubber goods. His available capital is £75,000.

The vendor is asking for £40,000 for fixed assets and £10,000 for goodwill. The stock in hand is to be acquired at cost and is estimated at £25,000. Other miscellaneous expenses of acquisition are estimated at £2,000. It is anticipated that all these costs will have to be met on or about the day of acquisition.

Forecasts have been prepared of the twelve months' transactions following 1 July 19X8, which is the proposed date of acquisition. These are as follows:

19X8	Credit sales £	Cash sales £	Expenses (excluding purchases) £
Jul.	25,000	1,000	1,500
Aug.	25,000	1,000	1,500
Sep.	24,000	800	2,100
Oct.	24,000	800	1,600
Nov.	23,000	800	1,600
Dec.	23,000	800	2,200

	£	£	£
19X9			
Jan.	23,000	800	1,700
Feb.	23,000	800	1,700
Mar.	24,000	800	2,000
Apr.	25,000	1,000	2,500
May	26,000	1,000	1,500
Jun.	26,000	1,000	2,100
	291,000	10,600	22,000

Creditors for goods purchased are paid at the end of the month following the one in which the goods are purchased. The gross profit on sales is approximately 20% and stock is replenished at about the same rate as goods are sold.

Debtors usually pay during the second month after the month of sale (e.g. July credit sales will be paid for in September).

Expenses listed above should be regarded as cash expenses and include wages, except for Tom Booth. Mr Booth will work full time in the business and will draw £1,000 per month for personal expenses.

Required:

(1) You are to prepare:

(a) A cash budget for the year ended 30 June 19X9 showing the maximum amount of overdraft required by Booth.

(b) A projected profit and loss account and balance sheet for the year ending 30 June 19X9. Fixed assets are to be depreciated at 5% and a provision is to be made for bad debts of 5% on debtors at the year end. It is also anticipated that £2,000 will need to be written off for obsolete stock.

(2) Should Tom Booth proceed with the purchase?

Solution:

1(a)

Cash budget for year ended 30 June 19X9

	Jul. £	Aug. £	Sep. £	Oct. £	Nov. £	Dec. £	Jan. £	Feb. £	Mar. £	Apr. £	May £	Jun. £
Receipts												
Cash sales	1,000	1,000	800	800	800	800	800	800	800	1,000	1,000	1,000
Credit sales			25,000	25,000	24,000	24,000	23,000	23,000	23,000	23,000	24,000	25,000
	1,000	1,000	25,800	25,800	24,800	24,800	23,800	23,800	23,800	24,000	25,000	26,000
Payments												
Assets	40,000											
Goodwill	10,000											
Stock	25,000											
Misc expenses	2,000											
Purchases –												
cash sales		800	800	640	640	640	640	640	640	640	800	800
credit sales		20,000	20,000	19,200	19,200	18,400	18,400	18,400	18,400	19,200	20,000	20,800
Expenses	1,500	1,500	2,100	1,600	1,600	2,200	1,700	1,700	2,000	2,500	1,500	2,100
Drawings	1,000	1,000	1,000	1,000	1,000	1,000	1,000	1,000	1,000	1,000	1,000	1,000
	79,500	23,300	23,900	22,440	22,440	22,240	21,740	21,740	22,040	23,340	23,300	24,700
Cash increase/ (decrease) during month	(78,500)	(22,300)	1,900	3,360	2,360	2,560	2,060	2,060	1,760	660	1,700	1,300
Capital available	75,000											
Closing cash-in-hand/(overdrawn) at end of month c/f	(3,500)	(25,800)	(23,900)	(20,540)	(18,180)	(15,620)	(13,560)	(11,500)	(9,740)	(9,080)	(7,380)	(6,080)

The maximum overdraft required will be £25,800 in August 19X8.

1(b)

Tom Booth

*Projected Trading and Profit and Loss Account
for the year ended 30 June 19X9*

	£	£
Sales – credit		291,000
cash		10,600
		301,600
Cost of goods sold		241,280
Gross profit		60,320
less Expenses		
On acquisition	2,000	
Miscellaneous (including wages)	22,000	
Depreciation	2,000	
Stock written off	2,000	
Bad debts provision	2,600	30,600
Net profit		29,720

Projected Balance Sheet as at 30 June 19X9

Assets	Cost £	Depreciation £	Net £
Goodwill	10,000	–	10,000
Fixed assets	40,000	2,000	38,000
	50,000	2,000	48,000
Current assets			
Stock		23,000	
Debtors	52,000		
less Provision	2,600	49,400	
		72,400	
Current liabilities			
Creditors	21,600		
Bank overdraft	6,080	27,680	
			44,720
			92,720
Financed by			
Capital			75,000
add Profit for year		29,720	
less Drawings		12,000	
			17,720
			92,720

Notes to Trading and Profit and Loss Account and Balance Sheet:

(i) Sales can be calculated by adding the original data in the question. Alternatively, the cash budget figures can be totalled across. It is important to remember that the final two months' credit sales are not included in the cash budget. Whichever method is adopted the final two months' credit sales (i.e. May and June) must be shown as debtors in the balance sheet.

(ii) Cost of goods sold can be calculated directly in this question by taking 80% of sales. Alternatively, the cash budget figures can be totalled across. It is important to remember that the final month's purchases (June) are not included in the cash budget. Whichever method is adopted, purchases in June must be shown as creditors in the balance sheet. In this example the stock has remained constant (except for the obsolete stock, £2,000, written off) and therefore no adjustment to purchases is required to arrive at cost of goods sold.

(1) Requirement (1) has now been completed. It will be noted that particular attention has been drawn in the answer to the fact that the maximum overdraft requirements will be in August 19X8, amounting to £25,800. It is not a good idea to expect an examiner to make his own interpretation.

(2) A net profit of £29,720 might superficially appear to provide a reasonable income for Tom Booth. Many questions do contain this sort of trap. Remember that in this case no charge has yet been made for the interest on the overdraft.

Furthermore the original £75,000 could have been invested very safely with a bank or building society to provide a reasonable income. If this loss of income is deducted from the net profit, along with an estimated amount of bank interest, Tom Booth does not look so well rewarded for working full time in the business. When discusssing something like requirement (2) it is important to bear in mind current interest rates and current wage/salary rates. The employment situation may be an influencing factor. If Tom Booth is unemployed, he may be prepared to accept a lesser reward for full-time work than he would otherwise. Questions of this nature are not always designed for straightforward, simple answers. They often require some thought and discussion.

Questions

24.1S   An accountant gathered together the following information regarding his company's cash position for the next six months:

	£
Cash/bank balance, 1 January 19X2	6,000
Monthly wages bill	40,000
Interest on debentures payable June	10,000
Rates payable in April	15,000
Dividend (anticipated) in June	30,000

	Jan.	Feb.	Mar.	Apr.	May	Jun.
	£	£	£	£	£	£
Cash sales	30,000	28,000	24,000	32,000	29,000	36,000
Credit sales	70,000	80,000	60,000	90,000	70,000	60,000
Purchases	25,000	30,000	30,000	25,000	25,000	30,000
Expenses	12,000	18,000	20,000	18,000	20,000	15,000

Credit sales are collected on average 80% in the month following that in which sales are made and 20% in the subsequent month. November 19X1 credit sales amounted to £70,000 and December 19X1 to £60,000. Purchases and expenses are usually paid in the month following that in which they are incurred. Expenses in December 19X1 amounted to £15,000 and purchases to £26,000.

Prepare a cash budget from January to June 19X2.

24.2S A company with predominantly seasonal summer sales manufactures mainly for stock in the early months of the year. For this purpose it is assisted by its bankers with overdraft arrangements. A cash budget is required for the first four months of the year (i.e. January to April) and the appropriate estimated figures are as follows:

	Sales	Purchases	Wages	Expenses
	£	£	£	£
November	63,000	42,000	4,600	4,000
December	61,000	50,000	4,500	4,000
January	38,000	78,000	5,000	8,000
February	54,000	84,000	5,200	6,000
March	70,000	84,000	5,200	6,000
April	80,000	60,000	5,000	5,000

Budgeted cash at the bank on 1 January is £9,000.

Credit terms of sales are payment by the end of the month following the month of supply. On average half of the sales are paid by the due date and the other half are paid during the next month. Creditors for purchases and expenses are paid during the month following the month of supply.

The company's bankers are usually prepared to accept a cash budget prepared on a monthly basis to determine the approximate amount of the overdraft required.

Prepare the required cash budget, and also discuss briefly whether the company's cash position is likely to improve in May.

24.3S On 31 March 19X5 the balance sheet of Schubert Ltd, retailers of musical instruments, was as follows:

	£		£	£
Ordinary shares of £1		Equipment at cost	2,000	
each fully paid	2,000	*less* Depreciation	500	
				1,500
Unappropriated profit	1,000	Stock		2,000
Trade creditors	4,000	Trade debtors		1,500
Proposed ordinary		Balance at bank		3,500
dividend	1,500			
	8,500			8,500

The company is developing a system of forward planning and on 1 April 19X5 supplies the following information:

(1)

Month	Credit sales £	Cash sales £	Credit purchases £
March 19X5 (actual)	1,500	1,400	4,000
April 19X5 (budgeted)	1,800	500	2,300
May 19X5 (budgeted)	2,000	600	2,700
June 19X5 (budgeted)	2,500	800	2,600

(2) All trade debtors are allowed one month's credit and are expected to settle promptly; the trade creditors are paid in the month following delivery.

(3) On 1 April 19X5 all the equipment was replaced at a cost of £3,000; £1,400 was allowed on the old equipment and a net payment made of £1,600. Depreciation is to be provided at the rate of 10 per cent per annum.

(4) The proposed dividend will be paid in June 19X5.

(5) The following expenses will be paid:

Wages £300 per month
Administration £150 per month
Rent £360 for year to 31 March 19X6 (to be paid in April 19X5).

(6) The gross profit percentage on Sales is estimated at 25%.

You are required to:

(a) prepare a cash budget for each of the months April, May and June 19X5;

(b) prepare a budgeted Trading and Profit and Loss Account for the three months ended 30 June 19X5; and

(c) explain the reasons for the difference between budgeted profitability and budgeted liquidity for the period.

(Institute of Chartered Accountants in England and Wales)

24.4 The month by month forecast of profitability of a company for the five months May to September is given below:

			£000s		
	May	Jun.	Jul.	Aug.	Sep.
Materials consumed	60	70	80	102	90
Wages	32	32	32	40	32
Depreciation	7	7	7	7	7
Factory expenses	5	5	5	5	5
Rent	3	3	3	3	3
Salaries and office expenses	32	32	32	32	32
Advertising and publicity	12	14	10	16	20
Sales commission	8	9	10	13	11
	159	172	179	218	200
Sales	160	180	200	260	220
Profit	1	8	21	42	20
Raw material stock (end-month)	70	80	90	70	60

The following additional information is given:

(1) On average payment is made to suppliers one month after delivery.

(2) The lag in payment of wages is 1/8th month.
(3) Factory expenses are paid during the month incurred.
(4) Rent is paid quarterly on the last day of March, June, September and December.
(5) Salaries and office expenses are paid in the month in which they arise.
(6) Advertising and publicity expenditure is paid monthly but 2 months' credit is taken.
(7) Sales commission is paid one month in arrear.
(8) On average debtors take two months' credit.
(9) Cash balance at 1st July is £52,000.
(10) In September, £30,000 will be paid for machinery. A dividend and tax thereon amounting to £6,000 will be paid in August. Investment grants of £20,000 will be received in September.

You are required to prepare a cash budget for each of the three months to 30th September. (Give figures to the nearest £1,000.)

(Institute of Chartered Accountants in England and Wales)

24.5 Hopeful Limited has recently been incorporated and intends to start business on 1 July 19X5.

The authorised capital consists of 100,000 ordinary shares of £1 each and these will be issued at £1.25 per share. In addition, an issue of 50,000 12% debentures of £1 each will be made at par, interest being payable on 31 December and 30 June, accruing from 1 July 19X5. The debentures are redeemable on or after 1 July 19XX at a price of £1.20 each.

The subscription moneys for both share and debenture issues will be received in full, one fifth of the total being invested in stocks and the remainder, with the exception of £10,000, in fixed assets. Of the stock, it is estimated that two-sevenths will form a 'base stock' and the remainder will be turned over completely every two months.

The preliminary expenses amounting to £3,000 will be paid and it is intended that these be written off in equal instalments over the first three years of operation.

You may assume the above transactions will be effected on 1 July 19X5.

In order to provide funds for the redemption of the debentures, a sinking fund is to be established by investing, on 31 December and 30 June in each accounting year, sums equivalent to 20% of the cash resources available on those days (commencing 31 December 19X5) until such time as a sufficient sum has been set aside to redeem the whole amount outstanding.

The following estimates have been made in respect of trading transactions for the twelve months to 30 June 19X6:

(1) Sales will all be on two months' credit and all purchases on one month's credit.
(2) Bad debts incurred will be 1% of sales.
(3) Gross profit earned will be 25% of sales.
(4) Trading expenses will amount to £12,000 per annum and will be payable one month in arrear.
(5) Depreciation of fixed assets will be provided at 10% per annum.
(6) An amount equal to 52% of the estimated profit after charging all trading expenses plus debenture interest, but before the write off of preliminary expenses and other appropriations, is to be set aside for corporation tax. No corporation tax will be paid in the year.
(7) Sales, purchases and expenses will accrue evenly throughout the year and stocks remain constant.

(8) The income tax on the debenture interest would be paid to the Inland Revenue 14 days after the respective quarterly dates concerned.

You are required to:

Prepare estimated accounts for the year ended 30 June 19X6, comprising

(a) a statement of receipts and payments
(b) a trading and profit and loss account
(c) a balance sheet

Take all calculations to the nearest £ and basic income tax rate at 33%. Ignore VAT and interest on sinking fund investments.

(Chartered Association of Certified Accountants)

25 Interpretation of accounts: an introduction

Aims of the chapter:

To identify the potential users of accounts
To explain how final accounts can be used as an aid in evaluating performance

The final accounts of any business can provide a substantial amount of useful information in addition to that described and considered in previous chapters.

Much of this information is provided by the use of ratio analysis which involves the calculation of ratios and/or percentages. Future references to *ratios* in this chapter will mean either a ratio or a percentage. Because of the wide use of ratios in the interpretation of accounts, students should not make the error of believing that accounts can be interpreted simply by calculating and producing a list of accounting ratios. The skill of interpretation lies in choosing or devising a suitable ratio for a particular task, making appropriate comparisons, and drawing the correct conclusion. A ratio simply reduces comparative information to a common denominator.

There are many pitfalls and hazards which await the unwary and need to be avoided. Students should be aware of the ratios in common use, understand any they use, and what, if any, are their limitations. A student should also be able to devise a simple appropriate ratio for a particular situation. He/she will probably be 're-inventing' a ratio, but no matter. A common sense approach is often more valuable than a list of half-understood accounting ratios learned by rote.

Many categories of user might be interested in information regarding a business. The owner/manager would wish to learn all he can about his own business. The intelligent owner/manager is in a favoured position in this respect. He knows what information he would like, and he has all the books and accounts of the firm at his disposal.

The owners of a limited company, i.e. the shareholders, are not normally in such a privileged position as an owner/manager. In the case of a public company the management and directors, neither of whom need necessarily be shareholders, will be much better informed than the shareholders.

Another possible interested party is the firm's banker. A request for overdraft facilities would very probably result in the banker requiring quite detailed information, so placing the banker in a somewhat privileged position.

Other parties interested in information, but whose access is likely to be restricted, include creditors, debenture holders, employees, trade unions and financial reporters. The sources open to these are likely to be limited to the published profit and loss accounts and balance sheets, directors' reports, chairman's statements, and interim reports. There are also firms such as Extel Statistical Services Ltd which specialise in providing information and ratios culled and computed from limited sources such as those listed above.

Whilst ratios can be very helpful in comparing the performance from year to year of a single firm, their usefulness is much more restricted when making inter-firm comparisons.

The classification of expenditure and the methods of valuing the stock and fixed assets of different firms are rarely comparable. The Centre for Inter-firm Comparisons does organise comparative studies for some industries. Firms involved in comparative studies have to submit information on the basis of standard definitions, which will usually require adjustments to a firm's normal accounts.

The following accounts relate to an imaginary departmental store for which the most recent three years' final accounts are summarised. Following the accounts, many of the more important accounting ratios are set out and commented upon.

Trading and Profit and Loss Accounts

	Year 1		Year 2		Year 3	
	£000s	£000s	£000s	£000s	£000s	£000s
Sales						
Cash		1,530		1,850		1,280
Credit		470		650		520
		2,000		2,500		1,800
Cost of sales						
Stock b/f	290		302		400	
Purchases	1,512		2,038		1,410	
	1,802		2,340		1,810	
less Stock c/f	302	1,500	400	1,940	390	1,420
Gross profit		500		560		380
General expenses	360		380		340	
Debenture interest	20	380	20	400	20	360
Net profit		120		160		20
Corporation tax		48		64		8
Proposed dividends		49		56		14
		97		120		22
To reserves		23		40		−2

Balance Sheets

	Year 1 £000s	Year 1 £000s	Year 2 £000s	Year 2 £000s	Year 3 £000s	Year 3 £000s
Net fixed assets		980		1,000		990
Current assets						
Stock	302		400		390	
Debtors	40		57		54	
Bank/cash	110		135		16	
	452		592		460	
Current liabilities						
Proposed dividend	49		56		14	
Tax	48		64		8	
Creditors	145		242		200	
	242		362		222	
Working capital (net current assets)		210		230		238
		1,190		1,230		1,228
Share capital (ordinary)		700		700		700
Reserves (including profit and loss a/c)		290		330		328
Shareholders' funds		990		1,030		1,028
10% debentures		200		200		200
		1,190		1,230		1,228

Profitability on sales

The most important ratios in this respect are

	Years 1	2	3
Gross profit as a percentage of sales (gross profit margin)	25	22.4	21.1
Expenses as a percentage of sales	19	16	20
Net profit before tax as a percentage of sales (net profit margin)	6	6.4	1.1

The ratios calculated above show some cause for concern. The management of the firm should of course be aware of developing problems in advance of the final accounts, and they ought to have received interim statements.

An examination of the accounts together with the ratios above shows that year 2 appears to have been a much better year than year 1 in terms of profitability. Turnover (i.e. sales) in year 2 has increased and net profit has increased in absolute terms and as a percentage of sales. Expenses, though increasing in absolute terms, have reduced as a percentage of sales. Gross profit, although it has improved in absolute terms, has reduced as a percentage of sales. This reduction in gross profit margin may have been due to a deliberate decision, in that management decided to reduce prices in the hope that this would attract an increase in turnover which would more than offset the reduced profit margins. If it were a deliberate decision, it appears to have been successful.

Year 3, however, shows a much changed picture. Turnover is now down below year 1. The gross profit as a percentage of sales (or gross profit margin) is also down once again. This could be due to sales resistance and/or increased competition forcing a reduction in selling prices. Expenses have been reduced slightly in amount, though as a percentage of sales they have risen considerably when compared with year 2. The result is a dramatic reduction in the net profit.

A major problem of trading companies is that many of their expenses are relatively fixed and cannot easily be reduced in response to reducing sales. In this example the debenture interest is obviously fixed. But other expenses such as rates, heating and lighting, and cleaning are also very difficult to reduce. It is also comparatively easy to increase staff in response to increasing sales, but difficult to shed staff quickly in more difficult times.

Profitability on capital employed

The ratios used in the last section concentrated on examining the degree of profitability obtained from sales. The expenses incurred in making those sales were also considered.

This section is concerned with the return that the firm attains on the capital that it uses or employs, that is the funds that have been invested in the firm. For this purpose the net asset value of the firm is often equated with capital employed, i.e. fixed assets plus current assets less current liabilities. This is of course equal to shareholders' funds plus long term debt.

Since capital employed has been defined as shareholders' funds plus long term debt, it is necessary in looking at the return on capital employed that the interest on long term debt should be added back to the profit before taxation.

	Years		
	1	2	3
Capital employed – £000s	1190	1230	1228
Profit plus debenture interest – £000s	140	180	40
Return on capital employed	11.76%	14.63%	3.26%

The above figures show that a very poor return is being obtained on the net assets of the firm in year 3. Year 1 and particularly year 2 are more satisfactory, but there have been many years when an investment in government stock, or a building society, or a bank deposit account would have produced a better return than this firm obtained from its assets in year 1.

Rather than use capital employed as defined above, many claim that a better measure of the efficiency of the firm is shown by using total assets, i.e. fixed assets, plus current assets. These are the assets being used by the firm and they should be utilised efficiently irrespective of how they are financed. This basis is used in the following table, and shows the previous remarks to have been apposite.

	Years		
	1	2	3
Total assets (fixed assets + current assets) £000s	1432	1592	1450
Profit plus debenture interest £000s	140	180	40
Return on total assets	9.78%	11.31%	2.76%

Another useful measure of profitability is the return obtained on shareholders' funds measured as below.

	Years		
	1	2	3
Shareholders' funds £000s	990	1030	1028
Net profit £000s	120	160	20
Return on shareholders' funds	12.12%	15.53%	1.95%

It is interesting to compare the return on shareholders' funds with the return on capital employed. The return on shareholders' funds is greater than the return on capital employed for year 1 and year 2 but less for year 3. The reason for this is that the debenture holders receive interest at a fixed rate of 10%. If the firm earns more than 10% on its assets (which are partly financed by the debentures), the shareholders will benefit. But if the firm earns less than 10%, the 10% interest still has to be paid on the debentures and consequently the shareholders suffer. This is associated with *gearing*, mentioned later.

It should be mentioned that all the returns calculated above are based on the depreciated historic cost of the assets. It might be more realistic to revalue the assets to determine whether a reasonable return is being obtained. A firm may also lease or rent assets and these may not be reflected in the balance sheet, so further reducing the value of the above ratios as measurements of efficiency.

Efficiency in the use of stock

The aim of all concerns should be to turn stock into sales as quickly as possible. Stock unsold or unused is earning nothing, but it has to be financed from shareholders' funds or borrowed money. A reduction in stock could lead to a reduction in borrowed monies, or further investment in profit-earning ventures.

Most manufacturing concerns now seek to keep their stocks of raw materials and parts at a minimum, whilst at the same time trying to avoid the possibility of a stock shortage interrupting production.

A departmental store as described and analysed here is in a different position. It will also wish to turn its stock into sales as quickly as possible, but at the same time a store must look well stocked, and possibly overstocked, with a wide range of goods in order to attract customers. It will certainly not wish to be found short of goods in regular demand, and it will wish to anticipate and therefore take advantage of new trends and fashions. Stock levels will therefore be relatively high.

The ratio used for comparison purposes is the number of times the stock has been completely sold in the year (or other appropriate period), i.e.

$$\frac{\text{Cost of sales in period}}{\text{Average stock}}$$

The average stock would be best calculated on a weekly or monthly basis, but if only the annual accounts are available the opening and closing stocks should be averaged. The use of opening and closing stocks for this purpose does have dangers in that it is an average of stocks taken at the same time of the year. In the case of a seasonal trade the figures may give an artificially low or high average.

The stock turnover for the departmental store was as follows:

	Years		
	1	2	3
Cost of sales £000s	1,500	1,940	1,420
Opening/closing stock £000s	290/302	302/400	400/390
Stock turnover per annum	5.07	5.53	3.6
Stock turnover in days	72	66	101

The above ratios show, as would be expected, that the stock was turned over more rapidly in the successful years. One would anticipate management attempting to reduce stock levels in and after the third year, without at the same time reducing the appeal of the store.

Efficiency in the collection of debts

Efficiency in the collection of debts can be determined by calculating their average collection period as follows:

	Years		
	1	2	3
Credit sales £000s	470	650	520
Credit sales ÷ 365 (i.e. credit sales per day) £000s	1.288	1.781	1.425
Debtors at year end £000s	40	57	54
Collection period for debtors	$\frac{40}{1.288}$	$\frac{57}{1.781}$	$\frac{54}{1.425}$
= days	31	32	38

The above table shows that debts are not being collected as efficiently in year 3 as in year 1 and year 2. Alternatively, the longer period for collection may be due to extended credit being offered so as to encourage sales.

Liquidity or solvency

The capital invested by the owner(s) of a firm, together with any long-term debt, should be sufficient to finance the fixed assets of the firm and also provide the necessary working capital. If the capital and long-term debt is not sufficient to finance the fixed assets, some of the fixed assets are being financed from current liabilities. A bank overdraft, being theoretically repayable on demand, is usually regarded as a current liability and many large firms at some time or other have relied on bank overdrafts to finance their capital expansion in terms of fixed assets. This is rather a precarious situation which might be best avoided except as a short-term expediency.

One test of a firm's ability to meet its financial obligations is to compare its current assets with its current liabilities and to compute a *current ratio*. The current ratios of the firm under consideration are

	Years		
	1	2	3
Current assets £000s	452	592	460
Current liabilities £000s	242	362	222
Current ratio, i.e. current assets/current liabilities	1.86	1.65	2.07

The firm's current assets are considerably in excess of its current liabilities in each year (i.e. the current ratios exceed 1) and this would seem to show that it could quite readily meet its liabilities as they fall due in all the years under scrutiny.

However, stock is not always easily turned into cash or debtors, and so a further ratio can be calculated excluding stock from the current assets. This is called the *liquid ratio* or the *quick ratio*. It is also sometimes described as the *acid test ratio*, though some literature excludes debtors from the *acid test ratio*.

The liquid ratios or quick ratios for the departmental store under analysis are

	Years		
	1	2	3
Current assets *less* stock £000s	150	192	70
Current liabilities £000s	242	362	222
Quick ratio	0.62	0.53	0.32

A minimum quick ratio of 1 is sometimes regarded as necessary if a firm is to be able to meet its liabilities as they fall due. But this assumes that all stock has to be first turned into debtors before it becomes cash. In fact more than two-thirds of the sales of the firm under consideration were cash sales. Some of the stock will be directly turned into cash each day. Again not all of the current liabilities, e.g. corporation tax, may be immediately payable.

On the other hand, there is little cash immediately available to pay the creditors and the dividends outstanding at the end of year 3. The current ratio has improved to 2.07, but most of this is in the form of stock which is turning over very slowly in year 3. In contrast the quick ratio has deteriorated to 0.32, and this probably gives the better guide to solvency at the end of year 3. An adaptation of the quick ratio to include a proportion of stock and exclude current liabilities not immediately payable might prove an even better indicator.

Both the current ratio and the quick ratio should be calculated in examination questions. But great care is required, as evidenced above, in their interpretation. The type of business under analysis should always be borne in mind.

Gearing

Gearing or *leverage* refers to the proportion of capital employed that is provided by fixed interest capital. In the example under consideration the position is as follows:

	Years		
	1	2	3
Capital employed £000s	1,190	1,230	1,228
Fixed interest capital £000s	200	200	200
Gearing ratio (%)	16.81	16.26	16.29

In this instance the fixed interest capital is entirely composed of debentures. For the purpose of calculating gearing it should be noted that preference shares are also regarded as fixed interest capital.

The importance of gearing is in the effect it has on profits available for distribution to ordinary shareholders. The payment of interest on fixed interest capital is a first charge on the firm. But if money can be borrowed at 10% and re-invested in a project to earn 12%, there is a distinct advantage to the ordinary shareholder who benefits from the excess 2%. On the other hand, if only 8% is earned on this money borrowed at 10%, the ordinary shareholder suffers in the form of reduced profits available for his benefit.

The larger the proportion of fixed interest capital, the more pronounced are the benefits or disbenefits outlined above. A firm with a high proportion of fixed interest capital is referred to as being highly geared.

Public companies

The financial press gives financial statistics which are mainly related to the current stock market price of securities. These are produced to assist potential buyers and sellers of shares, rather than as an aid to management.

In addition to the previous day's market price of a share, there will often be given the forecast yield to an investor based on the latest market price rather than the nominal price of the share. The number of times that the dividends are covered by profits will sometimes be shown, and also the price:earnings ratio. The price:earnings ratio is the market price of each share divided by the forecast earnings per share. It indicates the market price of a share in terms of the number of years' profits it represents, i.e. a share with a P/E (price : earnings) ratio of eight indicates that the current market price of the company's shares equals eight years of its current profits after tax.

The formulae used in this chapter for calculating ratios are summarised below.

Formulae

Profitability on sales

1. Gross profit as a percentage of sales $= \dfrac{\text{Gross profit} \times 100}{\text{Sales}}$.

2. Expenses as a percentage of sales $= \dfrac{\text{Expenses} \times 100}{\text{Sales}}$.

3. Net profit before tax as a percentage of sales $= \dfrac{\text{Net profit (before tax)} \times 100}{\text{Sales}}$.

Profitability on capital employed (as defined)

1. Return on capital employed $= \dfrac{\text{Net profit (before tax)} \times 100}{\text{Capital employed}}$.

2. Return on total assets $= \dfrac{\text{Net profit (before tax)} \times 100}{\text{Total assets}}$.

3. Return on shareholders' funds $= \dfrac{\text{Net profit (before tax)} \times 100}{\text{Shareholders' funds}}$.

Measures of efficiency

1. Efficiency in the use of stock $= \dfrac{\text{Cost of sales}}{\text{Average stock}} = $ No. of times stock is turned over in a year.

2. Efficiency in the collection of debts $= \dfrac{\text{Debtors at year end}}{\text{Average daily credit sales}}$

$=$ Average length of credit taken by debtors in days.

Liquidity ratios

1. Current ratio $\qquad = \dfrac{\text{Current assets}}{\text{Current liabilities}}.$

2. Liquid or quick ratio $\qquad = \dfrac{\text{Current assets } less \text{ stocks}}{\text{Current liabilities}}.$

Gearing

1. High geared $=$ Where the proportion of fixed interest capital is high relative to the total capital of the company.
2. Low geared $=$ Where the proportion of fixed interest capital is low relative to the total capital of the company.

Questions

25.1S Shown below are the accounts of R.J. Smith, for the year to 31 March 19X5.

Trading and Profit and Loss Account
for the year to 31 March 19X5

	£	£	£
Sales			21,000
less Opening stock at cost	2,400		
Purchases	15,600	18,000	
deduct Closing stock at cost		2,250	15,750
Gross profit			5,250
less Rent and rates		600	
Light and heat		192	
Wages		936	
Part-time salesman's commission		420	
Delivery expenses		180	
Depreciation of fittings		120	
Office and sundry expenses		390	2,838
Net profit			2,412

Mr Smith plans to increase his sales by 10% during the year to 31 March 19X6, and assumes the following:

(i) His percentage of gross profit to turnover will remain the same as for the year to 31 March 19X5.

(ii) All expenses will remain the same as for the year to 31 March 19X5, with the exception of rent and rates, salesman's commission and delivery expenses. Rent and rates will rise to £800; the percentage of salesman's commission to turnover in 19X5–X6 will be the same as in 19X4–X5; it is estimated that delivery expenses will increase by £50 above the 19X4–X5 figure.

You are required to:

(a) Define what is meant by *gross profit ratio*.
(b) Answer the following questions on the accounts to 31 March 19X5:

(i) What is the percentage of gross profit to turnover?
(ii) What is the percentage of net profit to turnover?
(iii) What is the percentage of salesman's commission to turnover?
(iv) What is the value of stock at cost available for sale during the trading period?
(v) What is the cost of goods sold?

(c) From the information given, calculate:

(i) the expected gross profit for the year to 31 March 19X6;
(ii) in the form of a profit and loss account, the expected net profit for the year to 31 March 19X6.

25.2S The balance sheets and trading and profit and loss accounts for the year ended 30 June 19X8 of S. Ltd and T. Ltd are given below:

Balance Sheets as at 30 June 19X8

	S. Ltd £	S. Ltd £	T. Ltd £	T. Ltd £
Fixed assets, at cost	60,000		30,000	
less Provision for depreciation	20,000	40,000	10,000	20,000
Current assets				
Stocks	57,000		30,000	
Debtors	22,000		20,000	
Cash	11,000		10,000	
	90,000		60,000	
less Current liabilities	30,000	60,000	30,000	30,000
Net assets employed		100,000		50,000
Ordinary share capital, fully paid		95,000		45,000
Revenue reserve: Profit and loss a/c balance		5,000		5,000
		100,000		50,000

Trading and Profit and Loss Accounts for the year ended 30 June 19X8

	S. Ltd £	S. Ltd £	T. Ltd £	T. Ltd £
Sales		160,000		120,000
Stock at 1 July 19X7	39,000		20,000	
add Purchases	114,000		85,000	
	153,000		105,000	
less Stock at 30 June 19X8	57,000		30,000	
Cost of sales		96,000		75,000
Gross profit for the year		64,000		45,000
less General expenses		56,000		39,000
Net profit for the year		8,000		6,000

	£	£
add Balance brought forward	3,000	1,000
	11,000	7,000
less Dividends paid	6,000	2,000
Balance carried forward	5,000	5,000

You may assume that stocks have increased evenly throughout the year.

You are required to:

(a) calculate three of the following ratios separately for each company:

    (i) net profit for the year as a percentage of net assets employed at 30 June 19X8;

    (ii) net profit for the year as a percentage of sales;

    (iii) gross profit for the year as a percentage of sales;

    (iv) current assets to current liabilities at 30 June 19X8;

    (v) debtors and cash to current liabilities at 30 June 19X8;

    (vi) cost of sales to average stock held during the year;

(b) describe briefly the main conclusions which you draw from a comparison of the ratios which you have calculated for each company.

(Chartered Institute of Management Accountants)

25.3S Unigear Ltd is a high fashion retail trading company with an issued share capital of £200,000 in ordinary shares. The detailed profit and loss account for the year ended 31 December 19X2 showed the following:

19X1				19X2	
£	£			£	£
	1,500,000	Sales			1,000,000
		less Cost of sales			
250,000		Opening stock	300,000		
950,000		Purchases	760,000		
1,200,000			1,060,000		
		less Closing stock			
300,000			410,000		
	900,000				650,000
	600,000				350,000
		Deduct:			
10,450		Rent and rates	12,106		
3,608		Light and heat	4,942		
609		Telephone	718		
301,459		Wages and salaries	212,374		
40,216		Advertising	42,605		
2,600		Repairs and renewals	750		
4,224		Bad debts	12,943		
22,328		Bank interest and commission	46,420		
850		Audit fee	1,000		

£	£		£	£
		General		
5,960		expenses	7,240	
2,400		Depreciation	2,000	
	394,704			343,098
	205,296	Trading profit for year		6,902
	55,000	Deduct: Corporation tax		5,500
	150,296	Profit for year after taxation		1,402
	40,000	*less* Dividend		–
	110,296			1,402
	24,843	*add* Balance b/f		135,139
	135,139	Balance carried forward		136,541

Wages and salaries include directors' remuneration of £24,650 (19X1 £67,740), and the charge for corporation tax in the year to 31 December 19X2 includes an underprovision of £2,500 relating to the previous year.

You are required to write a short report to the directors giving your observations on the results for the year and the comparison with the previous year.

(Institute of Chartered Accountants in England and Wales)

25.4S The Alpha Co. Ltd, a retail business, has an authorised share capital of 200,000 £1 ordinary shares and 250,000 8% £1 redeemable preference shares.

(*a*) The trial balance of that company as at 31 December 19X5 (after preparing the trading, profit and loss account) was as follows:

	£
Provision for depreciation – Fittings	75,000
Vehicles	187,000
Goodwill	60,000
Issued share capital	
100,000 £1 ordinary shares	100,000
250,000 8% £1 redeemable preference shares	250,000
Share premium account	20,000
Trade debtors and prepayments	85,400
Land and buildings at valuation (cost £220,000)	270,000
Capital redemption reserve	150,000
Fittings at cost	175,000
Motor vehicles at cost	397,000
10% debentures	80,000
Trade creditors and accruals	48,000
Short term investments (market value £43,000)	39,000
Stock at 31 December 19X5	148,000
Bank overdraft	27,000
Revaluation reserve	50,000
Net profit for the year	72,000
Undistributed profit at 1 January 19X5	73,000
General reserve	55,000
Provision for doubtful debts	2,400
Interim dividends paid – Ordinary	5,000
Preference	10,000

The directors wish to:

(i)   Transfer £25,000 to general reserve.

(ii) Provide for a 5% final ordinary dividend, and the final preference dividend.

(iii) Write £20,000 off the goodwill account.

Required:

Prepare in good form the appropriation account of the Alpha Co. Ltd for the year ended 31 December 19X5, and a balance sheet as at that date. (Ignore taxation.)

(*b*) Write a *short* response to the following questions based on the above accounts.

(1) When can the company issue the balance of its share capital?

(2) What is the return on net capital employed (after making adjustment for debenture interest)? What is the significance of this figure?

(3) What is the company's working capital and what is the importance of this?

(4) How could the 'goodwill' have arisen?

(5) Assuming the company had the cash, what is the maximum amount which could be distributed by way of dividend?

(6) Why should the market value of the ordinary shares differ from their book value?

(7) What is the significance of the 'share premium' account?

(Chartered Association of Certified Accountants)

25.5   The following are the abridged accounts of A, B and C trading as R. B. & Company.

Balance Sheet as at 31 December

	19X9		19X0	
	£	£	£	£
Assets				
Fixed assets at cost		20,000		28,000
less Depreciation		4,000		5,000
		16,000		23,000
Current assets				
Stock at cost	8,000		11,000	
Debtors	5,000		7,000	
Cash at bank	1,600		–	
	14,600		18,000	
less Current liabilities				
Creditors	9,100		10,400	
Bank overdraft	–		5,300	
	9,100		15,700	
Net current assets		5,500		2,300
		21,500		25,300

			£	£	£	£
Financed by						
Capital accounts	A	9,000		–		
	B	6,000		6,000		
	C	3,000	18,000	3,000	9,000	
Current accounts	A	1,800		–		
	B	900		4,300		
	C	800	3,500	3,000	7,300	
Loan account	A				9,000	
			21,500		25,300	

Profit and Loss Account for the year ended 31 December

	19X9	19X0
	£	£
Sales	40,000	64,000
less Cost of sales	22,000	36,000
Gross profit	18,000	28,000
less Trading expenses	9,000	11,000
Net profit for the year	9,000	17,000

Notes:
1. During the year ended 31 December 19X0, A retired and withdrew the balance on his current account.
2. All sales were made on credit.
3. The stock at cost at 1 January 19X9 was £7,800.

You are required:

(a) to state the components of and to calculate four accounting ratios which help to assess the profitability and liquidity performance of R. B. & Company for both 19X9 and 19X0;

(b) using the above ratios and any additional information to comment on the position of the firm at 31 December 19X0.

25.6 You are required BRIEFLY to comment on the meaning and practical application of the following ratios:

(a) Capital gearing ratio
(b) Shareholders' funds: total assets (the proprietary ratio)
(c) Percentage of net trading profit to turnover
(d) Liquid ratio
(e) Yields.

(Chartered Association of Certified Accountants)

25.7 From the following information extracted from the accounts of Robin Company Limited as at 31 December 19X8, you are required:

(a) to draw up a vertical form of balance sheet with suitable sub-headings, and in a form suitable for analysis, and

(b) to comment on the position disclosed thereby.

Your comments in (b) should include the additional information you may require and any action you may consider the company needs to take.

	£		£
Bank overdraft	15,000	Plant and machinery	
Sundry creditors	25,000	at cost	200,000
Sundry debtors	7,500	Provision for	
General reserve	2,500	depreciation – on:	
Goodwill	40,000	Land and buildings	40,000
Investments at cost	22,500	Motor vehicles	16,000
Land and buildings		Plant and machinery	88,000
at cost	110,000	Profit and loss a/c –	
Motor vehicles at		debit balance	42,500
cost	20,000	Stock at valuation	24,000
6% mortgage debentures		Share capital, issued and	
19X4/X6 (i.e. 6–8 years		authorised –	
hence)	40,000	100,000 5% prefer-	
		ence shares of £1	
		each, fully paid	100,000
		140,000 ordinary	
		shares of £1	
		each, fully paid	140,000

(Chartered Association of Certified Accountants)

25.8   (a) The following balances have been extracted from the books of the Nemesis Company Limited as at 30 September 19X7:

	£
Creditors	6,300
Sales	80,000
Land at cost	18,000
Buildings at cost	38,000
Furniture and fittings at cost	22,000
Bank (credit balance)	6,000
Depreciation – buildings	6,000
– furniture and fittings	10,000
Discounts received	1,764
Unappropriated profit at 1 October 19X6	2,000
Provision for doubtful debts	816
Goodwill	16,400
Cash in hand	232
Stock at 1 October 19X6	14,248
Interim dividend on preference shares	600
Rates	2,124
Wages and salaries	8,000
Insurance	1,896
Returns inward	372
General expenses	436
Debtors	12,640
Purchases	43,856
Debenture interest	400
Bad debts	676
5% debentures	16,000
6% £1 preference shares	20,000
£1 ordinary shares	20,000
General reserve	10,000
Share premium	1,000

Additional information:

(i) Stock on hand at 30 September 19X7 was £15,546.
(ii) Insurance paid in advance – £100.
(iii) Wages owing – £280.
(iv) Depreciation is to be provided at 10% on cost of buildings, and at 20% on the written down value of furniture and fittings.
(v) Provision for doubtful debts is to be reduced to 5% of debtors.
(vi) Debenture interest outstanding of £400.
(vii) The directors propose to pay a 5% ordinary dividend and the final preference dividend, and to transfer £8,000 to general reserve.

Required:
Prepare the trading, profit and loss and appropriation account for the period ended 30 September 19X7 and a balance sheet as at that date.

(*b*) Examine the accounts you have prepared in (*a*) above and then answer the questions below:

(i) How did the share premium account arise?
(ii) How could the goodwill account have arisen?
(iii) What is the rate of return on net capital employed, and what is the significance of this figure?
(iv) Which of the reserves are capital reserves and which are revenue reserves, and what, in principle, is the difference between the two?
(v) The company is relatively highly geared: what does this mean?

(Chartered Association of Certified Accountants)

25.9 A. Williamson Ltd, was established in the retail trade in 19X1. Since that date, the company has shown increasing profits. The directors have asked for a detailed report on the current financial position of the company based on the accounts for 19X8, and recommendations regarding future activity.

Profit and Loss Account for the year ended 31 December

	19X7 £000s	19X8 £000s
Sales	800	900
less Cost of sales	480	525
Gross profit	320	375
less Expenses	160	165
Net profit before taxation	160	210
Taxation	68	94
Net profit after taxation	92	116
Dividends proposed	64	64
Retained profit for the year	28	52

Depreciation is included in the expenses figure. For 19X8, the total was £48,000 made up of £30,000 for furniture and fittings and £18,000 for motor vehicles.

Balance Sheets as at 31 December

	19X7			19X8	
	£000s	£000s	£000s	£000s	£000s	£000s

	19X7 £000s	19X7 £000s	19X8 £000s	19X8 £000s
Assets				
Fixed assets (net of depreciation)				
Furniture and fittings		300		380
Motor vehicles		93		141
		393		521
Current assets				
Stock at cost	180		240	
Debtors	83		93	
Cash at bank	70		7	
Cash in hand	57		5	
	390		345	
less Current liabilities				
Creditors	108		113	
Proposed dividends	64		64	
Taxation due 30 September 19X9 (19X8)	68	240	94	271
Net current assets		150		74
		543		595
Financed by				
Share capital – authorised and issued				
Ordinary shares of £1 each		400		400
Retained profits		93		145
		493		545
10% debentures		50		50
		543		595

You are required to prepare a report for the directors, including a statement of sources and application of funds, based on the figures given for 19X7 and 19X8.

26 Bills of exchange

Aims of the chapter:

To define a bill of exchange
To show how such bills are recorded in the books of account

The Bills of Exchange Act 1882 defines a bill of exchange as

> an unconditional order in writing, addressed by one person to another, signed by the person giving it, requiring the person to whom it is addressed to pay on demand or at a fixed or determinable future time a sum certain in money to or to the order of a specified person or bearer.

A bill of exchange works in the following manner.

The creditor (say H. Kells) is owed £500 for goods he has supplied to S. Lees. H. Kells, the creditor, writes out a bill of exchange and is the *drawer* of the bill. The wording of the bill is such that it will require S. Lees (the *drawee* and debtor) to pay £500 to H. Kells at a fixed or determinable future time. S. Lees signs his name across the face of the bill (usually, but not necessarily, including the word *accepted*) and so becomes the *acceptor* and returns the bill to H. Kells. S. Lees is not liable for the bill until he accepts it.

In the example given above, H. Kells is both the drawer and *payee* as the money is to be paid to himself. H. Kells could have required that S. Lees pay J. Campbell, in which case J. Campbell is the payee.

The advantages of a bill of exchange are as follows:

1. It is legal evidence of debt and it fixes the date of payment.
2. It can be cashed at a discount before the date of payment.
3. As a *negotiable instrument* it can be transferred by the payee to another person in settlement or part settlement of debts.
4. It is used mainly in trades where fairly long credit is given, and it assists in providing this credit.

Bills receivable

Since the amount of the bill is receivable by the drawer (or creditor), in the creditor's books of account bills of exchange are known as *bills receivable*.

In the previous example, where S. Lees accepted a bill from H. Kells for £500, the following entry would be made in the books of H. Kells on his receipt of the accepted bill.

	Dr. £	Cr. £
Bills receivable	500	
S. Lees (debtor)		500
Bill of exchange accepted by S. Lees.		

The ledger accounts at this stage would show

S. Lees

	£		£
Sales	500	Bills receivable	500

Bills receivable

	£	
S. Lees	500	

If a balance sheet was to be prepared now, the bills receivable would appear as a current asset immediately below debtors.

On the due date the bill would be presented for payment, and when the cash was received by H. Kells his bank account would be debited and the bills receivable account would be credited. The bills receivable account can be regarded, therefore, as another form of debtors account, except that the debt has been evidenced by a bill of exchange. A subsidiary book or *bill book* is kept to record the position of all bills in the bills receivable account.

Discounting bills receivable

As indicated in the list of advantages, a bill of exchange can be cashed or *discounted* before its due date of payment. This means that the bill is, in effect, sold to a banker or bill broker. The banker will deduct an amount from the face value of the bill. The amount deducted, called a *discount*, is based on current interest rates and the length of time to the maturity of the bill, and is equivalent to an interest charge. The holder of the bill who discounts the bill is paid the face value less the discount by the bank.

EXAMPLE 26.1

P. Tyson draws a bill of exchange on T. Charnley payable on 1 June for £600 for goods sold to Charnley on 1 April. Charnley accepts and returns the bill to Tyson. On receipt of the accepted bill on 10 April, Tyson discounts it with his bank at a cost of £15.

The following entries would appear in Tyson's books:

	Dr. £	Cr. £
Bills receivable	600	
T. Charnley		600
Bill of exchange accepted by Charnley.		
Bank	585	
Discount on bills	15	
Bills receivable		600
Bill of exchange (accepted by Charnley) discounted at bank.		

The bills receivable account and the discount on bills account would appear as follows:

Bills receivable

	£		£
Apr. 10 T. Charnley	600	Apr. 10 Bank	585
		10 Discount on bills	15
	600		600

Discount on bills

	£
Apr. 10 Bills receivable	15

At the end of the accounting year the balance on the discount on bills account is transferred as an expense to Tyson's profit and loss account. The bill would be presented, by the bank, on T. Charnley for payment on the due date, but this would not affect P. Tyson's books provided that the bill was paid by Charnley (see later).

A further use of a bill of exchange is that it can be transferred by the payee to another person in settlement or part settlement of a debt. The payee would endorse the bill by signing his name on it, usually indicating the new payee, and would pass the bill over to the new payee.

EXAMPLE 26.2

L. Middleton draws a bill of exchange on A. Bell payable on 1 September for £550 for goods sold to A. Bell on 1 July. Bell accepts and returns the bill to Middleton on 5 July. On 8 July Middleton endorses the bill to R. Lowe, to whom he owes £750.

The following entries would appear in Middleton's books:

	Dr. £	Cr. £
Bills receivable	550	
A. Bell		550
Bill of exchange accepted by Bell.		
R. Lowe	550	
Bills receivable		550
Bill of exchange endorsed to R. Lowe.		

The ledger accounts would show the following:

A. Bell

	£		£
Jul. 1 Goods	550	Jul. 5 Bills receivable	550

Bills receivable

	£		£
Jul. 5 A. Bell	550	Jul. 8 R. Lowe	550

R. Lowe

	£		£
Jul. 8 Bills receivable	550	Balance b/d	750

On 1 September, Lowe would present the bill on Bell for payment. Middleton would not be involved unless the bill was dishonoured.

Dishonoured bills

The major complication introduced in questions dealing with bills of exchange is where a bill is *dishonoured*. This is where a bill is presented for payment, but payment cannot be obtained from the acceptor. When a bill is dishonoured, notice of dishonour must always be given to prior parties to retain their liability.

The bill may be *noted*, and must be noted if it is a foreign bill. This means that it is re-presented by a public officer called a *notary public* to obtain legal proof of dishonour. If the bill is dishonoured again the notary public draws up a *protest*, which is an official certificate evidencing the dishonour.

A protest by a notary public is recognised all over the world and is demanded by international law as legal proof of dishonour. Unless a protest is obtained on dishonour of a foreign bill, all parties excluding the acceptor are released from their liability.

The holder of a bill has recourse against previous endorsers and the drawer. This means that any previous debts settled by the bill may have to be reinstated. Any noting charges are legally recoverable from the acceptor.

A typical examination question would cover a bill which had been discounted with a bank and then dishonoured. It is also fairly common practice to ask the examinee for journal entries rather than ledger accounts.

EXAMPLE 26.3

J. Brown receives an accepted bill of exchange from G. Walker for £400 on 1 October in respect of a debt. Brown discounts the bill with his bank at a cost of £10 on 3 October. The bill is subsequently dishonoured on 1 December, and noting charges amounted to £5 on 3 December. The entries in Brown's books would be as follows:

	Dr. £	Cr. £
Bills receivable	400	
G. Walker		400
Bill of exchange accepted by Walker.		
Bank	390	
Discount on bills	10	
Bills receivable		400
Bill of exchange accepted by Walker discounted at bank.		
G. Walker	400	
Bank		400
Debt re-raised on dishonour of discounted bill.		
G. Walker	5	
Bank		5
Noting charges on bill being dishonoured.		

The ledger accounts would show

G. Walker

	£		£
Balance b/f	400	Oct. 1 Bills receivable	400
Dec. 1 Bank	400		
3 Bank (noting charges)	5		

Bills receivable

	£		£
Oct. 1 G. Walker	400	Oct. 3 Bank	390
		3 Discount on bills	10
	400		400

Discount on bills

	£	
Oct. 3 Bills receivable	10	

Bank

	£			£
Oct. 3 Bills receivable	390	Dec. 1 G. Walker		400
		3 G. Walker (noting)		5

Note: Walker is required to meet the noting charges. However, the discount on bills is an interest charge made by the bank on Brown for advancing him cash: this is not recoverable from Walker as he played no part in the discounting arrangements.

Discounted bills receivable as a contingent liability

Where a firm has discounted bills and those bills have not reached the date of presentment for payment, there is a contingent liability. In the case of a limited company this contingent liability should be disclosed in the balance sheet.

Bills payable

In the acceptor's (or debtor's) ledger accounts, bills of exchange are described as *bills payable.*

All the previous illustrations and extracts from the ledger accounts have concerned the creditor's books and bills receivable. The records in the debtor's books are much simpler because endorsements of the bill, or discounting of the bill, do not affect the debtor. He is only required to meet the bill when it is presented for payment. The entries in Walker's books for the previous illustration would be as follows:

	Dr.	Cr.
	£	£
J. Brown	400	
Bills payable		400
Bill of exchange from J. Brown accepted.		
Bills payable	400	
J. Brown		400
Bill payable to J. Brown dishonoured.		
Noting charges	5	
J. Brown		5
Noting charges on bill dishonoured.		

The ledger would show

J. Brown

	£			£
Oct. 1 Bills payable	400		Balance b/f	400
			Dec. 1 Bills payable	400
			3 Noting charges	5

Bills payable

	£			£
Dec. 1 J. Brown (bill		Oct. 1 J. Brown	400	
dishonoured)	400			

Noting charges

	£
Dec. 3 J. Brown	5

The noting charges would be transferred as a charge in the profit and loss account at the end of the year.

Bills payable at the balance sheet date are shown as current liabilities next after creditors.

Questions

26.1S On 28 July 19X1 J. Conroy sells to B. Borne goods to the value of £1,200, receiving in payment a three months bill. The bill is dishonoured by Borne at maturity and is noted for a charge of £10.

You are required to enter the above transactions in Conroy's journal and make the postings to the ledger accounts.

26.2S Show the entries for the details given in Question 26.1S in Borne's ledger.

26.3S S. Smith sells to I. Nash goods to the value of £650 on 14 July 19X2, receiving in payment a two months bill. Smith discounts the bill with his bank for £635 on 16 July 19X2. At maturity the bill is dishonoured by Nash and is noted for a charge of £10.

You are required to show the entries in Smith's ledger and cash book recording the transactions.

26.4 On 1 January 19X5 A. Jones owes E. Coleman £400. Jones is allowed discount of 2½% and on 3 January 19X5, he accepts a bill of exchange at three months for the balance. The bill is discounted by Coleman for £375 on 6 January 19X5, but is dishonoured at maturity.

You are required to show the entries to record the above transactions in Coleman's books.

26.5 Show the entries for the details given in Question 26.4 in Jones' books.

26.6 Crerand, Pike and Bailey are in partnership. The trial balance on 31 December 19X6, was as follows:

	£	£
Capital accounts:		
Crerand		7,000
Pike		4,000
Bailey		3,000
Current account balances at 1 January 19X6:		
Crerand		2,600
Pike		1,420
Bailey		1,310
Drawings:		
Crerand	3,832	
Pike	2,167	
Bailey	1,820	
Furniture and fittings:		
Cost	2,500	
Depreciation		1,282
Motor vehicle:		
Cost	3,000	
Depreciation		2,760
Debtors and creditors	14,180	4,811
Bills receivable and payable	2,150	1,280
Provision for doubtful debts		1,242
Cash in hand	43	
Bank balance		1,084
Purchases and sales	12,712	23,316
Stock at 1 January 19X6	4,986	
Wages	4,741	
Rates	500	
Heat and light	517	
Motor expenses	520	
Bank interest	199	
Discount allowed	503	
Bad debts	735	
	55,105	55,105

Stock at 31 December 19X6 was valued at £5,824. The provision for doubtful debts is to be increased to 10% on the total of debtors and bills receivable.

Provide for £68 depreciation on furniture and fittings and 20% on the book value of the motor vehicle. The partners share profits and losses in proportion to their capital account balances.

You are required to prepare a trading and profit and loss account for the year ended 31 December 19X6, and a balance sheet as at that date.

27 Royalties

Aims of the chapter:

To explain the nature of royalties
To show how payments for royalties are recorded

Payments made to the owners of patents, or the owners of copyright, or the owners of mines and quarries are rarely fixed in amount, but vary according to the amount that the patent, copyright or mine is used. The owner of a patent will usually receive an amount based on the number of articles manufactured which incorporate his patent; an author's rewards will be based on the number of books sold; and the owner of a mine or quarry will receive a rent based on the quantity or weight of mineral extracted. Rents or payments calculated in this way are usually described as *royalties*. The use of the word *royalty* dates back to payments made to the Crown for the use of mineral rights.

The basic accounting for royalties is very simple. The user (or lessee, or licensee) will open a royalties account in his books to which will be debited all amounts due for royalties; the credit entry is to the *landlord* or *owners account*. At the end of the year the balance on the royalties account will be transferred as an expense to the manufacturing account, or trading account, or profit and loss account, whichever is appropriate to the type of business.

In many agreements there is a clause requiring that a *minimum rent* shall be paid to the owner of the patent or copyright or lease. This type of clause is often inserted to guarantee a minimum income to the owner, and also prevent under-usage of the right. Under-usage might prevent the landowner of a leased quarry from reinstating his land as quickly as he would wish. Rights of various kinds could also be acquired relatively cheaply and deliberately under-utilised to obviate competition if a minimum rent were not payable.

Where there is a minimum rent, the amount by which the minimum rent exceeds the royalty calculated according to the agreed scale is called *short workings*. There is sometimes a right to recover these short workings from subsequent royalties, provided the minimum rent is maintained. The right to recover short workings is usually for a limited initial period so as to allow time for the build up of production or output.

The accounting entries for royalties where short workings are involved are as follows:

	Dr.	*Cr.*
Royalties	With the amount of royalties due	
Short workings	With the amount required to make up the royalties to minimum rent	
Landlord		Minimum rent

The accounting entries where short workings can be recovered are as follows:

Royalties	Debit	
Landlord		Credit
With the amount of royalties due		

Landlord	Debit	
Shortworkings		Credit
With the amount of shortworkings recoverable		

Any short workings which become irrecoverable should be charged as an expense to profit and loss account in the year in which they become irrecoverable.

Most literature on this topic uses the generic term *landlord* to include patent owners, authors and lessors.

EXAMPLE 27.1

R. Bowker arranged a ten year agreement to incorporate a patented device into the sub-aqua equipment he manufactures. He agreed to pay £0.10 for each unit he produced which included the device, with a minimum payment of £500 per year. Short workings can be recovered within two years of the year end in which they occurred.

The units produced incorporating the device over the first six years were 4,300, 4,700, 5,500, 4,900, 5,050, 5,300.

Solution:
A tabulation is set out below showing the amount payable by Bowker in each of the six years:

Year	Units produced	Royalty	Short workings	Short workings recoverable	Amount payable	Short workings irrecoverable
		£	£	£	£	£
1	4,300	430	70		500	
2	4,700	470	30		500	
3	5,500	550		50	500	20
4	4,900	490	10		500	30
5	5,050	505		5	500	
6	5,300	530		5	525	

The accounts in the books of R. Bowker would be as below. The owner of the patent is described somewhat inaccurately in the following accounts as the *landlord*; if this were an examination, *patent owner* would be a more apt description.

Royalties

	£		£
Year 1 Landlord	430	Year 1 Manufacturing	430
2 Landlord	470	2 Manufacturing	470
3 Landlord	550	3 Manufacturing	550
4 Landlord	490	4 Manufacturing	490
5 Landlord	505	5 Manufacturing	505
6 Landlord	530	6 Manufacturing	530

Short workings

	£		£
Year 1 Landlord	70	Year 1 Balance c/f	70
2 Balance b/f	70	2 Balance c/f	100
Landlord	30		
	100		100
3 Balance b/f	100	3 Landlord	50
		Profit and loss	20
		Balance c/f	30
	100		100
4 Balance b/f	30	4 Profit and loss	30
Landlord	10	Balance c/f	10
	40		40
5 Balance b/f	10	5 Landlord	5
		Balance c/f	5
	10		10
6 Balance b/f	5	6 Landlord	5

'Landlord'

	£		£
Year 1 Bank	500	Year 1 Royalty	430
		Short workings	70
	500		500
2 Bank	500	2 Royalty	470
		Short workings	30
	500		500
3 Short workings	50	3 Royalty	550
Bank	500		
	550		550
4 Bank	500	4 Royalty	490
		Short workings	10
	500		500
5 Short workings	5	5 Royalty	505
Bank	500		
	505		505
6 Short workings	5	6 Royalty	530
Bank	525		
	530		530

Note that the royalties have been charged in this case to the manufacturing account as it appears the most appropriate.

Short workings irrecoverable have, however, been charged to profit and loss account. This is because short workings would not usually be regarded as a manufacturing expense.

Questions

27.1S The K. Dodd Treacle Mine Co. took a lease of a mine at a minimum rent of £4,500 a year, merging into a royalty of 7½ pence per ton. The output for the first six years was 35,000, 43,000, 57,000, 63,000, 67,000 and 70,000 tons respectively. Short workings were recoverable during the first five years of the lease.

Prepare the accounts necessary to show the transactions in the firm's books.

27.2S Shipton, who had patented an automatic door closer, granted Doors Ltd a licence for ten years to manufacture and sell the closer on the following terms:

(1) Doors Ltd to pay royalty of £1 for every closer sold with a minimum

payment of £500 per annum. Calculations to be made annually as on 31 December and payment to be made on 31 January.

(2) If, for any year, the royalties calculated on closers sold amount to less than £500, Doors Ltd may set off the deficiency against royalties payable in excess of that sum in the next two years.

With effect from the end of the second year the agreement was varied and a minimum annual payment of £400 was substituted for £500, the other terms of the agreement remaining unchanged.

The numbers of closers sold were:

Year ended 31 December 19X2	200
Year ended 31 December 19X3	400
Year ended 31 December 19X4	600
Year ended 31 December 19X5	500

You are required to show the ledger accounts recording the above transactions in respect of royalties in the books of Doors Ltd, which are closed annually on 31 December.

(Institute of Chartered Accountants in England and Wales)

27.3   Close, who had patented an automatic dish washer, granted Sinks Ltd a licence for ten years to manufacture and sell the washer on the following terms:

(1) Sinks Ltd to pay a royalty of £1 for every washer sold with a minimum payment of £5,000 per annum. Calculations to be made annually as on 31 December and payment to be made on 31 January.

(2) If, for any year, the royalties calculated on washers sold amount to less than £5,000, Sinks Ltd may set off the deficiency against royalties payable in excess of that sum in the next two years.

As from the commencement of the third year the agreement was varied, and a minimum annual payment of £4,000 was substituted for £5,000, the other terms of the agreement remaining unchanged.

The number of washers sold was:

Year ended 31 December 19X6	2,000
Year ended 31 December 19X7	4,000
Year ended 31 December 19X8	6,000
Year ended 31 December 19X9	5,000

You are required to prepare the following ledger accounts recording the above transactions in respect of royalties in the books of Sinks Ltd which are closed annually on 31 December:

(a) royalties account,
(b) short workings account, and
(c) the account of Close.

(Institute of Chartered Accountants in England and Wales)

27.4   White, who manufactured fasteners, uses leased machines for this purpose. The terms of the lease for each machine provide that:

(1) The lessee should pay a royalty of £5 for every 100 fasteners produced.
(2) The minimum royalty should be £500 per annum.
(3) The lessee could recoup in the second year any short workings in the first year of leasing the machine.

Details in respect of three machines leased were as follows:

Machine number	1	2	3
Date lease commenced	1 Jan 19X4	1 Jan 19X5	1 Jan 19X6
Production of fasteners:			
Year ended 31 December			
19X4	8,000	–	–
19X5	15,000	10,200	–
19X6	17,400	9,600	8,900
19X7	18,100	12,400	7,400

You are required to show the ledger accounts recording the above transactions in respect of royalties in the books of White, which are closed annually on 31 December.

(Institute of Chartered Accountants in England and Wales)

28 Departmental accounts

Aims of the chapter:

To introduce methods by which a business may identify the
profitable sections of the organisation

The basic idea of departmental accounts requires little explanation. A business which has several departments will be interested in the profitability of
each department, as well as in the profitability of the business as a whole.

The same reasoning applies to a business with several branches. The
accounting arrangements for branches could in their simplest form be very
similar to those described below for departments. However, accounting
arrangements for branches are usually more complex. Branches are more
remote and there is greater difficulty in establishing effective controls. The
accounting systems for branches will be met in later studies but the division
between *departmental accounts* and *branch accounts* is somewhat arbitrary.
Additionally, many large stores with branches, and a branch accounting
system, will probably require a departmental analysis within those
branches.

The calculation of departmental gross profit is primarily a question of
analysis. It should be relatively simple to analyse purchases and allocate
them to the appropriate department and so, in effect, maintain a separate
purchases account for each department. If the system is kept by hand, the
purchases day book can be designed with a column for each department; if
the system is computer based, a method of coding will take care of the
analysis. Stock taking should be so arranged that each department's stock is
recorded separately.

The recording of departmental sales might be more difficult. If the
departments are physically separated by walls or screens, each department
may have its own cash tills and also record its own credit sales. A trend
now is to avoid physical barriers to customer circulation which might deter
impulse buying, and to have central cash points. Under these circumstances
a coding system for sales will need to be introduced and applied at the cash
points.

No attempt has been made here to define a *department.* It is a function
of management to decide the degree of analysis of its activities that it
requires. Sufficient information should be available to ensure that correct
managerial decisions are taken, whilst bearing in mind the cost of providing
that information.

Shown below is a departmental analysis of the year's gross profit of Emporium Ltd.

	Mens-wear £	Ladies-wear £	Furni-ture £	Shoe repairs £	Total £
Sales	53,200	67,500	90,000	12,000	222,700
Stock b/f	6,100	8,200	20,000	700	35,000
Purchases	42,500	50,500	50,200	2,500	145,700
	48,600	58,700	70,200	3,200	180,700
less Stock c/f	6,400	8,600	19,700	800	35,500
Cost of sales	42,200	50,100	50,500	2,400	145,200
Gross profit	11,000	17,400	39,500	9,600	77,500
Gross profit as a percentage of sales	20.7	25.8	43.9	80	34.8

It will be noted from the analysis that the gross margins in percentage terms vary widely, with shoe repairs taking first place. The shoe repairing department, however, is a service department much more than it is a sales department, and is not really comparable at this stage of analysis to the others. Labour costs, which are not shown above, are likely to be much heavier in shoe repairing than in any of the other departments. It could be that the other departments are comparable at the gross profit stage, and furniture therefore appears an outright winner in relative gross profits in both monetary and percentage terms. But what of other costs? And how does furniture rank in terms of monetary profit per square metre of floor space?

To answer these questions, departmental accounts usually provide for a greater degree of analysis than simple gross profit. But to be strictly comparable, one with another, the same degree of allocation of expenses should be applied to each department. If wages are to be allocated to shoe repairing, then they should similarly be allocated to menswear, ladieswear and furniture. This may be rather difficult if some of the departments are organised on an open plan basis with central cash points. Some staff may service more than one department. In these circumstances a reasonable basis of salary apportionment should be applied.

Other expenses such as rent and rates and heating and lighting can probably be equitably apportioned on a floor space basis. Many examination questions require that the whole of the expenses, including administration expenses, are apportioned on a predetermined basis.

The effect of attempting to allocate all expenses over all departments could be to show a particular department as making a loss. This can be misleading. If a department is more than covering all the expenses which can be attributed to it alone, i.e. those expenses which could be avoided if the department were to close, it is making a contribution to general overhead expenses. It should only be closed down if the floor space can be operated more profitably by a new department, or by expanding an existing department.

The example of Emporium Ltd is now continued below. Departmental wages have been allocated on the basis of actual cost, as have other miscellaneous expenses which can be attributed to the departments.

Rates, heating and lighting, and repairs to buildings have been apportioned on the basis of floor area occupied, i.e. menswear : ladieswear : furniture : shoe repairing, 4 : 4 : 8 : 1.

Administration and office wages and expenses have been apportioned on the basis of sales.

Emporium Ltd

	Mens-wear £	Ladies-wear £	Furni-ture £	Shoe repairs £	Total £
Sales	53,200	67,500	90,000	12,000	222,700
Stocks b/f	6,100	8,200	20,000	700	35,000
Purchases	42,500	50,500	50,200	2,500	145,700
	48,600	58,700	70,200	3,200	180,700
less Stock c/f	6,400	8,600	19,700	800	35,500
Cost of sales	42,200	50,100	50,500	2,400	145,200
Gross profit	11,000	17,400	39,500	9,600	77,500
Wages (departmental)	5,300	6,400	7,900	6,300	25,900
Miscellaneous direct expenses	210	370	530	90	1,200
	5,510	6,770	8,430	6,390	27,100
Surplus after direct expenses	5,490	10,630	31,070	3,210	50,400
Rates	1,012	1,012	2,024	252	4,300
Heating and lighting	1,694	1,694	3,388	424	7,200
Repairs to building	871	871	1,741	217	3,700
Administration and office wages and expenses	2,437	3,092	4,122	549	10,200
	6,014	6,669	11,275	1,442	25,400
Net profit/(loss)	(524)	3,961	19,795	1,768	25,000

The bases of apportionment of expenses which have been used in this example would be generally accepted as reasonable. The results show an apparent loss on the menswear department of £524.

However, the table has also been arranged to show that menswear has a surplus of £5,490 after direct expenses and before the general overhead expenses have been apportioned. Menswear has then to bear a share of £6,014 of the apportioned general expenses. But it is unlikely that much of this £6,014 could be avoided if menswear were to close, because rates would have to be paid and buildings heated and lit and repaired. It is possible that administration costs might be slightly reduced.

If menswear were to simply close down, and the space remain unoccupied, the other departments would have to bear the bulk of the £6,014. Alternatively, the other departments might expand, or a new department might be opened. But whatever the alternative strategy adopted, that alternative must make a contribution of more than £5,490 to overhead expenses before it becomes superior to menswear. Careful thought is required rather than hasty action.

Examination questions at foundation level rarely require much discussion. An analysis of departmental income and expenditure is normally required, based on explicit or implicit instructions in the question. The student may be given various alternative bases which could be used for apportioning expenses, and the most appropriate base has to be selected for the various types of expenses.

Questions

28.1S John Dobson is the proprietor of a retail business which has two main departments which sell respectively hardware and electrical goods. He had previously prepared his annual accounts in such a way that the relative profitability of the two departments was not ascertainable, but now he wishes to attempt to identify the profit attributable to each in order that he may pay a bonus to the more successful of the departmental managers. At 30 September 19X5, the balances in the books of the business were as follows:

	£	£
Capital		71,000
Sales – Hardware		59,000
Electrical		29,500
Purchases – Hardware	20,000	
Electrical	10,000	
Stocks at 1 October 19X4 – Hardware	2,320	
Electrical	2,136	
Salaries and wages – Hardware	20,560	
Electrical	15,440	
Advertising	615	
Discounts allowed – Hardware	400	
Electrical	200	
Drawings	3,000	
Premises (cost)	43,000	
Shopfittings and equipment – Hardware	18,000	
(at cost *less* depreciation) Electrical	7,000	

	£	£
Debtors and creditors	10,200	5,319
Bank	5,600	
Rent and rates	1,580	
Canteen charges	875	
Heating and lighting	880	
Insurance of stock	940	
General administrative salaries and wages	2,073	
	164,819	164,819

Notes:
(i) At 30 September 19X5 the following amounts were owing:

	£
Wages – Hardware	250
Electrical	170
Heating and lighting	20

(ii) The general administration expenses and the rent and rates included prepayments of £33 and £80 respectively.
(iii) Stocks at 30 September 19X5 were:

	£
Hardware	2,800
Electrical	2,450

(iv) Depreciation is to be provided on shop fittings and equipment at 10% of the written down value.
(v) The managers of the hardware and electrical departments are to be paid a commission of 5% of the net profit (prior to the commission payment) of the respective departments.
(vi) In apportioning the various expenses between the two departments due regard is to be had to the following information:

	Hardware	Electrical
Number of workers	9	6
Average stock levels	£2,500	£2,200
Floor area (square yards)	4,000	2,000

The general administration salaries and expenses are primarily incurred in relation to the processing of purchase and sales invoices.

Required:
(a) Prepare a schedule showing the basis on which you have apportioned the various expenses between the two departments.
(b) Prepare the departmental and total departmental trading and profit and loss accounts for the year ended 30 September 19X5. (*Note:* A balance sheet is *not* required.)
(c) Mr Dobson considers that the profit performance of the electrical department is far from satisfactory. What are the main issues he should investigate before judging the manager incompetent?

(Chartered Association of Certified Accountants)

28.2S   Allsports Limited are retail traders whose store has two departments dealing in clothing and sports equipment respectively. The following trial balance was extracted from the company's books at 30 April 19X0, the accounting year end.

	£	£
Sales: Clothing		120,000
Sports equipment		160,000
Stock at cost at 30 April 19X9: Clothing	10,000	
Sports equipment	16,000	
Purchases: Clothing and sports equipment	192,000	
Establishment expenses: Clothing	15,000	
Sports equipment	16,920	
Sales and administrative expenses: Clothing	7,400	
Sports equipment	5,840	
Ordinary share capital		20,000
Share premium account		2,000
Retained earnings at 30 April 19X9		19,460
Creditors		5,800
Bank overdraft		2,300
Debtors	8,600	
Freehold property: at cost	20,000	
provision for depreciation		800
Fixtures and fittings: at cost	26,000	
provision for depreciation		9,000
Motor vehicles: at cost	42,000	
provision for depreciation		20,400
	359,760	359,760

Additional information:

(a) Gross profit is earned as follows:

Clothing department – one-third of sales

Sports equipment department – three-tenths of sales.

(b) Stock in trade was valued, at cost, at 30 April 19X0:

	£
Clothing department	8,000
Sports equipment department	14,000

(c) Amounts prepaid at 30 April 19X0:

Establishment expenses – Clothing department £300.

(d) Accrued charges at 30 April 19X0:

Sales and administrative expenses – Clothing department £200
Sports equipment department £700

(e) The sales staff receive commission in June of each year based on the gross profit earned in their department in the previous financial year:

Clothing department	2% of gross profit
Sports equipment department	3% of gross profit

(f) In October 19X9, additional fixtures and fittings acquired at a cost of £4,000 were debited to purchases.

(g) Depreciation is provided annually on fixed assets at the following percentages of the cost of assets held at the relevant accounting year end:

Freehold property	2%
Fixtures and fittings	10%
Motor vehicles	20%

(h) In December 19X9 a motor vehicle which had been bought in January 19X5 at a cost of £6,000 was scrapped; the company did not receive anything for the scrap.

(i) The fixed assets depreciation is apportioned to departments as follows:

	Clothing department	Sports equipment department
Freehold property	$1/2$	$1/2$
Fixtures and fittings	3/5	2/5
Motor vehicles	5/12	7/12

(j) It is not proposed to pay any dividends to shareholders for the year ended 30 April 19X0.

Required:

(a) The trading and profit and loss account for the year ended 30 April 19X0 of (i) the clothing department, and (ii) the sports equipment department.

(b) The balance sheet as at 30 April 19X0 of Allsports Limited.

(c) Give reasons why it is useful to determine the gross profits/losses and net profits/losses of departments or sections of a business.

(Chartered Association of Certified Accountants)

28.3 Brian and Trevor are in partnership managing a small retail store which specialises in sweets and confectionary – managed by Brian – and newspapers and periodicals – managed by Trevor. The partnership agreement provides for Brian to receive three-fifths of the profit, and Trevor two-fifths, each partner to be allowed 8% interest on capital, and each to receive a commission of 10% of the profit of their respective sections prior to any other appropriation of profit. During the year to 31 March 19X8, a trial balance extracted at that date revealed the following financial features.

	£	£
Capital – Brian		14,000
Trevor		8,000
Current accounts – Brian		2,020
Trevor	250	
Drawings – Brian	1,100	
Trevor	900	
Freehold shop premises	10,000	
Equipment (at written down value)		
Confectionery section	4,500	
Periodical section	3,500	
Purchases – Confectionery section	15,900	
Periodical section	17,700	
Stock at 1 April – Confectionery section	2,300	
Periodical section	3,100	

	£	£
Sales – Confectionery section		18,500
Periodical section		21,500
Wages – Confectionery section	1,175	
Periodical section	1,470	
Miscellaneous expenses	230	
Rates	500	
Light and heat	400	
Advertising	250	
Debtors and creditors	1,800	2,100
Bad debts – periodical section	95	
Cash in hand	950	
Cash at bank	50	
Provision for doubtful debts – periodical section		50
	66,170	66,170

Additional information available:

(i)   Stock at 31 March 19X8 was £3,600 in the Confectionery section, and £4,400 in the Periodical section.

(ii) The partners have agreed that rates should be apportioned between the Confectionery and Periodical sections on a 3 : 2 ratio, advertising on a 1 : 1 ratio, lighting and heating on a 2 : 3 ratio, and miscellaneous expenses on a 1 : 1 ratio.

(iii) Wages owing at 31 March 19X8 amounted to £25 for the Confectionery section and £30 for the Periodical section.

(iv) Advertising prepaid at 31 March 19X8 amounted to £100.

(v)   The provision for doubtful debts is to be increased to 5% of the debtors of the Periodical section, which amount to £1,500 at 31 March 19X8.

(vi) Equipment of both sections is to be depreciated at 10% of the written down value at 1 April 19X7.

Required:

(a) Prepare a trading and profit and loss account for the Confectionery and the Periodical sections, and also for the business as a whole, for the year ended 31 March 19X8. (*Note:* A balance sheet is NOT required.)

(b) Prepare an appropriation account for the year ended 31 March 19X8.

(c) Prepare the partners' current accounts for the year ended 31 March 19X8.

(Chartered Association of Certified Accountants)

28.4   The profit and loss account for the year ended 31 December 19X8 of DQ Holidays Limited, a company which provides holidays at several resorts in Spain, is as follows:

	£		£
Agents' commission	90,600	Sales of holidays	906,000
Hire of aeroplanes	105,000	Net loss for the year	10,000
Coaches from airport to			
resort	7,000		
Hotel accommodation	581,400		
Salary and expenses of			
resort representatives	32,000		

	£	£
Brochures, advertising, head office and other common costs	100,000	
	916,000	916,000

The managing director has complained to you, as chief accountant, that the form of presentation of this profit and loss account does not tell him where or why the net loss has been incurred and is of little use for management purposes.

You are required to re-design the profit and loss account, using also the information given below, so that it will overcome the complaints of the managing director.

You are given the following information:

1. The public book their holidays with the company through local travel agents who were paid a commission of 10% of the gross price of the holiday.
2. Holidays were offered at six resorts in Spain, namely P, Q, R, S, T and U.
3. Only one hotel was used in each resort.
4. Flights were from Luton Airport to three airports in Spain, as follows:

Airport	For resorts	Annual cost £
X	P and Q	30,000
Y	R and S	40,000
Z	T and U	35,000

5. Separate coaches were used for the journey from the Spanish airport to each resort hotel. The annual costs of these were:

To resort	£
P	1,100
Q	900
R	1,400
S	1,100
T	1,700
U	800

6. The annual costs of hotel accommodation at each resort were:

Resort	£
P	305,900
Q	153,200
R	22,600
S	45,400
T	10,200
U	44,100

7. A separate representative was employed at each resort, and the annual costs were:

Resort	£
P	5,000
Q	4,500
R	6,000
S	5,500
T	5,700
U	5,300

8. Sales of holidays at the various resorts were:

Resort	£
P	480,000
Q	244,000
R	30,000
S	60,000
T	24,000
U	68,000

(Chartered Institute of Management Accountants)

29 Joint ventures

Aims of the chapter:

> To define a joint venture
> To explain the accounting procedure

A joint venture is a partnership which is limited to a single venture. On completion of the venture the partnership is concluded. There is little to distinguish a joint venture from any other partnership except that it is essentially of a limited nature. It is limited in that there is a separately identifiable activity or speculation and there is an assumption that the venture will not operate indefinitely.

There may be many reasons for a joint venture. An individual may be in a particularly advantageous position regarding the purchase of goods, but lack capital. An associate might agree to provide that capital in return for a share of the profits.

Alternatively one party might be in an advantageous position regarding the purchase of goods, whilst another party is well situated to dispose of the goods and a third party possesses the necessary capital.

Again, individuals may come together for a specific venture because they have different skills or attributes which will be required in the venture if it is to succeed.

The accounts for a joint venture might be kept in the same way as those of a partnership, i.e. a separate set of books is opened and maintained until the end of the venture.

The more usual method is that each party keeps a record of the expenses he has incurred and the income he has received in the venture. At the completion of the joint venture a summary is made of all the expenses and income, and a final settlement is made between the parties.

EXAMPLE 29.1

R. Moon and E. Bice entered into an agreement to buy and sell road construction equipment available at the completion of a motorway project. Moon, in the south of England, was responsible for purchasing suitable equipment and £30,000 was paid to him by cheque by Bice to assist in financing the purchases. Bice, in Scotland, had the main responsibility for selling the equipment, and instructed Moon in the type of equipment required. Profits were shared two-thirds to Bice and one-third to Moon.

Moon purchased two road rollers for £9,000, one lorry for £6,000, tarmac laying plant for £14,000 and three vans for £3,500. He also incurred various transport charges amounting to £2,300.

Bice sold one road roller for £5,000. Moon received an offer of £6,500 for the second roller. As Bice had not finalised the sale of this roller and it was still in England, it was agreed that Moon should accept the offer.

The tarmac plant was sold by Bice for £16,300 and he also sold two of the vans for £3,000. It was agreed that Bice could retain the third van at a value of £1,400. The lorry eventually brought £5,900 received by Bice.

Solution:

To record the expenses and income each party opens a *joint venture account* in his own books. In Moon's books it is called 'Joint venture with E. Bice', and in Bice's books it is called 'Joint venture with R. Moon'. The entires are as follows:

Books of Moon

Joint venture with E. Bice

	£		£
Bank – road rollers	9,000	Bank – cheque from Bice	30,000
lorry	6,000	road roller	6,500
tarmac plant	14,000		
vans	3,500		
Cash – transport	2,300		

Books of Bice

Joint venture with R. Moon

	£		£
Bank – cheque to Moon	30,000	Bank – road roller	5,000
		tarmac plant	16,300
		vans	3,000
		Motor vehicles – van	1,400
		Bank – lorry	5,900

The above accounts assume that each party has his own set of double entry books. All the transactions entered into by a party are fully recorded through his own books. The joint venture account at this stage is effectively a creditor/debtor account. It shows whether the joint venture has a creditor or debtor relationship with the party concerned.

To operate the joint venture efficiently and profitably each party will need to be continuously informed of the other's transactions. On completion of the venture a memorandum joint venture account is drawn up to determine whether there is a profit or loss, and to show the division of profits or losses. It is called a *memorandum* account because it is not part of the double entry system.

Memorandum Joint Venture Account

	£		£
Expenses of Moon:		Income of Moon:	
Road rollers	9,000	Cheque from Bice[1]	30,000
Lorry	6,000	Road roller	6,500
Tarmac plant	14,000		
Vans	3,500		
Transport	2,300		
Expenses of Bice:		Income of Bice:	
Cheque to Moon[1]	30,000	Road roller	5,000
		Tarmac plant	16,300
		Vans	4,400
Profit:		Lorry	5,900
Moon $\frac{1}{3}$ 1,100			
Bice $\frac{2}{3}$ 2,200	3,300		
	68,100		68,100

Note 1: As this amount is self-cancelling, it need not be included.

The share of profits as determined above are now debited in each party's joint venture account, as shown below, and credited to that party's profit and loss account.

Books of Moon

Joint venture with E. Bice

	£		£
Bank – road rollers	9,000	Bank – cheque from Bice	30,000
lorry	6,000	road roller	6,500
tarmac plant	14,000		
vans	3,500		
Cash – transport	2,300		
Profit and loss	1,100		
Balance c/d	600		
	36,500		36,500
		Balance b/d	600

Books of Bice

Joint venture with R. Moon

	£		£
Bank – cheque to Moon	30,000	Bank – road roller	5,000
Profit and loss	2,200	tarmac plant	16,300
		vans	3,000
		Van account	1,400
		Bank – lorry	5,900
		Balance c/d	600
	32,200		32,200
Balance b/d	600		

The position now is that E. Bice is shown as a creditor for £600 in Moon's books, whilst Bice's books show Moon as a debtor for £600. A cheque for £600 would be sent from Moon to Bice. This would conclude the venture and close the accounts as below.

Books of Moon

Joint venture with E. Bice

	£		£
Bank	600	Balance b/d	600

Books of Bice

Joint venture with R. Moon

	£		£
Balance b/d	600	Bank	600

Questions

29.1S   Port and Starboard agreed to enter into a joint venture to buy and sell speedboats. Profits and losses were to be divided: Port two-thirds, Starboard one-third.

On 3 May 19X9, Port purchased three speedboats for £730, £820 and £950 respectively. He bought a reconditioned engine costing £120 which he installed in one of the boats, the old engine being scrapped. On 31 May 19X9, he sold two of the boats for £900 each, paying the proceeds into his private bank account.

On 15 June 19X9 he sold the other boat for £1,000, which amount he paid over to Starboard, who paid it into his bank account.

On 4 May 19X9, Starboard purchased a speedboat for £675 and, having incurred expenditure of £40 on repainting, sold it on 12 May 19X9 for £750, paying the proceeds into his own bank account. This boat developed mechanical trouble and on 25 May 19X9 Starboard agreed to take the boat back at a price of £720, which he paid out of his bank account. The boat was still unsold at 30 June 19X9, and it was agreed that Starboard should take it over for his personal use at a valuation of £700.

Other expenditure incurred was as follows:

	Port	Starboard
	£	£
Harbour dues	10	3
Marine insurance	20	6

Port paid into his bank net receipts of £24 in respect of speedboat trips.

On 1 July 19X9, the sum required in full settlement as between Port and Starboard was paid by the party accountable.

You are required to prepare:

(a) the account of the joint venture with Port as it would appear in the books of Starboard, and

(b) the memorandum joint venture account, showing the net profit.

(Institute of Chartered Accountants in England and Wales)

29.2S G and H decide to undertake a joint venture in which they agree to buy and sell electrical products in the United Kingdom. No partnership books were to be kept, and each transaction is to be recorded in the individual books of the partner concerned. Profits and losses are to be shared equally and there is to be no partnership salary or interest on capital. Each partner is, however, to be entitled to a *del credere* commission (not specifically paid in cash) of 5% on the gross amount of sales made by him.

The following transactions occurred:

19X5

Jan.   8 G bought a stock of electrical products and paid cash of £8,300.
29 H sold goods on credit to J for £6,000.
Feb. 12 G sold goods on credit to K for £4,000.
26 H received the amount due from J in respect of his debt.
Mar. 19 H sold goods on credit to L for £2,000.
26 G received the amount due from K in respect of his debt.
Apr. 30 L was declared bankrupt, and a final dividend of £0.50 in the £ was received by H.
30 The balance of the stock was taken over by H at an agreed valuation of £1,500. No cash was paid specifically for this item, and no commission is applicable.
30 A memorandum joint venture account was prepared, the profit or loss was divided, and a cash payment in final settlement of the venture was made between the partners.

You are required to:

(a) journalise in the books of H those of the above transactions (including cash) as are relevant to him;
(b) prepare a memorandum joint venture account.

(Chartered Institute of Management Accountants)

29.3   Smith and White agreed to deal in stocks and shares on joint account and to share any profits or losses equally.

The following transactions in connection with the venture took place:

(1) On 10 January 19X7 Smith purchased 3,000 ordinary shares of £1 each in Tinkers Ltd at £1.25 per share, expenses amounting to £55.
(2) On 18 January 19X7 White purchased £1,000 (4,000 £0.25 units) ordinary stock in Metals Ltd at £0.60 *cum* div. per unit, expenses amounting to £35.
(3) On 20 February 19X7 White purchased a further £250 (1,000 £0.25 units) ordinary stock in Metals Ltd at £0.52½ *ex* div. per unit, expenses amounting to £12.
(4) On 20 March 19X7, a dividend of 10% for the year ended 31 December 19X6 on £1,250 (5,000 £0.25 units) Metals Ltd ordinary stock was received by White, who immediately paid over to the broker the amount due to the seller.
(5) On 31 May 19X7, Smith received an allotment letter from Tinkers Ltd in respect of an issue out of the capitalisation of reserves of one new ordinary share of £1, credited as fully paid, for every three shares held, the new shares not to rank for the dividend to be paid for the year ended 31 December 19X6. Smith sold 500 of these new shares for £1 each, expenses of sale being £10.

(6) On 31 May 19X7, a dividend of 20% for the year ended 31 December 19X6, was received by Smith from Tinkers Ltd.

(7) On 11 July 19X7, White purchased £400 (400 £1 units) ordinary stock in Reefers Ltd at £1.75 per unit, expenses amounting to £23.

(8) On 25 July 19X7, Smith sold the shares held by the venture in Tinkers Ltd for £1.10 per share, expenses amounting to £40.

On 31 July 19X7, it was agreed to terminate the venture, White taking over the Metals Ltd ordinary stock at a valuation of £0.75 per unit and Smith the Reefers Ltd ordinary stock at a valuation of £1.87$\frac{1}{2}$ per unit, the balance between them being settled in cash on the same date.

You are required to prepare:

(a) the memorandum joint venture account, and

(b) the joint venture account with White as it would appear in the books of Smith.

Ignore income tax and capital gains tax.

(Institute of Chartered Accountants in England and Wales)

29.4   Brown and Turner agreed to enter into a joint venture to buy and sell second-hand ice cream vehicles and to share profits and losses in the ratio 5 : 3 respectively. It was agreed that Brown would record all details of the venture in his books of account.

On 21 December 19X5, Turner purchased two vehicles and paid cash of £2,000. On 2 January 19X6, he spent sums of £248 on repairs, £24 on drivers' wages and £36 on temporary insurance cover. He sold the vehicles a week later for £2,800 subject to a 2% cash discount if paid within seven days. He paid the proceeds of sale into his bank account on 10 January 19X6.

On 31 January 19X6, Brown purchased five vehicles for £5,000, of which he managed to sell three for £3,600 for cash on the same day, without incurring any expenses. The fourth vehicle was sold for £1,350 and, on 7 February 19X6, he received a bill receivable to be presented for payment in three months' time.

On 31 March 19X6, the fifth vehicle was still unsold and it was agreed that Turner should take over this vehicle at a valuation of £750.

On 31 March 19X6, the parties made a settlement between each other, Brown agreeing to take the bill receivable at a value of £1,318.

You are required to prepare:

(a) the joint venture account, and

(b) Turner's account.

as they would appear in the books of Brown.

(Institute of Chartered Accountants in England and Wales)

Appendix

Accounting conventions and concepts

The word *convention* has been used in this book when referring to the rules governing accounting. This is not due to conviction, but mainly for convenience. No two writers agree precisely on what are the major rules, or how they should be described or classified. Some texts refer to *concepts*. Some talk of *conventions*. Others refer to various combinations of concepts, conventions, postulates, doctrines and assumptions. The Companies Act 1985 refers to certain accounting *principles*, whilst the same principles are described as concepts in a statement of standard accounting practice.

The rules or conventions briefly described below are the most generally accepted.

The accounting entity (or business entity)

Each set of accounting records should deal with a specific and identifiable business activity. It should deal with only the financial transactions, facts and events relating to that specific activity, and it should deal with all the financial transactions, facts and events relating to that activity.

The accounting entity is not necessarily a separate legal entity. A sole trader cannot legally separate his business affairs from his personal assets should he be unable to meet either business debts or personal debts. In a partnership, the partners are jointly and severally liable for its debts.

A limited company can be both an accounting entity and a legal entity, provided that it is not a holding company.

Money measurement

Only transactions, facts and events which are recordable in monetary terms should be brought into the accounts. This has advantages in that money is a common measure or common denominator in terms of which transactions, facts and events can be recorded. It has disadvantages in that money does not tell the whole story regarding the quality of a business, or its products, or its management, or its public image. Another major disadvantage is that money is not a stable unit of measurement, as witness recent rates of inflation.

Going concern (or continuity of activity)

A business is assumed to have an indefinite life unless there is clear evidence to the contrary. If this assumption were not made the possibility of immediate cessation of business would always have to be borne in mind. Depreciation could not be regarded as the allocation of the cost of an asset over its useful life. Stock would not be valued by, say, FIFO or AVCO but rather on what it would realise by immediate disposal under constraint. Debtors would present a very similar problem.

The going concern convention is not, of course, applied where there is definite evidence of the cessation of business, e.g. in bankruptcy or insolvency. Nor should it be applied where there is a definite intent that the entity should have a short life, e.g. a joint venture.

Periodicity (or period of account)

A profit statement and balance sheet together with other relevant or required financial reports should be produced at regular and frequent intervals. Accounts of yesteryear might only have been closed down and reported on at the completion of an adventure, or at the end of the contract for which they were set up, or at the sporadic request of a landowner.

However, with the development of more permanent businesses and the growing acceptance of the going concern convention, the necessity for regular and frequent reporting became apparent.

The law has also influenced the period of account and the period of reporting in that the Companies Acts require annual reports to be submitted to shareholders and the Finance Acts require the annual determination and reporting of profit for income tax purposes.

Statutory reporting periods are usually annual, but most public companies also provide a half-yearly interim report to investors. In most businesses, management would require reports much more frequently than yearly or half-yearly.

Matching (or accruals)

The matching convention results from the periodicity or period of account convention. It means that the expenses for a period should be matched against related income, rather than cash payments being compared with cash receipts. The periodicity convention does not necessarily require matching *per se*; entities which keep accounts on a receipts and payment basis will also report periodically. But most businesses keep accounts on an income and expenditure basis, and proper matching is therefore required.

Matching is not always an easy exercise. There is always the possibility that an item should have appeared in a previous period or should be deferred until a future period. The treatment of long-term contracts can be a particularly difficult problem. Depreciation can also create problems when determining the life of an asset, or its residual value. It is sometimes difficult to interpret correctly the position of a firm at the end of an arbitrary period such as a year.

The accruals convention can be distinguished somewhat artificially from the matching convention, but they are usually regarded as meaning very much the same thing.

Consistency

A business should be consistent in the way in which it applies its internal accounting policies. Despite legal requirements, statements of standard accounting practice, financial reporting standards and generally accepted rules and conventions, a good deal of discretion is still available to accountants in the way in which they interpret events and present accounting statements. Once methods and policies have been adopted, they should be adhered to. If there is a compelling reason for a change in practice, that change should be disclosed and reported.

Consistency is important in that a firm's profit statements over the years should be capable of comparison, one year with another.

Cost (or historic cost)

Assets and expenses are conventionally brought into the accounts at cost price. This is based on the view that cost is the most objective measurement as it is evidenced by an actual transaction. Any subsequent accounting treatment (e.g. depreciation) will be based on original or historic cost. This convention is also very convenient in that it does nothing to disturb the double entry system. Unfortunately, as mentioned previously under money measurement, money is not a stable unit of measurement. In times of high inflation the application of the cost convention leads to accounts which do not accurately reflect profits or asset values. The problem of accounting in times of high inflation is one which is yet to be resolved.

Conservatism (or prudence)

In essence this means that an accountant should take the pessimist's view. He should never anticipate profits, and he should make provision for all losses whether actual or anticipated. Where there is an alternative choice of values to be placed on an asset, the lower should be used.

Realisation

This is very much linked to the conservative approach described above. A profit should only be brought into account when it is actually realised. However, it is not always easy to determine when a profit is realised. Credit sales are normally taken into account in determining profits, and yet it is doubtful if the profit has been actually realised before the cash is received. However, a provision is usually made for bad debts. Long-term constructional contracts lasting over several years can also cause problems, but it is normal practice to take a proportion of the profits as the work progresses.

Materiality

Despite the matching convention mentioned earlier, accrual adjustments would not normally be made for trivial amounts which could be regarded as insignificant. What is material is largely a matter of judgement. What would be material for a small company might be insignificant for a large company. The cost of making trivial adjustments might far outweigh the benefits of increased and possibly spurious precision. There will almost always be some degree of approximation in accounting statements.

Statements of standard accounting practice, and financial reporting standards

There have always been 'grey areas' in accounting. By using alternative methods, companies can show significantly different results derived from the same figures, and by the 1960s it was becoming clear that remedial action was needed. One instance which helped to bring the debate into the public arena was the GEC takeover of

AEI. The directors of AEI forecast a profit of £10 million before tax. After the successful takeover the redrafted accounts showed a loss of £4.5 million. Roughly one-third of this discrepancy was found to be due to 'matters . . . of fact' and two-thirds to 'matters . . . of judgement'.

A greater standardisation of accounting treatment was introduced through a system of *statements of standard accounting practice* (known for short as SSAPs or *accounting standards*) issued by the Accounting Standards Committee which operated on behalf of the major accounting bodies. Before a standard was issued the profession when through a process of discussion and debate and the publication of an *exposure draft*. This was considered carefully by people with a particular interest or expertise in the topic under consideration. After consultation, and amendment to the original draft where necessary, an accounting standard would then be issued. Some 25 SSAPs were issued.

In 1990, arising from the Companies Act 1989, the Accounting Standards Committee was replaced by an independent body known as the Financial Reporting Council which became responsible for overseeing the work of an Accounting Standards Board. The Accounting Standards Board agreed to adopt the 22 extant SSAPs, but intends to review all of them in due course.

The Accounting Standards Board also intends to undertake a fundamental review of accounting practice. It will issue *financial reporting exposure drafts* for discussion. These will then be followed by *financial reporting standards* (FRSs). It has been suggested that the new system will radically restructure the form of British accounts. The chairman of the Accounting Standards Board has been reported as saying that 'there is an evasion industry out there'.

For some considerable time, therefore, there will exist both statements of standard accounting practice and financial reporting standards. Since the Companies Act 1985 there has been a legal obligation for all medium- to large-sized companies to follow standard practice. In addition, any member of an accounting body who fails to follow the guidelines may be subject to the profession's own disciplinary measures.

Solutions guide

A note for students

As stated in the text, the questions at the end of each chapter should be regarded as an integral part of that chapter. This student's guide gives suggested solutions to the 'S' suffixed questions. The same style and manner of presentation has been used in the solutions to the questions as is used in the examples in the main text. Students should be aware that there are different ways of setting out an answer to an accounting question, many of which would be considered correct.

Suggested method of working

Before attending a lecture

Read the appropriate chapter so that you will have some idea of the topic.

During the lecture

Make notes, particularly of any examples.

After the lecture

Read the appropriate chapter again together with your lecture notes, making sure you *understand* all the examples. Do not attempt to learn solely by rote – it is a mistake!

Before attempting the homework required by your tutor, work as many of the 'S' suffixed questions as time will allow. Do not consult the solution to a question until you have independently attempted a solution of your own. When you are satisfied that your solution is correct, or you understand where you have gone wrong, attempt the next question. The questions have been arranged in order of increasing difficulty to help your understanding, and to enable you to build on a firm foundation. When you have worked as many of the 'S' suffixed questions as time permits, attempt your homework problems. Remember that understanding *why* an answer you submitted was wrong is part of the learning process. If you do not understand why your solution is incorrect, ask your tutor.

1 Introduction to the double entry system of book-keeping

1.1S (a) Assets – property owned (and amounts owed to the business)
  (b) Liabilities – amounts owed by the business
  (c) Capital – owner's or proprietor's interest

1.2S The *accounting equation* is

$$\text{Capital} = \text{Assets} - \text{Liabilities}.$$

It means that the amount invested in the business by the proprietor is equal to the assets owned by the business less the amounts owed by the business.

1.3S

	Assets	Liabilities	Capital
(a) Buildings	√		
(b) Loan to the firm		√	
(c) Equipment	√		
(d) Cash	√		
(e) Cash paid into the firm's bank account by the proprietor	√		√

1.4S A. Sparrow. Balance Sheet as at 31 Jan. 19X1

Assets	£
Shop premises	21,000
Motor van	3,500
Fixtures and fittings	3,000
Office equipment	250
Bank	27,250
	55,000

Financed by	
Capital	50,000
Loan – C. Gull	5,000
	55,000

2 Ledger accounts or 'T' accounts

2.1S

	Debit	Credit
(a)	Bank	Capital
(b)	Shop premises	Bank
(c)	Fixtures and fittings	Bank
(d)	Bank	C. Gull – loan
(e)	Motor van	Bank
(f)	Office equipment	Bank

2.2S

Bank

19X1		£	19X1		£
Jan. 1	Capital	50,000	Jan. 3	Shop premises	21,000
17	C. Gull – loan	5,000	10	Fixtures and fittings	3,000
			24	Motor van	3,500
			31	Office equipment	250
			31	Balance c/d	27,250
		55,000			55,000
Feb. 1	Balance b/d	27,250			

Capital

			19X1		£
			Jan. 1	Bank	50,000

Fixtures and fittings

19X1		£			
Jan. 10	Bank	3,000			

Motor van

19X1		£			
Jan. 24	Bank	3,500			

Shop premises

19X1		£			
Jan. 3	Bank	21,000			

C. Gull – loan

		19X1	£
		Jan. 17 Bank	5,000

Office equipment

19X1	£		
Jan. 31 Bank	250		

Trial Balance – A. Sparrow

	Dr.	Cr.
	£	£
Bank	27,250	
Capital		50,000
Shop premises	21,000	
Fixtures and fittings	3,000	
C. Gull – loan		5,000
Motor van	3,500	
Office equipment	250	
	55,000	55,000

Balance Sheet as at 31 January 19X1

	£
Assets	
Shop premises	21,000
Motor van	3,500
Fixtures and fittings	3,000
Office equipment	250
Bank	27,250
	55,000
Financed by	
Capital	50,000
C. Gull – loan	5,000
	55,000

2.3S

Bank

19X9		£	19X9		£
Mar. 1	Capital	3,000	Mar. 2	Equipment	1,500
	Loan – father	2,000	5	Cash	100
12	Capital	5,000	9	Equipment	2,700
21	Equipment	400	12	Loan – father	2,000
			17	Motor vehicle	2,200
			31	Equipment	350
			31	Balance c/d	1,550
		10,400			10,400
Feb. 1	Balance b/d	1,550			

Cash

19X9	£	19X9	£
Mar. 5 Bank	100	Mar. 25 Equipment	90
		Balance c/d	10
	100		100
Apr. 1 Balance b/d	10		

Capital

19X9	£	19X9	£
Mar. 31 Balance c/d	8,000	Mar. 1 Bank	3,000
		12 Bank	5,000
	8,000		8,000
		Apr. 1 Balance b/d	8,000

Loan – father

19X9	£	19X9	£
Mar. 12 Bank	2,000	Mar. 1 Bank	2,000

Equipment

19X9	£	19X9	£
Mar. 2 Bank	1,500	Mar. 21 Bank	400
9 Bank	2,700	31 Balance c/d	4,240
25 Cash	90		
31 Bank	350		
	4,640		4,640
Apr. 1 Balance b/d	4,240		

Motor vehicles

19X9	£	
Mar. 17 Bank	2,200	

Trial Balance – G. Peake

	Dr.	Cr.
	£	£
Bank	1,550	
Capital		8,000
Cash	10	
Equipment	4,240	
Motor vehicles	2,200	
	8,000	8,000

Balance Sheet as at 31 March 19X9

	£	£
Assets		
Equipment	4,240	
Motor vehicles	2,200	
Bank	1,550	
Cash	10	
	8,000	
Financed by		
Capital		8,000

3 Trading

3.1S

The ledger of D. Johnstone

Bank

19X1		£	19X1		£
Jan.	2 Capital	50,000	Jan.	3 Shop premises	20,000
	19 Sales	8,500		5 Shopfittings	2,500
	31 J. Parker	2,000		9 Purchases	14,000
				10 Cash	100
				16 Van	2,500
				23 Van expenses	15
				31 Balance c/d	21,385
		60,500			60,500
Feb.	1 Balance b/d	21,385			

Capital

			19X1		£
			Jan.	2 Bank	50,000

Shop premises

19X1		£	
Jan.	3 Bank	20,000	

Shopfittings

19X1		£	
Jan.	5 Bank	25,000	

Purchases

19X1		£		£
Jan.	9 Bank	14,000	(Trading account	14,000)

Cash

19X1	£	19X1	£
Jan. 10 Bank	100	Jan. 12 Stationery	20
		28 Cleaning	20
		31 Balance c/d	60
	100		100
Feb. 1 Balance b/d	60		

Stationery

19X1	£		£
Jan. 12 Cash	20	(Profit and loss a/c	20)

Van

19X1	£		
Jan. 16 Bank	2,500		

Sales

19X1	£	19X1	£
Jan. 31 Balance c/d	12,000	Jan. 19 Bank	8,500
		Jan. 26 J. Parker	3,500
	12,000		12,000
(Trading a/c	12,000)	Feb. 1 Balance b/d	12,000

Van expenses

19X1	£		£
Jan. 21 Bank	15	(Profit and loss a/c	15)

J. Parker

19X1	£	19X1	£
Jan. 26 Sales	3,500	Jan. 31 Bank	2,000
		31 Balance c/d	1,500
	3,500		3,500
Feb. 1 Balance b/d	1,500		

Cleaning

19X1	£		£
Jan. 28 Cash	20	(Profit and loss a/c	20)

D. Johnstone
Extended trial balance

	Trial balance		Trading account		Profit and loss account		Balance sheet	
	Dr. £	Cr. £	Dr. £	Cr. £	Dr. £	Cr. £	Dr. £	Cr. £
Bank	21,385						21,385	
Capital		50,000						50,000
Shop premises	20,000						20,000	
Shopfittings	2,500						2,500	
Purchases	14,000		14,000					
Cash	60						60	
Stationery	20				20			
Van	2,500						2,500	
Sales		12,000		12,000				
Van expenses	15				15			
J. Parker (debtor)	1,500						1,500	
Cleaning	20				20			
Closing stock		4,000		4,000				
Closing stock c/f	4,000						4,000	
GROSS PROFIT			2,000			2,000		
NET PROFIT					1,945			1,945
	66,000	66,000	16,000	16,000	2,000	2,000	51,945	51,945

D. Johnstone
Trading and Profit and Loss Account
for the month ended 31 January 19X1

	£	£
Sales		12,000
Cost of sales		
Purchases	14,000	
less Closing stock	4,000	10,000
Gross profit		2,000
Stationery	20	
Van expenses	15	
Cleaning	20	55
Net profit		1,945

Balance Sheet as at 31 January 19X1

	£	£
Assets		
Fixed assets		
Shop premises		20,000
Shopfittings		2,500
Van		2,500
		25,000
Current assets		
Stock	4,000	
Debtor	1,500	
Bank	21,385	
Cash	60	26,945
		51,945
Financed by		
Capital		50,000
add Profit for the month		1,945
		51,945

3.2S

The ledger of P. Brown
Bank

19X2		£	19X2		£
Jul. 1	Capital	20,000	Jul. 1	Shopfittings	2,000
31	Cash	1,375	1	Van	3,200
			2	Rent	200
			10	Insurance	12
			17	J. Smith	1,500
			27	I. Thomas	700
			31	Balance c/d	13,763
		21,375			21,375
Aug. 1	Balance b/d	13,763			

Capital

		19X2	£
		Jul. 1 Bank	20,000

Shopfittings

19X2	£		
Jul. 1 Bank	2,000		

Van

19X2	£		
Jul. 1 Bank	3,200		

Rent

19X2	£		£
Jul. 2 Bank	200	(Profit and loss a/c	200)

Purchases

19X2	£	19X2	£
Jul. 3 J. Smith	2,500	Jul. 15 J. Smith	480
19 I. Thomas	1,400	31 Balance c/d	3,420
	3,900		3,900
Aug. 1 Balance b/d	3,420	(Trading a/c	3,420)

J. Smith

19X2	£	19X2	£
Jul. 15 Purchases	480	Jul. 3 Purchases	2,500
17 Bank	1,500		
31 Balance c/d	520		
	2,500		2,500
		Aug. 1 Balance b/d	520

Cash

19X2	£	19X2	£
Jul. 5 Sales	260	Jul. 8 Wages	35
12 Sales	400	15 Wages	35
19 Sales	480	22 Wages	35
26 Sales	600	24 Stationery	25
		29 Wages	35
		31 Bank	1,375
		31 Balance c/d	200
	1,740		1,740
Aug. 1 Balance b/d	200		

Sales

19X2	£	19X2	£
Jul. 31 Balance c/d	1,740	Jul. 5 Cash	260
		12 Cash	400
		19 Cash	480
		26 Cash	600
	1,740		1,740
(Trading a/c	1,740)	Aug. 1 Balance b/d	1,740

Wages

19X2	£	19X2	£
Jul. 8 Cash	35	Jul. 31 Balance c/d	140
15 Cash	35		
22 Cash	35		
29 Cash	35		
	140		140
Aug. 1 Balance b/d	140	(Profit and loss a/c	140)

Insurance

19X2	£		£
Jul. 10 Bank	12	(Profit and loss a/c	12)

I. Thomas

19X2	£	19X2	£
Jul. 27 Bank	700	Jul. 19 Purchases	1,400
31 Balance c/d	700		
	1,400		1,400
		Aug. 1 Balance b/d	700

Stationery

19X2	£		£
Jul. 24 Cash	25	(Profit and loss a/c	25)

P. Brown
Extended trial balance

	Trial balance Dr £	Trial balance Cr £	Trading account Dr £	Trading account Cr £	Profit and loss account Dr £	Profit and loss account Cr £	Balance sheet Dr £	Balance sheet Cr £
Bank	13,763						13,763	
Capital		20,000						20,000
Shopfittings	2,000						2,000	
Van	3,200						3,200	
Rent	200				200			
Purchases	3,420		3,420					
J. Smith (creditor)		520						520
Cash	200						200	
Sales		1,740		1,740				
Wages	140				140			
Insurance	12				12			
I. Thomas (creditor)		700						700
Stationery	25				25			
Closing stock				2,715				
Closing stock c/f	2,715						2,715	
GROSS PROFIT			1,035			1,035		
NET PROFIT					658			658
	25,675	25,675	4,455	4,455	1,035	1,035	21,878	21,878

P. Brown
Trading and Profit and Loss Account
for the month ended 31 July 19X2

	£	£
Sales		1,740
Cost of sales		
Purchases	3,420	
less Closing stock	2,715	705
Gross profit		1,035
Rent	200	
Wages	140	
Insurance	12	
Stationery	25	377
		658

Balance Sheet as at 31 July 19X2

	£	£
Assets		
Fixed assets		
Shopfittings		2,000
Van		3,200
		5,200
Current assets		
Stock	2,715	
Bank	13,763	
Cash	200	
	16,678	
less Current liabilities		
Creditors	1,220	15,458
		20,658
Financed by		
Capital		20,000
add Profit for the month		658
		20,658

3.3S   The ledger of Steve O'Hare
Capital

19X8		£	19X8		£
Jun. 30 Balance c/d		10,000	Jun. 1 Bank		10,000
			Jul. 1 Balance b/d		10,000

Bank

19X8		£	19X8		£
Jun.	1 Capital	10,000	Jun.	1 Rent	550
	7 Sales	1,500		Fittings	4,200
	14 Sales	2,400		Purchases	3,000
	21 Sales	1,900		4 Cash	600
	28 Sales	2,800		10 B. Whiteley	2,500
	30 D. Karsa	700		16 AB Cars	2,100
				18 Telephone	150
				30 Balance c/d	6,200
		19,300			19,300
Jul.	1 Balance b/d	6,200			

Rent

19X8		£	19X8		£
Jun.	1 Bank	550	Jun. 30 Profit and loss		550

Shopfittings

19X8		£	19X8		£
Jun.	1 Bank	4,200	Jun.	30 Balance c/d	4,200
Jul.	1 Balance b/d	4,200			

Purchases

19X8		£	19X8		£
Jun.	1 Bank	3,000	Jun.	14 R. Knowles	150
	3 B. Whiteley	4,000		30 Trading	10,650
	9 R. Knowles	1,500			
	23 R. Knowles	2,300			
		10,800			10,800

B. Whiteley

19X8		£	19X8		£
Jun.	10 Bank	2,500	Jun.	3 Purchases	4,000
	30 Balance c/d	1,500			
		4,000			4,000
			Jul.	1 Balance b/d	1,500

R. Knowles

19X8		£	19X8			£
Jun.	14 Returns	150	Jun.	9	Purchases	1,500
	30 Balance c/d	3,650		23	Purchases	2,300
		3,800				3,800
			Jul.	1	Balance b/d	3,650

AB Cars

19X8		£	19X8			£
Jun.	16 Bank	2,100	Jun.	16	Motor vehicles	8,400
	30 Balance c/d	6,300				
		8,400				8,400
			Jul.	1	Balance b/d	6,300

Motor vehicles

19X8		£	19X8			£
Jun.	16 AB Cars	8,400	Jun.	30	Balance c/d	8,400
Jul.	1 Balance b/d	8,400				

Cash

19X8		£	19X8			£
Jun.	4 Bank	600	Jun.	7	Wages	120
					Window cleaning	10
				14	Wages	130
				21	Wages	105
				28	Wages	135
				30	Balance c/d	100
		600				600
Jul.	1 Balance b/d	100				

Window cleaning

19X8		£	19X8			£
Jun.	7 Cash	10	Jun.	30	Profit and loss	10

Wages

19X8		£	19X8			£
Jun.	7 Cash	120	Jun.	30	Profit and loss	490
	14 Cash	130				
	21 Cash	105				
	28 Cash	135				
		490				490

Sales

19X8		£	19X8		£
Jun.	27 J. Markham	60	Jun.	4 D. Karsa	700
	30 Trading	9,860		7 Bank	1,500
				14 Bank	2,400
				21 Bank	1,900
				25 J. Markham	620
				28 Bank	2,800
		9,920			9,920

D. Karsa

19X8		£	19X8		£
Jun.	4 Sales	700	Jun.	30 Bank	700

J. Markham

19X8		£	19X8		£
Jun.	25 Sales	620	Jun.	27 Returns	60
				30 Balance c/d	560
		620			620
Jul.	1 Balance b/d	560			

Telephone

19X8		£	19X8		£
Jun.	18 Bank	150	Jun.	30 Profit and loss	150

Steve O'Hare's Trial Balance on 30 June 19X8

	Dr. £	Cr. £
Capital		10,000
Bank	6,200	
Rent	550	
Shop fittings	4,200	
Purchases	10,650	
Creditors: B. Whiteley		1,500
R. Knowles		3,650
AB Cars		6,300
Motor vehicles	8,400	
Cash	100	
Window cleaning	10	
Wages	490	
Sales		9,860
Debtor: J. Markham	560	
Telephone	150	
	31,310	31,310

S. O'Hare
Trading and Profit and Loss Account
for the month ended 30 June 19X8

	£	£
Sales		9,860
Cost of sales		
Purchases	10,650	
less Closing stock	5,320	5,330
Gross profit		4,530
Wages	490	
Rent	550	
Telephone	150	
Window cleaning	10	1,200
Net profit		3,330

Balance Sheet on 30 June 19X8

	£	£
Fixed assets		
Shop fittings	4,200	
Motor vehicles	8,400	12,600
Current assets		
Stock	5,320	
Debtors	560	
Bank	6,200	
Cash	100	
	12,180	
Less Current liabilities		
Creditors	11,450	
Working capital		730
		13,330
Financed by		
Capital		10,000
add Net profit		3,330
		13,330

4 Final accounts

4.1S

John Pink's ledger

Rent account

19X5		£	19X5		£
Mar. 30	Bank	100	Dec. 31	Profit and loss	400
Jun. 28	Bank	100			
Sep. 30	Bank	100			
Dec. 31	Amount owing c/d	100			
		400			400
			19X6		
			Jan. 1	Amount owing b/d	100

4.2S

Charles Indigo's ledger

Rent account

19X6		£	19X7		£
Sep. 28	Bank	250	Jun. 30	Profit and loss	1,000
19X7					
Jan. 3	Bank	250			
Mar. 28	Bank	250			
Jun. 30	Amount owning c/d	250			
		1,000			1,000
			Jul. 1	Amount owing b/d	250

Rates account

19X6		£	19X7		£
Jul. 28	Bank	220	Jun. 30	Prepayment c/d	140
19X7			30	Profit and loss	360
Apr. 30	Bank	280			
		500			500
Jul. 1	Prepayment b/d	140			

4.3S

J. Black
Trading and Profit and Loss Account
for the year ended 31 December 19X8

	£	£	£
Sales			63,000
Cost of sales			
Stock at 1 January 19X8		10,800	
Purchases	53,500		
less Purchase returns	2,000	51,500	
		62,300	
less Stock at 31 December 19X8		11,900	50,400
Gross profit			12,600
less Expenses			
Rent and rates		2,520	
Lighting and heating		470	
General expenses		1,000	3,990
Net profit			8,610

Note
Lighting and heating

	£
Per trial balance	440
add Amount accrued	30
	470

Balance Sheet as at 31 December 19X8

	£	£	£
Assets			
Fixed assets			
Fixtures and fittings			12,800
Motor vehicles			7,500
			20,300
Current assets			
Stock		11,900	
Debtors		4,450	
Cash in hand		80	
		16,430	
less Current liabilities			
Creditors and accrual	2,900		
Bank overdraft	4,780	7,680	
Working capital			8,750
			29,050

		£
Financed by		
Capital		
Balance at 1 January 19X8		30,000
add Profit for the year		8,610
		38,610
less Drawings		9,560
		29,050

Note
Creditors and accrual

	£
Creditors per trial balance	2,870
add Electricity accrued	30
	2,900

4.4S

S. White
Trading and Profit and Loss Account
for the year ended 30 June 19X6

	£	£	£
Sales			24,708
less Sales returns			180
			24,528
Cost of sales			
Stock at 1 July 19X5		7,296	
Purchases	17,434		
less Purchase returns	199	17,235	
		24,531	
less Stock at 30 June 19X6		7,144	17,387
Gross profit			7,141
add Discounts received			186
			7,327
less Expenses			
Salaries		1,245	
Rates		300	
Lighting and heating		200	
Sundry expenses		162	
Discounts allowed		330	2,237
Net profit			5,090

Notes

1. Rates

	£
Per trial balance	400
less Paid in advance	100
	300

2. Lighting and heating

	£
Per trial balance	172
add Amount accrued	28
	200

Balance Sheet as at 30 June 19X6

	£	£
Assets		
Fixed assets		
Freehold premises		15,000
Fixtures and fittings		6,750
		21,750
Current assets		
Stock	7,144	
Debtors and prepayment	3,280	
Cash at bank	2,908	
Cash in hand	30	
	13,362	
less Current liabilities		
Creditors and accrual	2,272	
Working capital		11,090
		32,840
Financed by		
Capital		
Balance at 1 July 19X5		30,000
add Profit for the year		5,090
		35,090
less Drawings		2,250
		32,840

Notes

1. Debtors and prepayments

	£
Debtors per trial balance	3,180
add Rates paid in advance	100
	3,280

2. Creditors and accruals

	£
Creditors per trial balance	2,244
add Electricity accrued	28
	2,272

4.5S

B. Riley's ledger

Rent and rates

19X3		£	19X3		£
Jan. 1	Rates prepaid b/d	88	Jan. 1	Rent outstanding	
4	Bank – rent	190		b/d	190
Mar. 29	Bank – rent	190	Dec. 31	Profit and loss	1,124
Jun. 26	Bank – rates	184			
Jul. 7	Bank – rent	190			
Sep. 30	Bank – rent	190			
Dec. 28	Bank – rent	190			
Dec. 31	Rates owing c/d	92			
		1,314			1,314
			19X4		
			Jan. 1	Rates owing b/d	92

Check of total charged to profit and loss account:

	£
Rent for the year (4 × £190)	760
Rates: for 3 months to 31 March 19X3	88
for 6 months to 30 September 19X3	184
for 3 months to 31 December 19X3	92
	1,124

5 Depreciation

Truck & Co.

Plant and machinery

19X7			£	19X8		£
Oct.	1	Balance b/d	10,000	Sep. 30 Balance c/d		10,000
19X8						
Oct.	1	Balance b/d	10,000			

Provision for depreciation of plant and machinery

19X8		£	19X7		£
Sep. 30 Balance c/d		4,000	Oct. 1 Balance b/d		2,000
			19X8		
			Sep. 30 Profit and loss		2,000
		4,000			4,000
			Oct. 1 Balance b/d		4,000

Balance Sheet (extract) as at 30 September 19X8

	Cost	Depreciation	Net
Fixed assets			
	£	£	£
Plant and machinery	10,000	4,000	6,000

D. Bird

Machinery

19X2			£	19X2		£
Jun.	30	Bank	3,000	Dec. 31 Balance c/d		3,000
19X3				19X3		
Jan.	1	Balance b/d	3,000	Dec. 31 Balance c/d		3,000
19X4				19X4		
Jan.	1	Balance b/d	3,000	Dec. 31 Balance c/d		3,000
19X5				19X5		
Jan.	1	Balance b/d	3,000	Dec. 31 Balance c/d		3,000
19X6				19X6		
Jan.	1	Balance b/d	3,000	Dec. 31 Balance c/d		3,000

19X7			19X7	
Jan. 1 Balance b/d	3,000		Dec. 31 Balance c/d	3,000
19X8				
Jan. 1 Balance b/d	3,000			

Provision for depreciation of machinery

19X2	£		19X2	£
Dec. 31 Balance c/d	750		Dec. 31 Profit and loss	750
19X3			19X3	
Dec. 31 Balance c/d	1,312		Jan. 1 Balance b/d	750
			Dec. 31 Profit and loss	562
	1,312			1,312
19X4			19X4	
Dec. 31 Balance c/d	1,734		Jan. 1 Balance b/d	1,312
			Dec. 31 Profit and loss	422
	1,734			1,734
19X5			19X5	
Dec. 31 Balance c/d	2,051		Jan. 1 Balance b/d	1,734
			Dec. 31 Profit and loss	317
	2,051			2,051
19X6			19X6	
Dec. 31 Balance c/d	2,288		Jan. 1 Balance b/d	2,051
			Dec. 31 Profit and loss	237
	2,288			2,288
19X7			19X7	
Dec. 31 Balance c/d	2,466		Jan. 1 Balance b/d	2,288
			Dec. 31 Profit and loss	178
	2,466			2,466
			19X8	
			Jan. 1 Balance b/d	2,466

Tutorial notes

1. Applying the formula given in the text, the rate per cent is found to be

$$1 - \sqrt[6]{\frac{534}{3,000}} = 1 - 0.75 = 25\%.$$

2. Since the depreciation is to be calculated on the reducing value of the asset, the charge to profit and loss will obviously reduce each year, viz.

		£
Year 1	Cost	3,000
	Depreciation 25% × £3,000	750
Year 2	Book value	2,250
	Depreciation 25% × £2,250	562
Year 3	Book value	1,688
	and so on	

5.3S (a)   Machine tools

19X4			£	19X4			£
Jan.	1	Balance b/d	10,000	Jan.	1	Disposal of machine tools	5,000
Jan.	1	Bank	8,000	Dec. 31	Balance c/d	13,000
			18,000				18,000
19X5							
Jan.	1	Balance b/d	13,000				

Office machinery

19X4			£	19X4			£
Jan.	1	Balance b/d	2,000	Dec. 31	Balance c/d	2,000
19X5							
Jan.	1	Balance b/d	2,000				

Provision for depreciation of machine tools

19X4			£	19X4			£
Jan.	1	Disposal of machine tools	1,000	Jan.	1	Balance b/d	2,000
Dec. 31	Balance c/d	3,400	Dec. 31	Profit and loss	2,400
			4,400				4,400
				19X5			
				Jan.	1	Balance b/d	3,400

Provision for depreciation of office machinery

19X4			£	19X4			£
Dec. 31	Balance c/d	600	Jan.	1	Balance b/d	300
				Dec. 31	Profit and loss	300
			600				600
				19X5			
				Jan.	1	Balance b/d	600

Disposal of machine tools

19X4		£	19X4			£
Jan. 1	Machine tools	5,000	Jan. 1	Provision for depreciation of machine tools		1,000
			Jan. 1	Bank		2,750
			Dec. 31	Profit and loss		1,250
		5,000				5,000

(b) Depreciation may be defined as the apportionment of the cost of an asset, less any residual value, over its working life on a consistent, defined basis. It does not of itself provide any cash for replacement. A separate transaction transferring the cash from the bank to a special fund would be necessary. In any case, since the depreciation charge in conventional accounts is based upon the historic cost of the asset, such a transfer of cash, if based upon the depreciation charge, will not provide sufficient funds to replace an asset in times of inflation.

Tutorial note
The charge to profit and loss of £2,400 for the year to 31 December 19X4 shown in the provision for depreciation of machine tools account is calculated as 20% on £12,000 = £2,400, i.e.

£4,000	the written down value of the machine purchased on 1 January 19X3, and still held at 31 December 19X4, plus
£8,000	the cost of the machine tool acquired on 1 January 19X4
£12,000	

5.4S (a)   Motor vehicles

19X6		£	19X6		£
May 31	Bank – NOL 862V	18,000	Dec. 31 Balance c/d		42,000
Oct. 31	Bank – NOM 760W	24,000			
		42,000			42,000
19X7			19X7		
Jan. 1	Balance b/d	42,000	Sep. 1 Motor vehicle disposals		18,000
			Dec. 31 Balance c/d		24,000
		42,000			42,000
19X8					
Jan. 1	Balance b/d	24,000			

(b)   Provision for depreciation of motor vehicles

19X6	£	19X6	£
Dec. 31 Balance c/d	2,900	Dec. 31 Profit and loss	2,900
19X7		19X7	
Sep. 1 Motor vehicles		Jan. 1 Balance b/d	2,900
disposals	4,500	Dec. 31 Profit and loss	7,200
Dec. 31 Balance c/d	5,600		
	10,100		10,100
		19X8	
		Jan. 1 Balance b/d	5,600

(c)   Motor vehicles disposals

19X7	£	19X7	£
Sep. 1 Motor vehicles	18,000	Sep. 1 Provision for	
		depreciation of	
		motor vehicles	4,500
		Sep. 20 Bank – insurance	
		proceeds	12,500
		Dec. 31 Profit and loss	1,000
	18,000		18,000

Tutorial notes:

1. The depreciation charge is calculated as follows:

Vehicle No.	Cost		19X6		19X7
	£		£		£
NOL 862V	18,000	7 months at		8 months at	
		20% p.a.	2,100	20% p.a.	2,400
NOM 760W	24,000	2 months at		12 months at	
		20% p.a.	800	20% p.a.	4,800
			2,900		7,200

2. Since the first vehicle purchased, NOL 862V, is no longer held by the firm, the balance on the motor vehicles account at 31 December 19X7 should be the cost of the second vehicle purchased, NOM 760W, and the balance on the provision for depreciation of motor vehicles account at the same date should be the depreciation provided to that date on that vehicle. An examination of the two accounts will confirm their correctness.

5.5S
F. Robinson
Trading and Profit and Loss Account
for the year ended 30 June 19X9

	£	£	£
Sales			164,720
less Returns inwards			1,330
			163,390
Cost of sales			
Stock at 1 July 19X8		14,864	
Purchases	116,230		
less Returns outwards	1,910	114,320	
		129,184	
less Stock at 30 June 19X9		10,280	118,904
Gross profit			44,486
add Discount receivable			816
			45,302
less Expenses			
Salaries and commission		18,600	
Rent, rates and insurance		2,050	
Lighting and heating		1,510	
Sundry expenses		802	
Discount allowed		1,220	
Depreciation of fixtures and			
fittings		400	24,582
Net profit			20,720

Notes
1. Salaries and commission

	£
Per trial balance	18,360
add Commission owing	240
Profit and loss a/c	18,600

2. Rent, rates and insurance

	£	£
Per trial balance		2,600
add Rent owing		250
		2,850
less Rates prepaid	700	
Insurance prepaid	100	800
Profit and loss a/c		2,050

3. Depreciation of fixtures and fittings 10% per annum on £4,000 = £400.

Balance Sheet as at 30 June 19X9

Assets

Fixed assets	Cost £	Depreciation £	Net £
Freehold premises	16,000		16,000
Fixtures and fittings	4,000	2,000	2,000
	20,000	2,000	18,000

Current assets		
Stock	10,280	
Debtors and prepayments	13,010	
Cash at bank	2,164	
Cash in hand	50	
	25,504	
less Current liabilities		
Creditors	12,184	
Working capital		13,320
		31,320

Financed by		
Capital		
Balance at 1 July 19X8		21,800
add Profit for the year		20,720
		42,520
less Drawings		11,200
		31,320

Notes

1. The figure of £2,000 shown as depreciation of fixtures and fittings is the accumulated amount to date, i.e. £1,600 to 30 June 19X8 plus £400 for the year to 30 June 19X9.

2. Debtors and prepayments

	£
Per trial balance	12,210
add Rates prepaid	700
Insurance prepaid	100
	13,010

3. Creditors

	£
Per trial balance	11,694
add Rent owing	250
Commission owing	240
	12,184

5.6S

S. Barnard
Trading and Profit and Loss Account
for the year ended 31 December 19X8

	£	£	£
Sales			38,700
less Sales returns			1,650
			37,050
Cost of sales			
Stock at 1 January 19X8		8,200	
Purchases	26,100		
less Purchase returns	1,300	24,800	
		33,000	
less Stock at 31 December 19X8		11,500	21,500
Gross profit			15,550
add Discount received			1,150
			16,700
less Expenses			
Wages		2,450	
Rent and rates		2,000	
Insurance		840	
Depreciation of – Van	550		
– Fixtures and fittings	250	800	6,090
Net profit			10,610

Notes
1. Rent and rates

	£
Per trial balance	2,110
add Rent owing	250
	2,360
less Rates prepaid	360
Profit and loss	2,000

2. Insurance

	£
Per trial balance	1,030
less Insurance prepaid	190
Profit and loss	840

3. Depreciation: The annual depreciation charge on the van is £$(2,500 - 300) \div 4 = £550$. The annual depreciation charge on the fixtures and fittings is £$(2,590 - 90) \div 10 = £250$.

Balance Sheet as at 31 December 19X8

Assets

Fixed assets	Cost £	Depreciation £	Net £
Fixtures and fittings	2,590	1,500	1,090
Van	2,500	1,650	850
	5,090	3,150	1,940

Current assets		
Stock		11,500
Debtors and prepayments		3,080
Cash at bank		8,750
Cash in hand		30
		23,360
less Current liabilities		
Creditors		3,000	20,360
			22,300

Financed by		
Capital		
Balance at 1 January 19X8		18,000
add Profit for the year		10,610
		28,610
less Drawings		6,310
		22,300

Notes

1. The depreciation to date is calculated as follows:

	Furniture and fittings £	Van £
Accumulated to 1 January 19X8	1,250	1,100
add Charge for the year	250	550
Balance sheet	1,500	1,650

2. Debtors and prepayments

	£
Per trial balance	2,530
add Rates prepaid	360
Insurance prepaid	190
	3,080

3. Creditors

	£
Per trial balance	2,750
add Rent owing	250
	3,000

6 Division of the ledger; books of original entry

6.1S

J. Mowbray
Cash book

19X2		Cash	Bank	19X2		Cash	Bank
		£	£			£	£
Jan.	1 Balances b/d	33	625	Jan.	4 J. Greaney		80
	3 V. Banyard	107			5 Bank	40	
	4 I. Watson	20			6 Wages	100	
	5 Cash		40		11 K. Walton		42
	12 W. Larkin		75		13 Cash		90
	13 Bank	90			Wages	100	
	15 A. Benthram		150		19 Office Equip-		
	18 J. Noble		86		ment Co.	8	
	20 J. Jones	106			20 Wages	100	
	25 P. Willey		152		24 A. Williamson		55
	27 Bank	110			27 Cash		110
					Wages	100	
					31 Balances c/d	18	751
		466	1,128			466	1,128
Feb.	1 Balances b/d	18	751				

6.2S (a)

A.M. Smith
Cash book

19X3		Dis-count	Cash	Bank	19X3		Dis-count	Cash	Bank
		£	£	£			£	£	£
Jan.	1 Balance b/d			520	Jan.	1 Cash			180
	Bank		180						
	2 N. Walton	26		494		3 Postages		15	
	10 W. Bolton			653		8 R. Hayton	18		342
	14 Bank		135			11 H. Vanstone			300
	21 D.Webster	21		399		Wages		120	
	28 Bank		174			14 Cash			135
						16 C. Yates	6		114
						25 Wages		120	
						Stationery		28	

£	£	£		£	£	£
			Postages	26		
			28 Cash			174
			Drawings			280
			30 F. Wilson			153
			31 Balances c/d		180	388
	47 489	2,066			24 489	2,066

Feb. 1 Balances b/d 180 388

(b) Discount allowed of £47 would be posted to the debit of the discount allowed account. Discount received of £24 would be posted to the credit of discount received account.

6.3S   Answer shown diagrammatically.

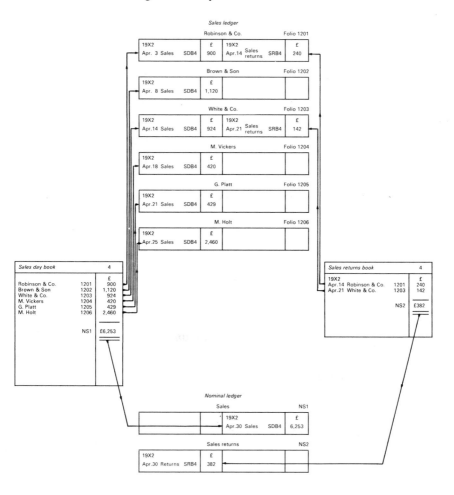

6.4S

E. Booth
Sales Day Book   Folio 10

19X8		Folio	£
Oct. 1	M. Greenwood	DG2	1,240
4	A. Gaston	DG1	746
6	E. Aldcroft	DA1	640
10	M. Daniels	DD1	480
14	M. Greenwood	DG2	420
16	A. Gaston	DG1	264
18	W. Pickles	DP1	336
24	E. Aldcroft	DA1	348
	M. Daniels	DD1	260
27	M. Heslop	DH1	760
30	A. Crompton	DC1	920
31	A. Gaston	DG1	647
		NS1	7,061

Purchases Day Book   Folio 10

19X8		Folio	£
Oct. 3	A. Hargreaves	CH1	800
4	R. Scruton	CS1	420
6	H. Smith	CS2	708
18	A. Hargreaves	CH1	680
21	B. Hubbard	CH2	2,240
27	P. Davies	CD1	520
30	E. Hull	CH3	1,460
		NP1	6,828

Debtors Ledger
E. Aldcroft   DA1

19X8			£	19X8		£
Oct. 6	Sales	SDB10	640	Oct. 31 Balance c/d		988
24	Sales	SDB10	348			
			988			988
Nov. 1	Balance b/d		988			

A. Crompton   DC1

19X8			£
Oct. 30	Sales	SDB10	920

M. Daniels   DD1

19X8			£	19X8		£
Oct. 10	Sales	SDB10	480	Oct. 31 Balance c/d		740
24	Sales	SDB10	260			
			740			740
Nov. 1	Balance b/d		740			

A. Gaston   DG1

19X8			£	19X8		£
Oct.	4 Sales	SDB10	746	Oct. 31 Balance c/d		1,657
	16 Sales	SDB10	264			
	31 Sales	SDB10	647			
			1,657			1,657
Nov.	1 Balance b/d		1,657			

M. Greenwood   DG2

19X8			£	19X8		£
Oct.	1 Sales	SDB10	1,240	Oct. 31 Balance c/d		1,660
	14 Sales	SDB10	420			
			1,660			1,660
Nov.	1 Balance b/d		1,660			

M. Heslop   DH1

19X8			£	
Oct. 27 Sales	SDB10	760		

W. Pickles   DP1

19X8			£	
Oct. 18 Sales	SDB10	336		

Creditors Ledger
P. Davies   CD1

	19X8		£
	Oct. 27 Purchases PDB10		520

A. Hargreaves   CH1

19X8		£	19X8		£
Oct. 31 Balance c/d		1,480	Oct. 3 Purchases PDB10		800
			18 Purchases PDB10		680
		1,480			1,480
			Nov. 1 Balance b/d		1,480

B. Hubbard   CH2

	19X8		£
	Oct. 21 Purchases PDB10		2,240

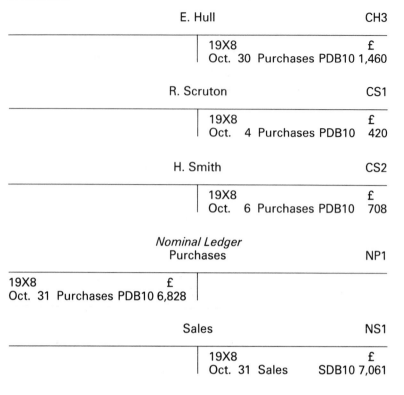

E. Hull   CH3

	19X8	£
	Oct. 30 Purchases PDB10	1,460

R. Scruton   CS1

	19X8	£
	Oct. 4 Purchases PDB10	420

H. Smith   CS2

	19X8	£
	Oct. 6 Purchases PDB10	708

Nominal Ledger
Purchases   NP1

19X8	£	
Oct. 31 Purchases PDB10 6,828		

Sales   NS1

	19X8	£
	Oct. 31 Sales	SDB10 7,061

6.5S   *J. Shaw*
                                    Journal

19X8		Dr.	Cr.
		£	£
Jan. 1	Freehold premises	25,000	
	Fittings	12,000	
	Stock	8,000	
	E. Booth	480	
	M. Greenough	360	
	Cash	200	
	Loan – J. Buckle		10,000
	Bank		6,800
	A. Hargreaves		260
	Provision for depreciation of fittings		3,000
	Capital		25,980
		46,040	46,040

Assets and liabilities at
1 January 19X8.

6.6S

J. Shaw
Journal

19X8

		Dr.	Cr.
		£	£
Jan. 1	Freehold premises	25,000	
	Fittings	12,000	
	Stock	8,000	
	E. Booth	480	
	M. Greenough	360	
	Cash	200	
	Loan – J. Buckle		10,000
	Bank		6,800
	A. Hargreaves		260
	Provision for depreciation of fittings		3,000
	Capital		25,980
		46,040	46,040

Assets and liabilities at
1 January 19X8.

Note
The journal entry to record the opening balances as required by Question
6.5S has been repeated above for illustration purposes.

Journal (cont.)

		Dr.	Cr.
Jan. 18	Fittings	1,200	
	N. Barrow		1,200
	Purchase of fittings –		
	see invoice dated		
	18 January 19X8.		

Sales Day Book

19X8		£
Jan. 2	E. Booth	290
5	M. Greenough	360
14	C. Leydell	420
22	C. Ingin	260
		1,330

Sales Returns Book

19X8		£
Jan. 26	C. Ingin	28
		28

Purchases Day Book

19X8		£
Jan. 8	A. Hargreaves	460
30	J. Gilpin	220
		680

Cash Book

		Dis-count	Cash	Bank				Dis-count	Cash	Bank
19X8		£	£	£	19X8			£	£	£
Jan.	1 Balance b/d		200		Jan.	1	Balance b/d			6,800
	11 Sales		320			12	Bank ₡		200	
	12 Cash ₡			200			Wages		120	
	29 E. Booth	12		468		26	Wages		120	
	M. Green-					29	A. Har-			
	ough	9		351			greaves			260
	31 Balance c/d			6,041		31	Balance c/d		80	
	D1	21	520	7,060					520	7,060
Feb.	1 Balance b/d		80		Feb.	1	Balance b/d			6,041

Note

₡ is the abbreviation for a contra entry.

Ledger
Freehold premises

19X8		£	
Jan.	1 Balance b/d	25,000	

Fittings

19X8		£	19X8		£
Jan.	1 Balance b/d	12,000	Jan. 31 Balance c/d		13,200
	18 N. Barrow	1,200			
		13,200			13,200
Feb.	1 Balance b/d	13,200			

Stock

19X8		£	
Jan.	1 Balance b/d	8,000	

E. Booth

19X8		£	19X8		£
			Jan. 29 Cash and		
Jan.	1 Balance b/d	480	discount		480
	2 Sales	290			

M. Greenough

19X8		£	19X8		£
			Jan. 29 Cash and		
Jan. 1	Balance b/d	360		discount	360
5	Sales	360			

Loan – J. Buckle

			19X8		£
			Jan. 1	Balance b/d	10,000

A. Hargreaves

19X8		£	19X8		£
Jan. 29 Cash		260	Jan. 1	Balance b/d	260
			Jan. 8	Purchases	460

Provision for depreciation on fittings

			19X8		£
			Jan. 1	Balance b/d	3,000

Capital

			19X8		£
			Jan. 1	Balance b/d	25,980

N. Barrow

			19X8		£
			Jan. 18	Fittings	1,200

C. Leydell

19X8		£		
Jan. 14 Sales		420		

C. Ingin

19X8		£	19X8		£
Jan. 22 Sales		260	Jan. 26	Sales	
				returns	28
			31	Balance c/d	232
		260			260
Feb. 1	Balance b/d	232			

J. Gilpin

		19X8	£
		Jan. 30 Purchases	220

Sales

19X8		£	19X8		£
Jan. 31 Balance c/d		1,650	Jan. 11 Cash		320
			31 Sales		1,330
		1,650			1,650
			Feb. 1 Balance b/d		1,650

Sales returns

19X8	£	
Jan. 31 Sales returns	28	

Purchases

19X8	£	
Jan. 31 Purchases	680	

Wages

19X8		£	19X8		£
Jan. 12 Cash		120	Jan. 31 Balance c/d		240
26 Cash		120			
		240			240
Feb. 1 Balance b/d		240			

Discount allowed

19X8	£	
Jan. 31 Discount allowed	21	

Trial Balance at 1 February 19X8

Name	Dr. £	Cr. £
Freehold premises	25,000	
Fittings	13,200	
Stock	8,000	
E. Booth	290	
N. Greenough	360	
Loan – J. Buckle		10,000
A. Hargreaves		460
Provision for depreciation on fittings		3,000
Capital		25,980
N. Barrow		1,200
C. Leydell	420	
C. Ingin	232	
J. Gilpin		220
Sales		1,650
Sales returns	28	
Purchases	680	
Wages	240	
Discount allowed	21	
Cash	80	
Bank		6,041
	48,551	48,551

7 Value added tax (VAT)

7.1S

J. Madden Ltd
Sales Day Book

	Net price	VAT	Total sale price
19X6	£	£	£
May 6 H. Smith Ltd	200	35	235
9 R. Scruton & Co.	320	56	376
13 R. Hollis & Co.	240	42	282
16 E. Aldcroft	400	70	470
20 M. Daniels & Co.	160	28	188
23 E. Seddon & Co.	280	49	329
27 H. Smith Ltd	360	63	423
	1,960	343	2,303

Debtors' Ledger
H. Smith Ltd

19X6	£	19X6	£
May 6 Sales	235	May 31 Balance c/d	658
27 Sales	423		
	658		658
Jun. 1 Balance b/d	658		

R. Scruton & Co.

19X6	£		
May 9 Sales	376		

R. Hollis & Co.

19X6	£		
May 13 Sales	282		

E. Aldcroft Ltd

19X6	£		
May 16 Sales	470		

M. Daniels & Co.

19X6	£		
May 20 Sales	188		

E. Seddon & Co.

19X6	£		
May 23 Sales	329		

Sales

		19X6	£
		May 31 Debtors	1,960

Value added tax

		19X6	£
		May 31 Debtors	343

7.2S

Stanley Jones
Cash book

19X1		Cash £	Bank £	Net of VAT £	VAT £
Jul. 1	Balance b/d	323	25,012		
	Sales	1,880		1,600	280
3	Bank (c)		1,880		
8	Sales	2,115		1,800	315
10	Bank (c)		1,500		
15	Sales	2,303		1,960	343
17	Bank (c)		2,000		
29	Sales	1,974		1,680	294
30	Bank (c)		2,000		
		8,595	**32,392**	**7,040**	**1,232**
Aug. 1	Balance b/d	401	5,842		

19X1		Cash £	Bank £	Net of VAT £	VAT £
Jul. 1	Shop fittings		4,700	4,000	700
	Purchases		18,800	16,000	2,800
	Ford Escort		2,350	2,350	–
3	Cash (c)	1,880			
7	Car expenses	47		40	7
	Wages	360		360	–
10	Cash (c)	1,500			
12	Norweb – electricity		480	480	–
17	Cash (c)	2,000			
21	Car expenses	47		40	7
	Wages	360		360	–
26	Brit Gas		220	220	–
30	Cash (c)	2,000			
31	Balance c/d	401	5,842		
		8,595	**32,392**	**23,850**	**3,514**

Contra items are marked (c).

The analysis of VAT can be checked as follows:

		£	£		£
Payments	Net cost	23,850		Decrease in bank balance	19,170
	VAT	3,514		Increase in cash balance	78
			27,364		
less Receipts net		7,040			19,092
	VAT	1,232			
			8,272		
Excess of payments			19,092		

Nominal ledger
Light and heat

19X1		£	
Jul.	12 Bank – Norweb	480	
	26 Bank – Brit Gas	220	

Motor car expenses

19X1		£	
Jul.	7 Cash	40	
	21 Cash	40	

Motor vehicles

19X1		£	
Jul.	1 Bank – Ford Escort	2,350	

Purchases

19X1		£	
Jul.	1 Bank	16,000	

Sales

		19X1		£
		Jul.	1 Cash	1,600
			8 Cash	1,800
			15 Cash	1,960
			29 Cash	1,680

Shop fittings

19X1		£	
Jul.	1 Bank	4,000	

Wages

19X1	£	
July 7 Cash	360	
21 Cash	360	

Value added tax

19X1	£	19X1	£
Jul. 31 Cash book	3,514	Jul. 31 Cash book	1,232

8 Bad debts; discounts on debtors

8.1S

Journal

	Dr. £	Cr. £
Bad debts account	630	
Sundry debtors account		630
Writing off of sundry bad debts.		
Profit and loss account	630	
Bad debts account		630
Transfer of balance on account.		
Provision for doubtful debts account	113	
Profit and loss account		113
Transfer of provision no longer required.		

Ledger
Provision for doubtful debts

19X5	£	19X5	£
Dec. 31 Profit and loss	113	Jan. 1 Balance b/d	725
Balance c/d	612		
	725		725
		19X6	
		Jan. 1 Balance b/d	612

Bad debts

19X5	£	19X5	£
Dec. 31 Sundry debtors	630	Dec. 31 Profit and loss	630

Sundry debtors

19X5	£	19X5	£
Dec. 31 Balance b/d	12,870	Dec. 31 Bad debts	630
		Balance c/d	12,240
	12,870		12,870
19X6			
Jan. 1 Balance b/d	12,240		

Workings
Provision for doubtful debts

	£
Balance at 1 January 19X5	725
Provision required at 31 December 19X5	
5% × £12,240	612
Balance – credit to profit and loss account	113

8.2S

W. Charnock
Provision for doubtful debts

19X7		£	19X7		£
Dec. 31	Profit and loss	350	Jan. 1	Balance b/d	1,400
	Balance c/d	1,050			
		1,400			1,400
19X8			19X8		
Dec. 31	Balance c/d	1,205	Jan. 1	Balance b/d	1,050
			Dec. 31	Profit and loss	155
		1,205			1,205
			19X9		
			Jan. 1	Balance b/d	1,205

Bad debts

19X7		£	19X7		£
Dec. 31	Sundry debtors	1,840	Dec. 31	Profit and loss	1,840
19X8			19X8		
Dec. 31	Sundry debtors	1,410	Dec. 31	Profit and loss	1,410

8.3S (a)

R. Young & Co.
Provision for doubtful debts

19X8		£	19X8		£
Dec. 31	Balance c/d	4,380	Jan. 1	Balance b/d	4,200
			Dec. 31	Profit and loss	180
		4,380			4,380
			19X9		
			Jan. 1	Balance b/d	4,380

(b)

Provision for discounts allowable

		19X8		£
		Dec. 31	Profit and loss	1,971

(c)   *Profit and Loss Account*
              for the year ended 31 December 19X8 (extract)

	£
Expenses	
Bad debts	1,200
Provision for doubtful debts	180
Provision for discounts allowable	1,971

Workings
1. Increase in provision for doubtful debts

	£
Sundry debtors before adjustment	45,000
less Bad debts	1,200
	43,800
Provision at 10% × £43,800	4,380
less Balance at 1 January 19X8	4,200
Charge for year	180

2. Provision for discounts allowable

	£
Sundry debtors after adjustment for bad debts	43,800
less Provision for doubtful debts	4,380
	39,420
Provision at 5% × £39,420	1,971

8.4S   *T. O'Keefe*
                         Discount receivable

19X1		£	19X1		£
Jan. 1	Provision b/d	600	Dec. 31	Sundry creditors	3,800
	Profit and loss	3,820		Provision c/d	620
		4,420			4,420
19X2					
Jan. 1	Provision b/d	620			

Profit and Loss Account
for the year ended 31 December 19X1 (extract)

	£
Receipts	
Discount receivable	3,820

8.5S

S. Urban
Trading and Profit and Loss Account
for the year ended 31 March 19X3

	£	£	£
Sales			83,580
less Sales returns			220
			83,360
Cost of goods sold			
Opening stock		18,400	
Purchases	60,080		
less Purchase returns	240	59,840	
		78,240	
less Closing stock		20,800	57,440
Gross profit			25,920
add Discounts received			1,840
			27,760
less Expenses			
Wages		10,700	
Salaries		3,500	
Lighting and heating		836	
Rent, rates and insurance		1,720	
Printing, stationery and advertising		112	
Discount allowed		2,520	
Bad debts		900	
Provision for doubtful debts		200	
Accountancy charges		656	
Depreciation on office furniture		125	21,269
Net profit			6,491

Note
Rent, rates and insurance

	£
Per trial balance	1,600
add Rent accrued	200
	1,800
less Insurance prepaid	80
Profit and loss account	1,720

Balance Sheet as at 31 March 19X3

Assets

	Cost	Depreciation	Net
	£	£	£
Fixed assets			
Freehold premises	15,440	–	15,440
Office furniture	2,500	625	1,875
	17,940	625	17,315

Current assets		
Stock	20,800	
Debtors	12,880	
Cash at bank	10,084	
Cash in hand	340	
	44,104	
less Current liabilities		
Creditors	12,068	
Working capital		32,036
		49,351

Financed by	
Capital	
Balance at 1 April 19X2	45,860
add Profit for the year	6,491
	52,351
less Drawings	3,000
	49,351

Notes

1. Debtors

	£
Per trial balance	14,400
less Provision for doubtful debts	1,600
	12,800
add Insurance prepaid	80
Balance sheet	12,880

2. Creditors

	£
Per trial balance	11,868
add Rent accrued due	200
Balance sheet	12,068

9 Control accounts

9.1S   (a) The sources from which a creditors control account would be compiled are

Credits
Purchase day book
Journal

Debits
Purchase returns book
Cash book
Journal

Purchases
Correction of errors

Purchase returns
Cash paid and discounts received
Contra entries and correction of errors

(b)   Debtors control account

19X5		£	19X6		£
Jul. 1 Balance b/d		32,170	Jun. 30 Sales returns		2,640
19X6				Cash received	290,040
Jun. 30 Sales		293,220		Discounts allowed	6,740
				Bad debts written off	3,200
				Balance c/d	22,770
		325,390			325,390
Jul. 1 Balance b/d		22,770			

9.2S   *S. Oldham & Co.*
                        Sales ledger control account

19X8		£	19X8		£
Jan. 1 Balance b/d		20,400	Jan. 1 Balance b/d		560
Jun. 30 Sales		126,400	Jun. 30 Cash received		119,390
Balance c/d		730		Discount allowed	3,840
				Sales returns	480
				Bad debts written off	402
				Contra entry	834
				Balance c/d	22,024
		147,530			147,530
Jul. 1 Balance b/d		22,024	Jul. 1 Balance b/d		730

Purchase ledger control account

19X8		£	19X8		£
Jan. 1	Balance b/d	120	Jan. 1	Balance b/d	14,680
Jun. 30	Cash paid	93,856	Jun. 30	Purchases	98,550
	Discounts			Balance c/d	126
	received	2,580			
	Purchase				
	returns	1,630			
	Contra entry	834			
	Balance c/d	14,336			
		113,356			113,356
Jul. 1	Balance b/d	126	Jul. 1	Balance b/d	14,336

9.3S (a)

Tipper
Reconciliation Statement
(adjustment to schedule of creditors)

		£	£
Original balance of schedule			12,560
add (4) Credit balances omitted		480	
(5) Cash purchase of goods wrongly			
dealt with		8	488
			13,048
deduct (1) Debit balance listed as credit (2 × £40)		80	
(4) Debit balances omitted		24	104
Corrected balance per purchase ledger control			12,944

(b)   Purchase ledger control account

19X7		£	19X7		£
Mar. 31	Goods returned		Mar. 31	Balance b/d	
	to Hector (2)	90		(derived)	13,014
	Purchases			Contra entry –	
	overcast (3)	100		Harrow (6)	120
	Balance c/d	12,944			
		13,134			13,134
			Apr. 1	Balance b/d	12,944

9.4S (a)   *Starling*
                                       Journal

	Dr. £	Cr. £
(1) B. Brown	20	
A. Brown		20
Correction of posting to wrong account.		
(4) Austin – Sales ledger account	60	
Sales returns		60
Cancellation of incorrect entry.		
Purchase returns	60	
Austin – Purchase ledger account		60
Credit for goods returned disallowed.		
(5) Cook – Sales ledger account	90	
Cook – Purchase ledger account		90
Contra entry not recorded in journal.		
(7) Purchases	3	
Brook – Purchase ledger account		3
Cash purchase posted incorrectly to Purchase ledger.		

(b)   Purchase ledger control account

19X4			£	19X4			£
Mar. 31	Purchase			Mar. 31	Balance b/d		
	returns (2)		84		(derived)		6,123
31	Balance c/d		6,289		Purchase returns		
					disallowed (4)		60
					Contra entry –		
					Cook (5)		90
					Purchases		
					undercast (6)		100
			6,373				6,373
				Apr. 1	Balance b/d		6,289

Workings

               Adjustment to schedule of creditors

	£	£
Original balance of schedule		5,676
add (3) Credit balances omitted	562	
(4) Increase in ledger account of Austin	60	
(7) Correction of balance – Brook	3	625
		6,301
deduct (3) Debit balances omitted		12
Corrected balance per purchase ledger control		6,289

9.5S (a)   Sales ledger control account

19X4		£	19X4		£
Jan. 1	Balance b/d	8,952	Jan./		
Jan./			Dec.	Bank	69,471
Dec.	Sales	74,753		Discounts allowed	1,817
			Dec. 31	Balance c/d	12,417
		83,705			83,705
Dec. 31	Balance b/d	12,417	Dec. 31	Bank-credit transfers (i)	198
	Transfer to car account (v)	1,173		Journal entries: Contra items (ii)	2,896
				Bad debts written off (ii)	640
				Balance c/d	9,856
		13,590			13,590
19X5					
Jan. 1	Balance b/d	9,856			

(b)   *Reconciliation Statement*
                   (adjustment to schedule of debtors)

		£	£
Original balance of schedule			9,663
add	(iii) Debit balances omitted	191	
	(iv) Balance incorrectly picked up	200	391
			10,054
deduct (i)	Credit transfers omitted		198
Corrected balance per sales ledger control			9,856

(c) The benefits that accrue from operating control accounts are
   (i) Errors are localised.
   (ii) Delay in producing final accounts is reduced because work is able
       to be carried out on a number of ledgers at the same time.
   (iii) The system of internal control is strengthened.
   (iv) There is immediate access to totals of debtors and creditors.

10 Bank reconciliation

10.1S

Bank Reconciliation Statement
as at 31 December 19X6

	£	
Balance per cash book	6,870	In hand
add Cheques not yet presented for payment	2,560	
	9,430	In hand
deduct Lodgments not yet recorded by bank	1,510	
Balance per bank statement	7,920	In hand

10.2S (i)

Cash book

19X2	£	19X2	£
Jun. 30 Balance c/d	356	Jun. 30 Balance b/d	262
		Bank charges	94
	356		356
		Jul. 1 Balance b/d	356

(ii)

Bank Reconciliation Statement
as at 30 June 19X2

	£	£	
Balance per cash book		356	Overdrawn
deduct Cheques not yet presented			
C Limited	727		
D Limited	641		
E Limited	218	1,586	
		1,230	In hand
deduct Lodgment not yet recorded by bank		184	
Balance per bank statement		1,046	In hand

10.3S (a)

A. Phillips
Cash book (bank columns)

19X1	£	19X1	£
Dec. 30 Balance b/d	461	Dec. 30 Debtor – cheque	
Dividends		dishonoured	73
received	38	Bank interest	
		and charges	42
		Trade subscription	10
		Balance c/d	374
	499		499
19X2			
Jan. 1 Balance b/d	374		

(b)

Bank Reconciliation Statement
as at 30 December 19X1

	£	
Balance per cash book	374	In hand
add Cheques not yet presented	630	
	1,004	In hand
deduct Lodgments not yet recorded by bank	250	
	754	
deduct Cheque charged in error (confirmed with bank)	27	
Balance per bank statement	727	In hand

10.4S *Tutorial notes*
The question should be tackled as follows:

1. Reconcile the balances at 1 December

	£
Balance per bank statement	1,011
Balance per cash book	985
Difference	26

Since there is one cheque debited in the bank statement for the exact amount of the difference, it is safe to assume that it is that cheque which accounts for the difference. Tick the figure of £26 on the bank statement.
2. Check the items in the cash book against items on the bank statement by ticking common entries. Note that debits in the cash book have been shown individually, but all cheques banked on a particular date are shown in one total figure on the bank statement.
3. Update the cash book by recording items shown on the bank statement and not recorded in the cash book:

Cash book

19X5	£	19X5	£
Dec. 31 Dividends		Dec. 31 Balance b/d	347
received	1,608	Charges	531
		Balance c/d	730
	1,608		1,608
19X6			
Jan. 1 Balance b/d	730		

4. Prepare the bank reconciliation statement.

Bank Reconciliation Statement
as at 31 December 19X5

	£	£	
Balance per cash book		730	In hand
add Cheques not yet presented			
Dec. 9 J & Sons	1,060		
Dec. 22 U & Sons	247		
Dec. 22 W & Sons	431		
Dec. 29 N Associates	65		
Dec. 30 P & Q	234		
Dec. 31 D Limited	1,145		
Dec. 31 L Limited	93		
Dec. 31 E Associates	162	3,437	
Balance per bank statement		4,167	In hand

10.5S   Cash book

(a) (i)

19X7	£	19X7	£
Jun. 30 Balance b/d	3,856	Jun. 30 A. Jones – dis-	
Cheque received		honoured cheque	48
understated	100	Bank interest	10
		Balance c/d	3,898
	3,956		3,956
Jul. 1 Balance b/d	3,898		

(ii)   Bank Reconciliation Statement
                          as at 30 June 19X7

	£	
Balance per cash book	3,898	In hand
add Cheques not yet presented	218	
	4,116	In hand
deduct Lodgment not yet recorded by bank	50	
	4,066	In hand
add Cheque credited in error by bank	95	
Balance per bank statement	4,161	In hand

(b) The basic reasons for preparing a bank reconciliation statement are to provide an independent check on the validity and accuracy of the transactions recorded in the cash book of the business.

1. *Validity* The bank statement provides an independent check on the validity of the entries shown in the cash book and provides an independent verification of the balance shown by the cash book at the end of the period.

2. *Accuracy* By comparing the items posted in the cash book with the bank statement, any errors can be identified, explained and corrected.

11 Partnership

11.1S

Hayton and Co.

	£	£
Net profit		18,000
Appropriation of profit		
Interest allowed on capital		
Hayton	600	
Webster	300	900
Share of remaining profits		
Hayton ½	8,550	
Webster ½	8,550	17,100
		18,000

Current accounts

19X6		Hayton £	Webster £	19X6			Hayton £	Webster £
Dec. 31	Drawings	6,000	5,000	Jan. 1	Balance b/d		1,500	200
	Balance c/d	4,650	4,050	Dec. 31	Interest on capital		600	300
					Profits		8,550	8,550
		10,650	9,050				10,650	9,050
				19X7				
				Jan. 1	Balance b/d		4,650	4,050

11.2S

Tilson and Hewitt
Trading and Profit and Loss Account
for the year ended 31 March 19X7

	£	£
Sales		78,000
Cost of goods sold		
Opening stock	4,950	
Purchases	36,750	
	41,700	
less Closing stock	4,050	37,650
Gross profit		40,350

	£	£
less Expenses		
Wages	3,300	
Rent and rates	8,550	
Heating and lighting	1,200	
Depreciation on shop fittings	1,500	
Depreciation on motor vans	2,250	16,800
Net profit		23,550

Appropriation of profit

Salaries		
Tilson	7,500	
Hewitt	10,500	18,000
Interest on capital		
Tilson	300	
Hewitt	150	450
Share of remaining profits		
Tilson	2,550	
Hewitt	2,550	5,100
		23,550

Balance Sheet as at 31 March 19X7

Assets	Cost	Depre-ciation	Net
Fixed assets	£	£	£
Shop fittings	15,000	6,750	8,250
Motor vans	11,250	6,000	5,250
	26,250	12,750	13,500

Current assets		
Stock	4,050	
Debtors	2,400	
Cash at bank and in hand	1,920	
	8,370	
less Current liabilities		
Creditors	1,320	
Working capital		7,050
		20,550

Financed by

	Tilson	Hewitt	
	£	£	£
Capital accounts	6,000	3,000	9,000
Current accounts			
Balances at 1 April 19X6	3,000	4,500	
Interest on capital	300	150	
Profit	2,550	2,550	
	5,850	7,200	
less Drawings	600	900	
	5,250	6,300	11,550
			20,550

Workings
1. Rent and rates

		£
	Per trial balance	9,300
	less Rent prepaid	750
		8,550

2. Debtors

		£
	Per trial balance	1,650
	add Rent prepaid	750
		2,400

11.3S

Hawes and Peters
Trading and Profit and Loss Account
for the year ended 31 December 19X5

	£	£
Sales		131,860
Cost of goods sold		
Opening stock	17,360	
Purchases	101,640	
	119,000	
less Closing stock	26,380	92,620
Gross profit		39,240
add Provision for doubtful debts no longer required		180
		39,420
less Expenses		
Wages	7,730	
Rent	928	
Insurance	550	
Office expenses	6,400	
Vehicle expenses	3,560	
Bank charges	70	
Discounts allowed	2,560	
Bad debts	200	
Depreciation on fittings	126	
Depreciation on vans	1,136	
Depreciation on car	160	23,420
Net profit		16,000
Appropriation of profit		
Interest on capital		
Hawes	1,640	
Peters	1,320	2,960
Share of remaining profits		
Hawes 3/5	7,824	
Peters 2/5	5,216	13,040
		16,000

Balance Sheet as at 31 December 19X5

Assets

	Cost	Depreciation	Net
	£	£	£
Fixed assets			
Fittings	2,400	1,266	1,134
Vans	11,600	7,056	4,544
Motor car	1,600	320	1,280
	15,600	8,642	6,958
Current assets			
Stock		26,380	
Debtors		11,770	
Petty cash		40	
		38,190	
less Current liabilities			
Creditors	5,498		
Bank	610	6,108	
Working capital			32,082
			39,040

Financed by

	Hawes	Peters	
	£	£	£
Capital accounts	16,400	13,200	29,600
Current accounts			
Interest on capital	1,640	1,320	
Profit	7,824	5,216	
	9,464	6,536	
less Drawings	4,160	2,400	
	5,304	4,136	9,440
			39,040

Workings

1. Provision for doubtful debts

	£
Debtors per trial balance	12,200
less Bad debts	200
	12,000
Provision of 2½% × £12,000	300
Existing provision	480
Credit to profit and loss	180

2. Wages

	£
Per trial balance	7,360
add Amount owing	370
	7,730

3. Insurance

	£
Per trial balance	620
less Amount prepaid	70
	550

4. Vehicle expenses

	£
Per trial balance	3,960
less Charged to Hawes	400
	3,560

5. Depreciation on fittings

	£
Cost	2,400
less Depreciation to 1 January 19X5	1,140
	1,260
10% × £1,260	126

6. Depreciation on vans

	£
Cost	11,600
less Depreciation to 1 January 19X5	5,920
	5,680
20% × £5,680	1,136

7. Depreciation on car

	£
20% × £1,600	320
less Charged to Hawes	160
	160

8. Debtors

	£
After writing off bad debts	12,000
less Provision for doubtful debts	300
	11,700
add Insurance prepaid	70
	11,770

9. Creditors

	£
Per trial balance	4,200
add Wages owing	370
Rent owing	928
	5,498

10. Bank

	£
Per trial balance	540
add Bank charges	70
	610

11. Hawes – drawings

	£
Per trial balance	3,600
add Vehicle expenses	400
Vehicle depreciation	160
	4,160

11.4S (a)
Rowe and Martin
*Summary of adjustments to the Profit and Loss Account
for the year ended 31 December 19X9*

	Add £	Deduct £	£
Net profit for the year (2 × £4,770)			9,540
Adjustments			
(1) Loss on sale of freehold premises		500	
(2) Net book value of plant and machinery scrapped		215	
(3) Motor vehicle licences prepaid – 6/12 × £100	50		
(4) Bad debts		291	
(5) Stocks – reduced to net realisable value		570	
Stocks – scrap metal omitted	330		
(6) Cash misappropriated		35	
	380	1,611	
		380	1,231
Adjusted net profit			8,309
Appropriation of profit			
Interest allowed on capital			
Rowe		1,629	
Martin		558	2,187
Share of remaining profits			
Rowe ½		3,061	
Martin ½		3,061	6,122
			8,309

(b)

Balance Sheet as at 31 December 19X9

Assets

	Cost £	Depreciation £	Net £
Fixed assets			
Freehold buildings	11,500	–	11,500
Plant and machinery	14,385	6,600	7,785
Motor vehicles	8,000	2,700	5,300
	33,885	9,300	24,585

Current assets		
Stocks at lower of cost and net realisable value	4,760	
Debtors	13,759	
Cash at bank	762	
Cash in hand	5	
	19,286	
less Current liabilities		
Creditors	11,262	
Working capital		8,024
		32,609

Financed by

	Rowe £	Martin £	£
Capital accounts	20,100	10,000	30,100
Current accounts			
Interest on capital	1,629	558	
Profit	3,061	3,061	
	4,690	3,619	
less Drawings	2,000	3,800	
	2,690	(181)	2,509
			32,609

Tutorial note

The overdrawn balance on Martin's current account is deducted from Rowe's current account balance in the balance sheet.

Workings

1. Bad debts

	£
Debts written off	521
Provision for doubtful debts	270
	791
less Existing provision	500
	291

2. Freehold buildings

	£
Per draft accounts	12,000
less Loss on sale	500
	11,500

3. Plant and machinery – cost

	£
Per draft accounts	15,000
less Cost of plant scrapped	615
	14,385

4. Plant and machinery – depreciation

	£
Per draft accounts	7,000
less Depreciation on plant scrapped	400
	6,600

5. Stocks

	£
Per draft accounts	5,000
add Stock omitted	330
	5,330
less Stock reduced in value	570
	4,760

6. Debtors

	£
Per draft accounts	14,000
less Bad debts, etc.	291
	13,709
add Motor vehicle licences prepaid	50
	13,759

7. Cash at bank

	£
Per draft accounts – overdrawn	2,700
add Cheques not mailed	3,462
	762

8. Petty cash

	£
Per draft accounts	40
less Cash misappropriated	35
	5

9. Creditors

	£
Per draft accounts	7,800
add Cheques not mailed	3,462
	11,262

12 Goodwill, with particular reference to partnership; revaluation of assets

12.1S

Edwards and Coleman
Balance Sheet as at 1 January 19X7

Assets

	£	£
Fixed assets		21,000
Current assets	12,000	
less Current liabilities	8,000	
Net current assets		4,000
		25,000

Financed by

	Edwards	Coleman	
	£	£	£
Capital accounts	7,000	8,000	15,000
Current accounts	7,500	2,500	10,000
			25,000

Workings

Journal

	Dr.	Cr.
	£	£
Capital account – Edwards	500	
Capital account – Coleman		500

Adjustments to capital accounts to record the agreed value of goodwill at 31 December 19X6, on a change in profit sharing ratio: viz.

	Old ratio	New ratio	Net
	Cr.	Dr.	
	£	£	£
Edwards	2,500	3,000	500 Dr.
Coleman	2,500	2,000	500 Cr.

12.2S (a)   Capital accounts

	Exe £	Wye £	Zed £		Exe £	Wye £	Zed £
Cash	6,000	3,000		Balances			
Balances				b/f	24,000	12,000	
c/d	24,000	12,000	9,000	Cash from			
				Zed	6,000	3,000	9,000
	30,000	15,000	9,000		30,000	15,000	9,000
				Balances			
				b/d	24,000	12,000	9,000

(b)   *Exe, Wye, Zed*
                       Balance Sheet as at 1 April 19X6

	£	£
Assets		
Fixed assets		24,000
Current assets (excluding cash)	54,000	
Cash at bank	15,000	
	69,000	
less Current liabilities	48,000	
Net current assets		21,000
		45,000
Financed by		
Capital accounts		
Exe	24,000	
Wye	12,000	
Zed	9,000	45,000
		45,000

Tutorial note
The cash at bank will increase by the same amount as the credit shown in
Zed's capital account. The balance of £9,000 introduced by Zed was with-
drawn by Exe and Wye.

12.3S (a)   *Doohan, Buckley and Mannion*
Capital accounts

	Doohan £	Buckley £	Mannion £		Doohan £	Buckley £	Mannion £
Adjustments for goodwill		4,000	2,000	Balance b/d	20,000	20,000	10,000
				Goodwill	6,000		
Transfer to loan account	26,000						
Balance c/d		16,000	8,000				
	26,000	20,000	10,000		26,000	20,000	10,000
				Balance b/d		16,000	8,000

(b)   *Balance Sheet as at 1 January 19X4*

	£	£
Assets		
Fixed assets		40,800
Current assets (excluding bank)	31,300	
Cash at bank	7,750	
	39,050	
less Current liabilities	26,800	
Net current assets		12,250
		53,050

Financed by

	Buckley £	Mannion £	£
Capital accounts	16,000	8,000	24,000
Current accounts	1,600	1,450	3,050
Loan – Doohan			26,000
			53,050

Workings

Journal

	Dr. £	Cr. £
Capital accounts – Buckley	4,000	
Mannion	2,000	
Capital account – Doohan		6,000

Adjustments to capital accounts to record
the agreed goodwill at 31 December 19X3.

	Old ratio Cr. £	New ratio Dr. £	Net £
Doohan	6,000		6,000 *Cr.*
Buckley	6,000	10,000	4,000 *Dr.*
Mannion	3,000	5,000	2,000 *Dr.*

Balance at bank

	£
Per balance sheet at 31 December 19X3	9,600
deduct Repayment of Doohan's current account balance	1,850
	7,750

12.4S (a)

Leech, Luff, Lee and Windward
Statement showing the division of profit
for the year ended 31 December 19X7

	£	£
Net profit		17,640
add Interest on current account debit balances		
Lee 8% on £792	63	
Windward 8% on £496	40	103
		17,743

Allocation of profit adjusted for interest on drawings	Leech £	Luff £	Lee £	Windward £	Total £
Interest on capital	1,080	540	180	180	1,980
Salary				1,500	1,500
Remaining profit 3 : 3 : 3 : 1	4,279	4,279	4,279	1,426	14,263
	5,359	4,819	4,459	3,106	17,743
Adjustment for guarantee	(74)			74	
	5,285	4,819	4,459	3,180	17,743

(b)   Current accounts

	Leech £	Luff £	Lee £	Windward £		Leech £	Luff £	Lee £	Windward £
Goodwill in new profit-sharing ratios	2,988	2,988	2,988	996	Balance b/f	5,000	1,000	1,200	
Balance c/d	7,988	1,000			Cash introduced				500
					Goodwill in old profit-sharing ratios	5,976	2,988	996	
					Balance c/d			792	496
	10,976	3,988	2,988	996		10,976	3,988	2,988	996
Balance b/d			792	496	Balance b/d	7,988	1,000		
Interest on current a/c			63	40	Profit	5,285	4,819	4,459	3,180
Drawings	6,320	4,900	4,900	2,193	Balance c/d			1,296	
Balance c/d	6,953	919		451					
	13,273	5,819	5,755	3,180		13,273	5,819	5,755	3,180
Balance b/d			1,296		Balance b/d	6,953	919		451

Notes

1. To determine the balances on the partners' current accounts at 1 January 19X7, the first part of requirement (b) must be prepared first.
2. It has been assumed that interest on capital is to be ignored in determining Windward's guaranteed aggregate of salary and share of profits of £3,000.

Workings

Valuation of Goodwill

	£	£
Profits, year ended 31 December:		
19X6	16,337	16,337
19X5	10,255	10,255
19X4	10,758	10,758
19X3	–	14,164
	37,350	51,514
Average	12,450	12,878
Goodwill is, therefore, 80% × £12,450	9,960	

12.5S (a)

Colours
Trading and Profit and Loss Account
for the year ended 30 September 19X2

	£	£
Sales		96,000
Cost of goods sold		
Opening stock	12,400	
Purchases	62,000	
	74,400	
less Closing stock	14,200	60,200
Gross profit		35,800

	Half year to 31 March 19X2		Half year to 30 September 19X2	
	£	£	£	£
Gross profit allocated on time basis		17,900		17,900
less Expenses				
Wages	7,300		7,300	
Salaries	3,450		2,250	
Trade expenses	765		1,015	
Rent and rates	500		500	
Bad debts	600			
Bad debts provision			230	
Depreciation:				
Plant and machinery	700		700	
Motor vehicles	775		600	
Interest on loan			540	
	——	14,090	——	13,135
		3,810		4,765
Appropriation of profit				
Interest on capital				
Brown	240			
Green	180		84	
Black			96	
	——	420	——	180
Remaining profits				
Brown	2,260			
Green	1,130		2,751	
Black			1,834	
	——	3,390	——	4,585
		3,810		4,765

(b)   Capital accounts

	Brown £	Green £	Black £		Brown £	Green £	Black £
Goodwill in new ratios		7,200	4,800	Balances b/f	8,000	6,000	
Transfer to loan account	16,000			Goodwill in old ratios	8,000	4,000	
Balances c/d		2,800	3,200	Cash – introduced			3,000
				paid to Brown			5,000
	16,000	10,000	8,000		16,000	10,000	8,000
				Balances b/d		2,800	3,200

Current accounts

	Brown £	Green £	Black £		Brown £	Green £	Black £
Car taken over	600			Balances b/f	2,400	1,600	
Drawings	1,800	2,400	900	Interest on capital	240	264	96
Transfer to loan account	2,500			Profit	2,260	3,881	1,834
Balances c/d		3,345	1,030				
	4,900	5,745	1,930		4,900	5,745	1,930
				Balances b/d		3,345	1,030

(c)   *Balance Sheet as at 30 September 19X2*
Assets

	Cost £	Depre- ciation £	Net £
Fixed assets			
Plant and machinery	14,000	4,200	9,800
Motor vehicles	4,800	3,975	825
	18,800	8,175	10,625
Current assets			
Stock		14,200	
Debtors		4,770	
Balance at bank		1,200	
		20,170	
less Current liabilities			
Creditors		6,380	
Net current assets			13,790
			24,415

Financed by

	Green £	Black £	£
Capital accounts	2,800	3,200	6,000
Current accounts	3,345	1,030	4,375
Loan – Brown			14,040
			24,415

Workings

1. Salaries

	£	£
Total per trial balances		10,800
Deduct: Partners drawings – Brown	1,800	
Green	2,400	
Black	900	5,100
		5,700

	£
Allocation:	
Half-year to 31 March 19X2:	
$\frac{1}{2} \times$ (£5,700 – £1,200) + Black's salary of £1,200 =	3,450
Half-year to 30 September 19X2:	
$\frac{1}{2} \times$ (£5,700 – £1,200) =	2,250
	5,700

2. Trade expenses

	£
Total per trial balance	1,600
add Accrual	180
	1,780

	£
Allocation:	
Half-year to 31 March 19X2:	
$\frac{1}{2} \times$ (£1,780 – £250)	765
Half-year to 30 September 19X2:	
$\frac{1}{2} \times$ (£1,780 – £250) + professional charges of £250	1,015
	1,780

3. Rent and rates

	£
Total per trial balance	1,400
deduct Rent paid in advance	400
	1,000

Allocation: 50 : 50

4. Depreciation
   Plant and machinery
      10% per annum on £14,000 = £1,400   Allocated 50 : 50
   Motor vehicles
      Half-year to 31 March 19X2: 25% per annum on £6,200 = £775
      Half-year to 30 September 19X2: 25% per annum on £4,800 =
      £600

5. Loan account and interest – Brown

	£		£
Cash from Black	5,000	Transfer from capital	
Balance c/d	14,040	account	16,000
		Transfer from current	
		account	2,500
		Profit and loss account	
		Interest at 8% p.a. on	
		£13,500 for six months	540
	19,040		19,040
		Balance b/d	14,040

6. Car taken over by Brown

	£	£
Cost		1,400
Depreciation – to 30 September 19X1	625	
to 31 March 19X2	175	800
		600

7. Motor vehicles

	Cost	Depreciation
	£	£
Per trial balance	6,200	3,400
less Vehicle sold	1,400	800
	4,800	2,600
Charge for year to 30 September 19X2		1,375
		3,975

8. Debtors

	£
Balance per trial balance	4,600
add Rent prepaid	400
	5,000
less Provision for bad debts	230
	4,770

9. Creditors

	£
Balance per trial balance	6,200
add Trade expenses accrued	180
	6,380

12.6S (a)

Lock, Stock and Barrel

Revaluation account

	£	£		£
Plant and equipment		700	Freehold premises	7,000
Motor vehicle taken			Goodwill	7,000
over by Lock		50		
Capital accounts:				
Lock (5)	6,625			
Stock (3)	3,975			
Barrel (2)	2,650	13,250		
		14,000		14,000

(b)

Capital accounts

	Lock £	Stock £	Barrel £		Lock £	Stock £	Barrel £
Adjustments to				Balances			
profit for year				b/d	12,000	6,000	4,000
ended 30 June				Profit on			
19X3	475	285	190	revaluation	6,625	3,975	2,650
Car taken over	400						
Goodwill							
written off		4,200	2,800				
Transfer to							
loan account	17,750						
Balances c/d		5,490	3,660				
	18,625	9,975	6,650		18,625	9,975	6,650
				Balances			
				b/d		5,490	3,660

(c)

Lock – loan account

	£		£
Repaid	3,000	Balance b/d	3,000
Balances c/d		Transferred from	
Current liability 10%	1,775	capital account	17,750
Deferred liability 90%	15,975		
	20,750		20,750
		Balances b/d	
		Current liability	1,775
		Deferred liability	15,975

(d)   *Stock and Barrel*
                    Balance Sheet as at 1 July 19X3
                                  £   £   £
Assets
Fixed assets at valuation on
  30 June 19X3
    Freehold premises   15,000
    Plant and equipment   3,500
    Motor vehicles   1,650
                                                   ───────
                                                   20,150
Current assets
    Stock   3,200
    Debtors   4,600
    Balance at bank   5,300
                                        ───────
                                        13,100
less Current liabilities
    Creditors   4,350
    Provision for repainting
      of premises   2,000
    Loan – Lock   1,775   8,125
                              ───────   ───────
Net current assets   4,975
                                                   ───────
                                                   25,125
                                                   ═══════
Financed by
                              Stock   Barrel
                                £   £   £
    Capital accounts   5,490   3,660   9,150
                             ═══════   ═══════
Loan – Lock   15,975
                                                   ───────
                                                   25,125
                                                   ═══════

Note
It has been assumed that the 10% of the outstanding balance on Lock's loan
account had not been repaid at 1 July 19X3.

Workings
1. Adjustment of profit 19X3
                                                            £
    Per draft accounts   8,150
                                          Add   *Deduct*
                                            £   £
    (3) Increase in provision for
          doubtful debts   200
    (4) Increase in provision for
          repainting   600
    (5) Damaged and obsolete stock   400
    (6) Creditors provision written back   250
                                          ─────   ─────
                                           250   1,200
                                          ═════   250   950
                                                              ───────
    Adjusted profit   7,200
                                                              ═══════

Apportionment of reduction in profit

		£
Lock	50%	475
Stock	30%	285
Barrel	20%	190
		950

2. Goodwill

	£	£
Profits year ended 30 June		
19X9		6,420
19X0		5,360
19X1	8,180	8,180
19X2	7,840	7,840
19X3	7,200	7,200
	23,220	35,000
Average	7,740	7,000
Goodwill		7,000

3. Motor vehicles

	£
Per draft balance sheet	2,100
less Book value of vehicle taken over by Lock	450
	1,650

4. Debtors

	£
Per draft balance sheet	5,200
less Provision for doubtful debts	600
	4,600

5. Balance at bank

	£
Per draft balance sheet	8,300
less Payment to Lock	3,000
	5,300

6. Creditors

	£
Per draft balance sheet	4,600
less Provision no longer required	250
	4,350

13 Partnership dissolution

13.1S (a)   *Anderson and Birch*
                              Realisation account

	£		£	£
Plant and machinery	8,500	Cash – sale of		
Stock	4,900	assets		14,000
Debtors	4,100	Creditors –		
Cash – realisation		discount		124
expenses	300	Loss on		
		realisation:		
		Anderson	1,838	
		Birch	1,838	3,676
	17,800			17,800

(b)   Cash account

	£		£	£
Balance b/d	1,600	Creditors		2,976
Realisation of assets	14,000	Realisation		
		account –		
		costs		300
		Capital accounts:		
		Anderson	6,162	
		Birch	6,162	12,324
	15,600			15,600

(c)   Capital accounts

	Anderson	Birch		Anderson	Birch
	£	£		£	£
Realisation – loss	1,838	1,838	Balances b/d	8,000	8,000
Cash	6,162	6,162			
	8,000	8,000		8,000	8,000

13.2S

Old and Young
Realisation account

	£			£
Warehouse	50,000	Old capital account –		
Retail shops	75,000	(warehouse +		
Fixtures	15,000	warehouse stock)		80,000
Motor vehicles	8,400	Young capital account –		
Stocks	75,000	(retail shops + shops'		
Debtors	2,400	stock + fixtures)		136,500
Cash – dissolution costs	1,200	Cash – motor vehicles		8,000
		Cash – debtors		2,400
		Loss on realisation:		
		Old	67	
		Young	33	100
	227,000			227,000

Cash account

	£		£
Balance b/d	2,700	Creditors	17,800
Realisation account		Realisation account –	
Sale of motor		dissolution costs	1,200
vehicles	8,000	Capital account – Old	60,193
Debtors	2,400		
Capital account – Young	66,093		
	79,193		79,193

Capital accounts

	Old £	Young £		Old £	Young £
Realisation			Balances b/d	75,000	50,000
account – assets			Transfer from		
taken over	80,000	136,500	current account	25,260	20,440
Loss on			Transfer from		
realisation	67	33	loan account	40,000	
Cash	60,193		Cash		66,093
	140,260	136,533		140,260	136,533

13.3S (a)   *Smart and Swift*
        Profit and Loss Account for the year ended 31 December 19X8

	£	£	£
Hotel takings			5,100
less Expenses			
Foodstuffs – Stock at 31 December 19X7	420		
Purchases	2,600		
	3,020		
less Stock at 31 December 19X8	300	2,720	
Wages		2,200	
General expenses		870	
Depreciation on motor vehicle		200	
Depreciation on fittings and fixtures		100	
Loan interest – Smart		180	6,270
Net loss			1,170
Dividend:			
Smart – 3/5ths			702
Swift – 2/5ths			468
			1,170

(b)   Realisation account

	£		£	£
Freehold premises	6,000	Smart's capital		
Fittings and fixtures	1,700	account		
Motor vehicle	500	Stock	250	
Stock	300	Fittings and		
Debtors	600	fixtures (part)	600	
Cash – dissolution		Sundry items	40	890
expenses	120			
Profit on realisation:		Swift's capital		
Smart (3/5)	462	account		
Swift (2/5)	308 770	Motor vehicle	400	
		Sundry items	20	420
		Cash – freehold		
		premises		6,800
		Cash – debtors		480
		Cash – fittings and		
		fixtures		1,400
	9,990			9,990

(c)   Cash account for January 19X9

	£		£
Realisation account		Balance b/d	4,590
Sale of freehold		Creditors	270
premises	6,800	Realisation account –	
Debtors	480	dissolution expenses	120
Sale of fittings and		Capital account – Smart	4,530
fixtures	1,400		
Capital account – Swift	830		
	9,510		9,510

(d)   Capital accounts

	Smart £	Swift £		Smart £	Swift £
Drawings	520	750	Balances b/d	3,000	500
Net loss for 19X8	702	468	Transfer from loan		
Realisation account –			account	3,000	
assets taken over	890	420	Loan interest	180	
Cash	4,530		Profit on realisation	462	308
			Cash		830
	6,642	1,638		6,642	1,638

13.4S   *Clark, Hibbert and Thomas*
                        Realisation account

	£		£	
Fixtures and fittings	2,000	Cash – sale of stock		6,800
Stock	9,000	debtors		4,650
Debtors	5,000	sale of fixtures		1,700
Cash – realisation		Creditors – discount		
expenses	400	received		100
		Loss – capital accounts		
		Clark	1,050	
		Hibbert	1,050	
		Thomas	1,050	3,150
	16,400			16,400

                          Cash account

	£		£	
Balance b/d	2,500	Creditors		7,150
Realisation account		Realisation expenses		400
Sale of stock	6,800	Capital accounts		
Debtors	4,650	Clark	4,900	
Sale of fixtures	1,700	Thomas	3,200	8,100
	15,650			15,650

Capital accounts

	Clark £	Hibbert £	Thomas £		Clark £	Hibbert £	Thomas £
Balance b/d		750		Balance b/d	7,000		5,000
Loss on				Deficiency			
realisation	1,050	1,050	1,050	shared by			
Hibbert's				Clark and			
deficiency	1,050		750	Thomas		1,800	
Cash	4,900		3,200				
	7,000	1,800	5,000		7,000	1,800	5,000

Note
The loss on realisation is shared between all three partners in their profit sharing ratios: Hibbert's total deficiency is then borne by Clark and Thomas in the ratio of their last agreed capital account balances.

14 Incomplete records

14.1S

P. Jennings
Trading Account for the year ended 31 December 19X2

	£	£
Sales		24,696
deduct Cost of sales		
Opening stock	6,933	
add Purchases	16,711	
	23,644	
less Closing stock	7,180	16,464
Gross profit		8,232

Workings

In trading account form the information given would show the following:

Trading Account for the year ended 31 December 19X2

	£	£
Sales		24,696
deduct Cost of sales		
Opening stock	6,933	
add Purchases	16,711	
	23,644	
less Closing stock		
Cost of sales		
Gross profit		8,232

The two missing figures, i.e. the cost of sales and the closing stock can be deduced and inserted and the trading account completed.

14.2S

G. Holt
Balance Sheet as at 31 December 19X2

	£
Capital employed	
Capital account balance as at 1 January 19X2	17,246
add Profit for the year	3,839
	21,085
deduct Drawings	3,120
	17,965

Represented by

	Cost	Depre-ciation	Net
	£	£	£
Fixed assets	20,000	10,000	10,000
Current assets			
Stock		4,838	
Debtors		2,856	
Bank		2,221	
		9,915	
deduct Current liabilities			
Trade creditors	1,568		
Expense creditors	382	1,950	
Net current assets			7,965
			17,965

Workings
In balance sheet form the information given would show the following:

	£
Capital employed	
Capital account balance as at 1 January 19X2	17,246
add Profit for the year	
deduct Drawings	3,120

	Cost	Depre-ciation	Net
	£	£	£
Represented by			
Fixed assets	20,000	10,000	10,000
Current assets			
Stock		4,838	
Debtors		2,856	
Bank		2,221	
		9,915	
deduct Current liabilities			
Trade creditors	1,568		
Expense creditors	382	1,950	
Net current assets			7,965
			17,965

By using the formula

$$\text{Capital} = \text{Assets} - \text{Liabilities}$$

the total capital employed figure can be inserted and, by deduction, the profit figure for the year obtained.

It is, of course, possible to calculate the above profit by using the formula

$$\text{Profit} = (A - L)_2 - (A - L)_1 + \text{Drawings for the year.}$$

Confirm this for yourself.

Also note that the balance sheet is presented in a slightly different form to that used consistently in the text.

14.3S

Bobbin
Trading and Profit and Loss Account
for the year ended 31 March 19X7

	£	£
Sales		13,645
Cost of sales		
Opening stock	1,250	
Purchases	10,426	
	11,676	
less Closing stock	1,456	10,220
Gross profit		3,425
less Expenses		
Wages and National Insurance	597	
Rent	400	
Rates	196	
Electricity	66	
Shop expenses	104	
Depreciation of fixtures and fittings	60	1,423
Net profit		2,002

Balance Sheet as at 31 March 19X7

Assets

	Cost	Depre-ciation	Net
	£	£	£
Fixed assets			
Goodwill	2,000	–	2,000
Fixtures and fittings	600	60	540
	2,600	60	2,540
Current assets			
Stock at cost		1,456	
Cash at bank		3,655	
Cash in hand		112	
		5,223	
less Current liabilities			
Creditors		385	

	£	£
Net current assets		4,838
		7,378

Financed by
   Capital account

	£
Amount introduced	6,000
add Net profit for the year	2,002
	8,002
less Drawings	624

	£
	7,378

Tutorial notes

1.   The amount of £3,750 paid to Reel Ltd is made up as follows:

	£
Fixtures and fittings	500
Goodwill	2,000
Stock	1,250
	3,750

The debit side of the transaction is shown in the three separate accounts; the credit entry is, of course, shown in the bank account.

2.   Cash payments made out of takings, plus the balance of cash in hand, represents cash received for sales. The double entry for this transaction is – debit cash account, credit debtors.

3.   Since there are neither opening debtors nor closing debtors in this question, sales for the year are simply the cash received, i.e. the figure which has been credited to debtors account.

4.   Purchases for the year are calculated as follows:

	£
Cash paid during the year	
From bank account	10,000
From cash account	158
add Closing creditors	268
	10,426

5.   Since Bobbin's lease is at £400 per annum, one quarter's rent has clearly not been paid at 31 March 19X7.

6.   The figure of £385 shown in the balance sheet for creditors is made up as follows:

	£
Trade creditors	268
Electricity outstanding	17
Rent owing	100
	385

Workings

Bank account

19X6		£	19X6			£
Apr. 1	Capital	6,000	Apr. 1	Reel Ltd		3,750
Apr. 1				Fixtures		100
to			Apr. 1	Purchases for		
Mar. 31	Shop bankings	12,050	to	resale		10,000
			Mar. 31	Rent		300
				Rates		196
				Electricity		49
			Mar. 31	Balance c/d		3,655
		18,050				18,050
19X7						
Apr. 1	Balance b/d	3,655				

Capital account

			19X6		£
			Apr. 1	Bank	6,000

Debtors

19X7		£	19X7		£
Mar. 31	Sales	13,645	Mar. 31	Bank	12,050
				Cash	1,595
		13,645			13,645

Stock

19X6		£	
Apr. 1	Bank – Reel Ltd	1,250	

Fixtures and fittings

19X6		£	
Apr. 1	Bank – Reel Ltd	500	
	Bank	100	

Goodwill

19X6		£	
Apr. 1	Bank – Reel Ltd	2,000	

Creditors

19X7		£	19X7		£
Mar. 31	Bank	10,000	Mar. 31	Purchases	10,426
	Cash	158			
	Balance c/d	268			
		10,426			10,426
			Apr. 1	Balance b/d	268

Rent

19X7		£	
Mar. 31	Bank	300	

Rates

19X7		£	
Mar. 31	Bank	196	

Electricity

19X7		£	
Mar. 31	Bank	49	

Cash

19X7		£	19X7		£
Mar. 31	Debtors	1,595	Mar. 31	Wages and National Insurance	597
				Purchases for resale	158
				Shop expenses	104
				Drawings	624
				Balance c/d	112
		1,595			1,595
Apr. 1	Balance b/d	112			

Wages and National Insurance

19X7		£	
Mar. 31	Cash	597	

Shop expenses

19X7		£	
Mar. 31	Cash	104	

Drawings

19X7	£		
Mar. 31 Cash	624		

Sales

		19X7	£
		Mar. 31 Debtors	13,645

Purchases

19X7	£		
Mar. 31 Creditors	10,426		

Bobbin
Trial Balance at 31 March 19X7

			Dr. £	Cr. £
Bank		B	3,655	
Capital		B		6,000
Stock		T	1,250	
Fixtures and fittings	A(4)	B	600	
Goodwill		B	2,000	
Creditors		B		268
Rent	A(3)	P	300	
Rates		P	196	
Electricity	A(2)	P	49	
Cash		B	112	
Wages and National Insurance		P	597	
Shop expenses		P	104	
Drawings		B	624	
Sales		T		13,645
Purchases		T	10,426	
			19,913	19,913

Accruals, prepayments, etc., at 31 March 19X7

1.	Stock, at cost	£1,456	T and B
2.	Electricity outstanding	£17	P and B
3.	Rent owing	£100	P and B
4.	Depreciate fixtures and fittings at a rate of 10% per annum		P and B

14.4S

I. Patchett
Profit and Loss Account for the period
1 July to 30 November 19X7

	£	£	£
Contract receipts			3,763
Materials consumed			
Opening stock		185	
Purchases		1,272	
		1,457	

	£	£	£
less Closing stock		200	
		1,257	
Wages and National Insurance		748	
Rent		85	
Rates		35	
Electricity		38	
Van expenses		74	
Sundry expenses		49	
Depreciation – Motor van	50		
Plant and equipment	25	75	
			2,361
Net profit			1,402

Balance Sheet as at 30 November 19X7

	£	£
Assets		
Fixed assets at valuation		
Motor van		250
Plant and equipment		75
		325
Current assets		
Stock at valuation	200	
Debtors	204	
Cash at bank	3,757	
Cash in hand	12	
	4,173	
less Current liabilities		
Creditors	394	
Net current assets		3,779
		4,104
Financed by		
Capital account		
Balance as at 30 June 19X7	2,654	
Amount introduced during the period	500	
	3,154	
add Net profit for the period	1,402	
	4,556	
less Drawings	452	4,104

Tutorial notes

1. The debit of £452 to drawings account from the cash account is the balancing figure.
2. You are required to prepare Patchett's *profit and loss account,* you are not asked to calculate a gross profit because obviously there is no such thing in a contractor's accounts.
3. Since Patchett was a contractor, his income would be receipts from contracts he carried out as opposed to 'sales' of some commodity or other. The calculation of contract receipts is made in the same way as the calculation of sales is made in a retail business, i.e. cash received + closing debtors − opening debtors.
4. In the capital account shown in the balance sheet, the amount introduced during the period is shown separately.
5. The fixed assets and stock are shown at valuation at the balance sheet date because the question states that this is to be done.
6. Debtors and creditors shown in the balance sheet are as follows:

	Debtors		Creditors
	£		£
Trade debtors	176	Trade creditors	349
Rates prepaid	28	Electricity owing	11
	———	Rent owing	34
	204		———
	════		394
			════

Workings

Since the balance sheet as at 30 June 19X7 is given, there is no necessity to prepare an opening statement of affairs. The T accounts can be opened from the figures given in the balance sheet.

Capital		Creditors		Rates		Electricity	
£	£	£	£	£	£	£	£
	2,654	1,023	256	84	21	41	14
	500	156	1,272				
		349					
		———	———				
		1,528	1,528				
		════	════				
			349				

Motor van at cost		Depreciation on motor van	
£	£	£	£
450			150

Plant and equipment at cost		Depreciation on plant and equipment	
£	£	£	£
250			150

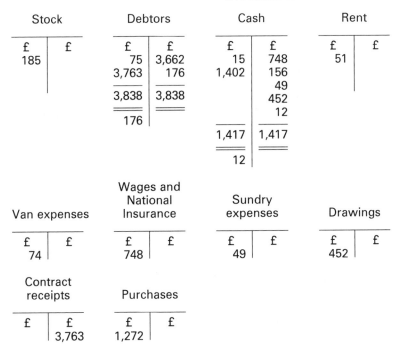

Stock		Debtors		Cash		Rent	
£	£	£	£	£	£	£	£
185		75	3,662	15	748	51	
		3,763	176	1,402	156		
					49		
		3,838	3,838		452		
					12		
		176					
				1,417	1,417		
				12			

Van expenses		Wages and National Insurance		Sundry expenses		Drawings	
£	£	£	£	£	£	£	£
74		748		49		452	

Contract receipts		Purchases	
£	£	£	£
	3,763	1,272	

The bank account has not been shown because it is analysed on the question paper.

Trial Balance as at 30 November 19X7

			Dr. £	Cr. £
Capital		B		3,154
Creditors		B		349
Rates	A(3)	P	63	
Electricity	A(2)	P	27	
Motor van at cost		B	450	
Depreciation on motor van	A(5)	B		150
Plant and equipment at cost		B	250	
Depreciation on plant and equipment	A(5)	B		150
Stock at 30 June 19X7		P	185	
Debtors		B	176	
Cash		B	12	
Bank		B	3,757	
Rent	A(4)	P	51	
Van expenses		P	74	
Wages and National Insurance		P	748	
Sundry expenses		P	49	
Drawings		B	452	
Contract receipts		P		3,763
Purchases		P	1,272	
			7,566	7,566

Accruals, prepayments, etc.	£	
1. Stock at valuation	200	P and B
2. Electricity outstanding	11	P and B
3. Rates prepaid	28	P and B
4. Rent owing	34	P and B
5. Depreciation to be provided:		
Motor van	50	P and B
Plant and equipment	25	P and B

14.5S

Angus
Profit and Loss Account
for the year ended 31 March 19X6

	£	£	£
Sales			
Crops		4,568	
Livestock		996	
Milk		3,111	8,675
Subsidies and grants			
Crop deficiency payments		217	
Ploughing grant		145	362
			9,037
Livestock expenses			
Purchases	426		
Feeding stuffs	2,026		
Veterinary fees	55	2,507	
Crop expenses			
Seeds and fertilisers	728		
Threshing and baling	273	1,001	
Establishment expenses			
Rent and rates	483		
Electricity	77	560	
Administration and general expenses			
Wages and National Insurance	1,109		
Tractor and machinery repairs	537		
Tractor and machinery depreciation	425		
Sundry expenses	29	2,100	
			6,168
Stock valuation adjustment			
Opening valuation	2,025		
Closing valuation	1,940	85	6,253
Net profit			2,784

Balance Sheet as at 31 March 19X6

Assets	Cost	Depre-ciation	Net
Fixed assets	£	£	£
Tractor	700	100	600
Machinery	1,625	325	1,300
	2,325	425	1,900

Current assets			
Stocks, at valuation:			
Livestock		1,700	
Crops, produce and fertilisers		240	1,940
Debtor			294
Cash at bank			668
			2,902
less Current liabilities			
Creditor			21
Net current assets			2,881
			4,781

Financed by		
Capital account		
Balance at 1 April 19X5		4,621
add Net profit for year		2,784
		7,405
less Drawings		2,624
		4,781

Tutorial notes

1. Although this question is for a specialist type of organisation, i.e. a farmer, the suggested method of dealing with incomplete record questions can and should be applied.
2. Angus receives his farm income from sales under three different heads, i.e. crops, livestock and milk. This fact is clearly shown in the profit and loss account where the sales for the year have been analysed under the headings given. Since there are no debtors at 31 March 19X6 for either sales of crops or of livestock the amount received under each of those heads is obviously the sales figure for the year. On the other hand, since there are both opening and closing debtors relating to milk sales, the milk sales figure for the year must be calculated using the formula given in the text.
3. Subsidies and grants are clearly income but just as clearly they do not represent income from sales. A separate heading is thus shown in the profit and loss account.
4. The expenses for the year have been analysed and shown in generally accepted categories.
5. Since a tenant farmer does not 'trade', it is not possible to include the stocks in a trading account. Obviously stocks must be taken into account in calculating profit for the year. Note that if the closing valuation had exceeded the opening valuation, the adjustment would have been deducted from the total of the expenses.

Workings

Statement of Affairs at 31 March 19X5

	£
Tractor	360
Machinery	1,500
Stocks – Livestock	1,825
Crops, produce and fertilisers	200
Debtor – Milk Marketing Board	267
Bank	492
	4,644
Creditor – Electricity	23
Capital – balancing figure	4,621
	4,644

Bank

£	£
492	340
3,084	728
145	1,296
217	537
570	55
1,724	125
	483
	2,000
	668
6,232	6,232
668	

Milk Marketing Board

£	£
267	294
3,111	3,084
3,378	3,378
294	

Electricity

£	£
79	23

Tractor

£	£
360	360
700	

Machinery

£	£
1,500	
125	

Stocks

£	£
1,825	
200	

Capital

£	£
	4,621

Ploughing grant

£	£
	145

Cereal deficiency payments

£	£
	217

Cattle auctions

£	£
996	570
	426
996	996

Crop sales

£	£
4,568	1,724
	1,841
	273
	730
4,568	4,568

Seeds and fertilisers

£	£
728	

Feeding stuffs		Tractor and machinery expenses		Veterinary fees	
£	£	£	£	£	£
1,296		537		55	
730					

Rent and rates		Drawings		Cash	
£	£	£	£	£	£
483		2,000		1,841	79
		624			1,109
					624
					29
				1,841	1,841

Wages and National Insurance		Sundry expenses		Threshing and baling	
£	£	£	£	£	£
1,109		29		273	

Sales		Cattle purchases	
£	£	£	£
	3,111	426	
	996		
	4,568		

The bank account has been included above in T account form for the convenience of students who wish to check the double entry of the transactions.

Trial Balance as at 31 March 19X6

			Dr.	Cr.
			£	£
Bank		B	668	
Milk Marketing Board		B	294	
Electricity	A(2)	P	56	
Tractor		B	700	
Machinery		B	1,625	
Stock at 31 March 19X5		P	2,025	
Capital		B		4,621
Ploughing grant		P		145
Cereal deficiency payments		P		217
Seeds and fertilisers		P	728	
Feeding stuffs		P	2,026	
Tractor and machinery expenses		P	537	
Veterinary fees		P	55	
Rent and rates		P	483	
Drawings		B	2,624	
Wages and National Insurance		P	1,109	

		Dr. £	Cr. £
Sundry expenses	P	29	
Threshing and baling	P	273	
Sales – Crops	P		4,568
– Livestock	P		996
– Milk	P		3,111
Cattle purchases	P	426	
		13,658	13,658

Accruals, prepayments, etc.	£	
1. Stocks, at valuation	1,940	P and B
2. Electricity outstanding	21	P and B
3. Depreciation to be provided:		
Tractor	100	P and B
Machinery	325	P and B

15 Income and expenditure accounts

15.1S (a)
Darset Old Comrades Club
Cash summary for the year ended 31 December 19X8

	£	£
Receipts		
Bar takings		40,612
Subscriptions		3,050
Cash from bank		5,848
		49,510
Payments		
Bank deposits	42,610	
Petty cash and wages	4,435	47,045
Claimable from insurance company		2,465

(b)
Income and Expenditure Account
for the year ended 31 December 19X8

	£	£
Income		
Subscriptions		3,050
Profit on bar (Note 1)		4,854
		7,904
less Expenses		
Wages and National Insurance	2,868	
Rent and rates	499	
Insurance	39	
Light and heat	152	
Glasses, crockery and maintenance	1,310	
Telephone	59	
Sundry expenses	257	5,184
Surplus of income		2,720

Note
1. Bar profit and loss account

	£	£
Takings		40,612
Cost of sales		
Opening stock	3,607	
Purchases	35,067	
	38,674	
less Closing stock	2,916	35,758
Profit		4,854

Workings

Rent and rates

	£		£
Rates prepaid b/d	26	Rent owing b/d	41
Bank	460	Rates prepaid c/d	28
Rent owing c/d	82	Income and expenditure	499
	568		568
Rates prepaid b/d	28	Rent owing b/d	82

Light and heat

	£		£
Bank	156	Electricity owing b/d	22
Electricity owing c/d	18	Income and expenditure	152
	174		174
		Electricity owing b/d	18

15.2S (a)

Seaside Golf Club
Income and Expenditure Account
for the year ended 30 September 19X0

	£	£
Income		
Subscriptions		5,920
Entrance fees		580
Green fees		4,012
Profit on bar (Note 1)		6,772
		17,284
less Expenses		
Wages and National Insurance	5,585	
Professional's retainer	1,500	
Rent and rates	1,652	
Light and heat	367	
Telephone	154	
Postage and stationery	182	
General expenses	362	
Fertilisers and seed	1,122	
Depreciation: Clubhouse	600	
Fixtures and fittings	750	
Equipment	1,580	13,854
Excess of income over expenditure		3,430
add Profit on sale of mower		100
Surplus of income		3,530

Note

1. Bar profit and loss account

	£	£
Receipts		28,805
less Stock at 1 October 19X9	414	
Purchases	21,974	
	22,388	
deduct Stock at 30 September 19X0	355	
Cost of sales		22,033
		6,772

Balance Sheet as at 30 September 19X0

Assets	Valuation	Depreciation	Net
	£	£	£
Fixed assets			
Clubhouse	30,000	600	29,400
Fixtures and fittings	7,500	750	6,750
Equipment	7,900	1,580	6,320
	45,400	2,930	42,470

Current assets		
Bar stock at cost	355	
Debtors	250	
Cash at bank	7,041	
Cash in hand	31	
	7,677	
Current liabilities		
less Creditors	550	
Net current assets		7,127
		49,597
Financed by		
Capital account		
Balance at 1 October 19X9		46,067
add Surplus for year		3,530
		49,597

(b) The receipts and payments account of the Seaside Golf Club would not be acceptable as an account of the transaction of the Club for the year, because of the following:

1. It does not show a true and complete picture of the income and expenses for the period, since (i) expenditure relating to periods other than the year to 30 September 19X0 is included, i.e. the accounts have not been prepared in accordance with the matching convention; (ii) capital expenditure is included in the account.

2. The assets and liabilities of the Seaside Golf Club as at 30 September 19X0 are not shown.

Tutorial notes
1. The subscription outstanding from one member for 19X8/19X9, £50, together with the 19X9/19X0 subscription for the same member, £55, have been written off.
2. Debtors

	£
Subscriptions due	70
Rates prepaid	180
	250

3. Creditors

	£
Rent owing	140
Bar purchases owing	410
	550

Workings
All workings are given in abbreviated form for this one solution.

Calculation of Capital Account at 1 October 19X9

	£	£
Cash at bank	2,548	
Cash in hand	65	
Subscriptions	150	
Rent		120
Rates	160	
Bar purchases		250
Bar stock	414	
Clubhouse	30,000	
Fixtures and fittings	7,500	
Equipment	5,600	
Capital account		46,067
	46,437	46,437

Subscriptions		Rent and rates		Bar purchases		Bar stock	
£	£	£	£	£	£	£	£
150	6,000	160	120	21,814	250	414	
		1,652					

Clubhouse		Fixtures and fittings		Equipment		Capital account	
£	£	£	£	£	£	£	£
30,000		7,500		5,600	200		46,067
				2,200			
				300			

Entrance fees		Green fees		Bar receipts		Telephone	
£	£	£	£	£	£	£	£
	580		4,012		28,805	154	

Light and heat		Postage and stationery		Wages and National Insurance		Professional's retainer	
£	£	£	£	£	£	£	£
367		182		5,585		1,500	

Fertilisers and seed		General expenses		Disposal of asset	
£	£	£	£	£	£
1,122		362		200	300

Trial Balance at 30 September 19X0

				£	£
Cash at bank		B		7,041	
Cash in hand		B		31	
Subscriptions		A(2)	I		5,850
Rent and rates	A(3)	A(4)	I	1,692	
Bar purchases		A(5)	I	21,564	
Bar stock at 1 October 19X9			I	414	
Clubhouse		A(6)	B	30,000	
Fixtures and fittings		A(6)	B	7,500	
Equipment		A(6)	B	7,900	
Capital			B		46,067
Entrance fees			I		580
Green fees			I		4,012
Bar receipts			I		28,805
Telephone			I	154	
Light and heat			I	367	
Postage and stationery			I	182	
Wages and National Insurance			I	5,585	
Professional's retainer			I	1,500	
Fertilisers and seed			I	1,122	
General expenses			I	362	
Profit on disposal of equipment			I		100
				85,414	85,414

Accruals, prepayments, etc.	£	
1. Bar stock at 30 September 19X0	355	I and B
2. Subscriptions due	70	I and B
		(write off £105)
3. Rent owing	140	I and B
4. Rates prepaid	180	I and B
5. Bar purchases owing	410	I and B
6. Depreciation:		
Clubhouse, 2% reducing balance		I and B
Fixtures and fittings, 10% reducing balance		I and B
Equipment, 20% reducing balance		I and B

15.3S (a)

Midon Cricket Club
Receipts and Expenditure Account
for the year ended 31 December 19X6

	£	£
Income		
Joining fees	56	
Subscriptions	412	468
Profit on bar (Note 1)		1,100
Surplus on cricket festival		196
Interest on investments		35
		1,799
less Expenses		
Wages and National Insurance	741	
Rent and rates	243	
Heating and lighting	108	
Postage and stationery	75	
General expenses	102	
Ground expenses	56	
Depreciation: Fixtures and fittings	63	
Machines	49	
Loss on sale of mowing machine	5	1,442
Surplus of income		357

(b)　　　　　**Balance Sheet as at 31 December 19X6**

Assets	Cost or valuation	Depreciation	Net
Fixed assets	£	£	£
Fixtures and fittings	504	63	441
Machines and equipment	270	48	222
	774	111	663
Investment – £1,000 7% Wessex			
Loan stock			1,000
Current assets			
Bar stock		426	
Debtors (Note 2)		21	
Cash at bank		362	
Cash in hand		36	
		845	
less Current liabilities			
Creditors (Note 3)		47	
Net current assets			798
			2,461
Financed by			
Accumulated fund			
Balance at 1 December 19X6			2,104
add Surplus income for the year			357
			2,461

Notes to the accounts

1. Bar profit and loss account

	£	£
Bar sales		5,200
less Stock at 1 January 19X6	397	
Purchases	4,129	
	4,526	
deduct Stock at 31 December 19X6	426	4,100
Profit		1,100

2. Debtors

	£
Rates prepaid	21

3. Creditors

	£
Rent owing	35
Heating and lighting owing	12
	47

Workings

1. Accumulated fund at 1 January 19X6

	£	£
Fixtures and fittings at valuation		504
Machines and equipment at valuation		200
Bar stock		397
Rates prepaid		19
Cash at bank		997
Cash in hand		21
		2,138
less Rent accrued	20	
Heating and lighting accrued	14	34
		2,104

2. Rent and rates

	£
Rates prepaid at 1 January 19X6	19
Paid during year	230
Rent owing at 31 December 19X6	35
	284

	£	
less Rent owing at 1 January 19X6	20	
Rates prepaid 31 December 19X6	21	41
		243

3. Heating and lighting

	£
Paid during year	110
Owing at 31 December 19X6	12
	122
less Owing at 1 January 19X6	14
	108

4. Depreciation of machines (at 20% per annum)

	£
On (£200 – £20) for 12 months	36
On £90 for 8 months	12
On £20 for 4 months	1
	49

5. Loss on sale of mowing machine

	£	£
Valuation at 31 December 19X5		20
less Depreciation for 4 months	1	
Trade-in allowance	14	15
		5

15.4S (a)

Alway Social Club
Estimated bank account
for the year ending 31 March 19X6

	£		£
Balance at 1 April 19X5	980	Clubhouse extension	1,000
Subscriptions	1,506	New sports equipment	340
Sale of sports equipment	50	Bar purchases	11,800
Bar sales	14,875	Bar steward's wages	1,200
Admission charges for		Commission	149
socials	2,400	Expenses of socials	1,680
		Insurance	80
		Bar licence	50
		Rates	500
		Heat and light	250
		Miscellaneous	70
		Balance at 31 March	
		19X6 c/d	2,692
	19,811		19,811
Balance b/d	2,692		

(b)   *Estimated Bar Trading and Profit and Loss Account
for the year ending 31 March 19X6*

	£	£
Sales		14,875
Cost of sales		
Opening stock	400	
Purchases	12,000	
	12,400	
less Closing stock	500	11,900
Gross profit		2,975
less Expenses		
Bar licence	50	
Wages	1,200	
Commission	149	1,399
Estimated profit		1,576

(c)   *Estimated Income and Expenditure Account
for the year ending 31 March 19X6*

Income	£	£
Subscriptions		1,498
Profit on bar		1,576
Surplus on social evenings		720
		3,794
less Expenses		
Rates	475	
Heat and light	220	
Insurance	75	
Miscellaneous	70	
Depreciation of equipment	597	
Loss on sale of equipment	50	1,487
Estimated surplus of income		2,307

Estimated Balance Sheet as at 31 March 19X6

Assets	Cost	Depre-ciation	Net
Fixed assets	£	£	£
Clubhouse	9,900	–	9,900
Equipment	2,390	1,547	843
	12,290	1,547	10,743
Current assets			
Stock		500	
Debtors (Note 1)		165	
Cash at bank		2,692	
Cash in hand		10	
		3,367	

	£	£
less Current liabilities		
Creditors (Note 2)	1,500	
Net current assets		1,867
		12,610
Financed by		
Accumulated fund		
Balance at 1 April 19X5		10,303
add Surplus income for the year		2,307
		12,610

Notes to balance sheet
1. Debtors

	£
Rates prepaid	125
Insurance prepaid	40
	165

2. Creditors

	£
Creditors for bar purchases	1,000
Clubhouse extension	500
	1,500

Workings
1. Accumulated fund at 1 April 19X5

Fixed assets	Cost	Depre- ciation	Net
	£	£	£
Clubhouse	8,400	–	8,400
Equipment	2,300	1,100	1,200
	10,700	1,100	9,600
Current assets			
Stocks		400	
Debtors		151	
Cash at bank		980	
Cash in hand		10	
		1,541	
less Current liabilities			
Creditors		838	

	£
Net current assets	703
Accumulated fund	10,303

Debtors	£	Creditors	£
Rates prepaid	100	Creditors for bar purchases	800
Insurance prepaid	35	Subscriptions in advance	8
Subscriptions in arrears	16	Electricity owing	30
	151		838

2. Subscriptions – cash received

	£
In arrears	16
Current – 298 members at £5 per annum	1,490
	1,506

3. Bar purchases

	£
Bar stocks at 31 March 19X5	400
Increase in costs from 1 April 19X5 – 25%	100
Equivalent to one-half of one month's purchases	500
Purchases for 12 months – 24 × £500	£12,000

4. Payments for bar purchases

	£
Outstanding at 31 March 19X5	800
Purchases for 11 months	11,000
	11,800

5. Bar sales

	£
Cost of sales per bar trading account	11,900
Gross profit at 20% on sales	2,975
	14,875

6. Equipment

	Cost	Depreciation
	£	£
Balances at 31 March 19X5	2,300	1,100
less Sold during year	250	150
	2,050	950
add New equipment	340	
At 31 March 19X6	2,390	
Depreciation at 25%		597
At 31 March 19X6		1,547

7. Clubhouse

	£
Cost	8,400
Extensions	1,500
	9,900

16 Manufacturing accounts

16.1S (a)

N. Jones
Manufacturing, Trading and Profit and Loss Account
for the year ended 30 April 19X1

	£	£
Sales		220,000
Cost of sales		
Materials consumed (Note 1)	80,000	
Manufacturing wages	40,000	
Prime cost	120,000	
Manufacturing expenses	20,800	
Depreciation (Note 2)	9,600	
Work in progress, 1 May 19X0	6,300	
	156,700	
less Work in progress, 30 April 19X1	6,300	
Manufacturing cost	150,400	
Stock of finished goods, 1 May 19X0	43,000	
	193,400	
less Stock of finished goods, 30 April 19X1	39,000	154,400
Gross profit		65,600
Selling and distribution expenses (Note 3)	24,050	
Administration expenses (Note 4)	15,250	39,300
Net profit		26,300

Balance Sheet as at 30 April 19X1

Assets	Cost	Depre-ciation	Net
	£	£	£
Fixed assets	120,000	60,000	60,000
Current assets			
Stock and work in progress (Note 5)		55,300	
Debtors (Note 6)		28,700	
Cash at bank and in hand		9,000	
		93,000	

	£	£
less Current liabilities		
Creditors (Note 7)	9,900	
Net current assets		83,100
		143,100
Financed by		
Capital account		105,000
Current account		
Balance at 1 May 19X0	21,800	
add Profit for the year	26,300	
	48,100	
less Drawings	10,000	38,100
		143,100

(b) 'Direct' means that the materials, labour and expenses involved in the manufacturing process are *traceable* to the particular unit of goods being made.

Notes

1. Materials consumed

	£
Stock at 1 May 19X0	8,000
Purchases	82,000
	90,000
less Stock at 30 April 19X1	10,000
	80,000

2. Depreciation

		£
10% × £120,000	=	12,000
Manufacturing 8/10	=	9,600
Selling and distribution 1/10	=	1,200
Administration 1/10	=	1,200
		12,000

3. Selling and distribution expenses

	£
Per trial balance	21,400
Bad debts written off	600
Increase in provision for doubtful debts	250
Depreciation	1,200
Accruals at 30 April 19X1	700
	24,150
less Prepayment at 30 April 19X1	100
	24,050

4. Administration expenses

	£
Per trial balance	13,950
Depreciation	1,200
Accruals at 30 April 19X1	200
	15,350
less Prepayment at 30 April 19X1	100
	15,250

5. Stock and work in progress at 30 April 19X1

	£
Materials	10,000
Work-in-progress	6,300
Finished goods	39,000
	55,300

6. Debtors

		£
Per trial balance		30,600
Prepayments: Selling and distribution		100
Administration		100
		30,800
less Bad debts	600	
Provision for doubtful debts	1,500	2,100
		28,700

7. Creditors

	£
Per trial balance	9,000
Accruals: Selling and distribution	700
Administration	200
	9,900

16.2S (a)

Black and White
Manufacturing, Trading and Profit and Loss Account
for the year ended 31 December 19X5

	£	£
Sales		20,250
Cost of sales		
Materials consumed (Note 1)	3,000	
Manufacturing wages (Note 2)	5,000	
Prime cost	8,000	
Factory overhead expenses (Note 3)	2,000	
Factory cost of goods produced	10,000	
Factory profit – 2/7 × £10,000	2,857	
	12,857	

	£	£
Stock of finished goods, 1 January 19X5 (Note 4)	2,572	
	15,429	
less Stock of finished goods at 31 December 19X5 (Note 4)	1,929	13,500
		6,750
Sales overhead expenses (Note 5)		2,200
Sales department profit		4,550
Factory profit		2,857
Provision for unrealised profit written back (Note 6)		143
		7,550
Allocation of profits (Note 7)		
Black		3,211
White		4,339
		7,550

(b)   *Black and White*
                    Balance Sheet as at 31 December 19X5

Assets	Cost	Depre- ciation	Net
	£	£	£
Fixed assets			
Freehold factory	8,500	550	7,950
Gas ovens and factory equipment	750	375	375
Delivery vans	1,250	750	500
	10,500	1,675	8,825
Current assets			
Stocks at cost (Note 8)		2,000	
Debtors (Note 9)		2,235	
Cash at bank		475	
		4,710	
less Current liabilities			
Creditors (Note 10)		2,175	
Net current assets			2,535
			11,360

Financed by	Black	White	
Capital accounts			
Balances brought forward	3,460	4,150	
Profit for the year	3,211	4,339	
	6,671	8,489	
less Drawings	1,700	2,100	
	4,971	6,389	11,360

Notes

1. Materials consumed

	£
Stock at 1 January 19X5	750
Purchases	2,750
	3,500
less Stock at 31 December 19X5	500
	3,000

2. Manufacturing wages

	£
Wages per trial balance	6,200
less Sales department wages (2 × £600)	1,200
	5,000

3. Factory overhead expenses

	£
Gas (£700 + £300)	1,000
Rates and insurance (£225 − £50)	175
Sundry expenses	700
Depreciation:	
Factory building 2% × (£8,500 − £6,000)	50
Gas ovens, etc., 10% × £750	75
	2,000

4. Stock of finished goods

   If finished goods are transferred from the factory to the sales department at cost plus two-sevenths, the factory profit must be included in the finished goods stock before the sales department profit can be calculated.

   Stock of finished goods at 1 January 19X5 will be shown as
   Cost + 9/7 = £2,000 + £572 = £2,572.

   Stock of finished goods at 31 December 19X5 will be shown as
   Cost + 9/7 = £1,500 + £429 = £1,929.

5. Sales overhead expenses

	£
Wages	1,200
Advertising (£225 + £75)	300
Delivery van running expenses (£485 − £35)	450
Depreciation on delivery vans –	
20% × £1,250	250
	2,200

6. Provision for unrealised profit written back

	£
Unrealised profit on finished goods	
Brought forward, 2/9 × £2,572	572
Carried forward, 2/9 × £1,929	429
	143

Whenever stock is shown at a figure above cost in the trading account, a provision must be made to reduce the stock to cost. Where the opening stock is greater than the closing stock, the provision required at the year end will be smaller than that required at the beginning of the year. As in this case, the provision no longer required will be written back.

7. Allocation of profits

	Black £	White £	Balance £
Factory profit – Black, 2/3 × £2,857	1,905		952
Sales department profit –			
White 2/3 × £4,550		3,033	1,517
Provision for unrealised profit			143
Balance allocated equally	1,306	1,306	2,612
	3,211	4,339	

8. Stock at cost

	£
Raw materials	500
Finished goods	1,500
	2,000

9. Debtors

	£
Per trial balance	2,300
Prepayments: Rates	50
Van licences	35
	2,385
less Provision for doubtful debts	150
	2,235

10. Creditors

	£
Per trial balance	1,800
Accruals: Gas	300
Advertising	75
	2,175

16.3S (a)
Field, Meadow and Park
Trading and Profit and Loss Account
for the year ended 31 December 19X2

	£	£
Sales (Note 1)		102,200
Cost of sales		
Materials consumed (Note 2)	44,200	
Manufacturing wages and bonuses	15,200	
Prime cost	59,400	
Factory overhead expenses (Note 3)	2,270	
Manufacturing cost		61,670
Gross profit		40,530
Administration expenses (Note 4)	7,550	
Finance expenses (Note 5)	1,350	
Depreciation of motor vehicles (Note 6)	300	9,200
Net profit		31,330

Appropriation of profit	Field	Meadow	Park	Total
	£	£	£	£
Interest on capital	1,000	700	300	2,000
Share of remaining profits				
(4:2:1)	16,760	8,380	4,190	29,330
	17,760	9,080	4,490	31,330
Adjustment for Park's				
guarantee in ratio 4:2	(340)	(170)	510	
	17,420	8,910	5,000	31,330

(b)
Balance Sheet as at 31 December 19X2

Assets	Cost	Depreciation	Net
	£	£	£
Fixed assets			
Freehold premises	22,000		22,000
Plant and machinery (Note 7)	16,000	4,860	11,740
Motor vehicles (Note 8)	2,000	900	1,100
	40,600	5,760	34,840
Current assets			
Stock (Note 9)		15,040	
Debtors (Note 10)		6,390	
Cash at bank		2,360	
		23,790	
less Current liabilities			
Creditors (Note 11)		6,800	
Net current assets			16,990
			51,830

	Cost	Depre- ciation	Net
	£	£	£
Financed by			
Capital accounts			
Field		10,000	
Meadow		7,000	
Park		3,000	20,000
Current accounts			
Field		18,620	
Meadow		9,290	
Park		3,920	31,830
			51,830

(c)   Current accounts

	Field £	Meadow £	Park £		Field £	Meadow £	Park £
Balance b/f			600	Balances b/f	2,400	1,100	
Drawings	1,200	720	480	Share of			
Balances c/d	18,620	9,290	3,920	profit	17,420	8,910	5,000
	19,820	10,010	5,000		19,820	10,010	5,000
				Balances b/d	18,620	9,290	3,920

Notes

1. Sales

	£
Per trial balance	104,000
less Goods on sale or return	1,800
(see Tutorial Note 1 p. 522)	
	102,200

2. Materials consumed

	£
Stock, 1 January 19X2	12,400
Purchases and carriage inwards	46,840
	59,240
less Stock at 31 December 19X2 (Note 9)	15,040
	44,200

3. Factory overhead expenses

	£
Repairs	1,210
less Amount capitalised	600
	610

	£
Depreciation on plant and machinery –	
10% × £16,600	1,660
	2,270

4. Administration expenses

	£
Salaries and bonuses	
Salaries per trial balance	6,100
less Partners' drawings	2,400
	3,700
Bonuses	1,400
	5,100
Office expenses	2,450
	7,550

5. Finance expenses

	£
Discounts allowed	980
Bad debts written off	210
Increase in provision for doubtful debts	160
	1,350

6. Depreciation of motor vehicles

	£
Charge for year	500
less Overprovision on vehicle sold	
during the year	200
	300

7. Plant and machinery – cost

	£
Per trial balance	16,000
Repairs capitalised	600
	16,600

8. Motor vehicles

	Cost	Depreciation
	£	£
Per trial balance	3,400	1,400
deduct Sale of vehicle	1,400	1,000
	2,000	400
Depreciation for year		500
		900

9. Stock

	£	£
Stock per Note 1 to trial balance		13,600
add Stock in customers hands at		
selling price	1,800	
less Mark-up	360	1,440
		15,040

10. Debtors

	£	£
Per trial balance		9,400
less Goods on sale or return	1,800	
Bad debt written off	210	
Provision for doubtful debts	1,000	3,010
		6,390

11. Creditors

	£
Per trial balance	4,600
add Bonuses	2,200
	6,800

Tutorial Notes

1. When goods are sent to customers on 'sale or return', the profit should not be taken until the customer acknowledges his intention to keep the goods and pay for them. Where the goods remain unsold at the balance sheet date and they have been invoiced to customers through the normal sales procedure (as in this question), it is necessary for the sales account to be reduced by the selling price of those goods and the closing stock to be increased by the cost price of those goods. The double entries are as follows:

Sales account	Debit	
Debtors		Credit

With the selling price of the goods.

Stock account (i.e. closing stock)	Debit	
Trading account (through the closing stock)		Credit

With the cost price of the goods.

2. Although the question did not ask for a manufacturing account, the partners were in a manufacturing business. In such cases, it is suggested that answers should be prepared in a manufacturing format so far as the information given will allow.

17 Limited companies

In many questions set prior to 1985 the word 'issued' rather than the word 'allotted' is used in respect of share capital. Answers have been amended and 'allotted' has been used where appropriate, in line with the Companies Act 1985.

17.1S

Derby Dale Plc
Trading, Profit and Loss and Appropriation Account
for the year ended 31 December 19X7

	£	£	£
Sales			175,600
less Returns			325
Net turnover			175,275
less Cost of sales			
Opening stock		20,520	
Purchases	100,400		
less Returns	475	99,925	
		120,445	
less Closing stock		19,242	101,203
Gross profit			74,072
less Expenses			
Salaries		15,480	
Rent and rates	2,800		
less Prepayment	150	2,650	
Lighting and heating	840		
add Accrual	142	982	
Depreciation – furniture and fittings		1,332	
Debenture interest accrued		1,500	
General expenses		4,700	26,644
Net profit			47,428
Transfer to general reserve			10,000
			37,428
Dividends proposed			
preference – 9%		1,800	
ordinary – 30%		12,000	13,800
			23,628
Undistributed profit brought forward			2,000
Undistributed profit carried forward			25,628

Balance Sheet on 31 December 19X7

Assets	Cost	Depreciation	Net
	£	£	£
Fixed assets			
Buildings	80,000	–	80,000
Furniture and fittings	13,320	2,832	10,488
	93,320	2,832	90,488
Current assets			
Stock		19,242	
Debtors	42,520		
less Provision for bad debts	3,000	39,520	
Prepayments		150	
Bank		11,850	
		70,762	
less Current liabilities			
Proposed dividends			
Preference	1,800		
Ordinary	12,000		
Debenture interest accrued	1,500		
Creditors	20,180		
Accruals	142	35,622	
Net current assets			35,140
Net worth			125,628
Financed by			
Share capital – authorised and allotted			
9% £1 preference shares		20,000	
£1 ordinary shares		40,000	60,000
Reserves			
General		10,000	
Profit and loss		25,628	35,628
Shareholders' equity			95,628
Loan capital			
5% debentures			30,000
Capital employed			125,628

17.2S

VHR Limited

Operating Statement for the year ended 31 December 19X6

		£	£	£
Sales				400,000
Cost of sales				
(a)	Raw materials consumed (Note 1)		150,000	
	Manufacturing wages		60,000	

		£	£	£
(b)	Prime cost		210,000	
	Manufacturing overhead expenses (Note 2)		89,200	
	Manufacturing cost		299,200	
	add Work in progress, 1 January 19X6		16,000	
			315,200	
	less Work in progress, 31 December 19X6		18,200	
(c)	Cost of finished goods produced		297,000	
	Finished goods stock at 1 January 19X6	51,000		
	Purchases	9,000		
		60,000		
	less Finished goods stock at 31 December 19X6	57,000	3,000	
(d)	Cost of finished goods sold			300,000
(e)	Gross profit			100,000
	Administration expenses (Note 3)		22,000	
	Selling and distribution expenses (Note 4)		41,000	63,000
(f)	Net profit before taxation			37,000

Notes

1. Raw materials consumed

	£
Stock at 1 January 19X6	39,000
Purchases	152,000
	191,000
less Stock at 31 December 19X6	41,000
	150,000

2. Manufacturing overhead expenses

	£
Manufacturing expenses	25,300
Repairs and maintenance of plant and machinery	13,500
Depreciation of factory	38,000
Power	10,000
Light and heat: factory	2,400
	89,200

3. Administration expenses

	£
Light and heat: general office	800
Depreciation of general offices	5,000
Miscellaneous	16,200
	22,000

4. Selling and distribution expenses

	£
Light and heat: sales warehouse and offices	1,300
Depreciation of sales warehouse and offices	7,000
Carriage outwards	6,600
Miscellaneous	26,100
	41,000

17.3S (a)

D. Yorke Ltd
Profit and Loss Appropriation Account
for the period ended 30 June 19X5

	£	£
Net profit for the period (Note 1)		12,670
Undistributed profit at 1 July 19X4		12,126
Profit available for distribution		24,796
Transfer to general reserve	6,000	
Dividends proposed		
Preference of 8%	1,600	
Ordinary of 10%	6,000	13,600
Undistributed profit carried forward		11,196

Tutorial note

Many accountants, including the authors, prefer the undistributed profit brought forward to be shown in the appropriation account after the appropriations for the year have been made. In this question, however, the appropriations made exceeded the net profit for the period ended 30 June 19X5. To avoid showing a debit balance on the profit and loss account, albeit a temporary one, the undistributed profit brought forward at 1 July 19X4 was added to the net profit for the period before the appropriations were made.

There is no legal reason to prevent the undistributed profits being shown as above; it is simply a matter of preference.

Balance Sheet as at 30 June 19X5

Assets	Cost	Depreciation	Net
	£	£	£
Fixed assets			
Land and buildings	66,100	–	66,100
Office fittings and equipment	22,320	11,948	10,372
Vehicles	9,700	8,240	1,460
	98,120	20,188	77,932

	£	£	£
Current assets			
Stock		41,926	
Debtors (Note 2)		13,675	
Cash at bank		3,898	
		59,499	
less Current liabilities			
Creditors (Note 3)	10,635		
Proposed dividends	7,600	18,235	
Net current assets			41,264
			119,196
Financed by			
Share capital – authorised and allotted			
8% £1 preference shares		20,000	
£1 ordinary shares		60,000	80,000
Reserves			
General reserve		20,000	
Profit and loss account		11,196	31,196
Shareholders' funds			111,196
Loan capital			
10% debentures			8,000
			119,196

(b) Directors' fees are treated as an expense when measuring profit because the directors, as directors, are employees of the company. They may also be part owners of the company as shareholders, but the fees they receive are for their work in the capacity of employees.

In a partnership business, all the profit belongs to the partners who between them own the whole of the business. The way in which the profit is appropriated between the partners is for the partners themselves to decide and partnership salaries are simply part of that appropriation.

Notes

1.   Net profit for the period

	£	£
Gross profit for the period		40,754
less Expenses		
Wages and salaries	14,100	
Directors' fees (£1,250 + £2,500)	3,750	
Rates and insurances (£705 − £75)	630	
Light and heat (£608 + £274)	882	
Postage and telephone	310	
General expenses	1,554	
Depreciation – office fittings and		
equipment	3,348	
– vehicles	1,940	
Debenture interest	800	
Audit fee	600	
Bad debts	170	28,084
		12,670

2. Debtors

	£
Per question	13,600
Insurance prepaid	75
	13,675

3. Creditors

	£
Per question	6,861
Electricity owing	274
Directors' fees	2,500
Audit fee	600
Debenture interest	400
	10,635

17.4S (a)

Skyblue Ltd
Trading and Profit and Loss Account
for the year ended 31 October 19X0

	£	£
Sales (Note 1)		1,821,000
Cost of goods sold		1,210,000
Gross profit		611,000
Discounts received		8,500
		619,500
less Expenses		
Wages and salaries	340,000	
Directors' emoluments (Note 2)	45,000	
Repairs and renewals (Note 3)	44,000	
Advertising (Note 4)	32,000	
Debenture interest (Note 5)	6,400	
Bank overdraft interest	4,300	
Discounts allowed	1,700	
Depreciation – of freehold property	14,000	
of fixtures and fittings	38,600	
Loss on sale of fixtures and fittings (Note 6)	15,000	541,000
Net profit		78,500
Dividend paid – interim of 5%	20,000	
Dividend proposed – final of 2½%	10,000	30,000
		48,500
Undistributed profit at 31 October 19X9		158,300
Undistributed profit carried forward		206,800

Balance Sheet as at 31 October 19X0

Assets	Cost	Depre-ciation	Net
	£	£	£
Fixed assets			
Freehold property	280,000	105,000	175,000
Fixtures and fittings (Note 7)	386,000	179,600	206,400
	666,000	284,600	381,400
Current assets			
Stock at cost		230,000	
Deferred revenue expenditure (Note 4)		60,000	
Debtors (Note 8)		173,000	
Cash at bank		3,600	
		466,600	
less Current liabilities			
Creditors (Note 9)	32,200		
Bank overdraft	89,000		
Proposed dividend	10,000	131,200	
Net current assets			335,400
			716,800
Financed by			
Share capital			
£1 ordinary shares fully paid			400,000
Reserves			
Share premium		30,000	
Profit and loss account		206,800	236,800
Shareholders' funds			636,800
Loan capital			
8% debentures 19X9–19X0			80,000
			716,800

(b) Working capital is the excess of current assets over current liabilities – another name for net current assets. The importance of working capital lies in the ability of a business to pay for labour and goods and services as and when required and to take the benefit of available cash discounts. To be able to achieve these objectives will usually necessitate an adequate amount of cash within the current assets. But in considering working capital, attention must be given to the nature of the business as well as to the nature of the current assets and current liabilities.

Inadequate working capital is often the cause of business failures but businesses in different industries will have different working capital structures.

Notes

1. Sales

	£
Per trial balance	1,830,000
less Receipt from K. Bone wrongly credited	9,000
	1,821,000

2. Directors' emoluments

	£
Per trial balance	41,000
Amount accrued	4,000
	45,000

3. Repairs and renewals

	£
Per trial balance	60,000
less New fixtures and fittings	16,000
	44,000

4. Advertising

	£
Per trial balance	92,000
less Deferred revenue expenditure	60,000
	32,000

The deduction of deferred revenue expenditure will, of course, be in agreement with the 'matching concept'.

5. Debenture interest

	£
Per trial balance	3,200
Amount accrued	3,200
	6,400

6. Loss on sale of fixtures and fittings

	£	£
Cost		40,000
deduct Depreciation 10% × £40,000 ×		
3 years	12,000	
Sale proceeds	13,000	25,000
		15,000

7.   Fixtures and fittings

	Cost	Depreciation
	£	£
Per trial balance	410,000	153,000
Additions during year	16,000	
	426,000	
Sales during year	40,000	12,000
	386,000	141,000
Depreciation for the year		38,600
		179,600

8.   Debtors

	£
Per trial balance	182,000
less Receipt from K. Bone	9,000
	173,000

9.   Creditors

	£
Per trial balance	38,000
Directors' emoluments owing	4,000
Debenture interest owing	3,200
	45,200
less Receipt from sale of fixtures and fittings	13,000
	32,200

17.5S (a)

Greater Bargains Limited
Trading and Profit and Loss Account
for the year ended 31 March 19X0

	£	£
Sales		500,000
less Cost of sales		350,000
Gross profit		150,000
less Expenses		
Salaries	21,000	
Directors' emoluments	12,000	
Rates, light and heat (Note 1)	9,100	
Telephone and postages (Note 2)	6,500	
Motor vehicle expenses (Note 3)	25,900	
Depreciation – of fixtures and fittings	6,000	
– of motor vehicles	14,400	
Loss on sale of motor vehicle	1,700	96,600
Net profit		53,400

	£
Dividend proposed	
Ordinary of 15%	30,000
	23,400
Undistributed profits at 31 March 19X9	15,000
Undistributed profits carried forward	38,400

Balance Sheet as at 31 March 19X0

Assets	Cost/ valuation £	Depre- ciation £	Net £
Fixed assets			
Freehold property (Note 4)	190,000	–	190,000
Fixtures and fittings	120,000	78,000	42,000
Motor vehicles	72,000	25,600	46,400
	382,000	103,600	278,400
Current assets			
Stock in trade, at cost		38,000	
Debtors (Note 5)		24,000	
Cash at bank		7,000	
		69,000	
less Current liabilities			
Creditors (Note 6)	9,000		
Proposed dividend	30,000	39,000	
Net current assets			30,000
			308,400

Financed by		
Share capital	Authorised	Allotted and fully paid
	£	£
Ordinary shares of £1 each	250,000	200,000
Reserves		
Share premium	20,000	
Revaluation reserve (Note 4)	50,000	
Profit and loss account	38,400	108,400
Shareholders' funds		308,400

(b) The functions of the profit and loss appropriation account in limited company accounts is to show the following: (1) the total net profit for an accounting period; (2) the amounts 'appropriated' for taxation, transfers to reserves and payment of dividends; (3) the undistributed profits carried forward.

Notes

1. Rates, light and heat

	£
Per list of balances	11,400
less Prepayment	2,300
	9,100

2. Telephone and postage

	£
Per list of balances	5,600
add Accrued charges	900
	6,500

3. Motor vehicle expenses

	£
Per list of balances	24,100
add Accrued charges	300
Sale of proceeds of vehicle credited in error	1,500
	25,900

4. Revaluation reserve

	£
Freehold property valuation	190,000
less Cost	140,000
	50,000

5. Debtors

	£
Per list of balances	21,700
Rates, light and heat prepaid	2,300
	24,000

6. Creditors

	£
Per list of balances	7,800
Accrued charges	
Telephone and postage	900
Motor vehicle expenses	300
	9,000

18 Suspense accounts and the correction of errors

18.1S (a)

Suspense account

Error no.		£	Error no.		£
	Trial balance	218	(i)	Bank	35
(iv)	Discounts received	426	(iii)	M. Smith	94
	Balance – unexplained		(iv)	Discounts allowed	396
	difference c/d	188	(v)	Bank	111
			(vi)	Carriage outwards	196
		832			832
				Balance b/d	188

Error (ii) will not affect the trial balance since no entries have been made in the books for the goods taken by the owner of the business.

Error (vi) will not affect the trial balance since the error is merely a switch between two debit balances.

All the above errors should be corrected by means of journal entries.

(b) The balance of a trial balance is only a check on the arithmetical accuracy of the postings to the ledger accounts and is not evidence of the absence of error. Certain types of error will not affect the trial balance, viz.

1. Errors of omission – where the transaction is completely omitted from the ledger
2. Errors of commission – where both the debit and the credit are posted but to the wrong account
3. Errors of principle – where revenue expenditure is classified as capital expenditure or vice versa
4. Compensating errors.

18.2S (a)

Misbal Co.
Journal

		£	£
1.	Suspense account	100	
	Purchase ledger control account		100
	Invoice from J. Smith omitted from control account.		
2.	Debtors control account	240	
	Sales		240
	Undercast of sales day book.		
3.	Discount allowed account	489	
	Suspense account		489
	Discount allowed not posted to nominal account.		

		£	£
4.	Purchases	2,410	
	Purchase ledger control account		2,410
	Invoice from Why Ltd received late.		
5.	Sales	192	
	Sales ledger control account		192
	Cheque from J. Jones treated as sale.		
6.	Sales	250	
	Disposal of motor van account		250
	Trade in allowance wrongly treated.		

Tutorial note
It has been assumed that the difference in the trial balance figures has been posted to a suspense account.

(b)   *Profit Adjustment Statement*

		Increase £	Decrease £
2.	Sales day book undercast	240	
3.	Discount allowed not posted		489
4.	Purchase invoice from Why Ltd		2,410
5.	Sales incorrectly credited		192
6.	Sales incorrectly credited		250
		240	3,341
			240
	Net decrease in profit		3,101

Note
Item 1 will not affect the profit.

(c)   *Trial Balance Adjustment Statement*

		Increase debit or decrease credit £	Increase credit or decrease debit £
1.	Invoice omitted from purchase ledger control account		100
3.	Discount allowed not posted	489	
		489	100
		100	
	Net difference to trial balance	389	

Tutorial note
The other items will not affect the trial balance.

18.3S (a)

ABC Limited
Journal

			£	£
(a)	Profit and loss account		350	
	Sales ledger control account			350
	Correction of rent payment debited to sales ledger control account in error.			
(f)	Profit and loss account		1,000	
	Purchases ledger control account			1,000
	Correction of cash purchase debited to purchase ledger control account.			
(i)	Difference on balances suspense account		1,900	
	Bank account			1,900
	Correction of overcast of bank debit column in March 19X0.			

(b)   Corrected List of Balances at 30 April 19X0

	Note	£	£
Fixed assets: at cost	1	68,640	
provision for depreciation			31,000
Ordinary share capital			35,000
Retained earnings	2		9,930
Stock in trade, at cost		14,000	
Sales ledger control account	3	9,810	
Purchases ledger control account	4		6,240
Balance at bank	5		9,980
Difference on balance suspense	6		300
		92,450	92,450

Notes
1. Fixed assets: at cost

	£
Per list of balances	60,000
Fixtures and fittings purchased (j)	8,640
	68,640

2. Retained earnings

	£	£
Per list of balances		12,000
add Cash sales (g)		2,450
		14,450
less Rent (a)	350	
Discounts allowed (c)	500	
Purchases (e)	300	
Purchase ledger control (f)	1,000	
Bank charges (h)	910	
Stationery (k)	1,460	4,520
		9,930

3. Sales ledger control account

	£	£
Per list of balances		9,600
add Refund to L. Green (d)		2,620
		12,220
less Rent (a)	350	
B. Bell (b)	1,560	
Discounts allowed (c)	500	2,410
		9,810

4. Purchase ledger control account

	£
Per list of balances	6,500
add Correction of purchase day book (e)	300
Payment to K. Bloom (f)	1,000
	7,800
less B. Bell (b)	1,560
	6,240

5. Bank

	£	£	
Per list of balances		1,640	in hand
add Cash sales (g)		2,450	
		4,090	
less Refund to L. Green (d)	2,620		
Bank charges (h)	910		
Overcast of debit column (i)	1,900		
Fixtures and fittings (j)	8,640	14,070	
		9,980	overdrawn

6. Difference on balance suspense account

	£	
Per list of balances	740	credit
add Stationery not posted (k)	1,460	
	2,220	
less Bank cost (i)	1,900	
	300	credit

Note
The trial balance in this question implies that the sales ledger control account and the purchases ledger control account have been regarded as an integral part of the double entry system.

(c) The reasons for preparing bank reconciliation statements are as follows:

(i) To check that all items shown on the bank statement have been recorded in the cash book.
(ii) To identify unpresented cheques.
(iii) To verify the balance shown in the cash book.

18.4S (a)

Perrod and Company
Debtors' control account

	£		£
Balance per schedule	1,891	Bad debts	68
Cheque returned	110	Discount allowed –	
Sales omitted – A. Jones	97	M. Smith	43
		Balance c/d	1,987
	2,098		2,098
Balance b/d	1,987		

Creditors' control account

	£		£
Invoice overstated	9	Balance per schedule	2,130
Balance c/d	2,121		
	2,130		2,130
		Balance b/d	2,121

(b) *Journal*

		£	£
(iii)	Office equipment	240	
	Purchases		240
	Invoice wrongly analysed.		
(iv)	Drawings	320	
	Wages		320
	Drawings of owner included in wages.		
(v)	Capital account	40	
	Provision for depreciation of office equipment		40
	Depreciation charge for 19X7 calculated at 10% on cost instead of 12½% on cost.		
(vi)	Drawings	45	
	Stationery		45
	Personal notepaper included in stationery.		
(vii)	Returns inwards	90	
	Returns outwards		90
	Goods returned to a creditor posted to wrong returns account.		

(c)   *Balance Sheet as at 31 December 19X8*
Assets

	Cost	Depreciation	Net
	£	£	£
Fixed assets			
Premises	7,000	–	7,000
Office equipment (Note 1)	1,840	750	1,090
	8,840	750	8,090
Current assets			
Stock		1,400	
Debtors		1,987	
Cash in hand		56	
		3,443	
less Current liabilities			
Creditors	2,121		
Bank overdraft	980	3,101	
Net current assets			342
			8,432
Financed by			
Capital account			
Balance at 1 January 19X8 (Note 2)			8,400
add Profit for the year (Note 3)			2,332
			10,732
less Drawings (Note 4)			2,300
			8,432

Notes
1. Office equipment – cost

	£
Per schedule	1,600
From purchases	240
	1,840

2. Capital – balance brought forward

	£
Per schedule	8,440
less Depreciation for 19X7	40
	8,400

3.   Profit for the year

	£	£	£
Sales			14,003
less Returns inwards (£310 + £90)			400
			13,603
Cost of sales			
Stock at 1 January 19X8		1,200	
Purchases (£9,480 − £240)	9,240		
less Returns outwards	90	9,150	
		10,350	
less Stock at 31 December 19X8		1,400	8,950
Gross profit			4,653
Discount received			121
			4,774
Wages (£1,540 − £320)		1,220	
Commission		160	
Heating and lighting		375	
Postage and stationery (£224 − £45)		179	
Discount allowed		210	
Bad debts		68	
Depreciation on office equipment		230	2,442
			2,332

4.   Drawings

	£
Per schedule	1,935
From wages	320
From stationery	45
	2,300

19 Issue and forfeit of shares

B. Booth Ltd
Journal

19XX		£	£
May 13	Bank	212,000	
	Application and allotment account		212,000
	Amount received on applications for 424,000 shares of £1 each – £0.50 per share.		
May 31	Application and allotment account	300,000	
	Share capital account		225,000
	Share premium account		75,000
	Amounts due on application and allotment of 300,000 shares of £1 each including a premium of £0.25 per share.		
	Application and allotment account	12,000	
	Bank account		12,000
	Money received on application refunded to unsuccessful applicants.		
Jun. 3	Bank account	100,000	
	Application and allotment account		100,000
	Money received on allotment of 300,000 shares of £1 each.		
Jul. 31	Call account	75,000	
	Share capital account		75,000
	Amount due on call of £0.25 per share on 300,000 shares of £1 each.		
Aug. 3	Bank	75,000	
	Call account		75,000
	Money received on call of £0.25 per share on 300,000 shares of £1 each.		

Cash book
Bank account

19XX		£	19XX		£
May 13	Application and allotment	212,000	May 31	Application and allotment	12,000
Jun. 3	Application and allotment	100,000	Aug. 3	Balance c/d	375,000
Aug. 3	Call account	75,000			
		387,000			387,000
Aug. 4	Balance b/d	375,000			

Tutorial note

Where the question asks for the entries on an issue of shares to be shown in the company's journal, it is usual to show all the entries, including those relating to cash, in the journal.

19.2S (a)   *K. Boydell Ltd*
                                   Journal

19XX	£	£
Investment-own shares	600	
First call account		300
Second call account		300
Transfer of the calls unpaid on ordinary shares in the name of . . . now forfeited.		

(b)   *Balance Sheet (extracts)*

Assets

	£	£
Investment-own shares		600

Financed by
    Share capital
        £1 ordinary shares

Authorised	200,000	
Allotted and fully called		100,000

19.3S   *Grobigg Ltd*
                        Application and allotment

19X8		£	19X8		£
Apr. 30	Bank – cash returned to unsuccessful applicants	6,000	Apr. 1	Bank – cash received on applications	135,000
	Ordinary share capital	120,000	May 3	Bank – cash received on allotment	13,500
	Share premium	22,500			
		148,500			148,500

Bank account

19X8		£	19X8		£
Apr. 1	Application and allotment	135,000	Apr. 30	Application and allotment	6,000
May 3	Application and allotment	13,500	Sep. 3	Balance c/d	172,780
Jun. 3	Call	29,920			
Sep. 3	Investment-own shares	80			
	Share premium	280			
		178,780			178,780
Sep. 4	Balance b/d	172,780			

Ordinary share capital

19X8		£	19X8		£
Sep. 3	Balance c/d	150,000	Apr. 30	Application and allotment	120,000
			May 31	Call account	30,000
		150,000			150,000
			Sep. 4	Balance b/d	150,000

Share premium

19X8		£	19X8		£
Sep. 3	Balance c/d	22,780	Apr. 30	Application and allotment	22,500
			Sep. 3	Bank	280
		22,780			22,780
			Sep. 4	Balance b/d	22,780

Call account

19X8		£	19X8		£
May 31	Ordinary share capital	30,000	Jun. 3	Bank	29,920
			Jul. 31	Investment-own shares	80
		30,000			30,000

Investment-own shares

19X8		£	19X8		£
Jul. 31	Call	80	Sep. 3	Bank	80
		80			80

20 Redemption of shares and the purchase by a company of its own shares

20.1S (a)

F. Davies Ltd

Redeemable preference share capital

19X3		£	19X3		£
Jul. 1	Preference share redemption	50,000	Jul. 1	Balance b/d	50,000

Premium on redemption of preference shares

19X3		£	19X3		£
Jul. 1	Preference share redemption	5,000	Jul. 1	Profit and loss	5,000

Profit and loss account

19X3		£	19X3		£
Jul. 1	Premium on redemption of preference shares	5,000	Jul. 1	Balance b/d	60,000
	Capital redemption reserve	50,000			
	Balance c/d	5,000			
		60,000			60,000
			Jul. 1	Balance b/d	5,000

Capital redemption reserve

			19X3		£
			Jul. 1	Profit and loss	50,000

Preference share redemption

19X3		£	19X3		£
Jul. 1	Bank	55,000	Jul. 1	Redeemable preference share capital	50,000
				Premium on redemption of preference shares	5,000
		55,000			55,000

Bank

19X3			£	19X3			£
Jul.	1	Balance b/d	85,000	Jul.	1	Preference share redemption	55,000
						Balance c/d	30,000
			85,000				85,000
Jul.	1	Balance b/d	30,000				

(b)   *Balance Sheet as at 1 July 19X3*

	£	£
Assets		
Fixed assets		105,000
Current assets (excluding cash)	95,000	
Cash at bank	30,000	
	125,000	
less Current liabilities	75,000	
Net current assets		50,000
		155,000
Financed by		
Share capital – authorised and allotted		
Ordinary shares of £1 each		100,000
Reserves		
Capital redemption reserve		50,000
Profit and loss account		5,000
		155,000

20.2S (a) Where shares are redeemed out of accumulated profits, it is necessary to transfer to a capital redemption reserve an amount equal to the nominal value of the shares so redeemed. Since a capital redemption reserve may only be used in paying up unissued shares to be allotted as fully paid bonus shares, the creation of such a reserve has the effect of preserving the interests of creditors.

(b) Where shares are redeemed out of the proceeds of a new issue of shares, the new shares take the place of the redeemed shares in the share capital structure and creditors' interests are protected in this way. In such a case, therefore, it is not necessary to create a capital redemption reserve.

20.3S   *Traders Ltd*
                                  Journal

19X3		£	£
May 31	Bank	18,000	
	Investments		14,000
	Profit and loss		4,000
	Sale of investments and transfer of profit on sale.		

		£	£
Bank		25,000	
	Application and allotment		25,000
	Amount received on application for 20,000 ordinary shares of £1 each issued to shareholders at £1.25 each.		
Application and allotment		25,000	
	Ordinary share capital		20,000
	Share premium		5,000
	Issue of 20,000 ordinary shares of £1 each at a premium of £0.25 per share.		

Jul. 1 6% redeemable cumulative preference

		£	£
shares		50,000	
Premium on redemption of preference shares		2,500	
	Preference share redemption		52,500
	Transfer of nominal value of redeemable preference shares plus premium payable on redemption.		
Share premium		2,500	
	Premium on redemption of preference shares		2,500
	Writing-off premium of £0.05 per share on redemption of preference shares.		
Preference share redemption		52,500	
	Bank		52,500
	Repayment of preference shares at £1.05 per share.		
Profit and loss		30,000	
	Capital redemption reserve		30,000
	Transfer of the nominal value of the preference shares redeemed otherwise than out of the proceeds of the new allotment.		

Sep. 30 Bonus shares

		£	£
		12,000	
	Ordinary share capital		12,000
	Issue of one ordinary share for every ten shares held in accordance with Directors' resolution no. _____, dated _____.		
Capital redemption reserve		12,000	
	Bonus shares		12,000
	Transfer of the bonus issue out of reserves.		

20.4S   *Barrows PLC*
                                            Journal

19X3		£	£
Jan. 31	Bank	90,000	
	Application and allotment		90,000
	Amount received on application for 75,000 ordinary shares of £1 each allotted at £1.20 each.		
	Application and allotment	90,000	
	Ordinary share capital		75,000
	Share premium		15,000
	Allotment of 75,000 ordinary shares of £1 each at a premium of £0.20 per share.		
Mar. 31	Redeemable share capital	100,000	
	Premium on redemption of share capital	10,000	
	Share redemption		110,000
	Transfer of nominal value of redeemable shares plus premium payable on redemption.		
	Share redemption	110,000	
	Bank		110,000
	Repayment of redeemable shares at £1.10 per share.		
	Profit and loss	10,000	
	Premium on redemption of share capital		10,000
	Writing-off premium of £0.10 per share on redemption.		
	Profit and loss	25,000	
	Capital redemption reserve		25,000
	Transfer of the nominal value of the shares redeemed otherwise than out of the proceeds of the new allotment.		

20.5S (a)   *Barrows PLC*
                                            Journal

19X3		£	£
Mar. 31	Redeemable share capital	100,000	
	Premium on redemption of share capital	10,000	
	Share redemption		110,000
	Transfer of nominal value of redeemable shares plus premium payable on redemption.		
	Share redemption	110,000	
	Bank		110,000
	Repayment of redeemable shares at £1.10 per share.		

	£	£
Share premium	5,000	
Profit and loss	5,000	
Premium on redemption of share capital		10,000

Writing-off premium of £0.10 per share on redemption.

(b) The whole of the premium on redemption of share capital would be debited to the share premium account. The aggregate of the premiums received on the issue of the shares redeemed would be less than the current amount of the company's share premium account after the premium received on the issue of the new shares had been credited to that account.

The journal entry would be:

19X3		£	£
Mar. 31	Share premium	10,000	
	Premium on redemption of share capital		10,000

Writing-off premium of £0.10 per share on redemption.

20.6S   Tutorial note

Where a company purchases its own shares out of the distributable profits, the premium payable on purchase is also paid out of the distributable profits. In the answer to part (a) therefore, the share premium account is not affected.

But where a company purchases its own shares out of the proceeds of a fresh issue of shares made for the purposes of the purchase, the premium payable on the purchase shall be paid out of the share premium account subject to the limitations given in the text – see page 278.

(a) *Workings*

Cash		£
Balance before purchase of shares		112,000
less Cost of shares		90,000
		22,000

Capital redemption reserve		
Nominal value of shares purchased		50,000

Profit and loss account		
Balance before purchase of shares		144,000
less Transfer to capital redemption reserve	50,000	
Premium on purchase	40,000	90,000
		54,000

Vincent Ganley PLC
Balance Sheet as at 31 March 19X5 (summarised)

Assets	£	£
Fixed assets		421,400
Current assets (excluding cash)	370,720	
Cash at bank	22,000	
	392,720	
less Current liabilities	260,120	132,600
		554,000

Financed by		
Share capital – allotted and fully paid		
Ordinary shares		300,000
'A' ordinary shares		50,000
		350,000
Capital redemption reserve		50,000
Share premium		100,000
Profit and loss account		54,000
		554,000

(b)   *Vincent Ganley PLC*
Balance Sheet as at 31 March 19X5 (summarised)

Assets	£	£
Fixed assets		421,400
Current assets (excluding cash)	370,720	
Cash at bank	122,000	
	492,720	
less Current liabilities	260,120	232,600
		654,000

Financed by		
Share capital – allotted and fully paid		
Ordinary shares		350,000
'A' ordinary shares		50,000
		400,000
Share premium		125,000
Profit and loss account		129,000
		654,000

The journal entries are given below:

	£	£
Bank account	100,000	
Ordinary share application account		100,000
Cash received on application for 50,000		
shares of £2 each.		
Ordinary share application account	100,000	
Ordinary share capital account		50,000
Share premium account		50,000
Allotment of fresh issue of shares and		
transfer of premium received.		
'A' ordinary share capital account	50,000	
Premium on purchase of shares account	40,000	
'A' ordinary share pruchase account		90,000
Transfer of the nominal value of the shares		
purchased plus premium payable.		
'A' ordinary share purchase account	90,000	
Bank account		90,000
Purchase of 50,000 'A' ordinary shares of £1		
each at a premium of £0.80 per share.		
Share premium account	25,000	
Profit and loss account	15,000	
Premium on purchase of shares account		40,000
Transfer of premium on purchase of 50,000		
'A' ordinary shares of £1 each. (Share premium		
account is debited in this case with the		
aggregate of the premiums received by the		
company on the issue of the shares redeemed		
because this figure is less than the current		
amount of the company's share premium		
account.)		

21 The issue and redemption of debentures

21.1S (a)

J. Pilling and Co. Ltd
Bank

19X2		£	
Jul. 1	9% debenture application – cash received on application	95,000	

9% debentures application

19X2		£	19X2		£
Jul. 1	9% debentures	95,000	Jul. 1	Bank – cash received on application	95,000
		95,000			95,000

9% debentures

19X2		£	19X2		£
Jul. 1	Balance c/d	100,000	Jul. 1	9% debentures application	95,000
				Discount on debentures	5,000
		100,000			100,000
			Jul. 1	Balance b/d	100,000

Discount on debentures

19X2		£	
Jul. 1	9% debentures	5,000	

(b)   *Balance Sheet (extract) as at 30 June 19X3*

	£	£
Assets		
Sundry assets		X
Discount on debentures not yet written off		4,750
		X

Financed by	£
Share capital	X
Reserves	X
Shareholders' funds	X
9% debentures	100,000
	X

21.2S (a)

Craft Ltd
Preference share redemption

19X6		£	19X6		£
May 1 Bank		132,000	May 1 7% redeemable preference shares		120,000
			Premium on redemption of preference shares		12,000
		132,000			132,000

Profit and loss

19X6	£	19X6		£
May 1 Premium on redemption of preference shares	12,000	May 1 Balance b/d		226,000
		General reserve		80,000
Capital redemption reserve fund	120,000			
Balance c/d	174,000			
	306,000			306,000
		May 1 Balance b/d		174,000

Capital redemption reserve fund

		19X6	£
		May 1 Profit and loss	120,000

Bank

19X6		£	19X6		£
May 1 Balance b/d		204,000	May 1 Preference share redemption		132,000
May 1 7½% debentures applications		147,000	May 1 Balance c/d		219,000
		351,000			351,000
May 1 Balance b/d		219,000			

7½% debentures application

19X6	£	19X6	£
May 1 7½% debentures	147,000	May 1 Bank	147,000

7½% debentures 19X0/19X2

19X6	£	19X6	£
May 1 Balance c/d	150,000	May 1 7½% debentures applications	147,000
		Discount on debentures	3,000
	150,000		150,000
		May 1 Balance b/d	150,000

Discount on debentures

19X6	£	
May 1 7½% debentures	3,000	

(b)   *Balance Sheet as at 1 May 19X6*

	£	£
Assets		
Fixed assets		429,000
Current assets		
Sundry	200,000	
Bank	219,000	
	419,000	
less Current liabilities	127,000	
Net current assets		292,000
		721,000
Financed by		£
Share capital – allotted and fully paid		
280,000 ordinary shares of £1 each		280,000
Reserves		
Capital redemption reserve fund	120,000	
Profit and loss account	174,000	294,000
		574,000
less Debenture discount not yet written off		3,000
Shareholders' funds		571,000
7½% debentures 19X0/19X2		150,000
		721,000

Tutorial notes
1. It has been assumed that the general reserve had been built up for the purposes of the redemption of the preference shares.
2. Note the treatment in this example of the balance on the discount on debentures account.

21.3S (a)   *Switch Ltd*
                                        Journal

19X1	£	£
Bank	120,000	
Ordinary share application and allotment		120,000
Amount received on application for 200,000 ordinary shares of £0.50 each offered at £0.60 each.		
Ordinary share application and allotment	120,000	
Ordinary share capital		100,000
Share premium		20,000
Issue of 200,000 ordinary shares of £0.50 each at a premium of £0.10 per share.		
Bank	145,500	
9% Unsecured loan stock 19X5/19X4 application		145,500
Amount received on application for £150,000 9% unsecured loan stock 19X5/19X4 offered at 97.		
9% unsecured loan stock 19X5/19X4 application	145,500	
Discount on loan stock	4,500	
9% unsecured loan stock 19X5/19X4		150,000
Issue of £150,000 9% unsecured loan stock 19X5/19X4 at 97.		
6½% redeemable preference shares	175,000	
Premium on redemption of preference shares	8,750	
Preference share redemption		183,750
Transfer of nominal value of redeemable preference shares plus premium payable on redemption.		
Share premium	13,250	
Discount on loan stock		4,500
Premium on redemption of preference shares		8,750
Writing-off discount on loan stock and premium on redemption of preference shares.		
Preference share redemption	183,750	
Bank		183,750
Repayment of preference shares at £1.05 per share.		
Profit and loss	75,000	
Capital redemption reserve fund		75,000
Transfer of the nominal value of the preference shares redeemed otherwise than out of the proceeds of the new issue.		

(b)   *Balance Sheet as at 1 July 19X1*
                            (after completing the above entries)
                                                            £   £

Assets
    Sundry assets   562,850
    Cash at bank (Note 1)   58,500
                                                                    ———————
                                                                    621,350
    less Sundry creditors   19,600
                                                                    ———————
    Net assets   601,750
                                                                    ═══════

Financed by
    Share capital – allotted and fully paid
        700,000 ordinary shares of £0.50 each   350,000
    Reserves
        Capital redemption reserve fund   75,000
        Share premium   6,750
        Profit and loss account   20,000   101,750
                                                        ———————   ———————
    Shareholders' funds   451,750
    9% unsecured loan stock 19X5/19X4   150,000
                                                                    ———————
                                                                    601,750
                                                                    ═══════

Note
1.   Cash at bank
                                                            £   £
    Received from allotment of:
        Ordinary shares   120,000
        9% unsecured loan stock   145,500
                                                                    ———————
                                                                    265,500
    less Redemption of preference shares   183,750
        Overdraft brought down   23,250   207,000
                                                        ———————   ———————
                                                                    58,500
                                                                    ═══════

21.4S (a)   *Tapical Ltd*
                                       Journal
19X7   £   £
Apr. 30 Share premium   90,000
        Profit and loss account   410,000
            Ordinary share bonus issue   500,000
        Transfer of reserves for bonus issue in
        accordance with resolution no. _____
        of the Annual General Meeting held on
        _____ 19X7.

        Ordinary share bonus issue   500,000
            Ordinary share capital   500,000
        Issue of bonus shares.

	£	£
Bank	936,000	
Application and allotment		936,000

Amount received on application for one-
for-four rights issue at £0.52 per share
for 1.8 million shares.

	£	£
Bank	120,000	
Application and allotment		120,000

Amount received on sale of 200,000
shares of £0.60 per share – rights
issues renounced.

	£	£
Application and allotment	16,000	
Bank		16,000

Amount of £0.08 per share on 200,000
shares paid to shareholders who
renounced their rights to the rights
issue.

	£	£
Application and allotment	1,040,000	
Ordinary share capital		500,000
Share premium		540,000

Rights issue of 2 million ordinary
shares of £0.25 each at a premium of
£0.27 per share.

	£	£
Issue expenses	53,000	
Bank		53,000

Payment of underwriting and other
expenses connected with the issue.

	£	£
Share premium	53,000	
Issue expenses		53,000

Writing off issue expenses.

	£	£
Loan stock purchase	51,220	
Bank		51,220

Payment for purchase of £60,000 loan
stock.

	£	£
7½% redeemable loan stock 19X7/19X2	60,000	
Loan stock interest	1,500	
Loan stock purchase		51,220
Profit and loss account		10,280

Cancellation of loan stock purchased
and transfer of interest on that stock to
date of purchase, i.e. 4 months'
interest.

(b) Before the one-for-four rights issue, the theoretical price of each £0.25
share was

$$\frac{£4,940,000 \text{ (net assets)}}{8,000,000 \text{ (shares in issue)}} = £0.62 \text{ per share.}$$

After the rights issue, the theoretical price of each £0.25 share was

$$\frac{£5,980,000 \text{ (net assets)}}{10,000,000 \text{ (shares in issue)}} = £0.60 \text{ per share.}$$

It can be seen that the theoretical price has fallen by £0.02 per share following the rights issue. The payment of £16,000 to the 0.8 million shareholders who renounced their rights is compensation for the fall in the theoretical price – (0.8m × £0.02 = £16,000).

22 Stock valuation

22.1S Smith
(a) Methods of computing the cost of stock on hand are as follows:

(i) *First in, first out (FIFO)*   Under this method, stock which is received first is regarded as being issued to production, or sold, first. For valuation purposes, the stock remaining at the end of the period will be deemed to be those goods which are the last to have been purchased.
(ii) *Last in, first out (LIFO)*   Under this method, stock which is received last is regarded as being issued to production, or sold, first. For valuation purposes, therefore, the stock remaining at the end of the period will be deemed to be those goods which are the first to have been purchased.
(iii) *Average cost (AVCO)*   Under this method, a new average unit cost of stock is calculated whenever there is a *receipt* of goods. The latest average unit cost so calculated is used for valuation purposes at the end of the accounting period.

(b) Effect of each method on Smith's results for the six months:

		FIFO		LIFO		AVCO	
	Tons	£	£	£	£	£	£
Sales	100		4,600		4,600		4,600
Cost of sales:							
Purchases	140	5,600		5,600		5,600	
less Closing stock	40	1,715	3,885	1,560	4,040	1,600	4,000
	100						
Gross profit			715		560		600

Comments
In times of rising prices, stock valued by the FIFO method will give both a higher closing stock valuation and a higher profit than stock valued by the LIFO method. Both methods have disadvantages: under FIFO sales are matched with purchases valued at out of date prices whilst under LIFO that part of the stock below which the level never falls could be valued at the prices which applied when the business commenced.

The AVCO method has the advantage of smoothing out fluctuations in the purchase price of goods and will usually result in a profit somewhere between the FIFO and LIFO figures.

Perhaps the most important point to make, however, is that whatever method of stock valuation is adopted, that method should be applied consistently.

Workings

1.   Purchases

	Tons	Price per ton £	Value £
1 July	20	38	760
5 August	30	40	1,200
12 September	25	35	875
20 October	40	42	1,680
11 November	15	43	645
10 December	10	44	440
	140		5,600

2.   Closing stock valuation

   (i)   FIFO

	£
10 tons at £44	440
15 tons at £43	645
15 tons at £42	630
40 tons	1,715

   (ii)   LIFO

	£
20 tons at £38	760
20 tons at £40	800
40 tons	1,560

   (iii)   AVCO

$$\frac{\text{Total cost}}{\text{Total units}} = \frac{£5,600}{140 \text{ tons}} = £40 \text{ per ton}$$

Stock = 40 tons at £40 per ton = £1,600

22.2S (a) Valuation of closing stock

		Transaction		Stock remaining					
				Valued at LIFO			Valued at FIFO		
		Units	Unit price £	Units	Unit price	£	Units	Unit price	£
Jan.	Bought	30	5	30	5	150	30	5	150
	Sold	20		10	5	50	10	5	50
Feb.	Sold	5		5	5	25	5	5	25
Apr.	Bought	40	6	40	6	240	40	6	240
				5	5	25			
	Sold	25		15	6	90	20	6	120
May	Bought	25	6.5	25	6.5	162.5	25	6.5	162.5
				5	5	25			
	Sold	30		10	6	60	15	6.5	97.5
Jun.	Bought	20	7	20	7	140	20	7	140
				5	5	25			
	Sold	20		10	6	60	15	7	105
	Closing stock					85			105

Gross profit

	LIFO basis		FIFO basis	
	£	£	£	£
Sales		811.00		811.00
Cost of sales				
Purchases	692.50		692.50	
less Closing stock	85.00	607.50	105.00	587.50
Gross profit		203.50		223.50

(b) *Balance Sheets as at 30 June 19X5*

	LIFO basis £	FIFO basis £
Assets		
Stock at cost	85.00	105.00
Cash	618.50	618.50
	703.50	723.50
Financed by		
Capital account		
Amount introduced	500.00	500.00
Profit for period	203.50	223.50
	703.50	723.50

Comments
In times of rising prices, which obtained during the six month period covered by the question, the FIFO valuation can be seen to give a higher closing stock valuation and a higher profit. The disadvantage of using the FIFO basis, that sales are matched with purchases valued at out of date prices, must be stressed as indeed must the disadvantage of an outdated stock valuation using the LIFO basis.

22.3S (a) Weighted average method (AVCO)

Date	Purchases			Issues			Balance		
	Quantity	Price £	Value £	Quantity	Price £	Value £	Quantity	Price £	Value £
b/f							100	39	3,900
May	100	41	4,100				200	40	8,000
Jun.	200	50	10,000				400	45	18,000
Jul.				250	45	11,250	150	45	6,750
Aug.	400	51.875	20,750				550	50	27,500
Sep.				350	50	17,500	200	50	10,000
Oct.				100	50	5,000	100	50	5,000

FIFO method

Date	Purchases			Issues			Balance		
	Quantity	Price £	Value £	Quantity	Price £	Value £	Quantity	Price £	Value £
b/f							100	39	3,900
May	100	41	4,100				100	41	4,100
Jun.	200	50	10,000				200	50	10,000
Jul.				100	39	3,900			
				100	41	4,100			
				50	50	2,500	150	50	7,500
Aug.	400	51.875	20,750				400	51.875	20,750
Sep.				150	50	7,500			
				200	51.875	10,375	200	51.875	10,375
Oct.				100	51.875	5,187.5	100	51.875	5,187.5

LIFO method

Date	Purchases			Issues			Balance		
	Quantity	Price £	Value £	Quantity	Price £	Value £	Quantity	Price £	Value £
b/f							100	39	3,900
May	100	41	4,100				100	41	4,100
Jun.	200	50	10,000				200	50	10,000
Jul.				200	50	10,000	100	39	3,900
				50	41	2,050	50	41	2,050
Aug.	400	51.875	20,750				100	39	3,900
							50	41	2,050
							400	51.875	20,750
Sep.				350	51.875	18,156.25	100	39	3,900
							50	41	2,050
							50	51.875	2593.75
Oct.				50	51.875	2593.75			
				50	41	2,050	100	39	3,900

(b)   *Trading Accounts for the 6 months to 31 October 19XX*

	Weighted average method £	£	FIFO method £	£	LIFO method £	£
Sales		47,900		47,900		47,900
Cost of sales:						
Opening stock	3,900		3,900		3,900	
Purchases	34,850		34,850		34,850	
	38,750		38,750		38,750	
less Closing stock	5,000	33,750	5,187.5	33,562.5	3,900	34,850
Gross profit		14,150		14,337.5		13,050

(c) The method in the situation depicted, which is regarded as giving the best measure of profit, is the LIFO method. When prices are rising the LIFO method matches the sales receipts with up to date costs of the goods sold.

Working
Sales

		£
Jul.	250 units at £64	16,000
Sep.	350 units at £70	24,500
Oct.	100 units at £74	7,400
		47,900

22.4S

	Product		
	A	B	C
	£	£	£
Sales – actual prices	172,500	159,400	74,600
add Discounts	2,500	600	400
	175,000	160,000	75,000
less Gross profit on normal selling prices	35,000	40,000	25,000
Cost of sales	140,000	120,000	50,000

(a) Values of stock at 31 December 19X7

	A	B	C
	£	£	£
Stock at 1 January 19X7	24,000	36,000	12,000
Purchases	146,000	124,000	48,000
	170,000	160,000	60,000
less Cost of sales	140,000	120,000	50,000
Stock at 31 December 19X7	30,000	40,000	10,000

(b) Gross profit by product

	A	B	C
	£	£	£
Sales – actual prices	172,500	159,400	74,600
less Cost of sales	140,000	120,000	50,000
Actual gross profit	32,500	39,400	24,600

23 Cash flow statements

J. Cook
Cash Flow Statement for year ending 31 December 19X2

	£	£
Net cash flow from operating activities		10,280
Returns on investments and servicing of finance		
Drawings	(8,890)	
Net cash flow from returns on investments and servicing of finance		(8,890)
Investing activities		
Payments to acquire fixed assets	(1,500)	
Net cash flow from investing activities		(1,500)
Net cash flow before financing		(110)
Decrease in cash (and cash equivalent)		(110)

Notes to the cash flow statement:
Reconciliation of operating profit to net cash flow from operating activities

	£
Profit for year	9,200
Depreciation charged	1,150
Increase in debtors	(30)
Increase in creditors	60
Increase in stock	(100)
Net cash flow from operating activities	10,280

Analysis of changes in cash and cash equivalents during the year

	£
Balance at 1 January 19X2	1,340
Net cash outflow	110
Balance at 31 December 19X2	1,230

Note:
A sole trader is not required to prepare a cash flow statement, though he may find it a useful and informative exercise. The above has been prepared using the standard headings where possible as useful practice. The position of 'Drawings' could be debated.

23.2S

D. Riggs

Cash Flow Statement for year ending 31 December 19X3

	£	£
Net cash flow from operating activities		20,613
Returns on investments and servicing of finance		
Drawings	(11,795)	
Net cash flow from returns on investments and servicing of finance		(11,795)
Investing activities		
Payments to acquire fixed assets	(14,400)	
Net cash flow from investing activities		(14,400)
Net cash flow before financing		(5,582)
Decrease in cash (and cash equivalent)		(5,582)

Notes to the cash flow statement:
Reconciliation of operating profit to net cash flow from operating activities

	£
Profit for year	16,225
Depreciation charged	6,200
Increase in debtors	(1,020)
Increase in creditors	58
Increase in stock	(850)
Net cash flow from operating activities	20,613

Analysis of changes in cash and cash equivalents during the year

	£
Balance at 1 January 19X3	1,690
Net cash outflow	(5,582)
Balance (overdrawn) at 31 December 19X3	(3,892)

Note: See the footnote to the answer to question 23.1S above.

23.3S (a)

MacDonalds Ltd

Cash Flow Statement for year ending 31 December 19X4

	£000s	£000s
Net cash flow from operating activities		508
Returns on investments and servicing of finance		
Dividends paid	(40)	
Net cash flow from returns on investments and servicing of finance		(40)
Taxation		
Corporation tax paid		(150)

	£000s	£000s
Investing activities		
Payments to acquire fixed assets	(1,150)	
Receipts from sales of fixed assets	17	
Net cash flow from investing activities		(1,133)
Net cash flow before financing		(815)
Financing		
Issue of debentures	150	
Cash flow from financing		150
Decrease in cash (and cash equivalent)		(665)

Notes to the cash flow statement:
Reconciliation of operating profit to net cash flow from operating activities

	£000s
Profit before tax	450
Depreciation charged	170
Loss on sale of asset	23
Increase in debtors	(180)
Increase in creditors	120
Increase in stock	(75)
Net cash flow from operating activities	508

Analysis of changes in cash and cash equivalents during the year

	£000s
Balance at 1 January 19X4	690
Net cash outflow	665
Balance at 31 December 19X4	25

Analysis of changes in financing during the year

	Debentures £
Balance at 1 January 19X4	350
Cash inflow from financing	150
Balance at 31 December 19X4	500

Note: Workings for plant and machinery

	£	Cost £
Balance 19X4		1,735
Deduct 19X3	655	
less Sales	70	585
		1,150

(b) It is important that a business should be profitable, but it is also important that it should generate enough cash to ensure its survival and success. Without cash a business will eventually fail, even though it may continue to report profits. A cash flow statement lists the cash inflows and outflows for the period, and indicates the ability or otherwise of generating cash.

23.4S

F. Jones Ltd

Cash Flow Statement for year ending 31 December 19X7

	£	£
Net cash flow from operating activities		291,750
Returns on investments and servicing of finance		
Dividends paid	(55,000)	
Net cash flow from returns on investments and servicing of finance		(55,000)
Taxation		
Corporation tax paid		(30,300)
Investing activities		
Payments to acquire fixed assets	(293,850)	
Receipts from sales of fixed assets	17,000	
Net cash flow from investing activities		(276,850)
Net cash flow before financing		(70,400)
Financing		
Issue of share capital	50,000	
Receipts from share premium	25,000	
Cash flow from financing		75,000
Increase in cash (and cash equivalent)		4,600

Notes to the cash flow statement
Reconciliation of operating profit to net cash flow from operating activities

	£
Profit before tax	152,200
Depreciation charged	136,450
Increase in debtors	(2,300)
Increase in creditors	3,900
Decrease in stock	1,500
Net cash flow from operating activities	291,750

Analysis of changes in cash and cash equivalents during the year

	£
Balance at 1 January 19X7	39,600
Net cash inflow	4,600
Balance at 31 December 19X7	44,200

Analysis of changes in financing during the year

	Share capital £
Balance at 1 January 19X7	550,000
Cash inflow from financing	50,000
Balance at 31 December 19X7	600,000

Workings

Profit for 19X7

	£
Increase in P and L a/c (£140,000 − £90,000)	50,000
Proposed dividends	65,000
Corporation tax	35,700
	150,700
add Loss on sale of assets charged against profits	1,500
	152,200

Fixed Assets

	Cost £	£	£	Depreciation £
Balances 19X7		1,279,300		283,100
Deduct 19X6	1,058,700		201,400	
Less sales	73,250	985,450	54,750	146,650
Purchases 19X7		293,850		
Depreciation 19X7				136,450

24 Cash budgeting

24.1S

Cash budget for period January to June 19X2

	Jan. £	Feb. £	Mar. £	Apr. £	May £	Jun. £
Receipts						
Cash sales	30,000	28,000	24,000	32,000	29,000	36,000
Credit sales[1]	62,000	68,000	78,000	64,000	84,000	74,000
	92,000	96,000	102,000	96,000	113,000	110,000
Payments						
Purchases	26,000	25,000	30,000	30,000	25,000	25,000
Expenses	15,000	12,000	18,000	20,000	18,000	20,000
Wages	40,000	40,000	40,000	40,000	40,000	40,000
Rates				15,000		
Interest						10,000
Dividend						30,000
	81,000	77,000	88,000	105,000	83,000	125,000
Cash increase/ (decrease) during month	11,000	19,000	14,000	(9,000)	30,000	15,000)
Cash brought forward	6,000					
Closing cash	17,000	36,000	50,000	41,000	71,000	56,000

Note
1. Credit sales

	Jan.	Feb.	Mar.	Apr.	May	Jun.
80% previous	48,000	56,000	64,000	48,000	72,000	56,000
20% penult.	14,000	12,000	14,000	16,000	12,000	18,000
	62,000	68,000	78,000	64,000	84,000	74,000

24.2S   *Cash budget for period January to April*

	Jan. £	Feb. £	Mar. £	Apr. £
Receipts				
Sales (Note 1)	62,000	49,500	46,000	62,000
Payments				
Purchases	50,000	78,000	84,000	84,000
Wages	5,000	5,200	5,200	5,000
Expenses	4,000	8,000	6,000	6,000
	59,000	91,200	95,200	95,000
Cash increase/(decrease)				
during month	3,000	(41,700)	(49,200)	(33,000)
Cash brought forward	9,000			
Closing cash-in-hand/				
(overdrawn)	12,000	(29,700)	(78,900)	(111,900)

Note
1. Sales

½ previous	30,500	19,000	27,000	35,000
½ penult.	31,500	30,500	19,000	27,000
	62,000	49,500	46,000	62,000

Cash receipts in May should amount to £75,000 (½ of March plus ½ of April sales). Cash payments will be for April purchases and expenses, i.e. £65,000 plus May wages. From the information provided for previous months it appears that May wages will be approximately £5,000. The cash position in May should therefore improve by about £5,000.

An alternative way of dealing with this part of the question would be to extend the cash budget to include May. A footnote would then be required to explain any assumed figures, and to draw conclusions from the tabulation.

24.3S (a)   *Schubert Ltd*

Cash budget for period April to June 19X5

	Apr. £	May £	Jun. £
Receipts			
Credit sales	1,500	1,800	2,000
Cash sales	500	600	800
	2,000	2,400	2,800

Payments			
Trade creditors	4,000	2,300	2,700
Wages	300	300	300
Administration	150	150	150
Rent	360		
Dividend			1,500
Equipment	1,600		
	6,410	2,750	4,650
Cash brought forward	3,500	(910)	(1,260)
Cash increase/(decrease) during month	(4,410)	(350)	(1,850)
Closing cash/(overdrawn)	(910)	(1,260)	(3,110)

(b)   *Schubert Ltd*

*Projected Trading and Profit and Loss Account for
period April to June 19X5*

	£	£
Sales		
Cash	1,900	
Credit	6,300	8,200
Cost of sales		
Opening stock	2,000	
Purchases	7,600	
	9,600	
less Closing stock (Note 1)	3,450	6,150
Gross profit (Note 1)		2,050
less Expenses		
Wages	900	
Administration	450	
Rent	90	
Depreciation	75	1,515
		535

Notes
1. Gross profit = 25% of Sales (£8,200) = £2,050.
    Cost of Sales = Sales (£8,200) less gross profit (£2,050) = £6,150.
    Closing stock = Cost of sales (£6,150) deducted from total of Opening
    stock (£2,000) and Purchases (£7,600) = £3,450.
2. There is a loss on the sale of the replaced equipment amounting to
    £100. This loss could be charged to this period, but would more likely
    be charged against the full year.

(c) At the commencement of the period, cash in hand amounted to £3,500, whereas at the end cash will be overdrawn £3,110, a reduction in cash of £6,610.

The reasons for the difference between budgeted profitability and budgeted liquidity are probably best explained by a flow statement.

In simple terms, it would appear that profits should produce a cash increase of £535, plus depreciation of £75 (depreciation is a non-cash expense), i.e. £610. However, cash has been paid out on dividends (£1,500) and equipment (£1,600). Stocks have also been increased, so decreasing cash, as have debtors and prepayments. Creditors have been reduced, again decreasing cash.

25 Interpretation of accounts: an introduction

25.1S   *R. J. Smith*

(a) 'Gross profit ratio' means the ratio of gross profit to net sales. It shows the percentage mark-up on selling price.

(b) (i) $\dfrac{5,250}{21,000} \times 100 = 25\%$

   (ii) $\dfrac{2,412}{21,000} \times 100 = 11.5\%$

   (iii) $\dfrac{420}{21,000} \times 100 = 2\%$

   (iv) £18,000, i.e. opening stock plus purchases

   (v) £15,750, i.e. opening stock plus purchases less closing stock

(c)   *Budgeted Trading and Profit and Loss Account*
            for the year to 31 March 19X6

		£	£
Sales			23,100
less Cost of sales			17,325
(i) Gross profit			5,775
	less Rent and rates	800	
	Light and heat	192	
	Wages	936	
	Part-time salesman's commission	462	
	Delivery expenses	230	
	Depreciation of fittings	120	
	Office and sundry expenses	390	3,130
(ii) Net profit			2,645

25.2S (a)   *S. Ltd and T. Ltd*
                                S. Ltd | T. Ltd

(i) Net profit as a
percentage of $\dfrac{8,000}{100,000} \times 100 = 8\%$ $\dfrac{6,000}{50,000} \times 100 = 12\%$
net assets

(ii) Net profit as a
percentage of $\dfrac{8,000}{160,000} \times 100 = 5\%$ $\dfrac{6,000}{120,000} \times 100 = 5\%$
sales

(iii) Gross profit as
a percentage $\dfrac{64,000}{160,000} \times 100 = 40\%$ $\dfrac{45,000}{120,000} \times 100 = 37.5\%$
of sales

(iv) Current assets
to current $90,000 : 30,000 = 3:1$ $60,000 : 30,000 = 2:1$
liabilities

(v) Debtors and
cash to current $33,000 : 30,000 = 1.1:1$ $30,000 : 30,000 = 1:1$
liabilities

(vi) Cost of sales
to average $96,000 : 48,000 = 2:1$ $75,000 : 25,000 = 3:1$
stock held

In item (vi) above, average stock is taken as (Opening stock + Closing Stock) ÷ 2.

(b) S. Ltd obtains a higher gross profit percentage than T. Ltd, but since the net profit percentage of both companies is the same the overhead expenses of T. Ltd must be lower than those of S. Ltd by a compensating amount.

The return on capital employed by T. Ltd is half as much again higher than that of S. Ltd. The reason for this better performance is shown in the other ratios:

(i) The stock of T. Ltd is turned over three times a year compared to S. Ltd's twice.
(ii) T. Ltd's cover of current liabilities by current assets of 2:1 is adequate.
(iii) S. Ltd has more investment in stocks than necessary: the money so tied up could be more profitably invested. Both companies' 'acid test' ratio is satisfactory.

25.3S   *Report to the directors of Unigear Ltd*

February 19X3

Gentlemen,

We submit our report on the results for the year ended 31 December 19X2, and a comparison with those of the previous year.

1. *Summary of results*   A brief summary of the results of the two years shows the following:

	%	19X2 £	%	19X1 £
Sales	100	1,000,000	100	1,500,000
Cost of sales	65	650,000	60	900,000
Gross profit	35	350,000	40	600,000
Overhead expenses	34.3	343,098	26.3	394,704
Net profit before tax	0.7	6,902	13.7	205,296
Corporation tax	0.3	3,000	3.8	57,500
Net profit after tax	0.4	3,902	9.9	147,796

The reduction in overhead expenses is accounted for, viz.

	19X2 £	19X1 £	Net £
Decreases:			
Directors' remuneration	24,650	67,740	43,090
Wages and salaries	187,724	233,719	45,995
Repairs and renewals	750	2,600	1,850
	213,124	304,059	90,935
Increases:			
Rent and rates	12,106	10,450	1,656
Light and heat	4,942	3,608	1,334
Advertising	42,605	40,216	2,389
Bad debts	12,943	4,224	8,719
Bank interest and commission	46,420	22,328	24,092
Other expenses	10,958	9,819	1,139
	129,974	90,645	39,329
Net decrease			51,606

2. *Observations on the results*
   (a) *Trading account*   Sales have fallen from £1.5m to £1m – a reduction of one-third. The probable reason for this reduction is the nature of the trade in which your company is engaged.
      Gross profit percentage has fallen from 40% to 35%. This reduction may be attributable to the following reasons:
   (i)   Deliberate reductions in selling prices in order to stimulate sales
   (ii) A change in the goods sold – more sales of those goods with lower mark-ups
   (iii) Losses from pilferage of stock and/or cash
   (iv) Significant mark down of stock at 31 December 19X2 resulting in a higher cost of sales figure for that year.
      The rate of stock turnover has decreased. Assuming that the average stock reflects the general stock levels during the year and that the sales accrue evenly over the year, the decrease can be shown as follows:

	19X2	19X1
Average of opening and closing stock	£355,000	£275,000
Cost of goods sold	£650,000	£900,000
Number of times stock turned over	1.8 times	3.3 times
Number of months sales in stock, at cost	6.6 months	3.6 months

It is obvious that stock levels have increased substantially during the current year. Holding stocks is an expense which should be reduced as soon as possible by reviewing the company's stock lines if necessary. In view of the nature of the business, it must be ensured that the stock at 31 December 19X2 is valued at the lower of cost or net realisable value for each line held.

(b) *Profit and loss account*   The decrease in directors' remuneration and wages and salaries obviously reflect the lower levels of business.

The increase in bad debts would suggest that the credit control procedures need reviewing as a matter of urgency.

Bank interest and commission has increased by a substantial amount and part of this must be due to the high cost of maintaining stock levels referred to earlier and part to capital expenditure (see below).

3.   *Corporation tax*   The adjusted corporation tax charge for 19X1 represents 28% of the net profit. Obviously, considerable capital expenditure relief was available to reduce the rate below the normal corporation tax rate. The cost of these new assets must have been financed by bank borrowing since no loan or hire purchase interest payable is shown in the accounts. In view of this, it is surprising to see a reduction in the depreciation charge for the current year. Perhaps this figure will need to be adjusted.

4.   *Dividends*   No dividend is proposed for the current year.

We shall be pleased to discuss the contents of our report with you in detail.

Yours faithfully,

25.4S (a)

The Alpha Co. Ltd

Appropriation Account
for the year ended 31 December 19X5

	£	£	£
Net profit for the year			72,000
Unappropriated profit brought forward			73,000
			145,000
Appropriation of profit:			
Transfer to general reserve		25,000	
Dividends:			
Paid – Interim preference – 4%	10,000		
Interim ordinary – 5%	5,000	15,000	
Proposed – Final preference – 4%	10,000		
Final ordinary – 5%	5,000	15,000	
Goodwill written off		20,000	
			75,000
Unappropriated profit carried forward			70,000

Balance Sheet as at 31 December 19X5

Assets

	Cost or valuation* £	Depre- ciation £	Net £
Fixed assets			
Land and buildings	270,000*	–	270,000
Fittings	175,000	75,000	100,000
Motor vehicles	397,000	187,000	210,000
	842,000	262,000	580,000
Goodwill not yet written off			40,000
Current assets			
Stock		148,000	
Debtors (Note)		83,000	
Short term investments (market value £43,000)		39,000	
		270,000	
less Current liabilities			
Creditors	48,000		
Bank overdraft	27,000		
Proposed dividends	15,000	90,000	
Net current assets			180,000
			800,000

	Authorised	Allotted and fully paid
Financed by		
Share capital		
8% £1 redeemable preference shares	250,000	250,000
£1 ordinary shares	200,000	100,000
	450,000	350,000
Reserves		
Capital redemption reserve	150,000	
Revaluation reserve	50,000	
Share premium	20,000	
General reserve	80,000	
Profit and loss account	70,000	370,000
Shareholders' funds		720,000
Loan capital		
10% debentures		80,000
		800,000

Note
Debtors

	£
Trade debtors and prepayments	85,400
less Provision for doubtful debts	2,400
	83,000

(b) (1) The balance of the share capital can be issued by the company at any time it wishes to raise additional finance.

(2) Return on net capital employed is given by

Net profit for the year + Debenture interest ÷ Net capital employed = £72,000 + £8,000 ÷ £800,000 = 10%.

This ratio measures the overall effectiveness of the company's operations.

(3) The company's working capital (or net current assets) is £180,000. The importance of working capital is that it shows whether a company is able to meet its debts as and when they fall due.

(4) In the case of Alpha Co. Ltd, the goodwill would have arisen on the purchase of another business where the purchase price exceeded the net assets acquired.

(5) Assuming the company had the cash, the maximum amount which could be distributed by way of dividend is given as follows:

	£
Profit and loss account balance	145,000
General reserve	55,000
	200,000
less Preference dividends	20,000
	180,000

The other reserves are non-distributable.

(6) The market value of the shares reflects the future expectations of the business whilst the book value is based on the historic cost of the assets.

(7) The share premium account has arisen because at some time the Alpha Co. Ltd issued shares at a price above their par value.

26 Bills of exchange

26.1S

J. Conroy

Journal

19X1		£	£
Jul. 28	Bills receivable	1,200	
	B. Borne		1,200
	Bill of exchange accepted by B. Borne.		
Oct. 28	B. Borne	1,200	
	Bills receivable		1,200
	Debt of Borne re-raised on dishonour of bill of exchange.		
Oct. 28	B. Borne	10	
	Bank		10
	Noting charges on bill of exchange dishonoured by Borne.		

Ledger

B. Borne

19X1		£	19X1		£
Jul. 28	Sales	1,200	Jul. 28	Bills receivable	1,200
Oct. 28	Bills receivable	1,200			
	Bank – noting charges	10			

Bills receivable

19X1		£	19X1		£
Jul. 28	B. Borne	1,200	Oct. 28	B. Borne	1,200

26.2S

B. Borne

Ledger

J. Conroy

19X1		£	19X1		£
Jul. 28	Bills payable	1,200	Jul. 28	Purchases	1,200
			Oct. 28	Bills payable	1,200
				Noting charges	10

Bills payable

19X1		£	19X1		£
Oct. 28	J. Conroy	1,200	Jul. 28	J. Conroy	1,200

Noting charges

19X1		£		
Oct. 28	J. Conroy	10		

26.3S

S. Smith

Ledger

I. Nash

19X2		£	19X2		£
Jul. 14	Sales	650	Jul. 14	Bills receivable	650
Sep. 14	Bank	650			
	Bank – noting charges	10			

Bills receivable

19X2		£	19X2		£
Jul. 14	J. Nash	650	Jul. 16	Bank	635
			16	Discount on bills	15
		650			650

Discount on bills

19X2		£		
Jul. 16	Bills receivable	15		

Bank

19X2		£	19X2		£
Jul. 16	Bills receivable	635	Sep. 14	J. Nash	650
			14	J. Nash – noting charges	10

27 Royalties

K. Dodd Treacle Mine Co.
Royalties account

Year		£	Year		£
1	Landlord	2,625	1	Operating account	2,625
2	Landlord	3,225	2	Operating account	3,225
3	Landlord	4,275	3	Operating account	4,275
4	Landlord	4,725	4	Operating account	4,725
5	Landlord	5,025	5	Operating account	5,025
6	Landlord	5,250	6	Operating account	5,250

Landlord's account

Year		£	Year		£
1	Bank	4,500	1	Royalties	2,625
				Short workings	1,875
		4,500			4,500
2	Bank	4,500	2	Royalties	3,225
				Short workings	1,275
		4,500			4,500
3	Bank	4,500	3	Royalties	4,275
				Short workings	225
		4,500			4,500
4	Bank	4,500	4	Royalties	4,725
	Short workings	225			
		4,725			4,725

		£			£
5	Bank	4,500	5	Royalties	5,025
	Short workings	525			
		5,025			5,025
6	Bank	5,250	6	Royalties	5,250

Short workings account

Year		£	Year		£
1	Landlord	1,875			
2	Landlord	1,275			
3	Landlord	225			
			4	Landlord	225
			5	Landlord	525
			5	Profit and loss (short workings irrecoverable)	2,625
		3,375			3,375

27.2S

Doors Ltd
Royalties

19X2		£	19X2		£
Dec. 31 Shipton		200	Dec. 31 Manufacturing a/c	200	
19X3			19X3		
Dec. 31 Shipton		400	Dec. 31 Manufacturing a/c	400	
19X4			19X4		
Dec. 31 Shipton		600	Dec. 31 Manufacturing a/c	600	
19X5			19X5		£
Dec. 31 Shipton		500	Dec. 31 Manufacturing a/c	500	

Shipton (patent owner)

19X3		£	19X2		£
Jan. 31 Bank		500	Dec. 31 Royalties	200	
				Short workings	300
		500			500
19X4			19X3		
Jan. 31 Bank		500	Dec. 31 Royalties	400	
				Short workings	100
		500			500

19X4		£	19X4		£
Dec. 31	Short workings	200	Dec. 31	Royalties	600
19X5					
Jan. 31	Bank	400			
		600			600
19X5			19X5		
Dec. 31	Short workings	100	Dec. 31	Royalties	500
19X6					
Jan. 31	Bank	400			
		500			500

Short workings

19X2		£			£
Dec. 31	Shipton	300			
19X3					
Dec. 31	Shipton	100			
			19X4		
			Dec. 31	Shipton	200
				Profit and loss (irrecoverable for 19X2)	100
			19X5		
			Dec. 31	Shipton	100
		400			400

28 Departmental accounts

28.1S (a)

Expense	Basis of apportionment
Advertising	Sales
Rent and rates	Floor area
Canteen	Number of employees
Heat and light	Floor area
Insurance of stock	Average stock levels
General administration	Sales

(b)

John Dobson
Trading and Profit and Loss Account
for the year ended 30 September 19X5

	Hardware £	Hardware £	Electrical £	Electrical £	Total £	Total £
Sales		59,000		29,500		88,500
Cost of goods sold						
Opening stock	2,320		2,136		4,456	
Purchases	20,000		10,000		30,000	
	22,320		12,136		34,456	
less Closing stock	2,800	19,520	2,450	9,686	5,250	29,206
Gross profit		39,480		19,814		59,294
less Expenses						
Salaries and wages	20,810		15,610		36,420	
Advertising	410		205		615	
Discounts allowed	400		200		600	
Rent and rates	1,000		500		1,500	
Canteen charges	525		350		875	
Heat and light	600		300		900	
Insurance of stock	500		440		940	
Administration	1,360		680		2,040	
Depreciation	1,800	27,405	700	18,985	2,500	46,390
		12,075		829		12,904
Commission 5%		604		41		645
Net profit		11,471		788		12,259

(c) Gross margins are approximately the same (i.e. 67%), but net margins are Hardware 19.4% and Electrical 2.6%. Expenses as a percentage of sales are Hardware 47% and Electrical 64.5%.

Electrical expenses are therefore proportionately too high. The apportionment of expenses has been carried out on a reasonably fair basis. Is the floor space allocated to Electrical too large?

Sales of Electrical department are only half sales of Hardware department. But sales staff of Electrical department are 2/3 in number and 3/4 in salaries and wages when compared with Hardware. Is staff of Electrical department too large? Can sales of Electrical department be increased without further staff costs? Salaries and wages are by far the major expense and close attention is required here.

How much of the above is due to manager of Electrical department, and how much is due to Dobson?

28.2S (a)

Allsports Ltd
Trading and Profit and Loss Account
for the year ended 30 April 19X0

	Clothing		Sports equipment		Total	
	£	£	£	£	£	£
Sales		120,000		160,000		280,000
Cost of goods sold						
Opening stock	10,000		16,000		26,000	
Purchases						
(Note 1)	78,000		110,000		188,000	
	88,000		126,000		214,000	
less Closing stock	8,000	80,000	14,000	112,000	22,000	192,000
Gross profit		40,000		48,000		88,000
less Expenses						
Establishment	14,700		16,920		31,620	
Sales and						
administrative	7,600		6,540		14,140	
Depreciation						
Freehold						
property	200		200		400	
Fixtures and						
fittings	1,800		1,200		3,000	
Motor vehicles						
(Note 2)	3,500		4,900		8,400	
Staff						
commission	800	28,600	1,440	31,200	2,240	59,800
Net profit		11,400		16,800		28,200

(b)

Balance Sheet as at 30 April 19X0

Assets

	Cost	Depreciation	Net
	£	£	£
Fixed assets			
Freehold property	20,000	1,200	18,800
Fixtures and fittings	30,000	12,000	18,000
Motor vehicles (Note 2)	36,000	22,800	13,200
	86,000	36,000	50,000

	Cost	Depre- ciation	Net
	£	£	£
Current assets			
Stock at cost		22,000	
Debtors		8,600	
Prepayments		300	
		30,900	
less Current liabilities			
Bank overdraft	2,300		
Creditors	5,800		
Accruals	900		
Staff commission	2,240	11,240	
Net current assets			19,660
			69,660
Financed by			
Ordinary share capital			20,000
Share premium account			2,000
Retained earnings (Note 3)			47,660
			69,660

(c) 1. To determine the profitability and contribution of each department.
2. To compare the profitability of different departments.
3. To assist in deciding future strategy.
4. As an aid to internal control and audit.

Notes
1.

	£
Purchases as per trial balance	192,000
less Transfer to fixtures and fittings	4,000
	188,000

Divided between Clothing and Sports Equipment as 'balancing figure'.

2. Depreciation on motor vehicles
   Motor vehicle purchased January 19X5
   20% depreciation charged year ended 30 April 19X6
   20% depreciation charged year ended 30 April 19X7
   20% depreciation charged year ended 30 April 19X8
   20% depreciation charged year ended 30 April 19X9
   Therefore final 20% to be charged year ended 30 April 19X0.

	Cost	Depreciation	Net
	£	£	£
Trial balance 30 April 19X0	42,000	20,400	21,600
Depreciation 19X9/X0		8,400	
	42,000	28,800	13,200
Written off	6,000	6,000	
Balance sheet 19X0	36,000	22,800	13,200

3. Retained earnings

	£
Brought forward	19,460
Net profit for year	28,200
	47,660

29 Joint ventures

29.1S (a)

Books of Starboard

Joint venture with Port

19X9		£	19X9		£
May	4 Bank – speedboat	675	May 12	Bank – sale of speedboat	750
	Cash – repainting	40	Jun. 15	Bank – Starboard	1,000
	25 Bank – repurchase of speedboat	720		30 Drawings account – boat taken over	700
Jun. 30	Bank – harbour dues	3			
	Bank – marine insurance	6			
Jul.	1 P and L – share of profit	60			
	Bank – settlement due	946			
		2,450			2,450

(b)

Port and Starboard

Memorandum joint venture account

		£		£
Expenses of Port			Income of Port	
Speedboat		730	Two speedboats	1,800
Speedboat		820	One speedboat	1,000
Speedboat		950	Boat trips	24
Reconditioned engine		120		
Insurance and harbour dues		30		
Expenses of Starboard			Income of Starboard	
Speedboat		675	Speedboat	750
Repainting		40	Speedboat for own use	700
Repurchase of speedboat		720		
Insurance and harbour dues		9		
	£			
Profit – Port	120			
Starboard	60	180		
		4,274		4,274

Workings

Books of Port
Joint venture with Starboard

19X9		£	19X9		£
May 3	Bank – speedboat	730	May 31	Bank – sale of two speedboats	1,800
	Bank – speedboat	820	Jun. 15	Bank – sale of one speedboat	1,000
	Bank – speedboat	950	30	Bank – boat trips	24
	Bank – recon- ditioned engine	120	Jul. 1	Bank – settle- ment due	946
Jun. 15	Bank – Starboard: receipts from one boat	1,000			
30	Bank – harbour dues	10			
	Bank – marine insurance	20			
Jul. 1	P and L – share of profit	120			
		3,770			3,770

Tutorial note
The above account is not required by the question, but it is a check on parts (a) and (b).

29.2S *(a)*   *Journal of H*

19X5		Dr. £	Cr. £
Jan. 29	J (debtor)	6,000	
	Joint venture with G		6,000
	Sale of goods.		
Feb. 26	Cash	6,000	
	J		6,000
	Cash received.		
Mar. 19	L (debtor)	2,000	
	Joint venture with G		2,000
	Sale of goods.		
Apr. 30	Cash	1,000	
	L		1,000
	Cash received.		
Apr. 30	Bad debts	1,000	
	L		1,000
	Bad debt written off.		
Apr. 30	Purchases	1,500	
	Joint venture with G		1,500
	Balance of stock taken over at agreed valuation.		

	Dr.	Cr.
	£	£
Apr. 30 Joint venture with G	2,700	
Profit and loss:		
Del credere commission		400
Share of profit on venture		2,300
Share of profit, etc. on joint venture.		
Apr. 30 Joint venture with G	6,800	
Cash		6,800
Cash paid to G in settlement (see workings).		

(b)   Memorandum joint venture account

	£			£
Purchases (G)	8,300	Sales (H)	6,000	
Del credere commission			2,000	8,000
H 5% of 8,000	400		——	
G 5% of 4,000	200	Sales (G)		4,000
Share of profit		Stock taken over by H		1,500
G	2,300			
H	2,300			
	——			——
	13,500			13,500
	═══			═══

Workings

Joint venture with G

	£		£
Profit and loss		J	6,000
Commission	400	L	2,000
Profit	2,300	Purchases	1,500
Cash – settlement with G	6,800		
	——		——
	9,500		9,500
	═══		═══

Tutorial note

A *del credere* commission is more usually met in consignment accounts. In this example it means that each party to the joint venture (i.e. G and H) will be personally responsible for bad debts on sales they have made. Therefore, although H has profits, etc., of £2,700 on the venture, the profits are offset by the £1,000 bad debt of L.

Index